FIGHT

ALSO BY JONATHAN ALLEN AND AMIE PARNES

HRC

Shattered

Lucky

FIGHT

★★★ INSIDE THE ★★★
WILDEST BATTLE
FOR THE WHITE HOUSE

JONATHAN ALLEN
& AMIE PARNES

WM
WILLIAM MORROW
An Imprint of HarperCollinsPublishers

HarperCollins books may be purchased for educational, business, or sales promotional use. For information, please email the Special Markets Department at SPsales@harper collins.com.

FIRST EDITION

Library of Congress Cataloging-in-Publication Data has been applied for.

ISBN 978-0-06-343864-4

25 26 27 28 29 LBC 7 6 5 4 3

For Stephanie, Asher, and Emma, the lights of my life

—*JA*

For the amazing Remy, my hero and champion prizefighter

—*AP*

★ CONTENTS ★

PART I: THE UNMAKING OF THE PRESIDENT

PART II: WHAT IT TOOK

PART I

THE UNMAKING OF THE PRESIDENT

"THE QUIET PART OUT LOUD"

THE SUN HAD JUST SET WHEN NANCY PELOSI SETTLED ONTO THE LIVING room couch in her seven-figure Georgetown condo overlooking the Kennedy Center and the Potomac River. The former House Speaker, still in perpetual motion at eighty-four, fixed her wide brown eyes on a rarely used television screen. If not for the vanishing supply of chocolate ice cream in the freezer, and the quick naps she caught between busy days, there was usually little evidence that anyone lived in her posh Washington crash pad at all. But this night, June 27, 2024, was different from all other nights. The television was on. She wanted to watch President Joe Biden debate former president Donald Trump without distraction, with a clear and focused mind. For that, Nancy Pelosi needed to be alone.

Months earlier, she had urged Biden, a friend of four decades, not to line up toe-to-toe with Trump. At the time, the president, First Lady Jill Biden, and a handful of top White House officials were in the midst of internal discussions about whether to debate. At one point, Anita Dunn, the president's senior adviser for communications, thought that Trump's decision to skip Republican primary debates might provide enough political cover for Biden to sidestep him. The idea betrayed concern that debates might not go well for Biden. He asked his aides to consider the pros and cons. "We just didn't feel like we could get out of it," said one top Biden adviser. "If we didn't debate, it would have added to the narrative that the president was hiding from people." Biden worried that Trump wouldn't debate on the level, but he loved the prospect of a fight he was sure he would win. Some outside allies, aware of the internal talks, weighed in with White House chief of staff Jeff Zients and other senior Biden aides to warn against debating Trump. Pelosi took her concerns directly to Biden.

"I know you can beat him," Pelosi said, playing to Biden's ego before leaning in on the notion that he should not lower himself by sharing a camera frame with Trump. "You just can't go onstage with him." Of the millions of voters who loathed Trump, none found him more repulsive than Pelosi. Her House impeached him twice—once, with a handful of Republican votes, after his supporters sacked the U.S. Capitol in a violent but vain attempt to stop the certification of his 2020 defeat. Trump had mocked her husband, Paul Pelosi, when an intruder bashed his head in with a hammer. She told Biden he should not dignify Trump by granting the equal footing of a presidential debate. Trump's affinity for rolling around in the mud would make it impossible for Biden to emerge unsullied, she told the president. Trump's *smell* would spread to him, she thought.

Biden disagreed. "No, no," he said. "I should go." In early March, a solid performance at the State of the Union boosted Biden's confidence. After that address to Congress, he gave Pelosi an update. "I'm going," he told her. "We're setting the terms." *He isn't resigned to debating Trump*, Pelosi thought. *He's really eager to do it.* "As long as State of the Union Joe Biden comes out," she replied to the president, "it'll be great."

In between roll call votes on the House floor several hours before the debate, lawmakers confessed their fears of a Trump romp to Pelosi. Biden did not look sharp. Some suspected that his limited contact with them—and avoidance of the media—suggested an even steeper decline. Others echoed the theory that Trump would bully and bluster his way to a victory that night. White House officials had tried to calm skeptics in private conversations, explaining their view that the debate was a necessary part of the presidential campaign process, that Biden would rise to the occasion, and that the contrast with Trump would be clear and convincing.

Pelosi deployed some of the same arguments to reassure worried colleagues. But she privately harbored concerns about the risk of resting the fate of the party and the country on the spectacle of a side-by-side of Biden and Trump—which was why she needed to watch by herself. In that, she wasn't alone.

Jim Clyburn, the eighty-three-year-old former House majority whip, turned down nearly a dozen invitations to join friends that night, including one from the Congressional Black Caucus, which he had once chaired. He attributed his apprehensiveness to the gut instincts acquired from a lifetime in politics. *If it doesn't go well*, he thought, *I don't want anyone to see me cry.* He sequestered at his Washington condo, mixing Diet Pepsi into a glass of Jack Daniel's before he settled in. Maybe that would settle his nerves. *Maybe.*

Dunn, the grand dame of Beltway public relations, locked her blue eyes on a videoconference from her Washington home. She had helped run Biden's prep sessions that week at Camp David. But instead of flying to the Atlanta debate with him and the rest of the campaign brain trust, she had driven back to the nation's capital. In private White House deliberations, her counsel had evolved. At first she entertained the idea of sticking a knife in presidential debates altogether. Once it was clear that Biden would not run from a fight, she argued, successfully, for an early first debate date. A big win might shake up a static race in which Trump held a small but stubborn lead. If things went sideways, as they often did for incumbents in the first debate of their reelection campaigns, it would give Biden more time to recover. Biden and the rest of his inner circle agreed with her reasoning.

Now Dunn homed in on a screen showing campaign pollster David Binder leading a small set of swing-state voters in a focus group. This way, she would be able to monitor the voters' reactions to the candidates in real time, measured by dials they used to rate responses. Dunn believed Biden had not practiced enough. But she soothed herself with the hopeful—perhaps revisionist—thought that he had a history of overperforming at crucial moments. Maybe he could dig down one more time to find a little Biden magic. *Maybe.*

In a luxury condo on the Upper East Side of Manhattan, a few blocks from his favorite cigar lounge, Rev. Al Sharpton held his expectations in check. The once-chubby radical activist now had a sleek frame and confirmed status in the political establishment. He had long since traded in tracksuits for three-piece suits, he counted presidents—including Biden—as friends, and he had become a fixture on MSNBC. Though his own presidential ambitions had fallen well short, he was an astute observer of political talent. *Joe can hold his own*, Sharpton thought as the zero hour neared. *But he's not a knockout-punch debater.* Perhaps the rules, particularly one silencing the microphone of the candidate who wasn't speaking, would cut to Biden's benefit and frustrate the interjection-happy Trump. *Maybe.*

Inside his Ponce Inlet, Florida, home, just south of Daytona Beach on the Atlantic coast, Democratic megadonor John Morgan drizzled butter into a deep bucket of fresh popcorn while pregame debate punditry droned in the background. Feeling a thrill of excitement, the nation's most prominent personal injury lawyer treated himself by pouring a full-calorie Coke over ice. *Biden's going to mop the floor with Trump*, he thought, popping a few kernels into his mouth as CNN co-moderators Jake Tapper and Dana Bash appeared on his screen to introduce the candidates.

Then a single camera shot focused on Biden for the first time that night, and the Democratic universe began to unravel. *His face is so pallid*, Pelosi thought. Biden, his hair wispy and white, walked gingerly toward his lectern, waving at an imaginary audience. Pelosi's concern grew. *He looks uncertain.*

At a restaurant in downtown Atlanta, where a couple dozen campaign officials and high-end donors gathered for a watch party, shoulders slumped, arms folded across chests, and heads shook in confusion in the opening minutes. Hearing audible gasps, one money bundler looked around the party and noticed no one was smiling. Not Jaime Harrison, the normally buoyant chair of the Democratic National Committee. Not Senator Amy Klobuchar, a Minnesota Democrat and former presidential candidate who had seen her share of good and bad nationally televised debate performances. And not Julie Chavez Rodriguez, the Biden campaign manager. A troubling thought popped into the money bundler's mind as he surveyed the macabre scene: *How in the hell can we survive this?*

Biden, a man who suffered through the premature deaths of his first wife and two of his children, and rebounded from a string of primary defeats to win the White House in 2020, had always found his moorings in the face of the most vicious winds nature and politics could summon.

But on debate night, with the eyes of the nation upon him and the hopes of the Democratic Party clinging to his frail body, the eighty-one-year-old Biden drifted in the crosscurrents of his own thoughts.

In his first rebuttal of Trump, Biden claimed that no American troops had died abroad during his presidency—appearing to forget the thirteen service members killed during an attack on Kabul International Airport during the August 2021 U.S. withdrawal from Afghanistan. That moment had been a major turning point for Biden with the American public, plunging his approval ratings. Moments later, he trailed off into nonsense midsentence, asserting that he would make "every single solitary person eligible for what I've been able to do with Covid."

Biden knew that didn't sound right. He cut himself off. His lids covered his eyes as he looked down to the lectern in front of him. He searched inside for an answer. As Biden paused in silence, millions of Democrats' hearts stopped. They stared at the expressionless face pale with horror-show makeup. They waited for him to say something—anything but the phrase that next escaped his dry lips. Lifting his chin, gathering his poise and a measure of familiar Biden brio, he reconnected with CNN moderators Jake Tapper and Dana Bash. Then, he misfired again: "We finally beat Medicare!"

He didn't beat Medicare. He didn't try to beat Medicare. No Democrat would try to beat Medicare. And perhaps most important, the off-target boast had little to do with what he had been talking about. Biden meant that he had outmaneuvered PhRMA, the drug lobby, to lower prescription prices for some seniors. It was one of his signature achievements. He wanted to accuse Trump of trying to kill Medicare, the federal health insurance program for the elderly, and its sister entitlement, Social Security.

On one level, Biden handed Trump a debate-night gift. "Well, he's right—he did beat Medicaid," Trump replied, mistakenly referring to the third major entitlement—the health insurance program for the poor and disabled. "He beat it to death. And he's destroying Medicare, because all of these people are coming in, they're putting them on Medicare. They're putting them on Social Security. They're going to destroy Social Security."

On a much deeper level, Biden altered the course of the 2024 election in a profound and permanent manner. In that moment, and in a cavalcade of stumbles that night, he showed voters that his faculties were diminished. It was impossible to unsee the president, the leader of the free world and the master of a nuclear arsenal, bereft of coherent thought. Biden's slow gait, wan complexion, and hoarse whisper of a voice completed the portrait of lifelessness. For four years, since they ran against each other the first time, Trump had claimed that Biden was enfeebled both physically and mentally, and incapable of running the country. Now Trump looked like the truth-teller—at least on that score.

Trump couldn't believe it. It took him some time to adjust to the idea that he had been right about Biden. His attacks went unanswered. Biden absorbed blows and didn't punch back. *How do I keep hitting him without coming off as an asshole?* Trump thought. *And if I stop hitting him, will viewers lose interest?* He suddenly became acutely aware of the optics of bullying a sitting president of the United States. He could go too far. *They all think I'm going to go off the rails,* Trump thought. Instead, he drew back. An odd note that sounded almost like sympathy touched Trump's voice after Biden spit forth word salad during an answer about border security. "I really don't know what he said at the end of that sentence," Trump said. "I don't think he knows what he said either."

In a nearby hold room, senior Trump advisers Susie Wiles, Jason Miller, and Stephen Miller sat speechless. Coming into the debate, they had worried that Trump was not taking his informal prep sessions seriously enough—and that Biden might exceed a low bar of expectations. This was too good to be true. *Holy shit!* thought Wiles, who seldom let profanity slip through her lips.

Back in Washington, Pelosi's phone exploded. Messages from alarmed Democrats poured in. She shot a text to Morgan, the donor in Florida. *What are you seeing? What are you thinking?*

This is a natural disaster playing out before our very eyes, wrote Morgan, who could be counted among Biden's staunchest loyalists. His phone pinged. It was Pelosi again. *John Morgan says this is a disaster.* The text was a mistake. She had intended to send it to her husband. Life was suddenly moving very fast for everyone but Biden, whose brutal night continued to unfold in ruthlessly slow motion.

Even as recently as the 2020 election, Biden had been capable of responding rapidly on a debate stage. During a primary debate in Miami in 2019, Representative Eric Swalwell, a California Democrat, suggested Biden was too old to represent his party against Trump. It was time for Biden to "pass the torch" to a new generation of leaders, Swalwell said. Not yet forty, Swalwell got a pointed rejoinder from his elder: "I'm holding on to that torch," Biden replied.

Like most lawmakers, Swalwell did not get invited to Biden's White House very often. It was not until June 2023, at the annual White House picnic for members of Congress, that he first became concerned about Biden's mental acuity. When they came face-to-face, Biden did not immediately recognize his onetime rival for the party's nomination. Swalwell had to cue Biden with personal details to remind him.

Watching the Biden-Trump contest with their wives, Swalwell and Arizona representative Ruben Gallego turned quickly to dark humor as they sat in the living room of Swalwell's Capitol Hill home. In the midst of Biden's stumbles, there was a loud knock on Swalwell's door. "They're already here for you," Gallego ribbed Swalwell, a favorite Trump target who had served as an impeachment manager. "It's over," Gallego said. "You're going to jail." The rap at the door had come from an Uber Eats driver with a dinner delivery. But Gallego, who was locked in a tough battle for an Arizona Senate seat, kept razzing his buddy. "I know folks in the tribes," he said. "I can hide you."

Delaware senator Chris Coons, one of Biden's closest confidants, missed the opening minutes of the debate as he shook hands and slapped backs at a campaign watch party in the Roxborough neighborhood of Philadelphia, a rich hunting ground for Democratic votes. But it didn't take him long to catch up to the catastrophe. Sitting down with a plate of snacks, he felt his phone buzz continuously in his pocket. A onetime Biden intern who held the president's former Senate seat, Coons was known as Biden's man on Capitol Hill. As he made quick work of his appetizer plate, the messages from fellow senators and colleagues arrived in rat-a-tat fashion. They all wanted him to answer for what they were witnessing. "Disaster!" "Terrible!" "What the hell is going on?"

Coons wasn't even supposed to be in the country. Innocently enough, he had called Anita Dunn earlier in the week to offer long-distance help. He was in Europe, and he could spin the media after the debate from Rome, he assured her. Dunn, ensconced in Biden's debate prep at the time, disagreed vehemently. "The hell you can," she replied, all but ordering the senator to find the nearest airplane and get on it. "We need you back here."

He canceled the rest of his trip, scrambled to book a flight across the Atlantic, and landed in Philadelphia hours before the debate. Now, jet-lagged, he found himself thrust into the unusual position of protecting Biden from Democratic senators. He knew, as Biden's guy in their chamber, he could give no ground. If he did, it would only feed the frenzy. He shot back texts accusing his colleagues of "bed-wetting," telling them to put their big-kid pants on and asking what was wrong with them that they would so easily go faithless on the president.

As his thumbs banged on the screen, he kept watching. He could see what they saw, even if he wouldn't say it. *This is awful*, he thought as the debate neared the halfway mark. *Damn, this really is not picking up.* The back half wasn't as bad, he convinced himself, but it was hardly good. He knew he would be a lead member of the cleanup crew. And while senators pissing their pants was nothing new, they were right that the president had shit the bed.

Coons briefly stopped replying to texts so that he could send a fresh one to former Delaware governor Jack Markell, the ambassador to Italy and another Biden ally. He wanted a gut check, and Markell had been with Biden at a G-7 meeting of the leaders of the world's top economies earlier in the month.

"Did you see anything like that?" Coons asked.

No, Markell told him. Nothing like this. Coons went back to triage on the frantic messages from colleagues that continued to pop up like hurricane warnings on his phone. The same scene played out on the screens of politicians, party operatives, and progressive pundits across the country—a widespread freakout unlike any other in American political history.

Biden's top White House and campaign advisers huddled around a television monitor in a small hold room outside the debate studio. Jennifer O'Malley Dillon, his campaign chief, dialed in to a Zoom meeting that connected the senior staff to aides at other locations. Within minutes, she was receiving text messages from donors and elected officials predicting doom for the campaign. She flipped her phone over so she could focus on damage control.

Vice President Kamala Harris was insulated from much of it as she watched in silence from a Los Angeles hotel conference room. As a security measure—and a godsend to staff—Harris's cell phone could not receive text messages. But she did not need color commentary to analyze the blow-by-blow takedown.

Harris had blindsided a more alert Biden in 2019, during the same primary debate in which Swalwell had told him to "pass the torch." Back then, Harris painted Biden as a segregationist—citing his opposition to school busing in the 1970s—in such coldblooded fashion that it almost cost her a spot on his ticket the following year. Jill Biden had never gotten over the attack on her husband or the raw ambition she saw behind it. But Joe Biden had looked past that moment to pick Harris and ultimately put her one heartbeat away from the most powerful job on earth. That was the root of her fealty to Biden, a degree of loyalty uncommon for politicians at her level. In her mind, he had earned it. Even when Washington's chattering classes were cruel to her, Biden was kind. He had been vice president for eight years, and he had taken her under his wing.

It pained Harris to watch him struggle against Trump. Sitting with her chief of staff, Sheila Nix, and communications aides Brian Fallon and Kirsten Allen, Harris kept her thoughts to herself—cross talk in the conference room would have made it harder to hear Biden and Trump—until the first commercial break.

But one thought kept running through her head: *Why did we put him out there?*

★

In June 2023, one year before the debate and two months after he'd formally announced that he would seek reelection, Biden entered a reception at the Pool Lounge, an elegant glass-and-steel-lined event space inside the Mies van der Rohe–designed Seagram Building, on Park Avenue. Biden arrived by motorcade as service workers arranged a dessert bar with an assortment of donuts: chocolate blackout, blueberry, and key lime. It was his second pitch for cash that night, this time with heavy-hitting Wall Street donors, and the president appeared to be out of sorts when investment banker Blair Effron introduced him to a crowd of about fifty donors at 7:30 p.m.

While wealthy contributors listened to Biden brag about "Bidenomics" and warn that "there's so much at stake," the president's muscles tightened. His speech slurred. His body locked up for a moment—just long enough to leave at least one audience member concerned that he might not make it to Election Day. Others wondered if he had the faculties to compete for the presidency. "It wasn't just physical," said one decades-long acquaintance of Biden who was at the reception and witnessed similar episodes from time to time during his presidency.

Hours earlier, Biden had curiously gotten up from his chair on the set of MSNBC's *Deadline: White House* and wandered off behind host Nicolle Wallace before she could transition from their interview to a commercial break. A clip of the disoriented president instantly went viral on social media, racking up more than 2 million views.

Throughout his term, Biden fed into Republican claims that the White House lights were on but no one was home. He seldom held press conferences or participated in extended interviews. He relied heavily on printed talking points with extra-large lettering when meeting privately with lawmakers and members of his Cabinet. He often tripped over his words during public remarks. His aides wrote off these episodes as unreflective of the sharp mind they said they encountered at the White House every day. They regaled reporters with stories of Biden poring over thick briefing books and driving action in his administration— protecting the president with a counternarrative—that were dutifully reported in print and on the air.

The gulf between Biden's obvious struggles and his fit-as-a-fiddle messaging should have been easy for Trump to exploit. But the former president couldn't resist hitting his rival from both sides. He accused

Biden of being a puppet of West Wing aides and, without evidence, also portrayed the president as the mastermind behind four separate criminal cases against him. The incongruity helped Democrats dismiss the attacks, along with their own doubts about Biden.

Publicly, Democrats scoffed at Republican claims that Biden wasn't up to the job. But privately, some of them worried all along that they were putting too much stock in an old man who, at best, had long since lost his fastball. During his 2020 campaign, aides tried to keep his calendar clear at night. That same year, the Covid pandemic restricted his contact with the outside world. Once he was elected, White House aides continued to limit his exposure—even to allies. Coronavirus protocols gave them a ready justification. But even when the rules eased, Biden remained closed off.

Ultimately, a core group of family and deeply loyal aides acted as gatekeepers, schedulers, and protectors of Biden. First Lady Jill Biden carried the most sway. Her chief of staff, Anthony Bernal, and White House deputy chief of staff Annie Tomasini—who had been at the president's side for years—helped manage his calendar and his personal needs. Successive White House chiefs of staff Ron Klain and Jeff Zients, along with presidential counselor Mike Donilon, senior adviser Steve Ricchetti, Anita Dunn, and Deputy Chief of Staff Bruce Reed, formed a cocoon around Biden that tightened and hardened with each passing month.

But his capabilities did not decline in a strictly linear fashion. There were good hours and bad hours, great days and lost days. Over time, he was foggy more often and sharp less often. The shift became more dramatic in the spring of 2024, according to an aide who saw Biden semiregularly. "Physically, mentally, there was definitely a drop," the aide said. The change was harder for Democrats outside his tight circle to detect. They had to rely on reports from the aides who were protecting him.

In that way, the White House team permitted the Democratic Party to shield itself from the hard reality of Biden's condition. Elected officials who believed he was losing altitude, either from personal interactions or from what they could glean by watching him on television, were reluctant to say so openly, fearful of being read out of their own party for heresy. They also protected Biden because they believed he was their best chance to stop Trump from taking the White House. But the signs of decline were clear to anyone who was willing to see them.

Behind the scenes, in brief interactions in the White House, lawmakers and aides outside of Biden's inner circle would occasionally gossip about what they had seen. In one West Wing meeting in September 2021, as he tried to convince Democratic holdouts to help advance his agenda, Biden rambled far off topic, telling unrelated stories about his days in the Senate. Some wrote it off as a sentimental trip down memory lane, while others took the departure from talks about his sweeping economic proposal as evidence that he was losing his grip.

In late September 2022, Biden invited members of the late representative Jackie Walorski's family to the White House. A couple of days earlier, he had searched a crowd for the Indiana congresswoman to credit her for cosponsoring legislation creating a conference on hunger. "Jackie, are you here?" Biden said. "Where's Jackie?" She had died in a car crash the previous month. To help make up for the gaffe, he invited her ninety-year-old mother into the Oval Office and gave her and other family members a tour of the White House. Biden took a small group of Walorski family members, lawmakers, and the first lady to the White House dining room.

"Do you want to go outside?" he asked the Walorski family.

"No!" Jill Biden interjected from the other side of the table. "They don't want to go outside."

The president looked at Walorski's mom as he opened a door to the South Lawn. "Are you sure you don't want to go outside?" he asked. She did.

California representative Kevin McCarthy, the House minority leader, tagged along as Biden led his tour group down to the White House swimming pool and to the changing rooms.

What the fuck is going on? McCarthy thought. *What could be so interesting about the lockers?*

Biden tried the door. It was locked, and he needed a Secret Service agent to unlock it. Inside there was nothing more exciting than two dressing rooms. McCarthy, thinking he had just become a temporary staff minder for the president, prompted Biden to head back into the White House. The tour continued into a small office Biden had set up adjacent to the Oval Office with a desk, a chair, and a valet. A wrinkled blue shirt hung on the valet. He pointed out a painting that he particularly liked.

Holy shit, McCarthy thought. *The president is not with it.*

The lawmaker wandered back into the Oval Office, effectively leading the tour out of the tighter space with Biden's smaller desk. The president perked back up as he walked into the Oval.

"Kevin, ask me why I have a painting of Abraham Lincoln," Biden said, before answering his own question. "It's because we've never been at a time like this since the Civil War." McCarthy walked out to his car that night feeling a hint of sadness. *This guy's literally lost his mind*, he thought to himself.

About a month before the New York fundraiser with Wall Street donors, Biden stumbled over a sandbag—literally—at the U.S. Air Force Academy graduation ceremony in Colorado. After that, he grudgingly made minor changes to his routine. He started wearing "maximum stability" HOKA shoes more often, and he began using a shorter flight of wheel-up steps to board Air Force One from under the plane's belly rather than the longer set of airstairs commonly used by departing and arriving presidents. His brother Frank told friends that the nerves in Biden's feet were often inflamed to the point that he felt a burning sensation as he walked, a neuropathy their father had endured and which explained the president's ginger tread.

In front of more than a hundred people at an off-the-record conference in Aspen, Colorado, in September 2023, Hollywood superagent Ari Emanuel confronted Klain about the president's fitness. It's grossly irresponsible for someone of Biden's age, who is already clearly slowing down, to run for president again, Emanuel asserted during a question-and-answer session. Beyond his standing as a party donor, Emanuel's brother Rahm was Biden's ambassador to Japan. Klain, who by that time had left the White House, brushed the concern aside. Biden wasn't going anywhere, he said.

At a February 2024 reception with governors, Biden refused to look at a GOP plan on border security—and then oddly clung to the folder containing it as aides tried to take it from him. For some, it was reminiscent of Biden's performance at a meeting with governors the year before, in the East Room of the White House, when White House staff coached Harris to be ready to step in for Biden if his remarks went sideways. As he trailed off, Harris, sitting next to him, silently rooted for him to finish smoothly. "Her face looked like 'C'mon, C'mon,'" said one Harris aide who was in the room. The same month as the 2024 governors reception, special counsel Robert Hur, tasked with recommending whether to prosecute Biden for retaining classified documents from his vice presidency when he was a private citizen, issued a damaging report to Attorney General Merrick Garland. Hur recommended that the Justice Department refrain from bringing charges against Biden because it would be difficult, if not impossible, to prove that he knowingly kept the documents. "Biden's memory was significantly limited," Hur wrote, both when he spoke with a ghostwriter for his book *Promise Me, Dad* in 2017 and "in his interview with our office in 2023." Biden is an "elderly man with a poor memory," Hur concluded.

Biden struggled to recall which years he served as vice president, details of the debate over withdrawing from Afghanistan in 2021, and even the year in which his son Beau died of brain cancer. At a press conference following the release of the findings, Biden responded defiantly and self-righteously, as his aides often did when his acuity was questioned. "Frankly, when I was asked the question," he said of the timing of his son's death, "I thought to myself, was it any of their damn business?" But Hur, who theorized that Biden would be treated like a kindly old man by a jury, had inflicted damage on the president.

"The special counsel said the quiet part out loud," a former lawmaker who had met with Biden at the White House earlier in his term said at the time. "I think I share some of the concerns of the American people. Because if it's really *Weekend at Bernie's*, who are the two guys carrying him along?" It was more than two guys who acted as crutches for Biden, but not much more.

In April or May of 2024, according to one aide who had recently returned to Biden's orbit after a hiatus, there was a marked difference in his performance. "I was struck by how much better he showed up on TV than he did in person," this aide said. Biden would frequently pause for minutes before exiting his limo and then emerge with a confused look on his face, the aide added. The stories weren't legion, but they were common enough for insiders to sense that Biden wasn't always in top form.

By the month of the debate, Biden's condition had grown worse. On June 10, at a White House concert celebrating the upcoming Juneteenth holiday, he froze for several seconds, standing motionless amid a sea of attendees swaying to R&B music. Vice President Kamala Harris and her husband, Doug Emhoff, danced next to Biden as he stared off into the distance, his arms and hands tense at his sides. At the G-7 meeting in Puglia, Italy, on June 13 and 14, Biden aides noticed that he was physically beat and mentally unfocused as he conversed with leaders of the world's powerhouse economies. "He was tired when he got there, and tired in most of those sessions," one of them said, describing various methods his team devised to keep him on track in the first half of 2024. "Everybody kind of woke up wondering if today was the day when something went sideways," the aide said. "It was like this mix of anxiety and 'let's minimize all the risks we can.'"

While aides spent the early hours of each day worrying about what might go wrong, Biden's mornings started with masking the physical signs of his age. When he traveled overnight, Biden would have a makeup artist meet him around 8 a.m. in a cleared-out hotel room on his floor to smooth out his wrinkles and cover the liver spots on his face. Usually, the room would be set up for Biden to participate in Zoom meetings with aides back at the White House, but he did not consistently do that. "He always made makeup, but the briefings were almost always pulled down," said one aide familiar with his schedule. "He was a late starter for sure." Vanity was nothing new for Biden, whose enhancements over time included hair plugs and veneers. But he and his aides knew that his age was a major issue for voters, and that meant his look mattered more than ever.

None of them said a word about trying to whitewash his age or hide his inability to concentrate on his meetings, but he had sown more doubt about his ability to perform his duties among some of the people who traveled with him.

The day after the summit, Biden appeared to lock up again at a tinsel-tinged Los Angeles fundraising extravaganza featuring former president Barack Obama and Hollywood A-listers. After the two presidents sat for a friendly interview with comedian Jimmy Kimmel, Biden stopped for more than a moment on his way off the stage. Obama walked over to him, took him by the wrist, and led him away. White House aides dismissed both freeze moments—at the Juneteenth concert and the $30 million Hollywood fundraiser—as fake news, arguing that Republicans were trying to turn normal pauses into a medical condition.

Silver screen idol George Clooney would later confide to the country in a *New York Times* op-ed that Father Time's toll on Biden was evident that day. He was no longer the Biden of 2010, or even of 2020, Clooney wrote: "He was the same man we all witnessed at the debate." For whatever reason—likely fear of enabling Trump—he had held his tongue and his pen for several weeks.

But for many Democrats around the country, even professional political operatives who supported Biden, the debate was the first incontrovertible evidence that his worst moments were so awful. At least, Democrats hoped, this is rock bottom. *Maybe.* The people closest to Biden would never cop to the complicity of their own silence. None of them wanted to take the blame for their collective neglect.

What many Democratic voters didn't grasp at the time was that Biden was already on track to lose, and the highest-ranking party insiders were well aware of that. He had won by a comfortable popular-vote majority in 2020—with more than 7 million votes separating him from Trump—which led his supporters to believe he had cruised to victory.

But in the only measure that matters, the Electoral College, Biden's spread in the three pivotal states of Wisconsin, Arizona, and Georgia amounted, cumulatively, to less than 44,000 votes. There was no room for slippage in swing states. Biden trailed Trump in enough of the seven major battlegrounds—Pennsylvania, Michigan, Wisconsin, Georgia, Arizona, North Carolina, and Nevada—that it was hard to see how he could change his trajectory against a rival who was equally well defined for the electorate.

His campaign leaders maintained tight control of internal polling and data analytics scores, leaving outsiders and even key staff in the dark about his standing in the horse race. Biden's own team in Pennsylvania, for example, had not been given a breakdown of the state of the race from headquarters since mid-April. "The numbers were not good," said one senior Biden campaign official. Between private and public polls—and the Biden high command's refusal to share internal surveys—it was clear to other top Democrats that he was on course to lose. The June debate was one of the few chances he would have to redirect the race. He did. Just not in the way that he wanted.

"Democrats just committed collective suicide," one veteran Democratic Party strategist wrote in a message to a reporter less than fifteen minutes into the debate. "President Biden can't win. This debate is a nail in the political coffin."

For some Democratic insiders, the debate was a startling alarm—the first sign of a crisis. For others it was the opportunity they had been looking for to force a change at the top of the ticket.

★

In the middle of the afternoon on Tuesday, June 25, two days before the debate, a sickly Biden ambled into the family-style Hickory Lodge theater at Camp David, the presidential retreat nestled on Catoctin Mountain in western Maryland. He was congested. His throat hurt. He couldn't stop blowing his nose into tissues. But he tried to answer the bell for what would be one of his last rounds of prep before he faced Trump. A small clutch of advisers strained to hear him through a raspy voice and incessant coughing. If he knew what he wanted to say, it was hard for them to tell. After forty-five minutes, Biden called an end to the rehearsal. The juice just wasn't worth the squeeze. He would try again the next day.

By the time he left Camp David, nearly a full week after Marine One had touched down on June 20 to deliver him to "debate camp," Biden had barely practiced. Fatigue permeated every fiber of his body. He was worn down from travel and spiritually exhausted from his son Hunter's trial on federal gun charges. He tried his best to juggle the demands of governing and campaigning, but the world didn't slow down for this octogenarian. It sped up. He'd zigzagged across the Atlantic twice in the last two weeks—commemorating the eightieth anniversary of D-Day in France and meeting with the G7 leaders—and popped out to the West Coast for the star-studded fundraising extravaganza featuring Obama, Clooney, and Kimmel. He relished his time on the world stage and in the Hollywood spotlight. One stroked his sense of global importance, the other his need to feel like a celebrity.

"Everyone knew it was insane," one Biden adviser said of crisscrossing the globe and the country in such a short time frame. His internal clock didn't have the chance to reset each time he landed in a new time zone. "If he had been forty-one, that would have been insane." But Biden had insisted on returning to Washington between his trips to Europe, concerned about the optics of leaving the country for so long in the throes of a reelection campaign. There was a price to pay for the jet-setting.

Hunter's trial, which resulted in three felony convictions that month, resurfaced lurid details of the presidential progeny's struggles with drugs and a prolific sex life that included separate relationships with his brother's widow and a stripper. It took a noticeable toll on the president and his family. As he ran for reelection, Biden had to walk a narrow line in embracing the son he loved and at the same time distancing himself from any perception that he was interfering in the prosecution.

Hunter had long felt that a handful of his father's aides were applying too much pressure to the president, and him, to keep a low profile. He blamed Dunn and her husband, Bob Bauer, in particular, because, respectively, they advised Biden on messaging and the law. Bauer, a former White House counsel for Obama, served as the president's personal lawyer. The verdict, rendered a day before Biden's second trip to Europe, magnified the president's pain. He avoided talking about the most salacious aspects of his son's private life, but his aides could see the effects of the turmoil in his manner. "He just shuts down," said one Biden aide who was at Camp David.

Dunn and Bauer had committed another sin in the eyes of some Biden family members. When the president began to plan his reelection bid in the fall of 2022, with Trump on the verge of announcing his own effort, internal talks centered on how to build the campaign, not whether to run it. Mike Donilon, a bushy-browed operative with thinning white hair who had served as the keeper of Biden's message for decades, explained the dynamics to friends and allies in starkly practical terms. "Nobody walks away from this," Donilon, a senior adviser at the White House, told one prominent Democrat. "No one walks away from the house, the plane, the helicopter."

That was doubly true for the first lady. Twenty years earlier, when Biden met with advisers to discuss a possible 2004 run for the presidency, his wife thought it was a bad idea. Jill Biden recalled in her memoir that she was standing by the pool outside their home in Wilmington, where she scrawled the word "NO" on her stomach, between the two pieces of her bikini, and then marched into the house to make her view clear to her husband. But after eight years as the second lady and nearly two more as the first lady, the trappings of the most elite levels of Washington power had grown on her.

For Donilon and White House counselor Steve Ricchetti, a classic D.C. operator who had made a fortune as a lobbyist in between stints in government, the Biden presidency represented a last hurrah at the top of the cottage industry of Washington staffers.

"Ricchetti was one hundred percent in. Donilon was one hundred percent in. All of the people around him. They're my friends but for a lot of them, this was job security and this was as good a job as they're ever gonna get," one Biden ally said. "And let's be honest, Jill was a thousand percent behind this. So, she was pushing it. The staff was all pushing it. At the end of the day, I don't think anyone in that inner circle was presenting the president any contrary advice that this thing is not going to be easy or maybe this is not the best thing for the Democratic Party."

But in 2022, Bauer sat down with the president and first lady to deliver a candid assessment of the punishing legal fights facing the first family, including Hunter Biden. Similarly, Dunn outlined the political challenges on the horizon, including voters' perceptions of Biden's advancing age. Neither of them told Biden not to run, but they also did not pump pom-poms with the vigor that the president's family expected of staff.

The 2022 midterm elections, in which Democrats lost the House but held the Senate, bolstered Biden's conviction about his course. He took the better-than-expected results as a sign that the electorate had shifted away from the MAGA movement and toward his more traditional brand of leadership.

There were plenty of reasons not to run, most notably stubbornly anemic private polling that was shared with his aides. One June 2022 survey, run by the pro-Biden super PAC Unite the Country and circulated at the White House, illustrated the steep mountain he faced. In four states crucial to his Electoral College coalition—Arizona and the three "Blue Wall" states of Pennsylvania, Michigan, and Wisconsin—only 11 percent of voters believed the economy was getting better. In those states, his rating on inflation stood at 26 percent and his overall approval weighed in at 41 percent. Many Democrats were sticking with him despite concluding that the country was headed in the wrong direction and that his policies weren't helping them.

By the spring of 2024, Biden still hadn't solved those problems. He believed that his record as president, including stimulus, infrastructure, and climate-change laws, boosted the economy. Voters didn't agree. But that wasn't his reason for running anyway. He was focused, again, on stopping Trump. It wasn't creative—and few people close to Biden believed he would simply leave office if not for Trump—but he thought it could be sold to voters. What better way than a debate to show he was better than Trump?

In March, as the GOP primaries wound down, Trump began goading Biden. His team wheeled out a second lectern at one of his rallies to provide a visual aid of Biden hiding from Trump. The words "Anywhere. Anytime. Anyplace." were emblazoned on the front panel of the empty lectern. Donilon had always been in favor of Biden debating Trump, believing that a powerful contrast would benefit the president. Dunn, who had been slow to come around on debating Trump at all, now pushed to put a date early in the calendar. Ron Klain, a former White House chief of staff who managed debate prep for Democratic candidates, agreed. Poll numbers had been static, and Democratic political professionals thought Trump held a small lead. "We really felt like the race was pretty stuck," said one Biden aide who was involved in the discussions. "There's a small percentage in there that we were all playing for, but it really wasn't moving."

It was not initially a unanimous call. Bruce Reed, the deputy chief of staff whose ties to Biden dated back decades to their work with the moderate Democratic Leadership Council, thought the president needed as much time to prepare as possible. But Jeff Zients, the chief of staff, prioritized giving the president a single recommendation from his staff whenever a consensus could be reached.

Ultimately, the advisers sided with Dunn and Klain. They believed that Trump's legal troubles were counterintuitively aiding him. And not just because they helped him raise money and stoke energy among his base voters. Because the criminal charges were such big news, the media ignored Biden and didn't cover the "crazy things" Trump said on the campaign trail, as one of his advisers put it. A debate might remind voters why they had sent Trump packing in 2020.

"We didn't think he could sustain ninety minutes without becoming that Trump," said one Biden aide who was involved in the discussions. An early debate, they believed, would refocus voters and create the kind of "big moment" that Biden desperately needed to energize his own voters and grassroots donors. They were also wary of the traditional schedule for debates. Holding them late in the fall meant pulling the candidate and key campaign aides off the trail, devoting resources to debate prep rather than voter turnout. They were a distraction. And, Biden's advisers agreed, according to one of them, debates "fundamentally don't ever really change anything—except in a few cases."

In late April, Biden ended the mystery, telling radio shock jock Howard Stern that he would be "happy" to face off against Trump. He and his closest advisers had essentially made the decision already, but they had not yet alerted the campaign or the White House press shop. Coincidentally, top Trump aides, in the midst of a round of off-the-record talks with network executives about the upcoming Republican National Convention, were leaving Fox News headquarters—in the same complex of buildings as Stern's Sirius XM studio—when Biden delivered the news. They were shocked. Senior advisers Susie Wiles, Chris LaCivita, and

Danielle Alvarez scrambled across the street to Avra, a Greek restaurant at Rockefeller Center, with Republican National Committee chief of staff Richard Walters in tow.

Wiles, a daughter of legendary football announcer Pat Summerall, had made her name in establishment politics in Florida before taking over as Trump's de facto campaign manager. Soft-spoken and grandmotherly in appearance, she cut a striking contrast in a Trumpworld stocked with men who looked like bouncers and women whose surgical enhancements were as garish as their clothing. She was tougher than the bro squad that surrounded Trump: at her father's alcohol-abuse intervention years earlier, he was read a letter from her that described her embarrassment at sharing his last name. Summerall got sober. As important for Trump, she was an expert inside player who maintained discipline better than any of her predecessors in his White House and campaign operations. "What's the move?" she asked the group around the table at Avra.

LaCivita looked up from his plate, over the antennae of a gargantuan shelled lobster that was split in half and covered in pasta. Technically he was Wiles's peer as a fellow senior adviser, but she was the undisputed queen of Trump's campaign apparatus. A veteran of the Persian Gulf War, the bald, bearded, and burly political operative had made the 2004 Swift Boat Veterans for Truth ads that distorted Democratic nominee John Kerry's war record. After helping Trump win the primary, LaCivita took over a role running the day-to-day operations of the RNC while continuing to advise Trump. As Walters and Alvarez conferred about how to respond to Biden, LaCivita went back to work on his own version of surf and turf.

Alvarez and Walters told Wiles that she should send a note to Biden campaign chair Jennifer O'Malley Dillon—her opposite number on the president's team—because, based on an outdated view of Dunn's position, they believed O'Malley Dillon was more amenable to debates than Dunn. Wiles had met O'Malley Dillon—known by the deity-like initials JOD in Democratic campaign circles—the previous month at Washington's annual Gridiron Dinner and had told her colleagues she was surprised to find that the Biden campaign chief was "so normal."

Alvarez took Wiles's phone and tapped out a message to O'Malley Dillon: *We'd like to have an off-the-record conversation about planning a debate.* O'Malley Dillon responded that she would need a day or two to socialize the idea with Biden's team. Biden had not given her a heads-up about agreeing to a debate on Stern's show, she said. That made two campaigns that were caught off guard by Biden's declaration. Both camps quickly found consensus on a pair of issues: neither wanted to use the long-standing Commission on Presidential Debates as a mediator and both wanted to exclude Robert F. Kennedy Jr., an independent candidate, from the stage.

In May, Biden's team negotiated rules for a June debate with CNN, came to an agreement, and then dared Trump to go back on his word. The Trump campaign accused the network of conspiring with Democrats to write the rules without them. That's what had happened, but Trump had given his team no room to maneuver. "We have no leverage," LaCivita acknowledged in a testy meeting with CNN executives. The Biden camp used its power to insist on all the protocols: no live audience, time limits for answers, and the muting of the opponent's microphone when a candidate was talking. Trump's aides came up with what they thought of as the most petty demands as a form of rebellion. For example, they pushed CNN to require that both candidates have the same number of steps from their cars to the debate stage. But Trump, certain he could trounce Biden, quickly accepted the date and basic terms.

Inside a helicopter hangar at Camp David, Biden's team built a full, made-to-measure, Hollywood-style debate set. Jeffrey Katzenberg, the billionaire co-chair of his campaign and longtime studio executive, helped oversee the production and sat in on prep sessions. But in the end, they completed just one mock debate in the extravagantly outfitted hangar—and that session, three days before the debate, would provide a hint of the trouble ahead.

Dunn, wearing a signature bob, which she had allowed to go white after years of blonde, sat at a moderators' desk to play CNN's Dana Bash. White House communications director Ben LaBolt sat next to her in the role of Jake Tapper. Biden took up his spot behind one lectern, while Bauer stood in for Trump at the other. Just before they began, deputy

White House chief of staff Annie Tomasini, Biden's longtime personal aide, circulated word that the president was feeling the beginnings of a cold. A five-foot-seven guard on Boston University's basketball team in the 1990s, Tomasini had grown so close to the Biden family that his aides rightly thought of her as the representative of the Biden clan's wishes. When Biden was homebound during Covid, Tomasini was one of a handful of outsiders who were allowed in his Wilmington house. She told Dunn to limit the session to an hour—two-thirds the length of the actual debate.

The president, low on energy and fighting back the cold, failed to hit back hard against Bauer's barrage of attacks. Dunn used her authority to let the mock debate play out for fifteen minutes longer than Tomasini prescribed. Never the most electric debater, Biden struggled to keep his answers concise. It wasn't the worst his longtime aides had seen him in a debate rehearsal, but it wasn't the best. *He's not in terrible shape*, one of them thought in a moment of self-reassurance. That was a low bar for a sitting president of the United States.

Biden family members thought his aides were running him down. His aides thought he needed more time to rehearse for one of the few major moments of the campaign. That tension point had been growing over the course of years, but it became particularly acute in the weeks leading up to the debate, as Biden trotted the globe in service of country and campaign.

Then everything went to shit. Biden woke up Tuesday morning with overwhelming cold symptoms, leading to the decision to limit his practice to the forty-five-minute round in the Hickory Lodge theater. No matter how much his mental capacity had diminished, neither the sickness nor the rehearsal time it stole would improve his performance. His team wouldn't see him again until the next day. Under normal circumstances, they would spend two or three hours with him a couple of times a day during debate camp. He was being robbed of essential rounds of mental exercise. "We weren't spending any time with him," one of them said later.

By Wednesday, the day before the debate, Biden's illness had grown serious enough that he tested for Covid. He pushed through another light round of questioning but couldn't muster the strength for a full mock. There was no serious consideration given to canceling the debate, just as there had been no real discussion about avoiding debates entirely or choosing to seek reelection. "That would have been a horrific disaster, suggesting the president couldn't debate because he had a cold," said one top Biden adviser. "Play that out for a minute. We would have been out of the race in twenty-four hours."

But to the extent that Biden's family and his aides worried about his state, they betrayed no concern to the outside world. On Thursday, the day of the debate, Biden practiced a little bit more on the flight from Camp David to Atlanta, and with a small set of aides at his hotel.

A couple of hours before showtime, Jill Biden strode confidently into a salon in the basement of the Ritz-Carlton hotel in downtown Atlanta. The campaign had brought its biggest cash bundlers to town for national finance committee meetings. The first lady was a surprise guest, a bit of a treat for the donor network to break up the drudgery of presentations.

"The president's feeling great," Jill Biden said. "He's ready. We're going to win this thing!" She didn't mention his cold.

CHAPTER 2

CONTINGENCY PLANS

FIX IT!" DANIELLE ALVAREZ DEMANDED IN A LOW BUT FIRM VOICE FROM the back of the O'Keefe Gymnasium on Georgia Tech's midtown campus. The audio wasn't working on a mammoth television monitor set on one wall of the volleyball arena, which had been piped and draped to give Trump's allies a place to watch together in privacy a short walk away from the postdebate spin room. About two dozen of them—vice presidential hopefuls, governors, senators, House members, and the like—had been bused in from a fundraiser and, sitting in rows of long tables in the gym, they couldn't hear the beginning of the debate. Biden's lips were moving, but there wasn't enough sound.

The VIPs, many of whom had pens ready to take notes, looked askance. Alvarez, thirty-five, with long, straight black hair parted in the middle, pressed Trump's operations team to find a technician. Then, when her boss spoke—clearly—it struck her in a flash that there was nothing wrong with the sound. *The audio isn't fucked-up*, Alvarez thought. *It's Biden*. Her deep brown eyes lit up. She broke into a smile as she looked at Brian Hughes, the flat-topped Trump adviser sitting next to her. Alvarez grabbed his shoulder and blurted out "It's *happening*!"

Trump aides scrambled to rewrite the top of a one-page set of talking points they distributed to the crew of VIP surrogates. Alvarez, a top communications adviser, stood in front of the surrogates during the final commercial break and hit the high points: Biden had lied by claiming the endorsement of the Border Patrol union and by asserting that no troops had died abroad on his watch. Trump's economic plans would rescue the country while Biden's would lead to higher prices for consumers. And, she emphasized, it's not just that Biden failed to perform; Trump, she said, was flawless.

The surrogates lined up to march across a long parking lot between O'Keefe and McCamish Pavilion, the Yellow Jackets' basketball arena, which housed the media spin room. A lost coin flip had relegated them to the volleyball court while Biden's surrogates had the ostensible advantage of space inside McCamish, closer to the media. Trump's foot soldiers would have to speed-walk to limit the amount of time Biden's allies would have alone with the press—or so they thought.

But, entering the spin room, the Trump surrogates—Senator JD Vance (R-OH), Senator Marco Rubio (R-FL), and Governor Doug Burgum (R-ND) among them—quickly realized they didn't have to compete for attention. Biden's allies weren't there. Minutes ticked by. Reporters eager for the Biden camp's reaction waited, impatiently, for interviews. Alvarez looked down at her watch. It had been nearly half an hour since the end of the debate. Finally, Biden campaign communicators emerged, briefly, to talk to the press. They exited as spontaneously as they had arrived.

Alvarez smiled to herself. *We just fucking won big*, she thought.

Leaving the stage, Trump sent word that he wanted to see Wiles. She made her way through a backstage maze to find the former president. As he walked toward her, Trump opened his eyes wide. *We got this*, Wiles thought, mirroring Trump's expression. *Biden is gone.*

Trump received a hero's welcome in the hold room, including from Jason Miller, the no-holds-barred senior adviser who had leapt to his feet during the opening moments of the broadcast to yell, "He's fucked-up, guys. Biden is fucked-up. Something is wrong." Now Miller wanted to know how Trump had perceived it from the stage. "I didn't really know until maybe fifteen or twenty minutes in," Trump said. "Then I realized there was something wrong with him. I know sometimes we say it, but I realized something was wrong."

★

Former president Barack Obama was shocked, if not surprised. The forty-fourth president never had much faith in Biden's political ability.

He'd skipped over Biden to bless Hillary Clinton in 2016 and stayed out of the Democratic primary in 2020 until it became a clear choice between Biden and Bernie Sanders, a self-described socialist. He thought there were better candidates in the field that year. When Biden implied to voters that he would serve just one term—even calling himself a "bridge" to the next generation of leaders—Obama told friends he thought that made the most sense. If Biden was lucky enough to win a first term, he shouldn't test fate again at eighty-one years old.

From his retreat on Martha's Vineyard, where he played golf almost daily with billionaires, entertainment icons, and sports stars, Obama liked to think of himself as floating above the fray. He kept tabs on politics, but he was no longer immersed in every twist and turn of national affairs. He chafed at his former vice president's oft-made claim to be the most successful president since at least Lyndon Johnson, but he worried more—in part as a Democrat, in part as a friend—about Biden's condition. Obama knew from experience how the job aged a man, and he could see the effects when he watched Biden on television and in their rare joint appearances. Less than two weeks earlier, at the Los Angeles fundraiser, Obama led Biden offstage by the wrist after the president stood frozen for a few moments while staring into the crowd.

The circle of Biden aides overlapped with the set of Obama White House veterans, and the former president had a pretty good handle on Biden's capabilities. It was not surprising to him at all that Biden was struggling in his rematch with Trump—a race Obama didn't think Biden should have run in the first place. He didn't even watch the debate live—he was alerted to the catastrophe by his phone—but the Biden he saw in clips was unrecognizable. It was stunning, all five alarms cranking at full volume long before the Democratic Party, and perhaps the republic, might be consumed by a November inferno. Obama kept his thoughts to himself that night, but his proxies didn't afford Biden the same courtesy.

"There are going to be discussions about whether he should continue," David Axelrod, one of Obama's top advisers on the campaign trail and in the White House, said on CNN immediately after the debate ended. As "Axe" surely knew, those conversations had already reached full cacophony.

Even some longtime Biden allies began to grapple with a reality they had long refused to confront: he might not be fit to run—or continue serving. But if Democratic officials spoke of the latter publicly, if they told voters the sitting president was in no shape to run the country, they would surely forfeit any chance at winning in November, whether it was Biden or another Democrat at the top of the ticket. Voters could forgive a lot in prioritizing partisanship over country, but not that.

Democratic leaders instantly grasped the peril they were in. He was no longer just playing with his own electoral fate. He represented an existential threat to his party's chances of winning up and down the ballot in November. The fear was particularly acute among congressional Democrats. He could pull them down with him, erasing their hopes of winning a House majority from a Republican Party so badly divided that it had recently executed a coup against its own Speaker. Senate Democrats owned a narrow majority but faced a tougher electoral map, with vulnerable seats in West Virginia, Montana, Ohio, and, if the bottom dropped out, in more reliably Democratic states. Pelosi didn't need fresh polling or a crystal ball to see the coming train wreck: a Republican trifecta of Trump in the White House and GOP majorities in both chambers of Congress.

One Democratic House member, knowing his words would be repeated as he texted a reporter, likened the president to a punch-drunk boxer. His team should "throw in the towel" on the election, the lawmaker wrote, just minutes after the debate's conclusion. In the electronic warrens of congressional text chains, fear and anger exploded.

"The chat groups are lighting up," said one House Democrat who described the messages from fellow lawmakers this way: "We're done." "We're fucked." "What the hell is happening?" "Is he really this bad?" "How could they have kept this from us?" "He's got to drop out." "We're going to lose 20 seats in the House."

In at least one private thread, the search for a replacement candidate had already begun. Representative Hillary Scholten, a freshman Democrat from a highly competitive district anchored in Grand Rapids, Michigan, was one of the first to abandon Biden. In a group chat with other Democratic women lawmakers that night, Scholten texted, *Whit-*

mer for president. One colleague quickly seconded her call for Michigan governor Gretchen Whitmer to take Biden's place atop the ticket. Members of the Congressional Black Caucus wasted no time in pushing back on Scholten. But they didn't do it to defend Biden. They laid down a marker: if Biden exited the race, they would accept no option other than Vice President Kamala Harris.

At that point, Biden had a claim on more than 90 percent of the delegates to the Democratic nominating convention in Chicago in August. Other than throwaway instant polls, no survey had been taken of voters. He hadn't even left Atlanta yet. But, unbeknownst to him, the rumblings of a political insurrection buzzed throughout the Democratic universe. Members of Congress weren't fighting over him. They were drawing battle lines, with more than a hint of racial subtext, on the question of who should take his place on the ballot. "I watched the black-white stuff start on Thursday night," said one lawmaker who was in the group chat.

★

At the Atlanta restaurant, the job of summing up the evening for Biden's financiers fell to Chavez Rodriguez as the ranking campaign official. She walked to the front of the party and looked out to see a mix of disappointment, frustration, and anger. For months, she and other campaign aides had worked to reassure these people that Biden was not only in good health but on track to win the election. They had repeated the guarantees as they lobbied deep-pocketed Democrats to keep giving money in increments of thousands of dollars, hundreds of thousands of dollars, and, in max-out cases, more than $900,000.

Chavez Rodriguez, the granddaughter of legendary labor leader Cesar Chavez, felt her throat clutch. Tears began to well in her eyes. She tried to speak, but no words came out. There was nothing she could say to explain away what everyone had just witnessed. Harrison and Klobuchar quickly came to her aid. Taking turns, they offered words of comfort to a small crowd eager to hear anything positive. Everything would be fine, they said.

But the Biden fundraisers voted with their feet. Given the opportunity to go see him at a postdebate stop, most chose to return to their hotel, according to one person who was at the restaurant. "The whole group was very demoralized," this person said. "They felt like they'd been hit by a truck."

In the middle of the night, one of the Biden buckrakers received a flurry of calls and texts that were "pleas for him to get out of the race" as soon as possible. "There's been lots of chatter about his age and whatnot," the fundraiser said. "But this was new. It was dramatic. It was pretty aggressive and pretty fast, and it hit me like a ton of bricks."

On the eighth floor at Biden campaign headquarters in Wilmington, Delaware, campaign aides knew they had watched a debacle as they grazed on the remnants of stir fry, salads, and granola lovers' desserts from Philadelphia-based Honeygrow. "We knew the coverage would be tough," one senior-level Biden adviser said of the gloomy mood at HQ.

White House and campaign officials understood they would have to push back to stabilize Biden, but they did not fully grasp the gravity of the situation. For Biden and his insular set of top advisers, the naysaying they heard on television, saw on their phones, and read in cutting anonymous quotes delivered swiftly to online publications amounted to more of the same skepticism they believed they had proved wrong when he won in 2020. In the first minutes after the debate, an old scab covering the distance between the Biden believers and doubters ripped open in spectacular fashion behind the scenes.

The further they were from Biden, the angrier Democrats were at his team. Surely they had been hiding his condition. "There's typical bedwetting, and then there's this," said one longtime Biden confidant who scoffed at the idea that Democrats were overreacting. "This was different."

In Los Angeles, Harris and her aides jumped on a conference call to hash out what she would say in an interview with CNN's Anderson Cooper. She did not like the campaign's talking points, which amounted to "slow start, stronger finish."

That's not credible, Harris thought. *It will hurt more than it helps.*

"I'm just not doing that," she told her aides. It made sense to acknowledge the slow start—everyone had seen that—but arguing that he ended on a high note sounded ridiculous. She and her team landed on what they thought was a better pivot from the bad beginning: a broader contrast between the two candidates. That might be the easiest way to drown ninety minutes of bloodletting in a sea of context.

An hour after the debate wrapped, at 11:30 p.m. on the East Coast, Harris, wearing a navy blazer with an American flag pin on the left lapel, readied herself for what she expected would be a testy exchange with Cooper. Aides in Wilmington stopped what they were doing to fix their focus on Harris. She had a well-earned reputation for bungling high-stakes interviews. In June 2021, when Biden had assigned her to run point on the administration's border policy, Harris pushed back on NBC's Lester Holt for pressing her on why she had not been there. "I haven't been to Europe either," Harris snapped. "And I mean, I don't understand the point you're trying to make." The White House and campaign often turned to other surrogates first.

But now she was in the hot seat, and she repeatedly tried to frame the debate as a blip. Cooper interrupted her. The contentiousness, aides in Wilmington thought, was good for the campaign. It was a distraction from the debate itself, and Cooper came off as dismissive and rude—perhaps a touch misogynistic—in his treatment of the vice president. Finally, Cooper asked her one more time whether she had any concerns about Biden.

"It was a slow start. That's obvious to everyone. I'm not going to debate that point," Harris said firmly. "I'm talking about the choice in November. I'm talking about one of the most important elections in our collective lifetime." Her words sent a jolt of relief through Wilmington. She was on message. She was fighting for Biden. It had been the right decision to send her out as the surrogate in chief. "That was a very heartening moment," one Biden campaign official said.

★

But longtime Democratic critics of Biden were piling on publicly and privately. Allies tripped over their feet as they attempted to retain their own credibility while looking for silver linings. Biden aides winced at the scraping sound of fellow Democrats sharpening their knives. They needed reinforcements, and fast.

Brooke Goren, the campaign's deputy communications director, fired off an email at 12:10 a.m. pressing Biden allies to jump on an emergency conference call with just a ten-minute notice. Then Goren sent out a lengthy memo with talking points. They landed in inboxes like a battery of stink bombs.

"The more voters heard from Donald Trump, the more they remembered why they dislike him," read the first bullet. Biden "started slow but finished strong." They went on like that. *It was also a slow finish*, thought one Biden loyalist who received the memo and joined the call. *He couldn't even finish his closing line right.*

The conference call was no better. Goren repeated the importance of highlighting Biden's strengths. She was doing her job, but she was also inadvertently sending a powerful message to the campaign's top talking heads. *They're living in a fucking alternate universe*, thought one surrogate as he listened to Goren.

The coalition of the willing was being sent into battle—against fellow Democrats—with twigs. Moreover, Biden and his team did not understand that they were fighting the wrong war. They didn't need to convince anyone that he had won the debate or even that he had held his own. He plainly had not. They didn't need to sell the case that Trump had lied repeatedly or held extreme views. This wasn't about Biden versus Trump anymore. They had to prove that Biden could—and should—survive as a candidate. They just didn't know it. Campaign operatives were trained to look at trees. Now the forest was burning.

At 1:10 a.m. Friday, Biden spokesman Seth Schuster sent a text to reporters. *Know it's late*, he wrote. *Because I saw concerns in your story, from me: "Of course he's not dropping out."* In just four hours, Biden's team went from predicting that the candidate would overperform expectations to casually insisting that he wouldn't abandon his bid. It should have been obvious that the need to push back on the idea of him exiting the race was reason to panic.

While Biden aides reassured themselves, but no one else, the president stopped in to visit with late-night diners at an Atlanta Waffle House. Back in Wilmington, campaign officials worked into the wee hours, waiting for Air Force One to land at Raleigh-Durham International Airport in North Carolina, where Biden planned to hold a rally the day after the debate.

As the president's plane cut through the early-morning air, his closest advisers knew they needed a cleanup in aisle Biden. Donilon plugged away at redrafting his remarks for the Friday rally. In the debate Trump had lied, a lot, and stuck to his guns on abortion, an issue that energized many Democratic voters. But Biden was going to have to give a nod in some way to his own failures and try to spin them into a positive. Air Force One landed safely, but Donilon undershot the runway. He added a few lines for Biden: "I don't walk as easy as I used to. I don't speak as smoothly as I used to. I don't debate as well as I used to. But I know what I do know: I know how to tell the truth." It sounded good. But a little age and a little rust weren't the truth voters had just witnessed.

Biden got a raucous reception at the airfield, further confirming his team's view that Democratic critics had gotten out way over their skis. Over the years, Biden and his aides had developed a dim view of Democratic doubts—and a certainty about their own instincts that bordered on dogma. Inside the Biden bunker, the president constantly proved his Democratic critics wrong, whether it was Obama backing Hillary Clinton in 2016 or party leaders searching for an alternative establishment candidate in 2020 or lawmakers assailing his strategy for delivering his agenda on Capitol Hill. Biden had outlasted them all, and this, they thought, was just another—albeit louder—example of skittish Democrats flipping out over nothing. In Wilmington, Biden aides left their stations after 2 a.m. satisfied that everything would return to normal.

It's been a hell of a three or four hours, one Biden official thought as she left the Wilmington office that morning. *That was really tough, but I think we're going to get through this.*

If Biden didn't get through it, a handful of Democratic National Committee officials already had considered contingency plans. In hush-hush talks starting in 2023, these officials gamed out Biden-withdrawal scenarios, according to two people familiar with them.

They wanted to make sure the party was ready for every possible circumstance: if Biden launched his campaign and then stepped aside before the primaries; if he won a bunch of primaries and then could not continue; if he secured enough delegates for the nomination but dropped out before winning a floor vote at the convention; and if he left a vacancy at the top of the ticket after taking the nomination.

The planning was less about who might replace Biden and more about what party rules said—and how they might need to be changed—if the president no longer had the desire, or the ability, to run. One official involved in the secret talks put a fine point on the fear that Biden would not make it to Election Day as the party's nominee: "It shows what we had to do to prepare with the unique circumstances we had, which was an eighty-plus-year-old president who was running."

The vice president's office also had strategized around the possibility that Biden might die in office. As Harris's White House communications director, Jamal Simmons had developed an entire messaging plan around that possibility. Simmons, a veteran of Bill Clinton's White House, who was familiar to CNN viewers as a political analyst, envisioned the powerful image of Lyndon Johnson being sworn in to the presidency aboard Air Force One after John F. Kennedy's assassination, with grieving widow Jackie Kennedy at his side.

Simmons believed Harris would be strengthened by an institutional stamp of approval if she were sworn in hurriedly because Biden had died unexpectedly. Her legitimacy might be questioned, he worried, recalling the January 6 effort to stop Biden from being certified as president. The Trump people are going to go *apeshit* if she's president, he thought. The strongest validator, he believed, would be a federal judge who had been appointed by a Republican other than Trump. He compiled a spreadsheet of those jurists across the country, down to a city-by-city breakdown, and carried it with him when he traveled with Harris. He never told the vice president about the death-pool roster before leaving her camp in January 2023, but he advised colleagues that he should be notified immediately if something happened to Biden, because he had worked out an entire communications strategy. And he left the spreadsheet with another Harris aide.

Anything can happen to any president, Simmons thought. *But the likelihood of Biden dying is greater.*

CHAPTER 3

"KEEP FIGHTING"

J OE BIDEN NEEDED HELP FINDING HIS PATH FORWARD—FIGURATIVELY and literally. The guests pumping $3.7 million into his campaign at a Saturday-night New Jersey fundraising dinner two days after the debate knew the former was true. They wondered if they were wasting their money on a soon-to-be-scratched stallion or, worse, encouraging a lame horse to keep running. But it only became clear how much assistance Biden physically required when they looked down at the floor.

Amid Andy Warhol originals and a custom-made dinner table that had been hauled into the living room of Governor Phil Murphy's early-twentieth-century Italianate home in Middletown, Biden aides had, hours earlier, placed strips of fluorescent tape on the carpet. These colorful bread crumbs showed the leader of the free world where to walk. "He knows to look for that," one aide explained.

Before Biden's motorcade pulled up for the two-tiered fundraiser, a patio reception followed by a sit-down dinner, one of the donors asked Murphy about the ground rules.

"Do you mind if we raise at the table that we think he should drop out?" the guest asked.

"You're welcome to do that privately," Murphy replied. "But you can't do that in front of everybody."

It was June 29, less than forty-eight hours after the New Jersey governor and First Lady Tammy Murphy had watched the debate on her phone during a Copa America soccer match. She had been able to secure the final $300,000 for the fundraiser despite his performance, a sign, perhaps, that he might regain his legs.

But tape wasn't Biden's only crutch. When he strode to the patio, he found a lectern and a teleprompter waiting for him. In an intimate space, the setup looked as awkward as an NFL lineman in a Mini Cooper. Biden peered out at about fifty contributors and read his machine-loaded remarks. "It wasn't my best debate ever," he told the crowd. "I get it. I didn't have a great night, but I'm going to be fighting harder." It was lost on none of the guests that he couldn't do the most basic of political tasks, speaking for a few minutes to contributors, without a script. Katzenberg and Donilon looked on approvingly. If not with flying colors, he had passed the first test of the night.

Biden, the Murphys, and about two dozen VIP-level spenders ducked back into the house to take seats in cocktail chairs, evenly spaced around the gargantuan rectangular dinner table, and make small talk across a centerpiece of scores of white roses. Putting pink napkins in their laps, the guests sipped wine from the Garden State and listened to Phil Murphy lead off a question-and-answer session by asking Biden about the status of the war in Ukraine.

In the same barely audible timbre from two nights earlier, the president ably gave a report on the allied effort to repel Russia. He didn't look well. He didn't sound vital. But his mind seemed sharper than it had during the debate. Then, as the evening wore on, Biden began losing his train of thought midstream. Self-aware, he paused. "You don't want to hear from me," he said at one point as plates of Jersey hothouse tomatoes, beets and berries, and locally sourced chicken awaited them for dinner. "I'm keeping you from eating your food."

That pattern repeated half a dozen times. For the uninitiated, these deflections registered as good-natured humility. But for closer observers of Biden, they were an obvious device, a way of halting the carousel when he found himself in a rhetorical roundabout.

Two hours after his arrival, when the donors had finished their last bites of cheesecake, Biden clambered into his limo, done with a whirlwind fundraising tour through Long Island's Hamptons and New Jersey. He had been strong enough at each stop to cheer the true believers but too weak to remove all doubt. Shortly before midnight, he landed at Camp David, where, removed from the public eye, he could weigh his options with his family. The past two days had been torture for Biden, his campaign, his party, and, in an odd way, for Donald Trump.

★

Chaos in Bidenworld should have thrilled Trump. But it didn't. He was mad as hell. He usually commanded the political spotlight with the ease and flair of P. T. Barnum. From the ashes of his 2020 defeat, and his failed campaign to overturn it, Trump rebuilt his MAGA empire in full public view. Not content to fade away, he turned his influence with GOP lawmakers into theater, forcing leaders like House Speaker Kevin McCarthy to make pilgrimages to Trump's Mar-a-Lago resort and residence in Palm Beach, Florida, and kneel at his feet. In similar fashion, he made his endorsement the coin of the realm in Republican primaries. Picking winners and losers, he managed to make himself the central character in midterm races across the country.

Even though Republicans lost some of those elections with Trump's handpicked candidates—including Herschel Walker in Georgia and Dr. Mehmet Oz in Pennsylvania—the mere act of flexing his muscles proved he still had the biggest guns in the GOP. By the time he launched his third presidential bid in the shadow of those midterms, only a fool would have dismissed his chances of winning the nomination and competing to become the second ousted president, following Grover Cleveland in 1892, to reclaim the White House. Truth be told, Trump had wanted to get into the race in the summer of 2022 to crowd out potential competitors long before the midterms but stood down on the counsel of his advisers. Though he wasn't much for lingering in regret, the results of those elections, and a gathering primary field, convinced him he had been right.

A showman in his bones, Trump knew the power of an improbable comeback story. He spun a tale of grievance, repeating debunked allegations of 2020 election fraud, and portrayed himself as an avenger for his Make America Great Again movement. When he was indicted in four separate criminal cases, he accused Democrats of "weaponizing government" against him and his voters.

Rather than making him into a pariah within his party, the criminal charges served to bind GOP primary voters to him. His omnipresence suffocated potential rivals. In the spring of 2024, he cruised past a field of Republican primary opponents that included Florida governor Ron DeSantis, former New Jersey governor Chris Christie, and his own former ambassador to the United Nations and governor of South Carolina, Nikki Haley. Through it all, and with Biden as a sitting president and candidate for reelection, Trump drove daily news cycles as if he were still in office. He had resurrected himself to win the nomination, and now he had dealt a devastating blow to Biden in their first battle.

But tuning in to cable news and checking social media in the hours after the debate, he absorbed the ultimate insult. No one was paying attention to him. All the coverage focused on Biden—and that infuriated Trump. He dialed up Steven Cheung, his bald mountain of a media aide, midmorning on Friday, June 28, the day after the debate.

"They're not talking about me anymore," Trump whined, his high-in-the-throat tone as recognizable as any on earth. "I won, and they're talking about him," Trump said, his voice growing more indignant and aggressive on Cheung's speakerphone. "I kicked his ass." Trump ordered Cheung to change the narrative. The story shouldn't be Biden's frailty, he said. It should be Trump's strength.

A former communications director for the Ultimate Fighting Championship, Cheung knew a thing or two about executing a reversal. But this was an impossible task. It was also a counterproductive one. Trump wanted to draw eyeballs away from his self-destructing rival. But the soft-spoken Cheung didn't put up a fight. It wasn't his job to tell Trump what to do. He was there to implement what the boss wanted. Cheung and his colleagues pitched friendly outlets on the idea that the former president had a "dominant debate performance." They knew they weren't going to get much traction with mainstream media, and they didn't. Breitbart, the right-wing Trump amplifier, did—to a degree—breathlessly reporting on the "master class" Trump had taught. But even the headline noted that Biden was "weakened."

For the next two weeks, Trump would face the same wrenching choice every minute of every day: he could either cede the spotlight or help Biden by taking it away. Some of that was out of his control. It would be difficult to break through a full-on Democratic cannibalization of Biden. But for the most part, Trump would take a rare detour into the land of conventional political wisdom. He would stand aside and watch Democratic vultures pick over Biden's bones.

At first, not everyone in the Republican Party was on the same page with Trump. Newly minted Speaker Mike Johnson (R-LA) told reporters on Friday that the Cabinet should consider invoking the Twenty-Fifth Amendment, which allows the top appointees in the executive branch to remove an incapacitated president from power.

"It's not just political. It's not just the Democratic Party. It's the entire country," Johnson said. "We have a serious problem here, because we have a president who, by all appearances, is not up to the task."

Not only did his tack diverge from Trump's, but it also provided preemptive political cover to Democrats if Biden left office early. The Twenty-Fifth Amendment would only be activated if the vice president and a majority of the Cabinet declared the president unfit. Johnson was suggesting that Harris should make herself president.

In politics, no invisible bar is higher than the commander-in-chief test—convincing voters that someone who has never held the office can be perceived as presidential. If Biden resigned, or the Twenty-Fifth Amendment were invoked, Harris would become president. That would put her on a glide path to take the nomination, and it would moot the commander-in-chief test.

Maybe she would be a bad president or a bad candidate, but Trump and most Republicans were quite confident at this point that Biden was both. They wanted him to stay put and in the race.

★

While Trump raged about the coverage, a feeling of stomach-clenching dread gripped Jennifer O'Malley Dillon, Julie Chavez Rodriguez, and Quentin Fulks—the top brass of the Biden campaign—when they walked through the doorway of the basement salon at the Atlanta Ritz-Carlton the morning after the debate.

It had been a brutal start to the day already. The Biden team awoke to *Morning Joe*, the virtual breakfast table of the left-of-center intelligentsia—and the president's favorite program—adding to their misery. In his opening monologue, cohost Joe Scarborough asked in a funereal tone whether Democrats should tell Biden that it was time to go. Liberal commentators took to social media to argue that the existential fight against Trumpism was too important to entrust to the shaking hands of an aging president. Biden "has no business running for re-election," *New York Times* columnist Tom Friedman, a Biden ally, wrote on the newspaper's website. It was one thing for Republicans to hammer away at him. This was the Team Biden booster club.

Perhaps no set was angrier than the national finance committee members who had come to hear O'Malley Dillon, Chavez Rodriguez, and Fulks explain just what had happened—and, more important, how the campaign planned to recover. These bundlers had put their own reputations on the line to secure the cash for expensive television ads, massive ground campaigns in swing states, and the salaries of high-priced operatives. Most of them wondered how they could, in good conscience, ask savvy donors for more money. They wanted answers. But the high command was in no mood to meet that demand.

O'Malley Dillon did not like to be questioned—not by her staff, not by other operatives, and certainly not by donors. At forty-seven, she was one of only a handful of living campaign managers who had guided a Democrat to the presidency, and she had done it with plenty of skeptics challenging her moves. By kissing up to Biden and his graying pooh-bahs on that campaign, and later at the White House, she amassed more power over the president's political operation than anyone outside his innermost circle. By setting up information silos that reported only to her, she maintained her authority over the 2024 campaign.

Over the years, JOD had earned a reputation as a polarizing force, inspiring deep loyalty among the staffers she empowered and alienating those she shunned. If she wasn't a master of the inside political game, it was only because she left too many adversaries in her midst. But she was not someone to be fucked with lightly. Under attack from the campaign's top donors, she refused to give an inch. She simply repeated the talking points of the night before, applying another layer of lipstick to the face of failure. A round of rapid-fire questions did nothing to dent her armor as she insisted that Biden's team did not think there was a larger problem with Biden than an unexpectedly bad debate night. "If we really were trying to hide him, we would have hidden him," she told them. "I never imagined he would have such a bad debate."

What do we say to people who think there's something wrong with the president? What's the plan to mitigate the damage from the debate? What changes need to be made to bounce back and win the election? O'Malley Dillon told the buckrakers to stop wringing their hands. You're either on the team, she told them, or you're not.

Not only did some of Biden's most important allies believe that O'Malley Dillon was gaslighting them, but they felt that she was treating them like traitors. *Incompetent*, one bundler thought as he listened to frustration mounting in the voices of his peers. *An honest assessment would go a long way to reassuring us.* O'Malley Dillon had become accustomed to watching elected officials, donors, and aides fall in line when she gave orders. Now, O'Malley Dillon taking a tough stand against the very people who paid her salary rated somewhere between chutzpah and hubris.

It wasn't the toughest morning of her career in politics, but it ranked high on the list. She had taken a reputational risk in leading Biden's campaign for the second time. Usually, winning campaign managers rode off into the sunset—or at least the greener pastures of lucrative consulting gigs. But O'Malley Dillon lived and breathed campaigns, and she believed she had a responsibility to Biden, her party, and her country to help deliver a second term. The grilling burned, but she thought it was a small price to pay in service of trying to stabilize the campaign.

A handful of the furious financiers calmed down. Most did not. The meeting backfired. "The vast majority of donors in that room left even more pissed-off than they were when they came in," one of them said.

★

Clarity was in short supply on Capitol Hill too. Before leaving his condo that morning, Representative Jim Clyburn of South Carolina took a call from Representative Hakeem Jeffries of New York, the first-term House minority leader. A year and a half earlier, Clyburn, Pelosi, and Representative Steny Hoyer of Maryland, all in their eighties, had stepped aside from leadership to clear a path for a new generation that included the fifty-three-year-old Jeffries. A smooth politician who delivered rhyming speeches with a thick Brooklyn accent and the cadence of a slam poet, Jeffries often leaned on mentors, particularly Clyburn and Pelosi, as he worked to assert control over the reins of a factionalized Democratic caucus. If Democrats could flip the House into their hands in November, he would become the first Black Speaker.

On this day-after morning, Jeffries was staring into the double barrels of a political shotgun. If he pressured Biden to leave the race, he would lose the president's remaining loyalists. If he didn't, he would anger the rest. Clyburn's endorsement had helped catapult Biden to the 2020 Democratic nomination with a door-slamming victory in South Carolina's primary. If the Palmetto State congressman turned on Biden, it would be both a major blow to the president and a bad omen for his chances of surviving.

Jeffries asked Clyburn where he stood, waiting for a sign in the tenor of a gravelly southern drawl. After deliberating for a moment, Clyburn said, "It was a bad night for Joe." The words were the indicator, an echo of the White House's preference for playing down the calamity. Jeffries agreed. Both men knew Biden's exit could open a party-shredding fight over Harris. She wasn't as popular as the president, according to polls, and his approval numbers had been underwater since 2021. They could debate whether that was fair—West Wing aides had done little to defend her against critics in both parties—but it was true. When Democrats were unsure that Biden would run again in 2022, Clyburn and Jeffries had watched next-generation white governors lay the groundwork to battle Harris for the nomination. She was untested. Her own 2020 bid for the presidency, beset by infighting and money problems, ended before the first contest.

Clyburn and Jeffries were sympathetic to her plight. They would not let their party skip over the first Black woman vice president, not without a fight. All of that led to an obvious conclusion. The question wasn't about that second move on the chessboard. It was about the one right in front of them. Both required the same cautious first step. "I'm sticking with Joe," Clyburn said. Jeffries quickly made the same commitment. But, Clyburn hedged, "Let's see how things shake out."

Clyburn left home for Capitol Hill and a quick series of morning votes. It was getaway day for lawmakers, who were heading out of town for a weeklong Independence Day recess. They wouldn't have much time to socialize before the gavel landed, freeing them to dash to Washington's National Airport for flights to their home districts. When Clyburn arrived on the House floor a few minutes before 11 a.m., the joint was buzzing with chatter about the previous night's debate. He knew the president about as well as any House member could know a former senator, and friends inundated him with their own opinions and questions about his confidence in Biden. Clyburn told them what he had told Jeffries: he would ride with Biden.

His sentiment was hardly universal. Representative Lloyd Doggett, an iconoclastic liberal seventy-seven-year-old in his fifteenth term representing Austin, Texas, was fit to be tied. Biden needed to drop out—now—he told colleagues. He wasn't alone, but he was in a more liberated political space than most of them because he had decided not to run for reelection. Most House Democrats who wanted Biden out were hamstrung by a basic political reality: their own voting bases would be split. They risked a backlash if they backed Biden aggressively or abandoned him publicly.

Doggett didn't have to worry about that because he wouldn't be on the ballot. He stirred the pot with his friends. It wouldn't be long before he made a public call for Biden to drop out, they concluded before casting their final votes of the morning and rushing for the exits. One lawmaker who spoke to the Texan that morning said there were "plenty in private" who agreed with him. Even among Biden's closest House allies, the lawmakers who would never betray him publicly, either out of loyalty or to protect themselves politically, concern about his fate began to creep in. "There was a lot of gallows humor," one of them said.

Once again in a time of crisis, Biden turned up lucky. It would have been difficult for him to stop a pitchfork parade from pushing him out if members of Congress weren't scattering to their districts. But the July Fourth break meant they couldn't form a mob in Washington. If the agitators were going to mount a campaign to oust him, they would have to do it remotely.

On their own, rank-and-file lawmakers could make life less comfortable for Biden, but they didn't have the formal power to knock out a sitting president. Only a few Democrats were in any position to put real pressure on him: the party's former presidents and its congressional leaders. But so far, they were largely avoiding major pronouncements.

★

With the rest of the Democratic Party agonizing over his future, Biden took the first tentative steps to restore his own credibility on the day after the debate. By the time the sun rose that Friday on what would become a sweltering day in North Carolina's high-tech Research Triangle, with the temperature reaching 97 degrees, there should have been no reason for Biden's team to doubt that his seat was getting hotter. One top Biden campaign official said their text messages looked "just like everyone else's." But there was only so much Biden's team could do for him. They could write his words. They could load the teleprompter. They could put night-glow tape on the ground. They could limit his exposure to tough questions. But they couldn't perform for him. Only he could do that. And, in a twist that surprised his critics, he did just that in Raleigh.

The Biden who walked onstage inside an expo building at the North Carolina Fairgrounds shortly after 1 p.m. that afternoon was virtually unrecognizable compared to the man who had debated Trump the night before. Relaxed, with two buttons undone at the top of his striped dress shirt, this version was fiery and defiant. *We're back, baby*, one of his senior campaign aides thought. *We've got a fighting chance.*

An adoring crowd interrupted him repeatedly with chants of "four more years" as he lit into Trump and promoted his own record. But something more significant than his demeanor had changed in the intervening hours. The president who struggled so much to grab the national spotlight from Trump now had it all to himself. His audience wasn't limited to the folks who skipped work and school to cheer him on in Raleigh.

The whole Democratic Party, friend and foe alike, suddenly watched his every move as if it might be his last in the political arena. So did the media. That night, the *New York Times* editorial board, the self-appointed conscience of the center-left, delivered a swift and vicious blow. "To serve his country," the paper of record wrote, "President Biden should leave the race."

Biden blamed himself. There were no other culprits. The Raleigh rebound did little to restore his shaken confidence. He needed to find his feet again. In the interim, he would have to make a good show of staying in the fight, prove his mettle. Deep down to his core, he had always believed in himself. But was he mistaken this time? He couldn't make that call on the fly. Biden wanted a minute—or a couple of days—to reflect and reassess. He would be able to huddle with his thoughts and his family soon. That would renew his sense of purpose.

First, though, he had a set of campaign appearances and fundraisers in Manhattan, the Hamptons, and at Governor Murphy's house in New Jersey, which would keep him mostly behind closed doors for the rest of Friday and Saturday. Ditto for Sunday, when he would pose for a long-planned shoot with Annie Leibovitz, the legendary photographer to the stars. He could have ripped up his schedule and spent those days barnstorming the country to demonstrate his vigor. Instead, for all intents and purposes, Biden went dark. The campaign throttled down as the candidate wrestled with his own political mortality. "We had the momentum," one aide said of the Raleigh rally. "And then everything stops."

As Biden stared at the imposing walls of a box canyon, Harris ascended Park City Mountain in Utah, a secluded haven for the elite dotted with homes valued between $10 million and $30 million. She arrived in the middle of the afternoon at a 9,000-square-foot, ski-in, ski-out mansion owned by Mark Gilbert, the former U.S. ambassador to New Zealand, and his wife, Nancy.

Harris had been a tough draw for this fundraiser, and organizers worked double time to assemble enough of a crowd to pull in seven figures for the campaign and the Democratic National Committee. Over and over, they heard a refrain of reluctance. Donors didn't want to hear from Harris. She was the second fiddle, and she didn't play all that well, they said. They didn't like her. Her reputation among the political elite was meh, at best. Gilbert told friends and acquaintances that they didn't know her. They would be surprised, he promised.

The debate made her a hotter act. "More people were trying to buy tickets," said one person familiar with the planning. "They really wanted to hear from her."

Ultimately, about two hundred people packed into the contemporary brick-and-wood home with soaring ceilings. Gigantic windows gave way to views of mountain ridges reaching more than 8,000 feet above sea level. Harris met one-on-one with a handful of VIPs and posed for snapshots against backdrops of opulence crafted by man and God. Upstairs, Second Gentleman Doug Emhoff entertained a group of Jewish donors at a roundtable.

Despondence hung like a cloud that had slipped inside from the mountain air. Harris decided she couldn't lead with anything but the elephant in the chateau: the debate. These were people with enough money to throw thousands of dollars at a political campaign. None of them were worried about making rent or covering the difference in the price of eggs. If Harris wanted them to give more, she could only bullshit them so much.

He'd had a bad night, she said when she addressed the full crowd. But after three and a half years at his side, she explained, she knew Biden was a "profound thinker." Harris ticked through the laws he had pushed through Congress and the executive actions he had taken to implement his agenda. "The list of accomplishments reads like a CVS receipt," she said with a familiar lilt in her voice. "It just goes on and on."

It was not lost on anyone in the room that there was a world in which Harris might end up at the top of the ballot. Her words and demeanor offered a measure of reassurance and a dose of optimism to a downtrodden lot. "People came concerned," said one person who watched Harris turn the bearing of the audience. "The vice president, in the most magnificent of fashions, completely changed everybody's mood." Donors who had to be badgered to attend in the first place walked into the summer evening feeling at least a little bit better about the chances of averting a second Trump presidency.

It had been an intense two days since Harris's last buckraking venture, a fundraiser in the San Gabriel Valley on the outskirts of Los Angeles. That night, she had said, "I will tell you the debate is going to frame the race." She could not possibly have known how much.

★

The night after the debate, Bill Clinton ducked and dodged through a crowd of celebrities and politicos at Barker Hangar, a massive event space at the Santa Monica airport, where talent agency chief Casey Wasserman threw himself a diamond-studded fiftieth birthday party. A-listers in Clinton's midst included Nancy Pelosi, California governor Gavin Newsom, Doug Emhoff, and actress Jessica Alba, who played Invisible Woman in Marvel films. The seventy-seven-year-old former president suddenly wished he was the Invisible Man.

Inside the 35,000-square-foot converted hangar, where Imagine Dragons played live, Clinton aimed to sidestep the folks who wanted to solicit his views on the debate—or share theirs. It was unusual for Bill, a man who loved nothing more than stopping to talk to people. But he knew all too well as he glad-handed, slapped backs, and moved on to the next greeting that anything he said to anyone could be misconstrued, accidentally or intentionally. One person who did catch up with Clinton: Nancy Pelosi. He was not in a frame of mind to entertain entreaties to intervene with Biden. That was particularly true when it came to political donors, who were well represented in the crowd of several hundred people. The easiest way to avoid them was to stay in motion. *Keep them away*, he told his aides.

No one in America had a better understanding of what it was like for a president to watch segments of his own party turn on him. It had happened to Clinton at times during his presidency, most painfully when he admitted to an affair with White House intern Monica Lewinsky. He would have no part in doing that to Biden.

Clinton had known Biden for decades. They came out of the same centrist wing of the Democratic Party, and Biden had been the Senate shepherd of landmark Clinton administration laws, including the 1994 crime bill and the Violence Against Women Act. On the campaign trail, Bill recognized Joe's appeal to his own core constituencies: African Americans and moderate whites. *We speak the same language*, Bill thought.

Their relationship had been strained by ambition. Biden held a grudge after Hillary Clinton, with the tacit backing of Obama, crowded him out of the Democratic primary fight in 2016. But Bill respected Biden's public service, the dignity he brought to the presidency, and his manner. In short, Bill liked Joe. So did Hillary. Early that morning, before 10 a.m., she became the first of the party's elite power brokers to signal her loyalty. "I'll be voting Biden," she wrote on X.

Hillary saw herself in the Republican attacks and TV punditry focused on Biden's condition. "She certainly didn't think there was anything wrong with him," said one person close to the former secretary of state. "She is someone who has had her health questioned for twenty years and knows that this kind of stuff is bullshit." But sympathy and personal affinity weren't the only reasons, or even the overriding ones, to stand by the president. In philosophical, political, and practical terms, Bill believed Democrats were best served by giving Biden space to make his own decision about his future. As a former president himself, he held deep reverence for the office and empathy for the man in it. Biden had stood by him during his impeachment ordeal. In that moment, and even when Democrats had fretted about his third-place standing during the 1992 campaign, Bill had survived slings and arrows from within the party. Maybe Joe could too. *Maybe.*

Most important, Bill Clinton knew the rules. He had been a delegate tracker at the 1972 Democratic National Convention, where he learned the mechanics of the nomination process. Biden held the votes he needed. No one could force him out of the race. Besides, knowing Biden and the instincts of a president, Bill believed any effort to pressure Biden would be counterproductive. Trying to strong-arm the most powerful person in the world was more likely to make him dig in. *Bloviating about it doesn't help*, Bill thought. *It only hurts.*

If Bill secretly believed that Biden should fall on his sword, he would never say it publicly. He didn't have to. Biden's White House and political operation were stocked with former Clinton aides. Steve Ricchetti, the counselor to the president, had been Bill's deputy chief of staff. Biden's deputy chief of staff Bruce Reed had been deputy campaign manager in Bill's first bid for the presidency and director of his domestic policy council at the White House. Harris's chief of staff, Lorraine Voles, had worked for both Clintons. The list went on and on, and it included the chair of the Democratic convention, Minyon Moore, and a co-chair of the convention's rules committee, Leah Daughtry, who had been tapped as the personnel chief on Hillary's 2016 presidential transition team.

Almost anyone with a strand of gray hair in Biden's orbit worked for at least one of the Clintons at some point in the previous thirty-five years. Ricchetti and Reed were Bill's main conduits to Biden. "Those guys weren't guessing where we were," said one person close to the Clintons. "They knew [Bill] was supportive." Part of that confidence came from the stark differences between the public posturing of the Clinton and Obama camps. In the hours and days after the debate, Obama's highest-profile former aides took potshots at Biden on television, on X, and on the *Pod Save America* franchise of podcasts. Clintonworld, with the exception of impossible-to-control veteran political operative James Carville, kept quiet. Biden and his team could divine the difference between Bill's silence and Obama's—one was friendly and one was not.

When Obama took to X that afternoon, in what would be his only public comment about the situation ripping his party apart at the seams, he echoed Hillary by framing the election as a choice between "someone who has fought for ordinary folks his entire life and someone who cares only about himself." But Obama did not follow her lead in vowing to cast a ballot for Biden.

The fact that it was necessary for the biggest names in the party to weigh in on Biden's behalf sent a subtle message about just how vulnerable he had made himself. But the show of force provided welcome relief. "It makes it harder for others in the party to publicly call for the opposite," one lawmaker said when he saw the tweets.

★

The Democratic donor world immediately split into roughly three groups: Biden Dead-Enders, the Wait-and-See set, and the Choke Him

Now camp. On Wall Street, there weren't many Dead-Enders. As CEO of the global asset management firm Lazard and a former director of the White House and congressional budget offices, fifty-five-year-old Peter Orszag harbored a deep aversion to throwing good money after bad. Sitting near the center of a circle of major Wall Street donors, and as one of the few who knew Biden well, he had seen the president's gradual decline up close. Like so many others, Orszag had held his breath, raised money for Biden, and hoped that the old man had one last winning sprint in him. But the debate was too much for Orszag to take.

Disqualifying, he thought, as he watched. It was a word he would use over and over in conversations with friends in the elite ring of presidential finance and with Biden's top advisers. Orszag quickly made two determinations: he would never call publicly for the president to exit the race and he wouldn't perpetuate the farce of a Biden candidacy by helping the campaign raise money.

Some of the Wall Street set agreed with him that Biden had to go. Others were more open to giving the president a chance to steady himself. There was no agreement on a Plan B. But one thing was clear from the get-go: Biden could no longer fill a room with New York donors. Finance world money is nothing if not a leading indicator in presidential campaigns. Usually, money talks. In this case, it walked. Biden's sudden cash crunch wasn't confined to New York.

Within days of the debate, major donors across the country canceled plans to give to the campaign. "We had a whole bunch of planned events," said one Biden aide familiar with his campaign's finances. "They weren't going well. So, the hosts essentially said they didn't want to do them anymore or they would do them but not now." Even the most loyal donors wanted to see the situation settle. The campaign had no choice but to accept cancellations, because, as the aide said, "We're not going to send the president around the country to raise a third of what he would typically raise because of all the uncertainty."

Campaigns plan their spending around projected fundraising. The Biden treasury was not out of money yet, but the expected shortfall in July—based first on top donors checking out and later grassroots givers following suit—threatened to bankrupt him in the fall. "It's not about making payroll now," one Biden fundraising aide said. "It's about making payroll at Labor Day, and that's fucking devastating."

Biden's team lobbied Orszag and other close allies to schedule new events. "I don't know why you're pressuring me," he told one Biden adviser. "You don't understand how much concern there is."

The fear that Trump would return to the White House was no longer an amorphous monster in the collective subconscious of the Democratic Party. It now looked like Godzilla knocking down skyscrapers and breathing fire at his political enemies. In each of the interlocking classes of Democratic insiders—party officials, donors, lawmakers, downballot candidates, and campaign operatives—there was a consensus that something had to be done to stop the pending disaster. But there was no party leader with the power to make decisions with a wave of his hand.

Biden had been that singular force for the past four years. Candidates could complain about Biden dragging them down. Lawmakers could call for him to leave. Donors could suffocate his cash supply. Operatives could provide a steady stream of blind quotes to the media to apply pressure. But while the circles of Democratic elites overlapped, they weren't coordinated in any real sense. "If you drew a Venn diagram, it would be a mess," said one former lawmaker who still raised money for the party.

Mary Landrieu, a Louisianan who maintained close ties to a set of fellow former moderate senators, felt urgently that Biden could no longer represent the party in the election. Her brother, former New Orleans mayor Mitch Landrieu, was a co-chair of the campaign. Her niece, Grace Landrieu, served as the campaign's policy director. She could not make her views known publicly without hurting her family. But she also believed she couldn't sit idly with so much riding on the election. She waited most of a day before emailing Coons, Ricchetti, and Dunn. It's over, she wrote. Only Coons responded, noting that he had received her message.

Many Democrats couldn't reconcile the two Bidens—the fading president of Thursday night and the rally-rousing candidate of Friday afternoon. The collision was almost as jarring as the debate, which is why his Raleigh speech had little measurable impact. If anything, it added to the sense of chaos.

Biden's campaign and the DNC threw together a series of weekend conference calls with major contributors. On one call, O'Malley Dillon dodged a question about Biden's mental capabilities. She did the same when she was asked about the backup plan if he dumped out. Like she had on Friday morning, O'Malley Dillon just enraged donors more in each successive session. *They're telling us not to believe our lying eyes*, one heavyweight Democratic fundraiser thought as he listened.

On another call with DNC members, Harrison and Chavez Rodriguez pushed past the president's performance and laid out an optimistic view of his path to reelection. Jaws dropped. DNC members felt that they were being treated like imbeciles. Worse, some felt infantilized. They soon realized that they were meant to listen, not be heard. Harrison and Chavez Rodriguez disabled the chat function on the conference call and refused to take questions. Rather than tamping down anxiety, they managed again to turbocharge it.

"We started to do some calls that were an unmitigated disaster," said one top Biden campaign official. "Our narrative coming out of the debate was 'the fundamentals of this race have not changed.' That is fucking bullshit. I understand that people still don't like Donald Trump and they're still concerned about the issues that poll well, but the fundamentals of this race just completely and totally turned on their head."

The official grew more frustrated with each call. *What the fuck are we telling these people? We are losing all credibility*, the official thought. *The more often you say that, the more people will not believe you anymore. So, stop saying it.*

On one of those calls, Chavez Rodriguez told a few dozen top contributors that only Harris could directly inherit the campaign treasury and operation if Biden stepped aside. Coons, who joined the call, told the donors that a Biden exit would create a "messy" process for replacing him and that it would likely end with Harris at the top of the ticket. They were sending a subtle but unmistakable warning to the Choke Him Now crowd to be careful what they wished for.

★

At an estate in East Hampton, New York, on Saturday, before his trip to Murphy's house, Biden addressed a crowd that included shock-jock-turned-serious-interviewer Howard Stern and actors Matthew Broderick and Sarah Jessica Parker. It was on Stern's show in April that Biden had first said he would debate Trump. As Biden delivered remarks to his star-studded Long Island audience, he seemed oblivious to the peril at the gates. He spun the campaign's talking points. "I understand the concern about the debate—I get it," he said. Then he demonstrated that he didn't really get it. "Here's what's not getting reported: voters had a different reaction than pundits."

Neither the voters nor pundits were the audience that mattered most. This was now a fight at the highest levels of the party. Though House leaders dutifully gave him public votes of confidence, Pelosi, Clyburn, and Jeffries all privately told friends they were worried about his ability to recover. In the way of seasoned politicians, they chose their words carefully—"concern" rather than "terror," "let's see what happens" rather than "stop agitating"—but the coded language was easy enough for their peers to understand. The party leaders were not defending the president.

As Democratic elites searched for an explanation—and a solution that didn't end with Trump winning—Biden's family trained its sights on his advisers. They were the ones who had thought a June debate was a great idea. They were the ones who had run rehearsals for his meeting with Trump. If they hadn't set him up for failure, they had certainly failed to get him set.

The Bidens congregated at Camp David that weekend for the photo shoot with Leibovitz. The president and the first lady landed back at Camp David late Saturday night, following the Murphy fundraiser. White House aides insisted there would be no talk about the future of Biden's campaign. But he had a heart-to-heart with his relatives.

Biden's aides had come to learn over the years that the president's family—the first lady, his sister Valerie Biden Owens, his children, and his grandchildren—had a way of planting ideas in his head when his staff wasn't there to temper them.

In particular, Biden leaned on Hunter, whom he saw as a savvy adviser in the way that only his doting father could. A decade earlier, it had been Hunter's older brother, Beau, who was a hotshot rising star in the electoral universe. The old man saw Beau as a future president. An Iraq

War veteran elected attorney general of Delaware, he was the first Biden to befriend Harris, when she held the same position in California.

Like his father, Beau seemed to get along well with everyone, both in politics and at home, acting as the nucleus of the Biden family. His father referred to him as a right hand—with Hunter the left—and he helped manage the relationships in a large, tight-knit family that, for the entirety of his adult life, had focused on the presidential ambitions of the patriarch. The title of *Promise Me, Dad* referred to the vow Beau elicited from Joe to stay engaged in public life as Beau was dying of brain cancer.

"Hunter, he sees as his best political adviser, which can be a little annoying," said one Biden aide. At Camp David, Hunter drove a wedge between Biden and two longtime advisers. Dunn and Bauer were to blame for the debate, Hunter argued. He already had an ax to grind with the power couple. They had devised a strategy of father and son lying low during Hunter's legal fight. Hunter thought it was a shitty tack that left him taking hits without punching back. Trump was able to rally his own base every time he was charged with a crime or turned up in a courthouse. His in-your-face public relations strategy, which included attacking anyone who didn't support his exoneration, seemed to be working. Why, Hunter wondered, shouldn't he do the same?

Eventually, he would pursue a more Trumpian path, which did not prevent him from being convicted on gun charges. Dunn and Bauer were easy targets for Hunter because Dunn had pushed the early debate and both of them had been at Camp David for the prep sessions. The D.C. publicity queen and her lawyer husband couldn't be trusted, Hunter suggested, because they had made a lot of money during Biden's time in office.

Hunter also cast a leery eye at Ron Klain, the debate-prep guru. The family piled on, casting Biden as a victim of advisers who had left him unprepared to take on Trump. Hunter seized the opportunity to bleed the influence Dunn and Bauer had with his father.

Holding the president blameless for his own misfortune, his family urged him to hammer back against his adversaries—external and internal, real and perceived. "Keep fighting," they told him. The truth was that only one person might have enough sway with Biden to convince him to give up his vision of a second term, and she wasn't at all interested in doing that. Jill Biden was, if anything, more firm than her husband about maintaining a residence at 1600 Pennsylvania Avenue.

It was settled. Biden would cling to the nomination he had won and blast any Democrat who stood in his way. But as his family boosted his morale at Camp David, Pelosi found a revealing venue to sow doubt about his viability. If the medium is the message, there was no more telling vehicle than MSNBC's *Inside with Jen Psaki*. The namesake host with the signature red bob gained fame and ultimately a cable platform by defending Biden from the podium in the White House briefing room as press secretary to the president. Before that, she had been one of Obama's most prominent spokespeople.

Pelosi was one of a phalanx of ostensible Biden allies who fanned out on television programs that Sunday to defend his performance and his standing as their nominee. But even as she did that, Pelosi opened the door to alternatives. "I'm not abandoning Joe Biden right now for any speculation," she told Psaki. *Right now.* One of her top allies, Representative Jamie Raskin (D-MD), pushed the line a little more on the same station. "There are very honest and serious and rigorous conversations taking place at every level of our party," said Raskin, who had developed his own following among the party faithful as a member of the committee that investigated the January 6, 2021, attack on the U.S. Capitol.

The Biden dam was springing leaks, but it was mostly intact. Coons pointed out in an ABC News interview that weekend that no Democratic lawmaker had put their name to a call for the president to exit the race. What none of them said, what Democrats refused to contemplate as some of them began to gently persuade Biden to drop his campaign, was the question of whether he was still fit to be president. Republicans had been harping on the idea that he no longer had the cognitive function necessary to run the country for most of his presidency. For Democratic politicians, there was no upside to entertaining the idea that the White House and their party had either hidden his decline or had been blind—willingly or unwittingly—to it.

Outside the realm of elected officials, the Democratic chattering class moved faster. Former Obama aides who host the popular podcast

Pod Save America openly discussed the possibility of replacing Biden on the ticket, effectively echoing Axelrod without explicitly demanding that he step aside.

If Obama didn't direct his former aides to wage a campaign against Biden—and few thought he was pulling their strings—he also didn't tell them to quit it. The former president had been willing to throw Biden a single lifeline with a social media post. Then he went quiet. "That silence was deafening," said one person who talked to Obama in the aftermath of the debate. "That was a message in itself."

In Obama's view, Biden was simply not the best candidate for the party. But if not Biden, who could defeat Trump? He liked Gretchen Whitmer, the Michigan governor, but he believed an open fight for the nomination was the best way for Democrats to replace Biden on the ticket.

★

On the last day of June, three days after the debate, Whitmer called Harris. Whitmer was the runner-up when Biden tapped his pick for vice president four years earlier. Whitmer, the popular governor of a Rust Belt state, appealed to many of Biden's white advisers. At the same time, Black elected officials and Biden counselors—including a legion of the most prominent Black women in Democratic politics—lobbied for Harris.

When Biden called Clyburn, his close friend and the highest-ranking Black member of Congress, two days before making his pick that year, he said he had a "real battle between my head and my heart." Clyburn, who believed it would be a "plus" to put a Black woman on the ticket, told Biden, "Whatever is in your head, let your heart take a look before you make that decision."

The selection process left a bad taste in Whitmer's mouth. She felt burned by what she saw as a racially charged behind-the-scenes campaign by Harris's allies to portray her in a bad light. In 2022, when some Democrats clamored for Whitmer to replace Biden on the ballot in 2024—or Newsom, Murphy, or Illinois governor J. B. Pritzker—the talk among political insiders heightened tension between the two women. The idea that someone other than the vice president would step in if Biden chose not to seek reelection did not sit well with the Harris camp. Now, with pressure mounting for Biden to abandon that bid, some of the talk among donors and other insiders was quickly turning to "Gretch" and the other governors. She was seeing her name catch fire on X and other platforms.

Two days earlier, Whitmer called O'Malley Dillon to say that she wasn't doing anything to encourage the party to draft her into a race that the president was still in. Something got lost in translation. Inherent in her message was the reassurance that she didn't intend to run if Biden exited the race. But some Harris advisers remained unconvinced that Whitmer would stand aside if the top spot on the ticket opened up. When Whitmer caught wind of that, she became determined to speak to Harris directly. She didn't want to reopen the scars of the hardball 2020 veepstakes.

Now the virtual cocktail party of Democratic social media was full of opinions on who should replace Biden, with the cast of governors at the forefront. The same conversations were going on behind closed doors. Much of the talk pointed to deep fears that Harris was an even weaker candidate than Biden. Polls showed that. Media coverage suggested it. And the 2020 election, in which she had not even made it to the opening contest in Iowa, seemed to prove it. One veteran operative summed up the sentiments of Democrats who worried they would get stuck with Harris but still wanted Biden out: "Well, at least she has a pulse."

Whitmer could do herself more harm than good by getting in the middle of the intraparty fight. She couldn't force a Biden exit. She couldn't run a campaign against Harris with Biden still in the race. There was no advantage to angling for the job.

When Whitmer reached Harris, she said she had no designs on the presidency in 2024.

"I won't run under any circumstances," she said.

It was possible at that moment that Whitmer and Harris would be competitors for the 2028 Democratic nomination. Both women were savvy enough to understand one unifying dynamic of the odd situation they found themselves in: any rivalry would hurt Biden—and both of them. What Whitmer left unsaid was whether she would endorse Harris if Biden surrendered the nomination.

"Gretchen was very clear about what she was, and was not, doing," said one person familiar with their discussion.

CHAPTER 4

"AN EPISODE OR A CONDITION"

BARACK OBAMA GENTLY POKED AT BIDEN, HIS EVEN TONE BETRAYING NO agenda.

"What is your path?" the forty-fourth president asked the forty-sixth. It was their first phone call since the debate, and Obama knew he couldn't strong-arm his former VP. Biden resented his old boss for "subtly weighing in" against him—and for Hillary Clinton—in the shadow primary phase of the 2016 Democratic nomination fight. "The president was not encouraging," Biden wrote in a memoir, recounting conversations he had with Obama about a possible run. "Obama was my friend, but I found myself unable to fully confide in him." Obama added insult to injury four years later, declining to endorse Biden in the 2020 primary and telling friends he had little faith in Biden's ability to beat Trump.

Biden had never gotten over the affronts, and he no longer trusted Obama's political judgment. After Hillary's shattering 2016 loss, Biden told everyone who would listen that he would have beaten Trump and that Obama had been wrong. In his mind, Obama was responsible, in no small part, for Trump's presidency. Obama knew his influence with Biden was diminished, but he hoped that, as a friend and a man who had sat at the Resolute Desk in the Oval Office, he might help Biden gain clarity.

Obama's question about the path forward was meant to suggest support and subtly guide Biden toward his own conclusion that there was no light at the end of this tunnel. To Biden, it only implied doubt, like when Obama had responded to Biden's prospective 2016 bid by asking,

"How do you want to spend the rest of your life?" Biden wasn't looking to play Socratic games with a Harvard Law grad summering on Martha's Vineyard. In one form or another, he had been having the same conversation with Obama for nearly a decade, like actors in a long-running Broadway production.

Biden thought he was on the right track. The polls he looked at showed a close race, and he was dead-ass certain that no one else in the Democratic Party would fare so well. His decline had not robbed him of the capacity for cogency or his belief in his own resilience. If anything, his bruised ego made him more defiant. And no matter how often he might lose his train of thought, he would never forget Obama's persistent dubiousness.

What's my path? Biden thought as he listened to Obama. *What's your fucking plan?*

"What do you need from me?" Obama tried. Aside from hitting the campaign trail later in the year, there wasn't much Biden thought Obama could do for him. He'd won without Obama's support in a competitive primary the last time. To Obama, Biden didn't seem to grasp the gravity of the situation. He hung up more convinced that Biden was out of touch with the harsh reality of certain defeat.

Biden lived in bubble wrap inside bunkers. The White House. Camp David. A primary home in Wilmington that his family called the Lake. And, increasingly, a beach house in Rehoboth Beach, Delaware. Withdrawn from the maddening crowd of professional Democrats, fat-cat donors, and prying reporters, he honed the chip on his shoulder. He was always right; *they* were always wrong. *They* always doubted him. *They* would never learn, no matter how many times they underestimated him. *They* were all Obama. *They* would pretend they had been with him all along when, inevitably, he rebounded to victory.

Like most politicians, Biden demanded absolute loyalty from the people he allowed into his physical and psychological circles. In turn, his family and closest aides reflected his us-versus-them paradigm. They too treated anyone who questioned him with suspicion and anyone who crossed him with spite. This was especially true within the tight-knit Biden family, which surrounded him at Camp David the weekend after the debate. The family trained their fire at the insiders, not the outsiders.

The campaign's spin galled Biden's family and some of his close friends. The idea that a cold had defeated him sounded ridiculous on its face. More than that, it put the blame at the president's feet and absolved his aides. Beyond Hunter's vendetta against Dunn and Bauer, the family developed a narrative that, rather than illness, Biden had been undone by overpreparation. In this telling, which would be spread to the media, his team had filled his head with so many facts, figures, and scripted lines that he couldn't process everything in real time.

Even if it wasn't true, that narrative provided an opening for his aides to fall on their swords, sparing the president. That was the right thing to do, at least from the perspective of Biden's family and friends. But his White House and campaign aides stuck to the story that nothing was amiss at debate prep, that there was no way to predict how poorly he would perform, and that the cold was the only explanation they could find. "None of those cocksuckers would take the blame," said one Biden ally who participated in debate prep.

The competing narratives played out in news reports, but the truth was less important than the backbiting. It subtly signaled that Biden's family was focused on the short-term damage while some of his aides were starting to wrestle with the possibility that his campaign was doomed. The last thing Biden and his family should have been worried about was the aptitude or loyalty of advisers who had been in the trenches with him for years.

But Biden didn't believe he was in serious trouble. His own instincts and experience told him that Democrats were given to fits of cowardice. Party luminaries and their big-dollar donors had searched for another candidate when it looked like he might lose to Bernie Sanders in the 2020 primary. Each time his major bills ran into obstacles on Capitol Hill, Democrats fretted to the press that his agenda was dead. Yet he had won the presidency, and he had enacted a Covid-relief measure, an infrastructure law, and a historic climate-change package. This too, he thought, would pass.

He wasn't just relying on his own perspective. Trusted advisers told him what he wanted to hear. Sure, the critics were a little louder and angrier this time, but they were singing the same old song. Eventually, after a few news cycles, their voices would fade into the background as they always did. Privately, they were all hearing from frightened allies. But no one of consequence had made a public stink. "We knew we were having a really bad weekend, but we're also Biden—we have terrible, terrible periods," said one adviser who described the thinking of the president and his high command as "Don't overreact."

Instead, Biden didn't act at all. Between the private fundraising events and the weekend at Camp David, he effectively fell silent for days. That added to the panic inside the party. It even rattled campaign officials in Wilmington, who were desperate to put him back on the trail. There was an obvious remedy for his problem. He had the nation's attention. He could hit the rally circuit, schedule wall-to-wall television interviews, and burn up phone lines with calls to top allies. But Biden didn't even bother to check in with congressional leaders.

For a brief moment on Monday morning, July 1, the Supreme Court effectively interrupted round-the-clock coverage of Biden's debate bomb with a decision that figured to give Trump another big boost. In a ruling decided along partisan lines, 6–3, the justices granted presidents broad immunity from prosecution. In historical terms, the decision would give even more power to the presidency. In immediate practical terms, it meant that two federal cases against Trump would, at the very least, be pushed back until after the November election. Voters would have their say before jurors did. If Trump won, he could halt the cases against him, on charges related to his efforts to overturn the 2020 election and his retention of classified documents, without lifting a finger. No one doubted that he would do just that.

More troubling for Democrats, they believed that the opinion would free Trump to act with impunity in a second term. His hand was growing stronger, and the Democrats' hand was getting weaker. The high court added its chips to the election kitty. Trump crowed on the Truth Social media platform, "BIG WIN FOR OUR CONSTITUTION AND DEMOCRACY." Liberal justices and the Biden White House didn't see it that way at all. Justice Sonia Sotomayor wrote in a dissent that the majority opinion amounted to "a mockery" of the principle that "no man is above the law." She concluded her opinion with a simple-yet-powerful sentence: "I dissent."

Biden was still at Camp David, but Democrats wanted to hear from him. Most Americans had not seen him since the debate five days earlier. His advisers sensed an opportunity to achieve three goals by putting him in front of a camera: reassure nervous Democrats, show him as the commander in chief, and use the presidential platform to lean heavily into the central narrative of his campaign against Trump—a battle for democracy. With a growing number of Democrats privately calling for him to step aside, and others pressing his aides to hold public events so that he could show he was still fit to run, West Wing officials scrambled to schedule a rare White House address.

"Let's have him go out there and be a strong president," one of his top advisers urged. With Congress out of town, and Trump lying low, Biden would speak for his party, for his country, and for his presidency from the most powerful pulpit in the world.

Campaign aides expected him to say, in no uncertain terms, that he was staying in the race. They readied a press release to blast out to reporters' inboxes and the social media universe. This was the kind of pop-off-the-canvas moment campaign aides in Wilmington had been waiting for while Biden had been out of sight.

Just before 7 p.m., Marine One, carrying the president and first lady, touched down at Fort McNair, an Army outpost at the southern tip of Washington, D.C., that was established shortly after the Revolutionary War. Biden emerged wearing his hallmark aviator sunglasses and stepped into his limousine for a three-mile motorcade to the White House. His aides loaded a four-minute speech into teleprompters in Cross Hall, an indoor boulevard connecting the State Dining Room to the East Room. Wearing a navy suit and a lighter blue tie, Biden delivered what amounted to a campaign speech. He used Trump's name five times, including in a warning that reflected the crux of his case for re-election. "I will respect the limits of the presidential power, as I have for three and a half years," he said, his eyes moving from the teleprompter on his right side to the one on his left side. "But any president, including Donald Trump, will now be free to ignore the law."

His White House aides believed it was a strong moment for him, just as they had planned. *Take that, coastal donors*, one of them thought as Biden wrapped up. No one else in the party could carry the message about democracy with the clarity and moral authority of Biden, they thought. But in Wilmington, campaign officials exchanged confused looks. "What the fuck?" one of them exclaimed. "He didn't say it." What Biden had left out was a powerful affirmation that he was still running. Biden hadn't liked the idea. This speech was about democracy, not a campaign. He was speaking from the White House, not the stump. Campaign aides, feeling defeated, rewrote the press release they had hoped would send a viral signal that Biden was in the fight.

Wilmington was equally shocked when he walked away from the lectern without taking questions. The whole damn country wanted to know whether he was going to run or bail out, including his own campaign aides. Biden didn't want to distract from his message about the high court and Trump. He and his White house aides thought he'd been plenty clear in hammering Trump. They believed his performance was good enough to answer Democrats' concerns. But his iron grip on the party was loosening. He hadn't satisfied his friends or his foes.

At 7:54 p.m., less than five minutes after Biden concluded, *Newsweek* posted an op-ed from former congressman Tim Ryan envisioning a Democratic ticket without the president. "That future begins with Kamala Harris," wrote Ryan, who had endorsed Biden after dropping his own 2020 bid for the presidency. "I hope the powers that be in our party have the guts and vision to make that happen." Biden was still not talking to most of those powers directly. One of them was determined to talk about him.

Back in San Francisco for the House recess, Pelosi told friends that she believed Biden should step aside. She was too shrewd to put her private thoughts in the public square. *If you want a certain path*, she thought, *don't announce it. That's not the way to get someone to go down your path, by making it look like you made it happen.*

Pelosi had dealt with plenty of powerful men in her time, including countless lawmakers who had to give up their seats under the cloud of scandal or the threat of certain defeat. These men had to be shown their dwindling options, given space to draw their own conclusions, and granted cover to explain their decisions on their own terms. Most important, they must be afforded dignity. Trying to force Biden's hand would boomerang. He was more stubborn than most, and the call rested entirely with him. For all those reasons, she would never tell him to get out—at least not that directly.

Moreover, Pelosi wasn't yet sure where the House Democratic caucus stood. Because they were out of session, and scattered to their districts, she didn't have a firm feel for the group dynamics yet. She also didn't want to get out in front of Jeffries, whom she was still grooming even as he held the titular leadership of that caucus. She wanted to protect him from an ugly family fight.

Andrea Mitchell, the legendary NBC News reporter with a list of contacts that rivaled God's, picked up intel on Pelosi's thinking in her conversations with sources that weekend and booked the former Speaker for an interview. If Pelosi wouldn't call for Biden's head, she still might make news. Shortly after midday on Tuesday, about sixteen hours after Biden's White House remarks, Pelosi beamed into Mitchell's show with the Golden Gate Bridge as her backdrop. She quickly delivered an elbow to Biden's ribs.

"I think it's a legitimate question to say, is this an episode or a condition?" Pelosi said. "And so when people ask that question, it's completely legitimate—of both candidates. . . . Both candidates owe whatever test you want to put them to, in terms of their mental acuity and their health—both candidates." *It is*, she thought, *the question the American people need answered.*

Around the same time, Doggett, the Austin congressman, released a statement urging the president to withdraw from the race. In doing so, he broke the seal, becoming the first sitting member of Congress to do so. Doggett expressed his appreciation for Biden's record, but he offered a brutal assessment of the electoral battlefield. The president, he said, was running behind Democratic Senate candidates in battleground states and lagging Trump in most polls. His hope that Biden would reverse that trajectory in the debate had been dashed, and now he worried that the president would "deliver us to Trump." The Supreme Court ruling the previous day had only crystallized for Doggett that Biden's exit was necessary.

During a tense session in the White House briefing room that afternoon, the president's press secretary, Karine Jean-Pierre, lightly pushed back on Doggett, saying he was entitled to "his opinion." But she drew a thick line at picking a fight with Pelosi. Biden believed Pelosi's query was a "fair question," Jean-Pierre said, adding that the White House viewed the performance as neither an episode nor a condition.

At a moment when Biden was benefiting from paralysis within his own party—a mix of clashing sentiments about his prospects and the silence of a Congress in recess—Pelosi delivered an electric shock to the Democratic central nervous system. Whatever bounce he thought he got from the White House address on the Supreme Court, she took it away in a single interview.

In Wilmington, senior campaign officials were at a loss. Biden's operation felt like Mount Olympus to some of them. At the top sat the president, the first lady, Donilon, Ricchetti, Reed, and the personal aides to Joe and Jill Biden—Tomasini and Bernal. At times, White House chief of staff Zients, Dunn, and O'Malley Dillon were invited to the peak. They would ferry messages down to the teams at the White House and the campaign. But on Monday and Tuesday, there was virtual radio silence. Calendars usually stacked with meetings at campaign headquarters suddenly cleared. At the White House, Dunn was being pushed to the side, and Hunter Biden joined strategy sessions.

"We weren't hearing from Washington anymore," said one top campaign official. Instead, they were reading stories about the chaos in their own party and within Biden's high command. They were hearing that Biden had cut himself off from top Democrats and cut O'Malley Dillon and Dunn out of the decision-making circuit. Biden's small circle drew even tighter, limited to only the most trusted advisers, and that left his campaign flying blind. "We're fucking fighting, man, and then all of a sudden there's nothing going on."

O'Malley Dillon and Dunn pressed their colleagues to put Biden in the spotlight. More press. More events. More Biden. If he stayed scarce, he couldn't fight the narrative. Both former Obama aides, who sensed their influence waning as the circle around Biden tightened, were largely rebuffed. Donilon and Ricchetti led the charge to ignore critics. "If Mike and Steve had said, 'You gotta be out there every day,' he would be out there," said one person who participated in strategy calls. "But those guys operate with a little chip on their shoulder, like 'Fuck them.'" Biden didn't want to embarrass himself with performative appearances. That did not sit well with the donor class. "The first time he took questions was more than a week after the debate," said one Biden fundraiser. "That was fairly fatal in my world."

O'Malley Dillon could feel the life draining out of her campaign team. She organized a Zoom call with the senior staff in Wilmington. She told them what she did and didn't know—and she didn't know much. She couldn't even be sure that Biden would stick it out until the end. *Irrespective of what these folks think about whether or not he should be running at this point*, she thought, *he is the nominee and he's going to be the nominee until he decides not to be. The only way we're going to defeat Donald Trump is if we do what we need to do to get Joe Biden over the finish line despite all of it.*

Her words were more carefully chosen, but that was the idea she conveyed to her top lieutenants. The truth was that everything they did to help Biden and fight Trump would benefit either him or a replacement candidate. The job was the same—though Biden's relative absence made it harder. So did the realization that they had to battle the haters in their own party. "Fuck it," one senior aide said of the mentality coming out of that Zoom meeting. "If we have to go to war with the *Pod Save* guys, then we're going to war with the *Pod Save* guys. Do we have to go to war with Nancy Pelosi? Fine, then fuck it. We've got to be as aggressive as possible."

O'Malley Dillon, who instituted daily calls to deal with the internal warfare, couldn't do anything to stop factions in the White House from leaking against each other. But she could try to keep the campaign focused on the blocking and tackling of winning an election. "Everyone else at the White House was fucking fighting with each other," said one insider. "Jen kept moving the ball forward."

Trump, in an uncharacteristic maneuver to stay out of Biden's spotlight, paused the public portion of the virtual beauty pageant he was running to select his vice presidential candidate. He felt betrayed by his vice president, Mike Pence, who resisted his private entreaties and public condemnations in choosing to certify their 2020 defeat in Congress.

On January 6, 2021, Pence had fled Trump supporters, some calling for his execution, inside the Capitol and then worked with Pelosi to ensure that Congress could do its work once the building was cleared of rioters. In choosing Pence, Trump had made a political determination, reaching out to the social conservatives who weren't sold on him in 2016. After four years in the White House, and three years of plotting to reclaim it, Trump saw his 2024 pick as a highly personal decision.

For weeks he had brought hopefuls to deliver tributes to him at campaign events and openly mused about their abilities. Now, though, the chatter around his pick, which would send a message to the country about his desire to tack toward the middle or double down on his MAGA movement, quieted.

"There is so much up in the air that there is no reason for them to act quickly after what happened in Atlanta," a veteran Republican operative familiar with the Trump team's internal deliberations told NBC News. "There could be someone else nominated by Democrats—how does that potentially change things? Waiting for now makes all the sense in the world."

Trump aides determined that the campaign should do as little as possible to interfere with the Democratic infighting. It had been a tactical error, they thought, to debate Biden in June. But they had little choice after Trump pledged to let Biden pick the time and place of a debate. His advisers did not want to compound that mistake. "We got quiet. We didn't want to accelerate the drama," one of his senior aides said. "We hoped he stayed in the race."

Inside the Democratic Party, deep divisions were forming over a series of interrelated questions. The first, of course, was whether there was any point in discussing a replacement candidate if Biden didn't decide on his own to step aside. What if party leaders and donors inflicted enough damage on him to ensure a defeat and he held on to the nomination anyway? Was there any polling—or just gut feeling—to indicate that he had lost ground because of the debate? If he left the race, should the party back Harris, whose approval ratings were below Biden's? Or should the party hold some sort of accelerated primary process—and, if so, how would that work? If it looked like Biden would lose, and he insisted on staying put, was it possible to rip his delegates away from him?

None of those questions could be answered immediately. It would take time to poll voters across the country and check in with delegates. One House member commissioned a survey three days after the debate that asked voters in his district about the head-to-head matchup of Trump and Biden, whether Biden should stay on the ballot, and how they viewed Harris. The poll had been in the works already, and he paused it in order to let the debate sink in and throw in the questions about Biden's candidacy and Harris. Biden was up 5 points on Trump in a district that he had won by about a dozen points in 2020, according to the lawmaker. What that suggested was erosion in Democratic support for Biden, but not enough to make it politically safe for the lawmaker to call for him to step aside.

That kind of uncertainty, which gripped many elected officials, cut to Biden's benefit. Because the closer the party got to its late-August convention without another plan, the more it was locked in to nominating him. The DNC determined that the window was shorter because of an Ohio law that required candidates on the state's ballot to be certified by August 7.

Even if Biden chose to withdraw, it made more sense, according to one senior party official, for him to take the nomination and then give it away. That's because party rules dictated that if a nomination was vacated, the chairman of the party—Biden ally Jaime Harrison—had sole authority to name a successor. Effectively, that would leave the choice to Biden. Democratic leaders representing different interests already were asking party elders for advice on how the rules worked. Sudden widespread interest in arcane rules pointed to the perception of Biden's weakness.

But Biden had another advantage, one that he had built in. In contrast to Obama, who set up his own shadow party operation, Organizing for America, as a rival to the DNC, Biden had spent years bolstering the party. Bill and Hillary Clinton, worried about Bernie Sanders acolytes working their way into the infrastructure and pulling the party hard to the left, had helped him do that with their own contacts in the states and at the national level. Harris too had focused on party-building during her years as VP.

The party leadership, which had control over the procedures for the nomination and the convention, was full of Biden loyalists. The chairman of the convention committee, Minyon Moore, was a former Clinton White House political director, and her close friend Leah Daughtry ran the convention's rules panel. Acting at Biden's direction, the DNC had changed the primary calendar to ensure that no one could mount a legitimate challenge to him in the winter and spring of 2024, and no one did. He had won almost all of the delegates, save for a handful who had been elected as "uncommitted" to any candidate. In practical terms, it would take a coup for anyone to beat Biden for the nomination in August.

That didn't stop Democrats from playing Fantasy Power Broker. Tom Friedman, the three-time Pulitzer Prize–winning *New York Times* columnist, who was close to Pelosi and Obama, wrote his second op-ed calling for Biden's exit that Tuesday. In this version, Friedman wrote that the nomination "must be decided by an open competition." Friedman didn't explain what that would look like, but it would undoubtedly give more power, formal or informal, to leaders like Pelosi. Biden aides, sick of Friedman's veneration among Democrats, derisively labeled him "Saint Thomas."

All the fogginess served to bolster Biden, whose team pitched memos and talking points to Democrats that falsely asserted there was no other option than Biden. "The only person eligible for nomination is Joe Biden," one set of talking points said. There were a million dream scenarios in which that wouldn't be the case—including the DNC changing the rules ahead of the convention—but it was accurate in the sense that Biden retained control over the official levers of power.

The day after her MSNBC appearance, Pelosi answered her phone to hear an unmistakably smooth and soothing baritone beckoning from the opposite coast. Long before Biden, Pelosi had adroitly laid the groundwork for Barack Obama's presidency by fighting George W. Bush tooth and nail over the Iraq War. In the first two years of his presidency, they had together delivered a massive economic stimulus measure, Wall Street reforms, and the federal health insurance expansion that would bear his name: Obamacare.

At times they had disagreed on tactics, but their partnership had been productive enough for progressivism that voters sent Obama a corrective message by taking away the Democratic House majority in the Tea Party midterms of 2010. If Pelosi didn't think Obama walked on water, she certainly believed he had wings. Everything he did seemed to turn out well, no matter how high he floated above the trenches, she thought.

There was neither hope in Obama's voice nor a clear plan for change in his words. At a loss for answers himself, he had called to pick Pelosi's brain. There was no one, he knew, who better understood the mores and folkways of insider politics. Pelosi might not be able to give a soaring speech like him, but time and again he had watched in awe as she maneuvered politicians around her chessboard. Depending on her target, she could persuade with a feather as deftly as she could bend with a sledgehammer. They were both feeling pressure from friends to step up as leaders of the party and fix the Biden problem.

What can we do to recover from the debate? Obama asked. *What is Joe's path forward? What if he can't bounce back? What do we do then? How do we win this election?*

All his questions pointed to a simple truth: Obama didn't think Biden could—or should—continue. Pelosi didn't have answers. But she knew they were running out of time to find them. The trajectory looked terminal. With Republicans primed to take control of the Senate, that meant winning the House was all the more important as a last line of defense against Trump. They did not, according to a person who heard their conversation, discuss replacements for Biden. But Obama already had determined that he didn't think Harris should take the president's spot on the ballot. That was his position "from the outset," according to one person who spoke to him at the time. Pelosi's biggest initial fear had been about Harris. "She actually was worried when people were panicking the night of the debate, saying 'Oh my God, it's going to be her,'" said a person who spoke to her. Pelosi, who had watched Harris's entire

career from a catbird seat in their shared San Francisco Bay area political circles, had about as much confidence in the vice president as Obama
had in the president.

That evening in the White House, Biden sat at the end of a long conference table in the Roosevelt Room, flanked by Harris and Minnesota
governor Tim Walz, the chairman of the Democratic Governors Association. In the days after the debate, Walz kept in close contact with his fellow
governors, some of whom were concerned about Biden and some of whom
saw opportunity in his troubles. Walz asked the White House to put the
Democratic governors on the president's schedule. About half of them had
come to the West Wing while the rest joined by videoconference.

Several of the governors unloaded on the president. New Mexico
governor Michelle Lujan Grisham, growing much taller than her four-
foot-ten frame in a video box, told Biden that he was putting her state
in play, threatening the party's chances not only at the presidential level
but down the ballot. "We haven't gone red," Lujan Grisham reminded
Biden, "since 2004." She stopped short of telling him to drop out, but
came close. "You should know what the ticket looks like in my state,"
she said, pointing to the tight rematch freshman representative Gabe
Vasquez faced against Republican Yvette Harrell in a race Democrats
were counting on to help take the majority. Biden might even imperil
the reelection of Senator Martin Heinrich, a seemingly safe Democrat
who held a seat that had been in the party's hands for more than forty
years. One fellow governor described the bleak picture she painted as
"the most graphic" of the appeals to Biden's sense of party loyalty.

Governor Jared Polis of Colorado, whose state played host to two
highly competitive House races, expressed similar concerns. Both had
cut their political teeth in Pelosi's House. Governors Janet Mills of
Maine and Ned Lamont of Connecticut, who worried about the House
seats represented by Democrats Jared Golden and Jahana Hayes, respectively, raised doubts as well.

Biden had come to the meeting ready for the governors. He told
them he was committed to running—"All in."

Harris sat silently for most of the meeting but interjected forcefully
when a point was made about the fate of democracy resting on the out-

come of the election. "It's more than our fucking democracy," she half-shouted before listing the threats she perceived in a Trump presidency that had more to do with policy than the sanctity of the republic. Her point was that on issues from abortion to taxation, Trump could do plenty of harm to Democratic constituencies without fundamentally changing the country's form of government.

A few governors emerged from the West Wing to talk with reporters in the White House driveway and praised Biden. But the group, like the rest of the party, remained fractured over Biden's future. During the meeting he told them that he would adjust his schedule to try to prevent another episode like the debate. He wouldn't plan events after 8 p.m., Biden said. The governors were like mini-presidents of their own states, always in motion. The early shutdown time sounded nuts to them. "It was awful," one of the governors later observed. "Somebody better tell the Chinese when they can attack us, because I don't want [them] to do that and wake him up."

Heading into the July Fourth holiday, Biden allies helped him stave off a full-on revolt by talking up future events. He had scheduled a Friday interview with ABC News' George Stephanopoulos and a rally in heavily Democratic Madison, Wisconsin. The following week, Biden was scheduled to play a starring role at a North Atlantic Treaty Organization conference in Washington. Talking to colleagues and reporters, Biden friends said the president should not be undercut before his turn on the global stage, especially with MAGA Republicans questioning U.S. support for Ukraine and the general value of the Western alliance. Just wait, his surrogates said. Just wait. Give him a chance to catch his balance.

Biden determined to do that by insisting that he wasn't going anywhere. On Wednesday, White House chief of staff Jeff Zients had convened an all-staff call to give Biden a platform to spread his message internally. "Let me say this as clearly as I possibly can, as simply and straightforward as I can," he said to his aides. "I am running." Biden picked up the phone to deliver the same defiant line to key members of Congress. But neither he nor his aides were able to convince Democratic insiders that he was fine.

That same day, Jean-Pierre told reporters that Biden had not seen a doctor since the debate. If White House officials thought that would calm antsy Democrats, they were wrong. How could he not have checked in with a physician after his performance? During the meeting with Democratic governors that night, he contradicted Jean-Pierre. He had, in fact, seen his doctor since the debate, he said. Either he was lying or Jean-Pierre had given false information. The conflicting stories didn't help. Nor did Biden's joke to the governors that there was nothing wrong with his health—"just my brain." Telling the governors that he would try not to schedule events after 8 p.m. only added to the concern about his status.

Still, Biden and his aides believed they were turning the tide on the rush to push him out. It was one thing for pundits and political operatives to call on him to abort his bid, but most of his doubters in Congress were still silent. If he wasn't winning the fight, he at least hadn't lost it yet. He pushed on the gas. At the White House Independence Day celebration on Thursday, he clasped Harris's hand in his own and raised them to the sky. "I'm not going anywhere," he replied to a supportive shout from the crowd. Pushing back on the idea that Biden was unable to perform his duties, White House officials told the media that he had spoken to Israeli prime minister Benjamin Netanyahu that day about negotiations over Hamas-held hostages and a long-sought cease-fire in a war that had raged since terrorists slaughtered and kidnapped Israelis eight months earlier.

Before the Wisconsin rally on Friday, July 5, Biden taped the ABC News interview with Stephanopoulos, a onetime aide to President Bill Clinton. The session aired that night, an odd time to project confidence. Many voters would be on day two of a four-day holiday weekend bender, uninterested in politics. But across the country, Biden campaign aides and Democratic activists apprehensively tuned in like they were watching Neil Armstrong take one small step for man. "It's a fucking moon landing," one senior Biden adviser said. "Will he be able to do it?"

Biden again appeared stiff and uncertain. He stumbled on the third question. "Did you ever watch the debate afterwards?" Stephanopoulos asked.

"I don't think I did, no," Biden said.

Only eight days had passed, and he couldn't seem to remember whether he had gone back to watch what so many Democrats couldn't wipe from their memory banks. No matter what Stephanopoulos threw at him in the rest of the interview, Biden kept repeating that he'd had a "bad night." He did manage to push back gently on Pelosi, saying that it was an "episode" and not "a condition." But if the interview suggested anything, it was that little had changed from debate night. The same text chains that had lit up eight days earlier juiced again with new messages of fear, anger, and disbelief.

The first week after the debate was like the opening phase of a tug-of-war. Biden and his Democratic detractors went back and forth, each side gaining an inch only to lose it in the next pull of the rope. Yet there were early signs that the traction on his side was beginning to slip.

Biden advisers knew that he had been much better in the interview than the debate. What struck one of them more squarely, though, was the tension of the moment. Biden had done "fine," the adviser said, but how could he win reelection if his own team was hanging on every word with bated breath? "If a single interview with George Stephanopoulos is that much of a 'Phew, he nailed it,' doesn't that call the question?" Most Democrats didn't think he had nailed it.

CHAPTER 5

THE ACE IN THE HOLE

OVER THE INDEPENDENCE DAY WEEKEND, BIDEN STARTED TO FEEL that the fever might pass. He had survived the Stephanopoulos interview, and adoring fans greeted him warmly in Wisconsin on Friday and Pennsylvania on Sunday. He had spoken that week to various congressional leaders, including Pelosi. Many lawmakers were concerned about his viability—and their own. But they had not piled on. The mob did not seem to be growing or getting particularly louder. At least not to him.

Biden had not overreacted. Now, he thought, it was time to act, to crush the haters. *This is the week we shut it down*, he thought. *End of discussion.* His private conversations with congressional leaders and donors hadn't done the trick. When the talks leaked out, they were distorted. Now he would speak to elected leaders and the public all at the same time, unfiltered. That way he couldn't be misinterpreted out of malice, callousness, or carelessness. *There can't be any distance between the cup and the lip*, he thought.

White House chief of staff Jeff Zients instituted a daily nighttime meeting with senior members of Biden's team after the debate, and the president's advisers kicked around ideas for executing on the plan to push back. At a time when Biden was struggling to communicate clearly on camera, there was an inherent risk in delivering a speech or sitting for an interview. He would undermine his own case if he stumbled—again—while speaking. Donilon believed he should write a letter—one designed to be made public—and Ricchetti argued for addressing it to Democrats in Congress. They were the noisiest bunch, with their proximity to the media and their own reelection fears. But the letter was meant to send a message to Capitol Hill and beyond, as one adviser put it, "he wasn't going anywhere."

"It was an effort to try to bring people together and stop questioning the basic proposition of whether he was staying in," said a second adviser who was in on the talks.

Biden was going on offense. Senior campaign officials liked the strategy but weren't sold on the tactic. Why send a letter? Why not put Biden in front of a camera to throw down the gauntlet with authority? Was he not capable of carrying his own message on TV? It was the ultimate Donilon move—the epitome of old-school politics—to show up to a sword fight with a quill pen. As usual, Biden's right-hand man won out. *God*, thought one top campaign adviser, *this is just not forceful.*

O'Malley Dillon secured one small concession on behalf of the campaign team. In addition to the missive, Biden would make an appearance on *Morning Joe* in an effort to set his narrative with the smart set in the anti-Trump coalition. Later in the week, he would be at the center of international attention during a NATO conference in D.C. Biden felt like a veteran horse jumping through brand-new hoops, and his aides hoped the NATO appearance would be the last one on the course.

While the dam still hadn't broken, the creek continued to rise. Just below the surface, it was full of hungry predators. California governor Gavin Newsom, Maryland governor Wes Moore, and Pennsylvania governor Josh Shapiro were among the prominent Democrats who dialed up elite operatives to game out scenarios that could land them on the ticket. Billionaire Illinois governor J. B. Pritzker, an heir to the Hyatt hotel fortune, lurked as the only prospective candidate who could fund a ten-figure presidential campaign with a single stroke of his check-writing pen. With the Democratic convention taking place in Chicago, he would have the home-field advantage to woo delegates before a possible floor fight for the nomination. New Jersey governor Phil Murphy, a Goldman Sachs alum, might at least be able to kick-start his own campaign with a hefty donation, and he also had one eye on the presidency.

"Suddenly, I had people who I hadn't seen in a while—aka the governors of states—starting to reach out to say, 'What's the process? What could happen at the convention?'" said one top campaign aide to a former Democratic nominee. That started "right after the debate." If Biden's delegates remained loyal to him, and most of the delegates to the convention were elected on pledges to support him, he would have no problem taking the nomination. None of the governors thought they could defeat him in a head-to-head matchup on the floor. But they were very interested in what would happen to his delegates if he stepped aside. That was a more open and loaded question. The set of delegates quickly became a behind-the-scenes battleground. The president's team rightly saw them as his base of power.

Anita Dunn, a veteran of the convention floor fight between President Jimmy Carter and Senator Ted Kennedy in 1980, told her colleagues that they should rally the New York and California delegations to make statements in support of Biden. It would be a show of force, she said, that would kill talk of a rebellion. In any event, they needed to know where his delegates stood. Biden's campaign had done little to organize its delegates, despite—and probably because of—his domination of the primary. Hunter Biden had pushed her out of the tightest circle of advisers, but she still worked at the White House, had close contacts at the campaign, and was active in broader discussions. Biden's campaign aides began checking in with delegates to make sure they were solidly behind him, but the whip operation was disorganized at best, and incapable of giving Biden's top advisers a quick and accurate assessment of his count. "There was no delegate strategy," one of the advisers said.

With Pelosi raising questions about Biden's "condition" and Newsom quietly testing the waters of his own run, there wasn't a snowball's chance in Death Valley that the California delegation—where they were the most powerful players—would bend its knee. New York's heaviest hitter, Senate Majority Leader Chuck Schumer, was keeping his powder dry. His reticence was its own statement about the softness of his loyalty to Biden, particularly because he was so vocal in private. "The one that was loudest internally but refused to say anything externally was Schumer," said one Democratic operative who spoke with him regularly. For months, Schumer, the seventy-three-year-old musterer of the Senate, fretted over the Biden drag on Democratic senators in tough re-election fights. "They couldn't get over Biden's numbers, and the whole theory was 'he'll fix it at the debate, he'll fix it at the debate,'" the operative said. "After the debate, it was like, 'Oh, my God, five-alarm fire.'" Rather than ringing a bell to warn the rest of the country, Schumer used his flip phone to complain to friends. The New York convention delegation would stay on the sidelines too.

Jeffries, new in his job as the top House Democrat, tried to balance the factions within his own caucus. On a conference call Jeffries convened Sunday, July 7, four Democrats, including two from his own home state—Representatives Jerrold Nadler and Joe Morelle of New York, Adam Smith of Washington State, and Mark Takano of California—said they thought Biden should drop out. Smith, the ranking Democrat on the House Armed Services Committee, and Nadler, the ranking Democrat on the House Judiciary Committee, were powerful senior members of the caucus. Smith would make his views public the following day.

Biden didn't give a shit about the House. He viewed it the way a thirty-six-year veteran of the Senate does: as an annoyingly hyperactive little brother. But the Senate mattered a lot to him. It was the more august body—serious, thoughtful, deliberative—and none of its members had called for him to wave a white flag. No one would listen to a handful of House no-names if the Senate was silent. He could stop the bleeding and start recovering, he thought.

Biden felt confident in his counterattack plan. *Fighting back will bring this nonsense to a close.* By the time his head hit the pillow in the private residence of the White House that Sunday night, he was ready for battle.

Biden sent his letter to Capitol Hill the next morning. His aides skipped the step of waiting for lawmakers to leak it to the press; the campaign posted it on his X account at 9:15 a.m. The White House gave short notice to the media that he would be on *Morning Joe* about thirty minutes later. But he wouldn't really be on *Morning Joe*. He literally phoned it in. Campaign aides were shocked. Democrats were demanding to *see* him, not hear his disembodied voice. Critics in both parties said he was hiding. This reinforced that idea. But Biden resisted voices on his own team that wanted him to show he was fighting hard. He didn't want to be in a fishbowl. He was disappointed—in his party, in his team, and, truth be told, in himself. His heart just wasn't fully into a fight he didn't think he should be forced to mount. One adviser described the phone-in as one of dozens of half measures that represented the furthest Biden would go to perform like a circus monkey.

Still, gamely enough, Biden used the preferred platform of Democratic insiders to chuck a brushback pitch at the donors, operatives, and elected officials lining up to push him out. "I'm getting so frustrated by the elites in the party," he said, noting that the voters had chosen him in the primary. "If any of these guys don't think I should run, run against me. Go ahead. Announce for president—challenge me at the convention."

Whether he didn't understand that many Democratic voters were worried, or simply glossed over it to make his point, Biden tried to position himself as a champion of the little guy against powerful, largely unseen forces working against him and them. It was more than a little Trumpy. Long before the debate, polls showed that most Democrats preferred "someone else" to Biden. Like most incumbents, he had stacked the primary process to ward off potential opponents, circumventing the possibility that voters would choose anyone else.

Biden's moves were more audacious than most. At his bidding, the Democratic National Committee approved a new primary calendar in 2023 that put South Carolina, arguably his strongest state, at the front of the line. The Iowa caucuses, traditionally the first contest of the nomination process and a political graveyard for Biden, were shifted back. Georgia and Michigan, two delegate-heavy states where he expected to do well, were moved into an early window.

The new order made an uphill battle against Biden even steeper. While most Democratic voters were open to alternatives in 2023, beating Trump was their top priority. Not only was there little point in running against Biden with the new calendar, but serious politicians worried that they would incur permanent damage to their reputations within the party if Trump won after they launched a divisive challenge to the sitting president. Biden understood those dynamics as well as anyone—he had won the 2020 Democratic nomination and the presidency by portraying himself as Trump's best foil—and exploited them to cut off any potential competition at the knees. He went back to the Trump well to convince fellow Democrats that he remained their top option in 2024.

"The question of how to move forward has been well-aired for over a week now. And it's time for it to end. We have one job. And that is to beat Donald Trump," he wrote in the letter to lawmakers. "Any weakening of resolve or lack of clarity about the task ahead only helps Trump and hurts us."

The letter hit Capitol Hill like a crate of rotten eggs. Rather than confident, Biden came off as delusional. Though he had used the word in his television appearance, rather than in the letter, lawmakers resented being lumped into a category of "elites." They represented the same voters who had elected Biden. He was the guy who had been in Washington his entire adult life. He was rich by most standards, a multimillionaire from book advances and speaking fees. As president, he was literally the most elite human on the planet.

They also rejected the idea that they were doing the bidding of their contributors. This was peak holier-than-thou Biden, and it betrayed either a fundamental misunderstanding of campaign finance or an intentional suggestion that any lawmaker who questioned him was bought and paid for. It was Biden who was more reliant on megabucks. House candidates needed money too, but not at the scale that the presidential candidate did.

"People are frustrated that the president appears defensive and in denial," one lawmaker said of the letter and the *Morning Joe* interview. "He's like the grandpa who refuses to give up the car keys even though it's not safe for him to drive anymore." Yet in the next breath, the lawmaker acknowledged that the relative quiet on Capitol Hill was helping Biden rebound. "There's also a growing resignation that, if Joe Biden insists on remaining our nominee, we will have to make the best out of a bad situation going into the most consequential presidential election in American history."

Senator Patty Murray (D-WA), the seventy-three-year-old president pro tempore of the Senate, who sat third in line to the presidency, found the letter infuriating. There were legitimate concerns about Biden, and she feared that he would destroy the party's chances in November if he couldn't turn things around quickly. Murray didn't think there was much hope for that, but she wasn't ready to say it out loud. Instead, she released a statement rebutting Biden's. "More than a week since the debate, and after talking with my constituents, I believe President Biden must do more to demonstrate he can campaign strong enough to beat Donald Trump," she said.

It was with reluctance that Murray became the point of the spear in the Senate. The baby boomer "mom in tennis shoes" who upset an incumbent in the Year of the Woman in 1992 had served with Biden for sixteen years in the Senate, eight years of his vice presidency, and three-plus years of his presidency. She was now an elder stateswoman. She had hoped that her colleagues would quickly come to a consensus that reflected her own thinking: Biden should go. She was livid at the cowardice she saw in fellow senators, many of whom griped about Biden privately but refused to take the political risk of airing their views. "These men aren't doing anything," she confided to a friend. "We need some backbone in here."

On Tuesday morning, July 9, House Democrats trudged down New Jersey Avenue and South Capitol Street to the DNC headquarters, gathering in the Wasserman Room, a space far too small to comfortably fit nearly two hundred adults. Veteran lawmakers took the back entrance to avoid the television cameras and print reporters waiting outside the front door to the DNC. The media hounds were hungry enough to wait for more than two hours to see what color smoke—and what kind of fiery quotes—would emerge from the high-stakes confab.

Inside the Wasserman Room, caucus chairman Pete Aguilar opened the discussion. Pelosi sat quietly in the front row, facing Aguilar, with a pained look, as though she were watching a nineteenth-century doctor saw off her child's leg. Representative Brendan Boyle, a Pennsylvania Democrat close to Biden, was one of the lawmakers who spoke on the president's behalf. He would stick by Biden, he said. He also argued that public betrayals wouldn't help those who sought to make a change at the top. "Look, in my view, coming from the same culture as the president, if you come out and call on him to resign or step down as the Democratic nominee, that will be counterproductive," Boyle told his colleagues. "He will get his back up."

The house was divided. Knowing that their words were likely to be repeated to the press, most lawmakers kept their opinions to themselves. But Representative Annie Kuster, a New Hampshire Democrat, stood up to relay the views of the New Democrat Coalition, a moderate caucus within the caucus. With her voice cracking and her hands shaking, Kuster announced that she believed Biden should step aside and that there were other members of her faction who felt the same way. Brittany Pettersen, a freshman who represented western Denver and its suburbs, broke down in tears as she pleaded with fellow Democrats to act to protect women who feared a second Trump presidency. "It's not about any of us as individuals," she said as she advocated for Biden's departure.

When the meeting wrapped up around noon, the only consensus was that there was no consensus among House Democrats. Boyle took that as a positive sign for Biden. He texted a senior White House official. *This morning wasn't pretty*, he wrote. *But I think this is going to be the end of it. I think Biden has survived.*

As the House Democrats emerged from their emergency meeting, Senate Democrats were gathering in the Capitol for a weekly luncheon. Of the fifty-one members of the Senate Democratic caucus, no more than a half dozen were still firmly in Biden's camp. For more than a week, Coons had been taking their temperatures and calmly urging them not to "get out ahead of this." Senator John Fetterman, a first-term antiestablishment Democrat from Pennsylvania, was one of the handful who stuck up for Biden. During his first campaign in 2022, Fetterman had suffered a stroke. Biden had stood by him at a time when other Democrats pined for a replacement candidate. Bald, goateed, and three-hundred-plus pounds, the six-foot-eight Pennsylvanian cut an imposing and unorthodox figure in the Senate, which changed its dress code to allow him to cast votes on the floor in a hoodie and shorts. He made clear his view that Biden was the only candidate who could beat Trump.

But most of the Democrats who spoke were no longer with Biden. Senators Jon Tester of Montana and Sherrod Brown of Ohio, both in danger of losing their seats in November, said Biden's presence on the ticket would sink them. For reasons of friendship, loyalty, and fear of dividing their own bases, neither wanted to say so publicly. Tester's advisers were already pushing him to rip the Band-Aid off and put distance between himself and Biden. He simply didn't want to do that. But he knew Biden was an anchor on him. Schumer was taken aback by the tenor of the discussion. These senators weren't just worried. They were mad, and they were scared. That went beyond the senators on the ballot. If Brown and Tester lost, the returning Democrats would find themselves in the minority. They would lose chairmanships, fundraising clout, and relevance in the nation's capital.

Leaving the luncheon, Majority Whip Dick Durbin of Illinois, the second-ranking Democrat in the chamber, told reporters "it remains to be seen" whether Biden could continue as the party's candidate. Schumer sent word to the White House that the president needed to dispatch his top political aides to Capitol Hill to address Senate Democrats pronto.

If Biden had swung the pendulum in his direction on Monday, and he had, it was now starting to speed backward. At the opening of the NATO conference that Tuesday evening, he awarded Secretary General Jens Stoltenberg the Presidential Medal of Freedom and gave remarks without incident. But it took him several awkward seconds to clasp the medal around Stoltenberg's shoulders. One Biden ally who attended the ceremony worried that the president would drop the medal.

Every time he does anything in public, there's a risk that he'll look out-of-it, the ally thought as he watched apprehensively. *Why can't his people see that problem? He needs to get out, and the longer he waits, the harder it will be to have a mini-primary. We're losing that option.*

The ally, who is Jewish, was startled when a senior member of Biden's team asked if he had been sent to the ceremony to represent "the New York delegation"—a jab that, in addition to having an anti-Semitic edge, underscored Biden's frustration with a donor class that was turning on him with increasing ruthlessness. "Look, I'm personally supportive," the ally told Biden's team repeatedly. "I'm not going to say anything publicly, but if you did an event in New York, I don't think you could fill the room—and that's embarrassing."

All across the country, prospective donors pulled out of planned Biden fundraisers that week. "Money is pretty bad across the board," one source with visibility into campaign, party, and super PAC fundraising said. "It's already disastrous," said a second person. Not only would Biden fall far short of his fundraising goals for July—threatening his ability to ramp up his campaign operations for the stretch run—but contributors to the main super PAC formed to bolster him, Future Forward, decided to cut off hundreds of millions of dollars.

Biden's biggest-swinging donors were trying to choke him out. They were doing it from the cash-rich enclaves that traditionally pumped the lifeblood of money into Democratic campaigns: Manhattan, Silicon Valley, Hollywood, and Austin. While each metropolis and industry had its own donor trees—connected to one another by fundraising consultants and a strange new breed of "donor advisers" who were hired to tell rich people where to invest in politicians—most of them were doing it at least semi-independently. To the White House, it felt like a cash czar conspiracy to derail Biden.

For more than a week, Biden aides had been frantically pushing back in phone calls and in text messages, accusing donors of promoting their own agendas at the expense of Biden, the party, and the country. It all sounded like a serial killer's conspiracy theory. *Donors want to scrap Biden so they can get his wannabe replacements—the governors, with power over state decisions—to beg them for cash,* Biden aides argued. *This isn't fucking Wall Street financiers versus Ivy League presidents. Our guy isn't scared of your money. We have grassroots donors. We have the support of the voters. We have the nomination in hand. All you're doing is fucking yourself and the president. We will remember this. Capisce?*

The last threat, the ace in the hole, was Kamala Harris. *Even if Biden did drop out and you got your dreamed-up open convention, you would only succeed in nominating the vice president. Is that what you want? You want her? Look at her polling. No one wants her. Forget it. It's never gonna happen.*

One donor on the receiving end of an electronic message summed up the sentiments of Biden's top aides: "They were aggressively saying that we would wind up with the vice president and that would be a mistake."

CHAPTER 6

ET TU, NANCY?

SHORTLY AFTER DAWN ON WEDNESDAY, JULY 10, PELOSI RODE WITH HER security team from Georgetown to NBC's Washington, D.C., bureau, with its sweeping views of the Capitol, for an interview on *Morning Joe*. She barreled into the eighth-floor makeup room uncharacteristically unassembled. Instead of a trademark tightly tailored suit, she was draped in a loose-fitting lavender dress that she wore for the very first time that day. The top of it was too slack, revealing more neck and shoulder than she usually did. Strands of dyed light brown hair shot away from her normally perfect bob. Pelosi's signature scarlet lipstick was nowhere to be found. A makeup artist hurriedly daubed foundation on her skin and painted her lips with a light gloss. Pelosi had left no minutes to spare before her TV hit.

It was time to head down the hallway to the studio for a joint interview with exiled Belarusian opposition leader Svetlana Tikhanovskaya. Pelosi had been working with Tikhanovskaya to elevate the cause of democracy, and they had planned the tandem interview to use NATO's meeting that week to highlight the issue. Of course, viewers would hang on Pelosi's every word about the internal politics—not of Belarus, but of the Democratic Party. Democrats wanted to know what she thought of the Biden situation. Pelosi didn't pause to assess herself in the mirror— *It's vain and it's rude to Svetlana*, she thought—before walking down a long hallway to a rendezvous with political destiny.

Born in the shadow of the Great Depression, one on each side of America's entry into World War II, Biden and Pelosi had more in common than most in their party. Pelosi, the Italian Catholic from Baltimore, and Biden, the Irish Catholic from Wilmington, came of age politically in machine-run cities just seventy-five miles apart. When a Catholic was elected president for the first time, Pelosi attended John F. Kennedy's 1961 inauguration at the Capitol. Biden, a senior in high school at the time, would later say that Kennedy's ideas "rhymed with the lessons I'd learned from the nuns at school and around my father's kitchen table."

Over decades in Washington, they toiled to enact the agendas of presidents Bill Clinton and Barack Obama, worked together to pass Biden's big-ticket legislative items, and crossed the aisle to compromise with Republican presidents when they believed it suited their own interests or those of the country. They came to power from opposite sides of the Democratic spectrum: Pelosi as the leader of liberals in the more partisan House; Biden as a Senate moderate picked to balance Obama's ticket and later as the establishment's choice for the 2020 presidential nomination. Yet their policy preferences overlapped far more than they diverged. Pelosi felt closer to Biden, who had been a governing partner, than to Obama, whose preference for detachment left the intense labor of passing his bills to her.

But what connected Biden and Pelosi most was the same deeply held conviction that hurtled them into a war over the party, the presidency, and the nation in July 2024. Biden and Pelosi both saw themselves as the sole savior of democracy, and both were committed to cementing that legacy for themselves.

In the back half of the Trump presidency, Pelosi led Democrats to victory in the House, held the line against his ideas, and impeached him twice. Hiding from the pro-Trump mob that stormed the Capitol on January 6, 2021, she coordinated with Vice President Mike Pence and Senate leaders to bring Congress back into session that evening and ensure that Biden's victory was certified on the constitutionally appointed day. Biden had come out of retirement, framing his 2020 campaign as a rejection of Trump's values and conduct, to defeat the sitting president. He had successfully defended what he called the "soul of America" once, and he saw himself as the only champion who could vanquish Trump a second and final time.

The Democratic universe was big enough for two archangels of salvation, so long as they both viewed Biden as the party's best hope for winning the presidency—and the White House—as the most important power center for combating Trump. Suddenly, though, that was no longer true. Pelosi harbored doubts about Biden's viability before the debate. Now, with donors and lawmakers in her ear, those doubts swelled. With a wounded candidate at the top of their ticket, Democrats wouldn't be able to turn out voters for downballot candidates. Trump could win the presidency and control both chambers of Congress—what she called the "trifecta" for Republicans. She would do anything to stop that. It didn't matter to her who was at the top of the ticket, as long as he or she was the best positioned to help Democrats win the House. It was the House that meant the most to her, and Biden was putting it in peril. Pelosi began to think that the country needed to be saved not *by* Biden, but *from* him.

That's how it came to be that, in a betrayal worthy of Brutus, the ever-put-together Pelosi slipped her blade between Biden's ribs with bloodless lips and one bra strap visible to her audience. Like Brutus, she too believed she acted in the interests of the republic as she gave permission to fellow Democrats to slash a thousand cuts in their president. "Every time it looked like we were picking up traction and we were going to get past it, we would have another brick drop on our heads," said one of Biden's closest advisers. "Pelosi was the biggest—on *Morning Joe.*"

After her whirlwind arrival at NBC's Washington bureau, Pelosi chose her words tentatively and carefully on *Morning Joe.* By now Obama had called her a second time, and she had spoken with Biden. She was in constant contact with donors and lawmakers on both sides of the Biden divide. Uniquely positioned either to help shut down the circular firing squad in the party or to give instructions on when and in which direction to shoot, she had done neither publicly. Often the signal was what she didn't say. For nearly two weeks, in private conversations, she declined to defend Biden's candidacy—an omission that savvy politicians understood as a stunning lack of support for the sitting president of her own party.

But television has a way of giving voice to the quiet parts. A *Morning Joe* panelist, *Politico* White House bureau chief Jonathan Lemire, put the key question to her succinctly: "Does he have your support to be the head of the Democratic ticket?" Pelosi, garbling her first few words, pivoted. To insiders, that was a clear no. "It's up to the president to decide if he's going to run," she said. "We're encouraging him to make that decision because time is running short." The calendar only mattered if he planned to step aside—she clearly feared the window for a mini-primary was closing—and he had just told congressional Democrats, and the rest of the world, that his decision was locked in. As she always did, Pelosi made sure to intersperse praise for Biden. But Lemire reminded Pelosi that Biden insisted he was staying in the race. She responded by repeating her view that it was still an open question. "I want him to do whatever he decides to do," she said.

Her words boomed through Wilmington, where the top tier of Biden's campaign aides were conducting a morning conference call. They had just been discussing their view that Biden's letter to Congress had bought him "some breathing room," according to one of his senior advisers. "Oh God," one of the aides said, responding to Pelosi. "We're going to have to end this call."

In Wilmington, the campaign's sentiment could be summed up in the three words that one Biden aide used to describe it: "FUCK YOU, NANCY!" It had only been two days since Biden, on the same show, vowed to defeat the "elites" who wanted him out. *She's not just refusing to defend him,* one top Biden aide thought as he watched the interview. *She's actively sabotaging him.* Campaign operatives couldn't help but laugh wistfully at Pelosi pretending that she was on his side, lauding his presidency while she plotted his downfall. They exchanged rough reviews of her performance: "Girl, you are telling on yourself," "You are waving a big flag," and "The lady doth protest too much." Biden and his longest-serving aides felt bruised by Obama's decision to step back from the public fight over his future. But what Pelosi did was different—so out front and inflammatory—and it infuriated the president. He thought he had suffocated the insurrection, and here she was rekindling it—again. "We were hurt by Obama," said one top Biden adviser. "We were fucking pissed at Pelosi."

Pelosi's move instantly reinforced the donors clamoring for Biden's departure and added to their numbers. "They were starting to realize that they had more power" and decided to "double down," said a Biden adviser with strong contacts in the fundraising world. The Biden adviser described major donors as organizing a union among themselves to increase their influence, pointing to Netflix cofounder Reed Hastings, a Pelosi ally who had called for Biden's ouster July 3, and venture capitalist Bradley Tusk, a former aide to Chuck Schumer, as influential players in that effort.

Late that morning, Biden took a three-minute ride in his motorcade to AFL-CIO headquarters, two-tenths of a mile across Lafayette Square from the White House, to meet with more than fifty union chiefs who formed the AFL-CIO's executive council. He was greeted with chants of "Four more years," and AFL-CIO president Liz Shuler introduced him by saying "This is your home," and "We have your back."

After brief opening remarks from Biden, reporters were shooed out of the session so that Biden could take questions from the labor leaders privately. Shawn Fain, president of the United Auto Workers, told Biden that his members had concerns about the president's ability to win, according to a person who was in the room. He stopped short of telling Biden to step aside, but clearly he planted his flag for the president and the other union presidents to see. Fain repeated the sentiments in a follow-up chat with Biden campaign officials that afternoon.

Within a few hours of Biden's visit, the New York Times posted an online story reporting that some of the union officials had expressed "serious concerns" to their counterparts about the president's perceived inability to explain his path to victory. The labor leaders were still in the midst of a day full of executive council meetings, and Shuler put the story up on a screen in the room.

"We were unified, and we were ready to release a statement saying that," said one furious union president. "One person leaking to a reporter shit all over that." One of the labor chiefs demanded accountability. "Everybody put your phone in the center of the room right now. We're going to go through and see who texted who," the labor chief said. "We're going to see who has talked to this reporter recently and who has a history of talking with this reporter."

They didn't end up going through with the test of loyalty. But the point was made. "It was a betrayal of trust," one of the union heads said. At the same time, the whole episode was a demonstration of the degree to which infighting was spreading like an infection through the political left.

Pelosi wasn't done for the day—not even close. At noon, the House's California Democratic contingent, some forty members strong, convened for their weekly meeting in a conference room in the Capitol. Technically, Representative Zoe Lofgren, a close ally of the former Speaker, was the chairman of the delegation, but Pelosi had been its main power broker for decades. Her words carried more weight with this group, representing nearly 20 percent of all House Democrats, than the Ten Commandments. They were waiting to hear from her.

One colleague asked what would happen if Biden stepped aside. "Many people," Pelosi said, "would like to see an open process." Those people, she added, want to "see our bench" and "all of the talent that we have." Finally, she said a mini-primary would be "time-consuming" and Democrats would have to "get on with it." What she hadn't said was "Harris." There wasn't much room for interpretation. Pelosi didn't want Harris, didn't think the vice president would prevail in a competition for the nomination, and didn't think she would beat Trump. More than that, one Pelosi confidant said, "She doesn't like Harris." The shorthand version of her view became a phrase that would forever be attributed to her by insiders loyal to Biden and Harris: "He goes. She goes."

The problem for Obama, Pelosi, and the other wish-casting Democrats who prayed for a contest to replace Biden—aside from the fact that the president hadn't budged and little more than a month remained before a nominee had to be picked at the convention—was that they hadn't identified anyone to take his spot. They hadn't done that, at least in part, because it would create even more dissent within the party. Without a clear plan for the day after, many Democrats were reluctant to execute a coup. Whether it was in Afghanistan, Libya, or Washington, D.C., most of the rank and file understood the risks of leaving a succession plan to chance.

What was more clear was that the internal warfare was taking a toll on the party. Biden's numbers hadn't fallen off a cliff in national polling.

Most surveys, including his campaign's internal tracking polls, showed him losing a point or two in the first weeks after the debate. But some of the swing-state numbers were far worse. Moreover, he had been trailing Trump before the debate, and fighting Democrats left him unable to prosecute the case against Trump. Even some campaign and party officials began to conclude that he couldn't recover. "No one involved in the effort thinks he has a path," one of them said that Wednesday, summing up the squeeze of lousy fundraising, polls that weren't getting better, and a party in utter chaos. "The question for me, and a lot of us, is 'Who is the best person to beat Donald Trump?'" said one senior Biden campaign aide. "There are a lot of us that are true blue that are questioning our initial thoughts."

Biden summoned Pelosi to his personal residence at the White House that evening. She had spoken to him by phone once already, and she regularly conveyed her thoughts to him on a wide variety of topics through Steve Ricchetti and Jeff Zients. Biden wanted to know why Pelosi was turning on him. In her mind, she wasn't doing that at all. She said she had been misinterpreted on *Morning Joe*. She wasn't trying to say that he had a decision to make—which was what she actually said—but that the decision belonged to him and no one else. It was a distinction without a difference, and one that was lost on everyone who watched the clip.

Biden felt confident that, despite all the noise, his polling numbers were basically holding. *I don't know what data he's looking at,* Pelosi thought, *but our members are taking a big hit.* In any event, she said, none of it was personal. She wasn't advocating for him to get out of the race. Instead, she wanted to be assured that the campaign would get better, that its messaging would improve, and that it would focus more urgently on keeping Trump—*that thug*—out of the White House. Keeping Trump at the forefront would help mobilize Democratic voters and sway independents in swing districts, she thought. But right now, the campaign was looking inward. The navel-gazing gave Trump a pass.

Pelosi was under no illusion that Biden would take her counsel on how to run his campaign. *They don't take any advice,* she thought of the many presidential candidates she had dealt with. *They don't care what outsiders have to say.* But she wanted to make sure Biden was clear on what her members were thinking—the good, the bad, and the traitor-ous. She could say all day long that she was just acting as a vehicle for the thoughts of others—that she wasn't applying pressure herself—but Biden didn't believe that for a second. He was all too familiar with the Washingtonspeak technique of a politician putting his or her own views in the voices of colleagues.

Pelosi infuriated Biden and his team. George Clooney scared them. A day or two earlier, White House and campaign officials had learned that the Hollywood heartthrob planned to savage Biden in the *New York Times*. Jeffrey Katzenberg, who served as a bridge between Biden and the entertainment industry, was given a copy of the op-ed as a courtesy. It didn't read as courteous. "We are not going to win in November with this president. On top of that, we won't win the House, and we're going to lose the Senate," Clooney wrote. "This isn't only my opinion; this is the opinion of every senator and Congress member and governor who I've spoken with in private. Every single one, irrespective of what he or she is saying publicly." He called on Pelosi, Schumer, and Jeffries to tell the president to abandon his bid and for the party to hold a mini-primary. He omitted Obama, his friend, from that list of Democratic muscle.

Clooney's certitude surprised one Democratic aide who had worked the fundraising event, because the actor had not spent much time inter-acting with the president directly. But the aide nonetheless recalled be-ing advised beforehand that Biden was exhausted from his travels. That was evident onstage, where Obama frequently jumped in to save Biden from trailing off and even answered questions directed at the president.

Katzenberg had tried to stop Clooney by himself and failed. By the time Biden aides caught wind of it, the *Times* already had the op-ed in hand. If Pelosi spoke in coded language to elites, Clooney, twice named *People*'s sexiest man alive, had an audience that numbered in the hundreds of millions of Americans. "Pelosi's approach was asphyx-iation. Clooney was a drone strike at Biden's front door," said a Biden adviser who read the *Times* piece as it circulated in the White House and through campaign inboxes before it was released. "The quick hit and the slow death arrived at the same time."

The incoming came in different forms. But once Biden had fired back in his letter to Congress, it never let up. Clooney's words so closely reflected Obama's thinking that the op-ed might as well have carried the former president's byline. Obama didn't want to get his own hands dirty—couldn't face leaving bloody fingerprints on Biden's political corpse—but he hoped others would shoulder the wet work. Clooney named them in his op-ed.

Three of Biden's top advisers—Donilon, Ricchetti, and O'Malley Dillon—huddled the following day with Democratic senators at the Democratic Senatorial Campaign Committee's headquarters, a stone's throw from the Supreme Court. In a contentious two-hour back-and-forth, the Biden team presented its view of his path to victory and listened to anxious senators challenge their premise. Several senators emphasized their fondness for Biden while making clear they thought he should drop out. Some teared up. But only a few, including Fetterman, spoke in favor of Biden, and "he wasn't taken all that seriously," said one person who was there. O'Malley Dillon felt a sense of empathy for the senators who struggled to reconcile their appreciation for Biden with their fear of defeat. *We don't want to be in this situation*, she thought. *And they don't want to be in this situation.* Donilon and Ricchetti were in a different place. Their attitude, according to the person in the room, amounted to "Fuck them."

Biden still had significant support among Black, Hispanic, and progressive white lawmakers in the House, as well as some of his longtime friends in the labor movement. When union leaders said he had been their best ally in the White House, they could point to hard-won policies like a $90 billion bailout of labor pensions that had been languishing in Washington for years. While it was clear that most of the union presidents were still with Biden, Fain's concerns hinted that some labor leaders were going soft on him. Sara Nelson, president of the flight attendants' union, had suggested privately to allies that she thought Biden was unfit for the nomination. Like Pelosi, these union officials worried that Trump and a Republican Congress would lay waste to labor rights. Unlike Pelosi, they had members who would vote for Trump.

Fain liked Biden, but he hated Trump more. Even before the debate, he was deeply concerned about the prospects that the president would lose Michigan, a "Blue Wall" state that had voted for the Democratic presidential nominee in all but one presidential election—Trump's 2016 victory—since 1992.

Headquartered in Detroit, the UAW has a well-organized corps of Arab American members. Many of them live in suburbs, like Dearborn, that typically provide big margins for Democratic candidates. But Biden alienated Arab American voters and their allies by backing Israel's war in Gaza following the October 7, 2023, terrorist attacks. In February, more than 100,000 Michigan Democrats voted for "uncommitted" over Biden, leaving him with barely more than 80 percent in a primary in which he faced no real competition. Besides the policy issue, Fain believed the Biden campaign's operation in the state was subpar. For him it all added up to a nightmare scenario in which Michigan might help Trump win back the White House, sink Representative Elissa Slotkin's Senate bid, and flip one or more House seats into GOP hands.

The board of the UAW splintered over whether to back Biden, rescind its endorsement of him, or call on him publicly to ride away in the first American-made car he could find. But there was a growing sentiment that Democrats stood a better chance of winning—that the union's interests would be best served—if he dropped out. Fain communicated all of this to Ricchetti and Chavez Rodriguez as Biden put together plans for a Friday rally in Detroit. Not only would Biden's appearance put pressure on a divided union, but it would do the same to the Democratic lawmakers and candidates who would be called on to stand by his side or come out against him. At best, that would be uncomfortable. At worst, it could do real damage to their own campaigns.

Fain reached out to White House officials on Friday morning and demanded to talk with the president. If Biden would not get on the phone with him, he said, the UAW would withdraw its endorsement. Shuler received a flurry of calls from White House officials that morning that accelerated quickly from urgency to anger: from "We're hearing Shawn is going to rescind the endorsement. Can you talk some sense into him?" to "This is unheard-of. Who the fuck does he think he is?"

Fain aired his grievances to Representative Debbie Dingell, a former automotive industry lobbyist whose district once included Dearborn, and let her know the union's endorsement of Biden was in jeopardy. She prevailed on him not to humiliate Biden, to at least wait until after the president's Michigan visit. In the end, Fain did not have the votes on his own board to pull the endorsement.

Like Fain, Dingell, seventy, thought Biden should step aside. But she also felt defensive of the president. She didn't like the way her party was ganging up against him behind the scenes. She had watched Pelosi align votes against her late husband, John Dingell, the longtime chairman of the House Energy and Commerce Committee, to strip him of his gavel and hand it to one of her friends. The two women had developed a solid working relationship in the years since, but White House officials now reminded Dingell that she had seen Pelosi star in this role before. "She's ruthless in a way that other people are not," one of the White House officials who spoke to Dingell said of Pelosi.

At the start of the week, Pelosi asked Dingell what she thought of the broader situation with Biden and about his chances in Michigan. "I was worried about Michigan before the debate," Dingell said. "And, Nancy, his team's been incompetent." Pelosi nodded her agreement. With Biden's Michigan trip fast approaching, Dingell had focus-grouped House elders on what she should say when she saw him. "Tell him the truth," Jim Clyburn said, knowing that meant she would share her fears about his chances and how he might hurt the party's congressional candidates. "Tell him the truth."

CHAPTER 7

"FIGHT! FIGHT! FIGHT!"

High above Manhattan, Susie Wiles had a terrifying premonition.

She had been Donald Trump's right hand since shortly after he left office in 2021. He was the architect of his own stunning political comeback—the visionary, the salesman, and the decision-maker—but Wiles, now his de facto campaign manager, served as the building engineer. As much as anyone, she knew that Trump frequently turned on his top aides. He had fired her before, at the behest of Governor Ron DeSantis, when she was Florida co-chair of Trump's 2020 campaign, and rehired her over DeSantis's objections.

DeSantis suddenly and surprisingly soured on her in 2019, after she had been the turnaround artist who helped guide him to gubernatorial victory in 2018, amid allegations that she leveraged her proximity to him to serve lobbying clients and place allies in government jobs. Bad blood fueled a vendetta-style campaign of retribution in which DeSantis successfully pushed Trump to oust her in late 2019 and then failed to block her rehiring the following year.

When Wiles built Trump's 2024 campaign, she did it with an eye toward fixing the problems of his past White House and political operations. Wiles kept the staff lean and free of the most provocative voices in his orbit. Not all political operatives were created equal, Wiles believed, and she hired with that in mind, mixing in longtime associates with a handful of newer faces. She watched the budget with precision, knowing that, more than anything, Trump hated the idea of being bilked. Perhaps most important, she designed a team willing to execute on his orders rather than try to make decisions for him.

That team had helped Trump dominate the Republican primaries, dispatching DeSantis, former governors Nikki Haley and Chris Christie, businessman Vivek Ramaswamy, and a handful of other candidates. It had defended Trump in the press in 2023, the year he was charged in four separate criminal cases and found liable in civil court for sexually abusing the writer E. Jean Carroll. In each instance, Trump's aides, following his messaging lead, used his travails to rally Republican voters around his campaign. They echoed and amplified his argument that Democrats weaponized the courts to beat him at the ballot box. It became a motif of his campaign; not as central as the economy and immigration, but a powerful rallying cry for his base. Wiles found herself awed by Trump's ability to withstand the heat of a campaign and criminal indictments at the same time. Her job, she thought, was to keep his schedule straight—finding ways for him to campaign between court dates—and marshal his troops to fight the political end of his legal battles.

That's what Wiles was doing inside the twenty-fifth-floor boardroom at Trump Tower one evening in early May, toiling for Trump rather than enjoying the sweeping view of Central Park through the floor-to-ceiling windows. Sitting at a conference table with two of the campaign's top comms aides, Danielle Alvarez and Karoline Leavitt, Wiles pushed back against an upcoming story about the adult film actress Stormy Daniels. Four miles south, in a historic courthouse, Trump stood trial for falsifying business records to hide an alleged 2006 sexual encounter with Daniels. Trump's aides, who had just returned from court, wanted a media outlet to hold its story until Judge Juan Merchan lifted a gag order, allowing them to respond. They knew they were fighting an impossible trench battle that would last deep into the night.

At around 6 p.m., Wiles got up to make herself a cup of coffee. Alvarez followed her boss into a closet-size kitchenette close to the offices of Trump's sons Don Jr. and Eric. Normally a stoic contrast to the mercurial Trump, Wiles hit her breaking point. *He's weathered so much and his enemies will never, ever stop*, she thought.

"I just wish people understood what this man goes through," Wiles said, her eyes watering. "You've been in court now. How awful is it—what they're doing to him?" The courtroom was a metaphor for the treatment he received from the judge, the jury, and the media—*Dirty and nasty*, she thought. And this was just one of the four criminal trials he faced. Tears rolled down Wiles's cheeks as Alvarez tried to console her.

"I know," Alvarez said, taking Wiles's hand in her own. "I know."

Choking up, Wiles could barely get out her next words. "I just worry that if they can't get him this way," she said, "they'll try to kill him."

Her own eyes now watering, Alvarez pulled Wiles into a hug. "We're going to make it through this," she said.

But every time Trump chipped away at a wall in front of him, it seemed, his adversaries built two more behind it. In early 2021, the bipartisan Washington establishment hoped it had finally rejected the transplanted Trump organ for good. His approval rating dropped to 34 percent in a Gallup poll conducted mostly after the January 6 riot at the Capitol. Seven Senate Republicans voted to convict him on House impeachment charges in February of that year. But there were signs— the vast majority of House and Senate Republicans stuck with him on impeachment—that he had enough oxygen to keep the fire going if he didn't let it die. "For four years, we had a fight to stay alive, we had a fight to keep the MAGA movement going," said one aide who was personally close to Trump. "We had to fight to get back in." Sustaining that spirit through trial and tribulation required a candidate who could emanate extreme confidence and infect his aides and supporters with it.

But a thick layer of fear lurked just beneath the bravado that Trump and his campaign team projected. For the most part, it was rooted not in death but in imprisonment. The candidate lived under constant threat of becoming the first former president to follow up his stint in the White House with a stretch in the Big House. He faced a battery of charges in two federal courts, the Manhattan hush-money trial and an indictment in Georgia over his efforts to overturn the 2020 election results there. If he won the presidency, it was inconceivable that he would serve time in jail. But if he lost, the odds seemed strong that he would land behind bars. The stakes of the campaign could not be more personal.

His campaign aides, in their darkest moments, believed those stakes extended to them. Former Trump aides Steve Bannon and Peter Navarro had been jailed for refusing to cooperate with Democratic-led congressional investigations into Trump. Paul Manafort, the chair of his 2016 campaign, and Roger Stone, a longtime adviser, won pardons from Trump after they were convicted of crimes related to probes of Trump's connections to Russia. Even Rick Gates, the 2020 deputy campaign manager who cooperated with prosecutors, served jail time.

Over drinks and dinners in 2024, senior Trump aides sometimes found themselves talking about the prospect that they might be prosecuted. It was a dark topic, but it served to bind them to one another—and to their boss—as they imagined the consequences of defeat. They weren't just trying to elect the next Republican president. They were trying to safeguard their own freedom and his. "It's a very real belief because it happened to the people who have come before us," one top Trump aide said. "If we don't win, they'll try to put us in prison."

But, as was often the case, Wiles had a knack for seeing into the future. Jail wasn't her worst fear for Trump.

By the time Trump took the stage at 6:03 p.m. on July 13 at an outdoor rally in Butler, Pennsylvania, the temperature had dropped just below 90 degrees for the first time in hours. He had every reason to be in a good mood as his walk-up music, Lee Greenwood's "God Bless the U.S.A.," blared from loudspeakers at Butler Farm Show, a rural venue about forty-five minutes north of Pittsburgh. He peered out at an excited crowd to see a sea of red MAGA hats, like the one on his head, and placards bearing slogans of support. Away from courthouses and critics, the rally circuit was his safe space.

More than that, he was on a hot streak. He'd cleaned Biden's clock in the June debate, sending Democrats into full-blown chaos. Polls showed him as a clear favorite to reclaim the Oval Office. And less than two weeks earlier, the Supreme Court handed him—and other presidents—broad immunity from prosecution. In two days he would name a running mate, and then, for the third time in a row, he would triumphantly accept the Republican presidential nomination.

Wearing a freshly pressed dark suit, with the top button of his white dress shirt open, Trump saw familiar faces in the crowd and pointed to them. Trying to get closer to his biggest boosters, he toured the edges of the stage, clapping his hands. He loved sprawling outdoor venues in the countryside. They provided pretty backdrops, and they were cheap to rent. Some of his advisers were less enamored of them. It was difficult to amplify his voice enough to be heard without losing sound quality. More troubling, they were harder to secure than indoor arenas and partially closed stadiums. But Trump's preferences took priority, and he had held countless rallies at venues like Butler Farm Show—all without a significant security breach—over the better part of a decade. That was about to change.

On the roof of an outbuilding less than one hundred and fifty yards from Trump's lectern, a twenty-year-old nursing home aide lay in wait. One week earlier, Thomas Matthew Crooks had begun stalking the former president. Raised in Bethel Park, a Pittsburgh suburb about an hour south of Butler, Crooks fit the stereotype of an outcast. Shy and disheveled, he made an easy target for high school bullies. When he tried to fit in—attempting to join the rifle team—he was rejected for being a poor shot. The oversize lenses of thin-framed glasses and unkempt stringy brown hair gave the slightly built young man an outdated look.

It will never be fully clear what motivated Crooks, but he was methodical in planning and attempting to execute his mission. A week before the rally, he searched the internet to find the distance between assassin Lee Harvey Oswald and President John F. Kennedy. The following day he spent twenty minutes scoping out Butler Farm Show, which sat adjacent to a small airfield and a bottle supplies company called AGR International. Crooks spent part of Friday, July 12, the day before the rally, at the Clairton Sportsmen's Club, practicing his aim. He told colleagues at work that he planned to take Saturday off.

Apparently worried about his whereabouts and his mental state, Crooks's parents called the police on Saturday to report him missing. He had driven to Butler with two explosive devices in his car, and walked into a local gun store. Inside he bought fifty rounds of ammunition and a ladder. He cased the rally site with a camera-equipped drone well ahead of Trump's arrival.

About an hour before Trump stepped out into view, a Beaver County countersniper noticed Crooks loitering outside one of AGR's buildings across a fence line from the rally site. Something didn't look right. From a window inside the AGR building, the countersniper snapped two pictures of Crooks, who was wearing a short-sleeved gray shirt and had grown his hair out as an engineering science student at Allegheny Community College.

The Beaver County countersniper kept an eye on Crooks over the next eighteen minutes. Zooming in with a monocular, he could see Crooks scrolling through a news feed on his phone. But what caught the officer's attention was another device in Crooks's possession. He had a rangefinder, the tool shooters use to gauge the distance to their targets, and he was aiming it toward Trump's stage. Six minutes later, at 5:38 p.m., the countersniper had lost track of Crooks. He texted other local snipers to make them aware of Crooks and suggested that someone notify the Secret Service. State and local police began a search for Crooks.

At 5:45 p.m., the team leader of the local countersniper unit texted his Secret Service counterpart, who was stationed atop a barn right behind Trump's stage. The Secret Service agent said he would alert colleagues on the AGR side of a fence line, which was meant to act as a barrier between the rally and the outside world. He later told congressional investigators he intended to say that he would give a heads-up to fellow Secret Service countersnipers positioned on a second barn.

By 6:02 p.m., it had been half an hour since the last sighting of Crooks. The Beaver County sniper then spotted him between two of AGR's buildings and reported that the individual had a backpack on and appeared to be headed toward a Sheetz gas station.

One minute later, Trump walked onto the stage and basked in the roar of the crowd. He gave a thumbs-up sign at 6:04 p.m. and then climbed a short armored staircase to his lectern. Little more than a football field away, Crooks scaled an air-conditioning unit to pull himself to the top of an AGR building at one end of the company's complex. From there Crooks moved stealthily from roof to roof to position himself closer to Trump.

A Secret Service countersniper noticed two law enforcement vehicles pull into a parking lot near the AGR complex. The countersniper radioed a Secret Service channel to report that local law enforcement appeared to be monitoring a situation about two hundred yards out and that one of the officers was "moving urgently." At 6:09 p.m., a Butler Township officer briefly spotted Crooks on the roof of one of the buildings.

Within a minute, the Secret Service countersnipers atop the southern barn behind Trump's stage repositioned themselves to face the AGR complex. On the ground, state and local police surrounded the AGR buildings. But they didn't have a bead on Crooks. They couldn't see him above. Still, no one had alerted Trump's protective detail—the Secret Service agents on the ground with him—of the threat. They were on a different channel than the countersnipers.

Getting a boost from another cop, a Butler Township officer pulled himself up and popped his head over the roof of one of the buildings. The officer saw Crooks lying down on the roof, pointing an AR-style rifle at him from no more than six feet away. *I'm fucked*, the officer thought. *All he has to do is pull the trigger.* The officer released his grip on the edge of the roof and fell to the ground. Scrambling for assistance, he radioed out. "I saw him! He's laying down . . . He's got a long gun!" It was three seconds after 6:11 p.m. On the stage, Trump had turned his body to look at a giant projection screen with a chart showing illegal immigration rates over time. Gripping the lectern with his left hand, he extended his right arm to point to the chart as he began to explain its significance to the crowd—his "favorite chart," he said. Trump had introduced the chart earlier in the speech than his technical team had expected. They had put it up on the wrong screen, the one to his right rather than the one to his left.

Twenty-two seconds later, Crooks fired three shots in quick succession. Trump flinched. He heard a whizzing sound before he felt pain from the bullet that tore into his right ear. He reached up to the side of his head and then quickly dropped to the ground amid shouts of "Get down! Get down!" Several Secret Service agents dived on top of Trump, piling their bodies one over the other to form a large human shield. Trump's shoes were knocked off his feet and his MAGA hat fell from his head. The force of the agents' weight severely bruised his arms.

Crooks kept shooting, popping off five more rounds. A Butler cop on the ground spotted Crooks's head and shoulders, saw gas coming from the muzzle of his rifle, and heard what would be the final shot. The Butler cop fired a round. Fifteen seconds after Crooks started shooting, one of the Secret Service countersnipers told his partner he had Crooks in his sights. "I got him," the countersniper said, firing a single fatal round at Trump's would-be assassin. Trump was still on the ground.

So were his staffers inside a nearby operations tent. When the shots rang out, Wiles was meeting there with the campaign's Pennsylvania state director. "Get down!" she shouted. Out in the crowd, fifty-year-old Corey Comperatore, who was attending the rally with his family, was struck by a bullet and killed.

As Trump lay still, agents squatting beside the pile surveyed the scene. Facial muscles pulled tight in expressions of intensity, their eyes darted around the venue. Barking out the equivalent of a play call, they determined they were clear to move Trump. Forming a tight circle around him with their bodies, the agents brought Trump to his feet. "Let me get my shoes," Trump said as he regained his bearings. Then, at 6:12 p.m., with blood streaked across his right cheek, his lips tightly drawn, and his square jaw set, Trump faced the crowd and extended his fist into the air.

"Fight! Fight! Fight!" he shouted.

The Secret Service agents, still encircling him, moved in unison to tug Trump to his left toward a staircase at the far edge of the stage. His expression of defiance morphed into one of angry bewilderment. Trump's MAGA hat, which an agent had picked up, fell to the ground. Trump stopped the human caravan so that his hat could be retrieved. Then the protective detail hustled him down the stairs. As the agents moved him through an aisle in the crowd and toward a waiting black SUV, Trump again pushed his fist high into the air. He would repeat the gesture a third time before getting into the vehicle.

Bobby Peede, who ran the audiovisual board for the campaign, dashed into the operations tent. He grabbed Wiles's tote bag and told her that cars would be leaving immediately. She needed to get in one of them. She hustled Trump aides Steven Cheung and Dan Scavino along with her.

On a wild ride to Butler Memorial Hospital, Trump could feel the

SUV humming as it sped down a gravel road, kicking up rocks and dirt. In their trail car, Trump's campaign aides heard loud pops to their right. Gunshots? No, they quickly determined. Firecrackers. The driver made one turn sharply enough to slide passengers toward the door.

Trump's injuries weren't life-threatening. But his ear was still bleeding, which surprised him. *I never realized how much blood is in an ear*, he thought. Inside the hospital, he looked around for patients and was surprised to find none. *Where is everyone?* Butler staff had cleared the area and diverted emergency cases to other facilities in the region.

Only Secret Service agent Sean Curran was allowed in the hospital room where medical staff treated the former president. Wiles, Cheung, and Scavino waited outside. Twenty minutes seemed like twenty hours. Scavino connected with Trump family members by phone to let them know the patriarch was okay. Cheung talked to reporters. Wiles dispatched aides to collect a polo shirt and a pair of sneakers for Trump, who was still missing a shoe.

Adrenaline still pumping, Trump was in a chatty mood. "I told them I didn't get shot anywhere else," he said when his aides were finally allowed to talk with him. "Thank God it's just my ear, but did you know the ear bleeds more than any part of the body? That's why I'm so bloody." He refused to change his clothes, leaving his blood-soaked dress shirt in place as he started to field phone calls. Former first lady Melania Trump called from Bedminster, New Jersey, where the couple maintained a home at Trump National Golf Club.

"You're not going back to Florida," she instructed her husband. "You're coming here." That meant authorities would have to clear out the club of golfers and diners, which delayed Trump's departure from the hospital to a fixed-base operator airport in western Pennsylvania. At the airport, he took calls from friends and from President Joe Biden.

Biden was at mass inside St. Edmonds, a church built a couple of years before his birth, in Rehoboth Beach, Delaware, when the shots rang out in Butler. The president could hardly have been in greater need of sanctuary. Earlier in the day, Senate Majority Leader Chuck Schumer, who insisted privately on Biden's exit but had said little publicly, visited Biden's beach house to deliver tough news.

In a one-on-one conversation, Schumer shared brutal polling numbers designed to show Biden that the party was on course to lose several competitive Senate seats. Schumer didn't have to tell Biden to drop out; the numbers carried that message.

Just before the president went to church, he jumped on a videoconference with members of the New Democrat Coalition in the House. His face was tight in the frame as he looked up toward the camera and began laying out his case for staying in the race: they had accomplished so much together and that gave him a robust record to run on, he hadn't lost much ground in polling, and he could see his path to victory. By now his explanation felt rote, and some of the lawmakers thought he was reading from a script as he spoke to them.

Representative Jason Crow, a Colorado Democrat who served tours in Iraq and Afghanistan as an Army Ranger, told Biden that his constituents were worried about the president's ability to keep them safe. Biden's eyes narrowed and his facial muscles contracted as it registered that Crow was sugarcoating a call for him to drop out.

"I don't want to hear that crap!" Biden shouted back. He challenged Crow to name another world leader who had done as much to bolster NATO. He said he wouldn't take a back seat to anyone on national security and referred to his late son Beau's military service. Other lawmakers jumped in to explain to Biden that they were also seeing evidence that he was hurting them in their districts. He cut short the conversation, telling the group he had to go to mass. But with Schumer inching off the sidelines, and rank-and-file lawmakers getting more aggressive with him, the writing on the wall at the Rehoboth Beach house came into sharper focus.

Most Democrats reacted to Trump's shooting in the way that Rob Flaherty's mom did. Flaherty, a deputy campaign manager responsible for the Biden campaign's digital strategy, was eating dinner with his brothers at his mother's kitchen table in the Boston suburbs when he saw the news. *Oh, fuck*, Flaherty thought. He jumped up from the table, turned on the television, and parked himself on the couch. As he tried to process what was unfolding, his mother and brothers offered their assessments.

"This means he's going to win," Flaherty's mom said.

He replied quickly: "Shut up, Mom!"

But he knew her political weather vane was pointing in the right direction. Flaherty had gone through a rapid progression in his own mind as he watched the news. *Thank God he's okay*, Flaherty thought. *That image of him with his fist in the air, oh my God. If Biden's age and strength are in question, holy shit.*

Like Flaherty, the rest of Biden's high command didn't have to think long before arriving at the conclusion that surviving an assassination attempt would benefit Trump. What they hoped to avoid was an unforced error. O'Malley Dillon and Chavez Rodrgiuez dashed off a memo ordering campaign staff to stay off social media. They paused advertising and anything that could be construed as an attack on the wounded former president.

Biden exited the church about six minutes after the shooting and told reporters he had not yet been briefed. Less than two hours later, he delivered a short statement at a Rehoboth Beach police department facility. He condemned violence and said he was praying for the Trump family.

Alvarez had been driving to the airport when Trump was shot, on her way to Milwaukee for the upcoming Republican National Convention. Sitting in a bulkhead seat, with a row to herself on the sparsely populated flight, Alvarez pulled out her phone to watch the assassination attempt for the first time. Pressed against the window, she replayed it over and over—ten times—as she softly sobbed to herself. From her corner, she could hear other passengers talking about the shooting in gleeful tones. She hoped no one would notice her crying.

Despite the millions of Trump voters—and millions more who could sympathize with him even though they would never vote for him—Alvarez felt alone on the plane as tears rolled down her cheeks. She remembered what Wiles had told her two months earlier in the kitchenette. Susie had been right that someone might try to kill Trump. Alvarez drew a deep breath and wiped her eyes. *All right*, she told herself. *You got it out. Now let's fucking get back to it.* She looked at her phone. It was full of text messages and emails from reporters. The campaign wouldn't wait. She started tapping out replies.

CHAPTER 8

A VERY IMPORTANT
PHONE CALL

JD VANCE BOARDED BILLIONAIRE STEVE WITKOFF'S GULFSTREAM JET early on the morning of Saturday, July 13, to be ferried to a clandestine meeting with Donald Trump at Mar-a-Lago. Vance needed the luxury air limo because Trump's camp had not reached out to him until late the day before—and because traveling on a commercial plane would have alerted the media to his destination and purpose.

The thirty-nine-year-old Ohio senator, a convert to the cause who became very popular with the ex-president's MAGA base in just a couple of years, knew he was one of three finalists for the vice presidential slot on the Republican ticket. Trump had teased him about it earlier in the year: "JD Vance. Everybody's talking about him. He's hot right now," Trump had said. "He's looking very good on TV." But Trump had not yet had an explicit conversation with Vance about the number two role. This, Vance understood, would be his last, best chance to seal the deal—or sink it.

Since late winter, when he wrapped up the nomination for all intents and purposes, Trump had run a very public version of *The Bachelorette* to help him winnow a list of more than a dozen hopefuls. In the final weeks, he was down to three—Vance, Florida senator Marco Rubio, and North Dakota governor Doug Burgum. Not sure when he would make his selection, or who it would be, his aides had made preparations for an announcement at each of his most recent rallies. He did as he pleased, and they weren't sure whether the big reveal would come at a rally, in a social media post, or in an answer to an interviewer. But Trump was down to his last big event before the Republican convention—after meeting with Vance, he would fly to Pennsylvania for an evening rally in Butler—and he had to make his pick in the next forty-eight hours or so.

Trump liked creating, stoking, and drawing out the drama around a decision that was his alone to make. He had solicited countless opinions from friends, allies, and donors over the course of months. Rupert Murdoch, the conservative media mogul who controlled Fox News and a variety of other right-wing establishment outlets, received a fence-mending call from Trump in the spring when it became clear Trump would win the Republican nomination and that he had to unify the Republican Party behind him. The two men had had a falling-out after the 2020 election, but Trump needed Murdoch back in his tent.

Murdoch weighed in repeatedly against Vance, as did his constellation of news outlets. Between Murdoch's strong anti-Russia bent and his probusiness leanings, he saw the more traditional Burgum as a better choice than Vance, who shared Trump's leeriness of American involvement in Ukraine and often railed against big business. Murdoch would have been fine with Rubio too. Just not Vance, he told Trump.

Tucker Carlson, the longtime Fox host who had been ousted in 2023, caught wind of Murdoch's moves and countered. He called Trump multiple times to lobby for Vance. "It became a Tucker-versus-Rupert thing, like a dick-measuring contest," said one person familiar with the jockeying. It was also a competition of bank accounts: Elon Musk, the richest man in the world, lined up with Vance. Ken Griffin, the billionaire hedge fund manager and major GOP donor, tried to torpedo the Ohio senator.

"Everybody that you can ever think of called him to offer an opinion, and he listened to it all because he loves it," said one Trump confidant.

All of the heat around Vance suggested the truth: he always had the inside track. That in and of itself was a surprise to some in Trump's orbit because the relationship between the two men had started out frosty. But Vance, author of the bestselling memoir *Hillbilly Elegy*, which was made into an Oscar-nominated film, spent more than two years courting Trump.

In 2021, when he was running for the Senate for the first time in a crowded primary, Vance visited Mar-a-Lago with tech billionaire Peter

Thiel, who had helped fund Trump's 2016 campaign. Vance had come to seek Trump's forgiveness for the nasty things Vance had said about him publicly in the past. Trump wanted Vance to grovel. The former president spent ten minutes "busting JD's chops." Vance bent his knee, pleading ignorance—not of his own commentary but of Trump's greatness. Trump would go on to endorse Vance, who ran as a MAGA populist and then voted in lockstep with Trump's base in the Senate.

Vance also formed a close friendship with Donald Trump Jr., with whom he shared a top consultant, former Trump White House official Andy Surabian. When it came time for his father to think about the vice presidential field, Trump Jr. campaigned for Vance in private conversations and in public comments.

But Trump wanted to pressure-test his early preference, and he listened to a parade of advocates for and against each of the hopefuls. Rubio had his fans too—many of them Trump friends from Florida. But Rubio, who had been short-listed for vice president in 2012, took a different tack than Vance. "This isn't a job you lobby for," he told one of his longtime advisers. "This guy needs to feel comfortable with me and feel that I'm going to be helpful to him and he needs to arrive at that conclusion on his own. And if he doesn't, I don't want to try to convince him of something that he's not already inclined to believe."

It was never clear that Rubio thought he had a real shot at the job—or even particularly wanted it. He was old enough to remember Trump supporters calling for Trump's last vice president, Mike Pence, to be hanged at the January 6 riot. Like Vance, Rubio had once been a harsh critic of Trump. When they ran against each other for the Republican nomination in 2016, Rubio said Trump had "small hands"—a clear metaphor for Trump's manhood.

But during Trump's first term, Rubio worked with the White House on a variety of agenda items, including a Child Tax Credit law championed by Trump's daughter Ivanka. With Trump looking to boost his performance with Hispanic voters, the Cuban American Rubio offered a potential opening to do that in 2024. On the other hand, the base didn't trust him. Rubio had tried and failed to pass an overhaul of the immigration system that included a path to citizenship for illegal migrants—a position he abandoned under political pressure—and often sided with the establishment foreign policy hawks anathema to the MAGA movement.

Rubio decided to hang a lantern on a major drawback of picking him that had nothing to do with ideology or personality. In a meeting with Trump's high command and lawyers, he raised his so-called residency issue. Under a traditional interpretation of the Constitution, a presidential candidate would forfeit electoral votes from his or her own home state if the vice presidential candidate lived in the same state. There were potential workarounds—Rubio could resign his Senate seat and move to another state, for example—and some lawyers thought it wouldn't end up being a problem. But Florida's thirty electoral votes were on the line. Rubio didn't want to be the reason Trump couldn't claim them in a state that was increasingly out of reach for Democrats.

"I want everybody in this room to be on the same page," Rubio said. "The reality is that if you pick me as the vice president, the Democrats are going to use that and we're going to spend the first week, if not months, litigating this in the news and not talking about issues or contrast." This was a counterintuitive strategy. Rubio wasn't making the case for himself at all. He was rendering the kind of advice he thought a president should get—honest, even at the cost of the person giving it. "If everybody's okay with that, I'm willing to serve," Rubio said.

Trump liked Burgum enough, but the sixty-seven-year-old North Dakota governor wasn't the face of MAGA's future, like Vance, and he wouldn't bring in a raft of nonwhite voters, like Rubio might. It never boded well for Burgum, as he sought the nod of a businessman who turned TV stardom into political currency, that he could put a roomful of hyperactive kids to sleep in a single sentence and came from a state that many Americans could identify only on a map of the Dakotas.

The night before Vance's arrival, a Friday, Trump's team snuck Rubio in through the back of Mar-a-Lago for a final meeting. The two men talked about their shared interest in sports, specifically about Rubio's son, a football player at the University of Florida. Trump had forgiven Rubio for their 2016 feud, and he respected the senator's expertise in the political and public policy arenas.

But his onetime rival felt more like a peer than a potential protégé. He might have an independent streak. Trump, confident in his chances of beating Biden or whomever Democrats might choose to replace him, was increasingly thinking about tapping an heir to his movement. *Besides*, Trump thought, *I just don't feel that comfortable with him*. The meeting lasted only twenty minutes. While Rubio remained in the running, Burgum was out. The North Dakota governor's last talk with Trump was over the phone.

Trump was working his way back to his initial instinct. Wiles, a longtime ally of Rubio who was running the selection process, had picked up on Trump's personal preference for Vance. She too thought the Ohio senator made the most sense for Trump, in part because their bond seemed more natural—chummy like older and younger brothers.

When the two men sat down on Saturday morning, Trump prodded Vance to sing for his supper.

"You're obviously interested in this," Trump said. "Tell me why it should be you?"

Vance walked Trump through the high points of his bio, including service in the Marine Corps in Iraq, and how he thought he could help the ticket. Vance leaned into the idea that he would be a good governing partner because his worldview aligned with Trump's. He had been early to endorse a Trump comeback bid—in January 2023—and he frequently and ably promoted the former president's message in hostile television interviews. *Anyone can deliver talking points in a friendly interview*, Trump thought, *but not everyone has the stones to go toe-to-toe with the haters*. As the hourlong meeting wrapped up, Trump dropped a few tantalizing hints.

Vance feigned amusement at the torture. "Look, JD," Trump said, finally relenting, "I'm not offering it to you right now, but I think you're going to be happy in the end. I didn't say that to the other two guys."

★

Everything and nothing had changed by the time Trump turned his focus back to the VP slot on Sunday, July 14. A failed assassin's bullet crystallized his own mortality and the consequence of picking the right potential successor. Vance, almost four decades younger and ostensibly cut from similar philosophical cloth, stacked up well as an heir to the MAGA movement. In that way, the shooting should have made Trump even more certain about the Ohio senator. But he still wanted to test his own gut.

With an oversize bandage on his ear, Trump sat in his leather throne in the main cabin of his private jet, Trump Force One, and quizzed friends and aides about the candidates. On decisions large and small, he loved to take informal polls of whoever happened to be around him. A favorite patio game at his Mar-a-Lago club, the device helped him gather input and smoke out the motives of the people around him.

Now, on the two-hour flight from Newark, New Jersey, to Milwaukee—host city for the convention—Trump listened to the competing cases for Vance and Rubio. It seemed to the cluster of passengers that this was the last chance to sway him.

He hasn't fully decided yet, one of them thought.

Truth be told, Trump didn't think much of the number two slot. Maybe Mike Pence had helped him lock down tepid conservatives in 2016. But he knew that most voters didn't care about the bottom of the ticket. No one would vote for or against the most controversial political figure in generations based on his pick of a sidekick. After four years in the White House, he understood that the vice president had no real power. Pence and his lawyers had determined that the vice president didn't even have the constitutional authority to intervene in the certification of the 2020 election. His vice president had stuck to the formal limits of the office's power back then, despite pressure applied by Trump and a mob of activists.

In Trump's mind, vice president simply wasn't the most significant job to fill. "He does not believe the VP position is as important as attorney general or secretary of state," said one longtime Trump confidant who spoke with him repeatedly about the topic. Trump felt betrayed when Attorney General Jeff Sessions recused himself from Democratic-fanned allegations of a conspiracy between his 2016 campaign and Russia, allowing for the appointment of a special counsel. Another attorney general, William Barr, infuriated Trump by telling him that claims of

2020 election fraud were "bullshit." For a man convinced that he was the victim of a "Deep State" cabal and titillated by the idea of waging lawfare against his adversaries, it mattered far more who sat in the big chair at the Justice Department than in the little one in the West Wing.

Yet if there was ever a time when the relative weights he gave those jobs shifted, it was in the hours after he survived being shot. Besides, the vice presidential pick had to come first, and watching proxies fight for Vance and Rubio provided great entertainment for him.

Senator Lindsey Graham (R-SC), a throwback from the out-of-favor internationalist wing of the GOP, argued for Rubio. The handsome, Miami-born fifty-three-year-old could deliver Trump a boost demographically, said Graham, who often found common cause with Rubio. He would be an olive branch to the establishment Republicans Trump still needed to bring back in the tent, whereas doubling down with Vance would bring him little new support. A Rubio pick would open up a Florida Senate seat, and Trump's daughter-in-law Lara could be appointed to it, Graham said. The former military prosecutor was going to work systematically with a point-by-point review of the Rubio pros and Vance cons.

As Trump listened, Vance fans on the plane dashed off texts to the Ohio senator's allies to apprise them of a situation that felt like it was starting to teeter—and to call for reinforcements. Graham had stuck his knife in Vance, and he was starting to twist it.

Vance's chief hype man, Donald Trump Jr., wasn't on the plane. In a sign of a major power shift within the Trump family, Don Jr.'s voice was the loudest and most influential in his father's ear. Ivanka, who'd worked in the Trump White House with her husband, Jared Kushner, kept her distance from this campaign. They were close to Rubio, but they were no longer involved. Don Jr. had become the most important lieutenant in his father's political army.

But his father knew exactly where he stood anyway. It might have been counterproductive for him to weigh in again. Instead, senior Trump adviser Jason Miller took it upon himself to lead the charge for Vance, facing off against the veteran senator. *Holy shit*, thought one of the passengers, *Jason is going to war with Lindsey.*

Trump had heard all the angles before, but one gained more traction than Miller expected: legacy. Trump would have just one term in the presidency, and his pick would make a powerful statement about his vision for the future direction of the party and the country. Taking Vance, who practiced MAGAism with the zeal of a convert and could translate it to party elites, would signal to the movement that it would be left in trustworthy hands.

Wiles, despite her affinity for Rubio, chose to keep her thumb off the scale while she ran the monthslong selection process. It wasn't clear that she could muscle Rubio into the number two slot. Whether or not she could, just trying would surely piss off Don Jr. "She's watched what's happened in the past," said one Trump confidant who kept close tabs on the process. "You know, you fight with the family, the family always wins." In the end, according to others, she was in Vance's camp, long since having sensed where her boss would land.

On the plane, Trump sat back and watched the fight. He even prodded his courtiers to throw out the names of VP options he hadn't considered. Answering his phone at one point, he asked the caller, "Do you want to be VP?" He was in a remarkably playful mood for someone who had nearly been assassinated less than twenty-four hours earlier. Trump tended to other matters on the flight, including a discussion of his convention speech. Following the shooting, he had to rethink what he wanted to say.

Representative Ronny Jackson, a Texas Republican who had been Trump's personal physician in the White House, re-dressed his wounded ear. If the chat about his VP pick wasn't pivotal, it at least reconfirmed his view that Rubio didn't stack up to Vance. Rubio risked alienating the base and failing to woo Hispanic voters. Vance would thrill the base, and Trump believed he was the best messenger to voters of all stripes.

By the time Trump Force One landed in Milwaukee on Sunday evening, most of the passengers thought Trump had made up his mind. But the Ohio senator's team kept pushing allies to call Trump to put in last-minute appeals for Vance. On Monday morning, Trump wavered as more allies weighed in for Rubio. Wiles told him he had run out of time. He had to decide.

"I'm going to go ahead and call JD," Trump said. Wiles texted Vance to let him know the former president was about to call—without saying why—and then launched the necessary preparations for an announcement. Trump called Rubio and Burgum to tell them he had decided to go in another direction.

In the bowels of Fiserv Forum, the site of the convention, senior aides gathered in the office of the Milwaukee Bucks coach. Justin Caporale, the deputy campaign manager, had set up shop in the office, and he sat behind the coach's desk as they received word, over the phone, that Vance was the pick.

Early in the afternoon, Trump called Vance. He didn't get an answer. One of Trump's aides texted Vance to ask why he had not picked up. The president is trying to reach you, the aide wrote. Vance was under a lot of stress and had not been sleeping well. *Did I somehow miss a call from Trump?* he thought. He swiped at his screen. No missed calls. *What the fuck? What do I do?* He called an adviser to ask. The adviser told him to stay calm and connect through the Trump aide.

"JD, you missed a very important phone call," Trump chided when he finally reached Vance. "Maybe I should be calling Marco right now." Then he made the offer, which Vance quickly accepted. In the background, Trump could hear one of Vance's sons playing with Pokémon cards.

"What's that?" Trump asked.

"It's my son," Vance replied. "I'm sorry he's being noisy."

"Put him on the phone," Trump directed. Trump read a proposed Truth Social post to Vance and his son. "What do you think of that?" the president asked. The Vances, more focused on the meaning than the content, agreed that it was a good statement. About twenty minutes later, at 3:04 p.m. eastern, Trump broke the news on the social media platform.

★

The moment, the convention, and the election weren't about the VP slot. The Republican activists gathered in Milwaukee wanted to see Trump, survivor of an assassination attempt and champion for their cause, in the flesh. For the first time in four years, the entirety of the GOP political class believed not only that Trump could win, but that he would. What didn't kill him, figuratively and literally, made him stronger.

His numbers soared when he came under legal scrutiny, both in terms of polling and fundraising. It looked like he had beaten Biden so badly in their debate that he would end up having knocked a sitting president out of the race. And when a failed assassin fired a bullet centimeters from his skull, the bloodied Trump issued a call to battle. Republicans openly said they thought the election was over the second he thrust his fist in the air in Butler—many Democrats said the same privately. Trump was the Republicans' ultimate fighter, and they wanted to celebrate him.

On Monday, three nights before his address to the convention, Trump walked into the hall, the bandage on his ear as clear as the moon on a cloudless night. The crowd roared its approval. Some in the audience punched their fists in the air, yelling "Fight! Fight! Fight!" Trump soaked in the adulation—he had missed this opportunity during the pandemic in 2020—and mouthed "Thank you!" to thousands of foot soldiers. Nearly five minutes into the ovation, the crowd chanted "We love Trump!" just before he took a seat next to Vance in his VIP box.

Looking down at his hands, Trump noticed the makeup covering bruises he'd sustained when Secret Service agents dived on top of him at the Butler rally. Peering at himself in a full-length mirror the next night, as he waited to make an entrance at a fundraising event at Milwaukee's Baird Center, Trump was reminded of his brush with death. As he chatted with LaCivita and pollster Tony Fabrizio, with valet Walt Nauta steaming his suit jacket in the same holding room, his personal protective agents stood watch.

Everywhere he looked, there were totems of his mortality. He wasn't a religious man, or one given to the role of luck. His ego was wrapped up in the idea that he had made his own way—created his own luck—on his way to wealth, power, and the presidency. Wiles often talked about "providence" in Trump's presence. He usually rolled his eyes. But he had stopped doing that after the shooting. Now he began to consider for the first time whether he was the beneficiary of divine intervention. *God saved me*, he thought.

During an Oval Office speech on Sunday night, Biden had called for Americans to remain civil in settling political disputes. "We resolve our differences at the ballot box—not with bullets," Biden said. His campaign had temporarily paused its political advertising. Through the week of the Republican convention, Trump aides signaled that his rewritten speech would emphasize unity. Trump too, they said, wanted to dial down political rhetoric. But the instinct to fight, among both Democrats and Republicans, proved irrepressible.

On the final night of the convention, Trump stood at the lectern with his speech loaded into the teleprompters. Drafted by advisers Vince Haley, Stephen Miller, and Ross Worthington, it timed out to twenty-two minutes. Everyone in Trumpworld knew the ratings would go through the roof for his first extended remarks since the shooting. Then, as he often did, he wrapped his scripted speech in a spiked leather jacket.

"I am running to be president for all of America, not half of America," said the former president, who had often described political opponents as "evil." "There is no victory in winning for half of America." He recounted in detail how he had dodged a bullet in Butler. Then he launched into more than an hour of his stump speech—a mix of policy promises, attacks on Democrats, and old grievances. In addition to vowing to boost the economy and stop illegal immigration, Trump called Pelosi "crazy," renewed his lie that Democrats cheated to beat him in 2020, and accused his adversaries of "weaponizing the justice system" against him.

Trump 3.0 was more willing to listen to his advisers and follow their guidance—to a point. Some of them described the way he fought self-discipline as malicious obedience. By the time the final convention gavel fell that night, the GOP was unified and confident that he was headed to victory. Most elites in the Democratic Party, which remained fractured, felt pretty certain Trump was on track to win too.

Five days earlier, Phil Murphy, the New Jersey governor, had been awoken in the middle of the night during a trip to Germany, to learn Trump had been shot. He reached out to Ivanka and Kushner, with whom he shared a warm relationship, to say that the former president was in his prayers. In meetings with German officials, including Chancellor Olaf Scholz, Murphy gave a sober assessment of the state of the race. "Trump has been deified," he said. "He's going to be the president. We're going to lose the Senate. We might hang on to win the House." During the week, Murphy and his wife, Tammy, relayed a message to Trump, that they wanted to see him and "give him a hug" on the Saturday after the Republican convention ended.

So, a week after the shooting, Trump hosted the Democratic governor and first lady at his private residence on the Bedminster golf club grounds. The Murphys walked through a pool area into a horseshoe of homes on their way to Trump's living quarters. Trump greeted them in good spirits, riding the high of his political surge and the flood of tidings he continued to receive from friends and strangers following the shooting. A painting of him holding his fist in the air leaned up against one wall. Wiles and LaCivita joined the meeting to pick up whatever political intel might be passed from one principal to the other.

Trump knew the Murphys well. He and Phil had been in very close contact during the opening stages of the Covid pandemic, when Trump was looking for Democratic governors to support his response and Murphy needed the federal government to help secure ventilators and other necessities for his state. But Trump kept up with almost everyone in his vast digital Rolodex—in a way that other presidents and former presidents did not—and the Murphys were no exception. Sitting around a table, Trump immediately launched into an animated re-creation of the shooting scene. He spared no detail, showing off the shoes that had come off his feet when he hit the ground. Trump rolled up one of his sleeves to reveal a massive bruise that, a week later, still looked angry. "Boy are they strong," he said of the Secret Service agents. His eyes growing bigger, he recounted the wild car ride to the hospital and how it seemed odd to him that no other patients were there when he arrived. Trump hardly let anyone else get in a word. But forty minutes after they had arrived, it was time for the Murphys to get on their way. Wiles stopped them.

"We can't let you go without telling us how you feel about the top of the ticket," she said.

Murphy told them he thought Trump would beat Biden.

"Do you think I could win New Jersey?" Trump asked. He was obsessed with the idea of winning another one of his home states—with Florida in the bag and New York out of reach.

Under normal circumstances, it would have been an absurd question. New Jersey had not voted for a Republican presidential nominee since George H. W. Bush in 1988. Trump had lost the state to Biden by 16 points in 2020, and Hillary Clinton had beaten him by 14 points when he had won the presidency in 2016. But the electoral map was now in flux. Coming off his convention, surviving a shooting, and winning the first debate convincingly, Trump could taste a mandate in the making. Republican and Democratic operatives could, for the first time, see the possibility of states outside the seven main battlegrounds shifting to Trump.

Murphy thought about it. Trump was within about 3 points of Biden in the last poll he'd seen. It would be a hell of a feat for Trump to win the Democratic bastion. But given the state of the Democratic Party at the time, anything was possible.

"You know what?" he said. "I'm not sure."

CHAPTER 9

"KARAOKE AT THE END OF THE WORLD"

OVER THE COURSE OF TWENTY-FOUR DAYS, IN FITS AND STARTS, THE Democratic Party turned on its leader.

Democratic voters had chosen Joe Biden in a crowded 2020 primary because they saw him as the best hope for beating Donald Trump. Together, Biden and his voters were rewarded with victory, and most Democrats looked favorably on his record as president. They liked him. They loved what he did for them—for the country, they believed—in ousting Trump.

But in a rapid cascade, the party faithful, led by elected officials, commentators, and donors, lost confidence in Biden. More than that, they were angry. They did not want to admit that he had deceived them—perhaps deceived himself—about his fitness to run. They did not want to believe that Biden, their savior of the republic, had put ego over party and country. They blamed his staff and family for hiding his frailties. And surely, there were few innocents in his midst. The psychic blow left most Democrats unwilling to wrestle with the question of whether he remained fit to serve. Only one Democratic member of Congress, Representative Marie Gluesenkamp Perez, had publicly suggested Biden should resign his office. Instead, Democrats focused on whether he could win another term.

Biden had lived by the electability sword in 2020. Now Democrats slashed him with it.

On a humid afternoon in East Hampton, New York—five hundred miles east of Butler, Pennsylvania, and less than an hour before Trump was shot—roughly four dozen Democratic donors chatted about the election over cocktails and crudités on a back porch. They had gathered to raise money for a pair of the party's promising Senate candidates: Elissa Slotkin of Michigan and Angela Alsobrooks of Maryland. Representative Adam Schiff, running for a Senate seat in California, attended as a lure to bring in new donors for the other two.

Schiff, a Pelosi protégé and a shoo-in to win Harris's old Senate seat, had told friends privately that Biden should drop out. But in public he was far more cautious. As guests filed into a large den, he changed course. "If he is our nominee, I think we lose," Schiff told the donors. "And we may very, very well lose the Senate and lose our chance to take back the House."

I don't know why he's doing this, thought former representative Steve Israel, a close friend of Schiff, who helped organize the klatch. *He's been so careful.*

Slotkin took a very different tack. "First of all, let me disabuse you of the fact that there's going to be some sort of fantasy football situation and some white knight is going to come in and be president," she told the donors. "It's either Joe Biden or Kamala Harris." She argued that Biden's biggest negatives—"his age and his capability, his acuity"—would not rub off on Senate candidates. Harris, on the other hand, "gets labeled with that progressive Democrat, that woke Democrat label" and "those negatives tend to spill downballot," Slotkin said.

In her perfect world, Biden would clear the way for Michigan governor Gretchen Whitmer to take the nomination. But she did not see that as a viable option. "If you want to break the Democratic coalition for a generation," she said, "try to skip over the first African American vice president."

She had no faith in Harris and little in Biden, and it frustrated her that Trump was able to sit with "his feet up" while Democrats pummeled one another. The party would not be able to survive a fight if it extended much past the GOP convention.

"We need to, like, make a call," Slotkin concluded. "And then we need to suck it up, buttercup."

Predictably, someone recorded Schiff's remarks and shared a tran-

the mountaintop of American power. Now she had to show loyalty and patience. At the same time, she would suffer if those traits allowed rivals to jump out in front of her. It wasn't exactly a catch-22, but it was the trickiest high-wire political act she had ever attempted. And there was no playbook. No president had dropped out after winning a majority of delegates to the party convention.

The delegates were the key to Harris's fortunes, and her allies targeted them in the third week of July. Nikki Fried had just settled into her third-row seat at a Janet Jackson show in West Palm Beach on Thursday night, July 18, when her phone buzzed. She looked down, saw the caller's name, and turned to her sister—wearing a matching Janet shirt—to say she needed a minute.

The last few weeks had been particularly rough on Fried, the preternaturally youthful forty-six-year-old chair of the Florida Democratic Party. Four days before the debate, Biden campaign chief Jennifer O'Malley Dillon had declared Florida a dead zone for Democrats. Then Biden belly-flopped. Reporters hounded Fried about Biden's performance, his campaign's decision to ignore her state, and why she was still supporting him. The day before the concert, Biden had been diagnosed with Covid. Fried needed a break from presidential politics. An escapade at a Janet Jackson show seemed like the perfect escape—until she put her phone to her ear.

Fried heard the voice of her friend Bakari Sellers, the thirty-nine-year-old former South Carolina state legislator and TV talking head. Sellers knew Fried leaned toward backing Harris if Biden stepped aside. He had felt her out in a conversation earlier in the week. Now it was time for a gut check, and for a personal touch from deep inside the Harris camp. Sellers handed his phone to Donna Brazile, the white-haired Democratic operative who had run Al Gore's 2000 presidential campaign.

"Florida is important," Brazile said, massaging the sore spot. "It will have a seat at the table." Whether Florida mattered for the general election was debatable, at best. The state had turned from toss-up purple to Republican red in recent statewide elections, and there was no reason to think Democrats would reverse that with Trump, a transplanted Floridian, on the ballot. But Fried badly wanted presidential campaign money to help build the party infrastructure in the state and help downballot candidates.

There was no question at all about the state's significance in a nomination fight. Florida would send 254 delegates to the Democratic convention in August, ranking behind only California, New York, and Texas. Its Democratic electorate was one of the most diverse in the country. If Harris hoped to beat big-state governors in an open contest for the nomination, Florida could be a cornerstone or a graveyard for her.

Suddenly, the fantasy-politics talk Fried and Sellers had engaged in earlier in the week seemed real. *This is happening*, Fried thought to herself, as Brazile double-checked that she was ready to push the Florida delegation toward Harris's column. Brazile didn't ask about Biden.

For the first time in as long as she could remember, Fried felt a spike of excitement about the race. She was weary of taking arrows for Biden, though she knew she would never abandon him. But until recently she had been of two minds about what should happen if he stepped aside. *What*, she had asked herself, *will move the needle most? Would Harris fire up the party or would an open convention provide more of a spark?*

All the Democratic infighting, and her memories of Harris's performances during the vice president's frequent trips to Florida, melted away the allure of an open fight. So did time. There wasn't enough of it. If Biden stood down, the new nominee would need Democrats to stand up for her. Fried assured Brazile that she was on board and believed her delegation would follow. The call lasted less than five minutes.

Fried went back to Janet. Brazile and Sellers went back to work. For two weeks, they had run a two-tiered whip operation focused on southern states, where Black voters often make up the lion's share of the Democratic coalition. On the surface, Brazile, with Sellers acting as her de facto chief of staff, was shoring up support for Biden. Below the waterline, they were measuring and building Harris's base among the delegates. The delegates would nominate Biden or, if he dropped out, pick his successor. Brazile and Sellers determined that going through state party chairs was the best way to get a whip count within delegations, secure an influential lieutenant in each state, and keep their operation under wraps.

At the same time, Megan Jones, a Harris campaign adviser, compiled a secret spreadsheet of the convention delegates—a call list for Harris, if and when the time came. California Harris allies took similar actions. Michael Kapp, a DNC member from the state, heard from multiple high-level party and campaign officials that Thursday that Biden's exit seemed imminent. He immediately typed up a letter thanking Biden for his service and endorsing Harris. If Biden dropped out, he would quickly circulate it to current and former party officials for their signatures.

Biden's Covid diagnosis had accelerated the whipping, and others close to Harris—including convention chair Minyon Moore—reached out to their contacts to take temperatures.

Brazile and Moore were well positioned to carry out the mission. As longtime DNC leaders, they knew all the players. As Biden allies, they could make calls on his behalf. And, as secret weapons for Harris, they could send a firm message about the vice president. The two were part of a larger group of Black women operatives—calling themselves "the colored girls"—who had helped convince Biden to pick a Black woman vice presidential candidate in 2020. Since then, they had been vital informal counselors and behind-the-scenes warriors for Harris.

"We're ridin' with Biden," Brazile, a New Orleans native, told state party chairs and trusted delegates over and over. "But if he makes this decision, we're not going to let anyone skip over the VP." Through their conversations, Harris's allies constructed a picture of who was with Biden, who hungered for the VP, who wanted an open competition, and who remained uncertain. Brazile regularly delivered updates to White House senior aide Steve Ricchetti on Biden's standing with delegates. The Harris part remained unspoken.

"No need to tell them the second half," said one person familiar with the ad hoc cloak-and-dagger outfit. In their early calls, Brazile and Sellers were pleased to discover that the overwhelming majority of delegates in these southern states were loyal to Biden—and warm to Harris. But there was one major sticking point: Barack Obama. Delegates with large Black constituencies were perplexed by Obama's silence. They asked slightly varying versions of the same question: *What the fuck is Obama doing on all of this?*

The former president hadn't said a word publicly since the day after the debate. His former aides and other proxies hammered Biden in the press and in private conversations. Many of those Obamaworld figures pushed for a mini-primary or a convention fight, a thunderous vote of no confidence in Harris.

Brazile, who had been hired onto Jesse Jackson's 1984 presidential campaign by Sellers's father, played the inside game. She worked the delegates and party rules that she knew by heart. She came from the old school, where party officials made decisions. The DNC was a structure that, before Obama, had empowered Black delegates—and, by extension, Black voters. If it was strong, Harris would skate to the nomination.

Obama, the nation's first Black president, didn't believe in the national party. He had run against the establishment in 2008 and won. Though Black voters had pushed him to victory that year, his original ties to the community were strongest among a class of Black professionals who seeded his campaign with money. It was a different base within the ranks of Black voters than the one that Jackson had built, that Bill Clinton had tapped into for his presidential bids, and that had bailed out Biden in the 2020 primary. When Obama won, he tried to build his own organization outside, and in conflict with, the DNC. Though Organizing for Action never realized his vision, it competed with the party for power and money. He left the Democratic Party far weaker than he found it. Or, as one Black party operative put it, "Obama destroyed that shit."

Biden, the Clintons, and the "colored girls"—Brazile, Moore, Yolanda Caraway, and Leah Daughtry—had been working to rebuild the party infrastructure ever since Obama left office. In particular, this reconstructed party had been fashioned with the intent of protecting Biden and, if he had not sought reelection, Harris. In large part, it was designed to stop the party's left wing from taking control. By helping install party loyalists at the national and state committees over the course of years, these establishment Democrats kept progressive outsiders at bay. "You know who did that?" said one Black Biden ally familiar with the maneuvering. "Bill and Hillary motherfucking Clinton."

This party organ was now getting an unexpected stress test. Biden and Harris both stood to benefit if it proved resilient. But Obama was the single most influential voice among Democratic voters and donors. If Biden stepped aside, the Biden-Harris-Clinton faction would have to beat him. On tiptoes, Harris's team had already started the race.

★

The same night that Brazile spoke to Fried, Biden campaign aides gathered in the Mill, a co-work office space that housed part of the operation. Ninety miles away, their boss battled with coronavirus and his conscience. But inside the campaign office, it was karaoke night.

Worried about keeping their team engaged during the dark weeks after the debate, O'Malley Dillon and her senior lieutenants wanted to boost staff morale. Aides had sobbed to their bosses, sent out résumés, and watched their candidate's comeback bid run smack into Covid. "A lot of people were like, 'He's dead. There's no way he's coming back from this,'" said one high-ranking campaign aide.

O'Malley Dillon tried to tune that out with a mix of fiats and festivities. She banned aides from watching cable news in the office in July, and offered distractions like karaoke night. What better way to wash away the week, the campaign leadership thought, than to get boozy and belt out the Beastie Boys?

The twentysomethings hectored the thirty-plus crowd into taking center stage to sing "Tubthumping," the 1997 Chumbawamba hit. Sipping cheap wine, beer, and hard seltzers to wash down mouthfuls of pizza, the youngsters reveled in watching their bosses try to match the bars of a Gen X anthem released before most of the singers were born. The lyrics had special resonance. "I get knocked down, / but I get up again. / You're never gonna keep me down. . . . / Pissin' the night away."

In Milwaukee, Trump was about to formally accept his party's nomination and declare that "with proper leadership, every disaster we are now enduring will be fixed, and it will be fixed very, very quickly." He described the Biden presidency as a failure on issues at the top of many voters' minds: the economy, immigration, and maintaining peace around the globe.

But with oldies blaring and alcohol flowing, Biden aides noticed a more ominous narrative circulating in the news media and on X: Biden planned to drop out soon. In one version, he had decided not to endorse Harris and there would be a floor fight for the nomination. Rob Flaherty, a deputy campaign manager, started receiving texts from friends outside the political arena. They wondered whether it was true. The story was breaking through. From Washington, White House officials pushed back publicly. Deputy press secretary Andrew Bates subtweeted one of the stories with a simple "No."

The music might be on the verge of stopping for Biden, but it kept playing at his campaign headquarters. "It felt like karaoke at the end of the world," said one person at the Mill that night.

Hours later, on Friday, July 19, O'Malley Dillon went on *Morning Joe* to tamp down reports of Biden's pending departure. She seldom acted as the face of the campaign on television, but she thought it was wrong to ask beleaguered colleagues to carry a message if she was unwilling to do that herself. *How can I ask them to be on the front lines if I'm not standing there with them,* she thought. "The president is in this race," she said on *Morning Joe.* "You've heard him say that time and time again." But she also conceded that her boss had seen a "slippage in support." Later in the day, she touched on similar themes in a video-conference call with campaign staff across the country, prefacing her remarks with details of her star turn on TV: "There was, like, a lot of drama because I didn't have my makeup with me here, and Julie had to lend me her curling iron. And my heart was racing so much that it kicked in my little activity guy on my watch!"

Rather than calming fears, her upbeat tone sparked suspicion in some of the campaign staff. "We can still have fun, and we can still have joy, and we can still be proud of the work we're doing, because that is what really matters," O'Malley Dillon said, just after mentioning trophies that had been awarded to some of the aides for their work. "The real world is the voters that are standing with us, the delegates that are with us, and we are going to weather this because of this organization."

The happy talk clashed so cacophonously with the dark mood music playing in the rest of the Democratic universe that it undermined O'Malley Dillon's purpose. "There is only one of two ways that happened," one senior state-level aide said. "One, she's so outside the fucking loop that she's not included, which means she should not be the campaign manager. Or two, she's just fucking lying. Either way, she doesn't really have the confidence of anyone."

That Friday, more than a dozen House and Senate Democrats added their names to the list of those urging Biden's exit.

★

By Saturday morning, Jim Clyburn, the de facto dean of the Congressional Black Caucus, concluded that Biden would wave a white flag. It was a painful realization. In 2020, Clyburn's endorsement vaulted Biden to a rout in the pivotal South Carolina primary. The two men had been personally close for decades, and Clyburn, two years older than Biden, had already felt the sting of handing over power to the next generation himself.

Biden's final decision had not been made, and no one told Clyburn that it had been. But he had a pretty good idea of what was going on in Rehoboth Beach that day. He picked up his phone and talked to a clout-packed roster of Black political elites: Representatives Hakeem Jeffries and Gregory Meeks of New York, Joe Neguse of Colorado, and Bennie Thompson of Mississippi; former Department of Housing and Urban Development secretary Marcia Fudge; DNC chairman Jaime Harrison; and Cedric Richmond, a co-chair of the Biden campaign.

Clyburn knew what he wanted to do—rally support for Harris. But he was well aware that Obama, Pelosi, and some major donors hoped to stop her from taking the nomination. *There are some powerful folks saying, "Off with both of their heads,"* Clyburn thought. *They're all planning to pass over Kamala.* Those forces would lobby some of the same people he was calling. "I expect Joe to drop out," he said, softly whipping votes for the vice president. "What are we going to do?"

The moment of inevitability had arrived, even if Biden didn't know it yet. The people Clyburn spoke with about the next steps included the House Democratic leader, the DNC chair, and one of Biden's campaign co-chairs—none of whom felt that, at this point, they were betraying Biden by talking about the succession plan.

"I'm going all in with Kamala," Clyburn said. "I don't want to look back and y'all ain't there." They would all march in lockstep behind Harris.

★

Joe Biden carried the weight of the world on his shoulders. Sitting on a screened-in porch at his Rehoboth Beach vacation house on Saturday, July 20, the smell of salt-water air was harder to detect through the filter of the mask covering his nose and mouth. Only a week earlier, his mortal foe, Donald Trump, had survived a sniper's bullet and risen back defiant. Now Biden found himself sidelined by Covid, cut off from all but a handful of family members and close advisers. He was worn down from the punishing cadence of demands on a president and candidate, more than three weeks of brutal criticism from within his own party, and the rough strain of the virus that attacked his body.

Biden bought the stately six-bedroom home by the ocean as a refuge from the noise of Washington. But the D.C. drumbeat was blasting at full volume now, so loud that he could no longer escape it—not even here at his surfside oasis.

The juxtaposition of the two presidential candidates—one looking virile in iconic images, the other sickly and out of sight—could not have been more acute. In 2020, when Biden's scarcity proved prudent, Trump had been hustled to the hospital with a bad case of the virus. Back then, Covid helped Biden win the presidency. It had allowed him to maintain a light schedule while ceding the spotlight to wild daily Trump press conferences that eroded public faith in the president's leadership. Now the virus put Biden at a disadvantage.

Earlier in the week, as he started to gather status reports on various aspects of his campaign, Biden spoke with Rufus Gifford, his finance chairman, by phone. It had become impossible for Biden to dismiss calls for his departure out of hand. He had been told by elected officials, with varying degrees of directness, that he should get out. He asked Gifford for a readout of the campaign's financial situation.

"We're not going to meet our projections," Gifford said, noting that major donors were withholding cash. "That's going to be a hard situation for us to deal with in the short term."

"Will the money come back after I have the nomination?" Biden asked.

"It will, but I can't tell you when," Gifford said. "The convention is late this year, and we might not get the money until then."

On Saturday, Biden summoned his two most trusted aides, Donilon and Ricchetti, to his porch so that they could walk him through his political outlook. It was morbid. Donilon, fresh off a meeting with campaign pollsters and data analysts, shared the latest numbers. The top lines weren't fatal. Biden had lost ground in the key swing states, particularly in the last week or so, but not enough to seal a defeat, Donilon told him. The country remained so evenly divided that major political events led to relatively small shifts in polling. That meant Trump's lead only grew so much, but also that it would be a more implausible chore to close the gap.

"We were down everywhere," said one person familiar with the polling who spoke to Donilon shortly before his meeting with Biden. "It's possible to come back from being down four or five points. But you need to have ways to do that, and you need to have a pathway to do that. And it was harder and harder to figure out what that would be, because the debate was supposed to be that."

In the Blue Wall states of Pennsylvania, Michigan, and Wisconsin, Biden was slipping further behind Trump. If Biden won all of them, along with Nebraska's Second Congressional District, he would secure exactly 270 electoral votes—the minimum number needed to capture a second term. The Sunbelt states—North Carolina, Georgia, Arizona, and Nevada—looked uglier. The raw data was bad.

Inside the polling, there was a more troubling trend. Age had always been Biden's biggest challenge with voters. More of them worried that he was too old or infirm to do the job after the debate. Donilon's presentation mixed the campaign's own polling with surveys from outside sources. Biden already knew that House and Senate candidates were panicking about their own races. Chuck Schumer, Hakeem Jeffries, and rank-and-file lawmakers had told him that.

Hunter Biden, the president's son, listened in to the conversation on speakerphone. First Lady Jill Biden and aides Annie Tomasini and Anthony Bernal milled about the living room and dining room, popping onto the porch on occasion. Ricchetti, a walking compendium of Biden's political network, told the president where he stood with members of his own party. Most of them had held off on calling for him to drop out. But, again, the trend line resembled a diver on her way into the pool.

In the past two days, two senators in brutal reelection fights—Jon Tester of Montana and Sherrod Brown of Ohio—had buckled and issued statements urging his withdrawal. They had stuck with Biden as long as they felt they could—in Tester's case, against the advice of political consultants who saw the president's poll numbers dip below 30 percent in Big Sky country. The senators mattered to Biden. That was his chamber. He understood how its members thought about elections. Dozens of lawmakers were ready to follow suit if Biden didn't pull the plug before Monday.

But Democratic members of Congress did not control his fate. Ricchetti told Biden that a majority of the pledged convention delegates—about 70 percent of them—still planned to vote for him. He would win the nomination in a floor fight. Still, the erosion was significant. Biden's sense of self was wrapped up in the idea that he could muscle through any hardship. He had been left for dead in the 2020 primary, told by a top aide that he should consider taking out a second mortgage on his home to meet payroll. He had come back to win that race and the White House.

Biden's advisers would never directly tell him to give up his bid. This was his decision, not theirs. But they went as far as they dared—or felt comfortable with—by painting a picture of his electoral chances in black tar. He could still win, they told him, but it would be a "hard slog." And he would have to do it with a fractured party, fighting his Democratic friends along with his Republican adversaries. This last point held currency with Biden.

The party didn't come together fast enough after the primary in 2016, he thought. *That's partly why Hillary lost. Is there enough time to sew it back together before November if I have to keep fighting my allies to win the nomination? Probably not.*

After fifty years in politics, Biden knew what Donilon and Ricchetti were telling him, and he appreciated both their candor and their diplomatic delivery. He didn't want to be the reason that Trump returned to the White House. Biden believed that his predecessor presented a unique threat to democracy. He thought he could still beat Trump again, but he was worn down from all the pressure on him, and from the virus. If he was wrong about his ability to come back, losing would permanently tarnish his legacy. He would be remembered by Democrats as a goat, not the GOAT.

"Let me sleep on it," he told his aides. "But I want you to think through the plan of what it would look like to drop out."

PART II

WHAT IT TOOK

CHAPTER 10

"YOU NEED TO ENDORSE ME"

Behind the gates of the naval observatory in Washington, D.C., nestled inside a white, one-story pool house beside the vice president's residence, a handful of Kamala Harris's closest confidants convened a secret meeting to answer the question that could never be spoken outside their circle: What do we do if Biden exits?

It was 11 a.m. on Sunday, July 21, and Harris was well aware of what was going on in her pool house. But this was a topic she would not touch. She felt deep loyalty to Biden, and even in private conversations she had lashed out at the way he was being treated by fellow Democrats. Harris could see that her boss was running out of options. But she needed his support to win the nomination if he got out. All of that left her in a bind: she could not afford to get caught flat-footed in a sprint for the nomination or red-handed in grabbing for his job. The vice president, like Caesar's wife, had to be above suspicion.

That is why Harris stayed away from the pool house as her Kitchen Cabinet plotted her next moves. Her brother-in-law Tony West, chiefs of staff Lorraine Voles and Sheila Nix, and communications aide Brian Fallon were among the group that gathered in the living room–style space for the first nuts-and-bolts meeting of what would be the most unusual bid for a presidential nomination in modern American history.

Sitting around a coffee table, with a television screen on the wall, the ragtag cabal connected with Minyon Moore, the chair of the Democratic convention and a longtime Harris adviser, by Zoom.

"What do we do if Biden drops out tomorrow?" West asked the group. "What's our plan?"

"He's not going to drop out tomorrow," one of the participants declared.

"Thursday at the earliest," another said, pointing to a Wednesday meeting with Israeli prime minister Benjamin Netanyahu.

Moore walked the group through the ins and outs of how the party would pick its new horse if Biden exited the race before the nomination or afterward. If he took the nomination, DNC chair Jaime Harrison would have the power to pick a successor, in consultation with other party leaders. But if he dropped out sooner, the process could get ugly. "There are two paths here," Moore said. "Biden can endorse, and that will send a signal for the person he chooses, or he can leave it open and everyone will fight."

Moore explained that there would be more than 4,500 delegates coming to the convention. "Some of them are beholden to labor, some of them are beholden to more progressive factions or various candidates," Moore said. "Some of them might be beholden to the vice president, but all of them are beholden to Joe Biden." Her point was clear: Biden's word mattered the most in a floor fight. But even he might not be able to prevent the party from leaving "a lot of blood on the floor" after an open convention—enough blood to doom the eventual nominee—Moore predicted.

"Okay, okay," West said. But what if Biden dropped out and did not endorse—or waited a while to do it? "I understand it's not going to happen tomorrow. But who are the first ten people we have to call? Who's going to whip the delegates?" Harris aide Megan Jones's list of elected officials and delegates—the call sheet—was ready to go.

West's son-in-law, Nik Ajagu, interrupted the meeting more than an hour after it started. Harris needed West, pronto. He hurried to the main house and up the stairs to the vice president's personal quarters, with Nix and Voles trailing. He found his sister-in-law in her study, dressed for a casual Sunday with her family. Harris wore a Howard University hoodie and sweatpants. Her hair, normally styled at shoulder length, was pulled back in a ponytail.

She was on the phone with Joe Biden, Mike Donilon, and Steve Ricchetti.

★

Biden had woken up that morning still reeling from the virus infecting his body. The small circle of aides returned to his house shortly before noon to receive the final verdict. Tomasini walked in carrying cups of coffee.

"Where are you, sir?" one of them asked.

For the first time in half a century of chasing the presidency—and taking it once—Biden would no longer have his eyes set on winning the highest office in the land. He had never lost a general election, not from the time he first ran for a New Castle County Council seat in 1970. He still believed he could beat Trump, but not with a drawn-out family fight dragging the party down. It was time, he said, to stand down.

This lion-in-winter moment, a rare decision by a sitting president to give up the most profound powers in the world, was delivered to a small clutch of trusted advisers in a beach house along the Atlantic Coast. But its implications for both political parties, the American people, and the presidency would reverberate across the land for years to come. A president could be forced to his knees not by voters, but by the donors and elected officials in his own party. They could see his frailties, personal and political, and push him out of a reelection bid. But they could not make him leave the White House, even if many Americans thought he was no longer up to the job. It meant that fair play was out the window—that the party trailing in a presidential election could simply switch horses at any time. All of this was without precedent. Once Biden announced his decision, it would radically alter the landscapes of the race and American politics.

As directed, Donilon and Ricchetti had developed an execution plan overnight. They showed him the draft of a statement, and he made minor edits to it. He agreed that it made sense to post the statement to X when he was ready, so that the American people would hear it from him first.

At noon, Biden picked up his cell phone to start spreading the news to a handful of insiders who needed to know ahead of the public announcement. He called his chief of staff, Jeff Zients.

"We still have six months left in office," Biden told Zients. "I want this next six months to be as productive, or more productive, as any other six-month period in my presidency." Zients set up a senior staff call for 1:45 p.m. so that Biden could address his advisers directly.

O'Malley Dillon was in the attic office of her home in Chevy Chase, Maryland, when Biden called. She had gotten a heads-up from inside the beach house. But knowing what was coming did not take away the sting. She had grown close to the first lady, who had attended her father's funeral, since joining the Biden ranks in 2020. Jill Biden was on the phone too. The president told O'Malley Dillon matter-of-factly that he did not see a path to reelection and did not want to harm the effort to defeat Trump. He said it was the best thing for the country.

It had been a hellstorm of a month, like nothing the veteran campaign chief had ever endured. She had been forced to turn away from Trump and keep an entire team focused on defending its candidate to fellow Democrats. She had led the group through political wilderness, internal tension, an assassination attempt against the opponent, and an unprecedented potential candidate swap. And she had managed the budget when black ink started turning toward red. Through it all, O'Malley Dillon had kept it together for her team, for her party, and for Biden.

Now, hearing the president tap out, she lost it. O'Malley Dillon broke down in tears. Joe Biden kept his emotions inside—tamping down the swelling disappointment of his life's work coming to a premature end—but O'Malley Dillon could hear the referred pain in the first lady's voice. Jill Biden fought back her own tears to reassure the woman nearly twenty-five years younger.

"I love you," the first lady said. "I care about you."

O'Malley Dillon felt her back stiffen.

"We're going to get through this," Jill Biden said. "We're gonna be okay."

★

Before 1 p.m., Biden connected with Harris. He had made thousands of calls to other politicians over the years—to plot, to congratulate, to console—but none quite like this one.

When Harris answered, he told her what he had decided to do. Harris contained a swirl of emotions long enough to pose an appropriately reverent question.

"Are you sure?" she asked.

"Yes," Biden said.

"Don't let them push you out," Harris told Biden. "Are you sure this is the decision you want to make?"

"It's getting untenable," Biden replied. "Will you step up?"

"If you're sure you want to do this, I will," Harris said. "But only if I have your support."

"You have my support, kid," Biden said.

She was his choice as the next-best person to carry the Democratic banner against Trump and serve as president. Endorsing her was more than just a middle finger to Obama, Pelosi, and the rest of the mini-primary crowd. It was a validation of his decision to put her one heartbeat away from the presidency, and it gave Democrats a fighting chance to beat Trump. *It will be harmful to the party if we have anything other than a unified front*, he thought.

But Biden wanted to make sure the framing of his withdrawal, of his historic decision to step aside, did not get lost in a Harris media frenzy. He was not ready to give up center stage. He deserved his due, he believed, and he told Harris that he would not include an endorsement in the statement announcing his exit.

Harris needed more than that. She knew that if Biden stepped aside without explicitly backing her, it would be taken as a statement that he lacked confidence in her ability to win or to do the job—or both. That could mean crib death for a battle that she had not yet begun to fight. She also knew that a failure to throw his weight behind her would suggest that he had made the wrong decision in choosing her as his number two in the first place.

"No, Joe, you need to endorse me," she replied, emphasizing the speed element. "This is important for your legacy—to show that you have absolute faith in your VP. The only way to do that is to make it clear. . . . If you're going to make a statement, does it mention me?"

It did not.

"I will do my statement today, and then maybe Wednesday . . ."

Biden's last moment in the spotlight mattered most to him. For Harris, timing was everything. "No, that won't work," Harris said. "That's too much daylight. There will be mischief and confusion. The whole reason you're doing this is to maximize our chances of winning in November."

"You make a lot of good points," Biden said. "I'll send you my statement. Let me talk to my guys, and I'll call you back." Then he hung up.

Harris studied Biden's statement. If he released it and then waited to endorse her, all hell would break loose in the Democratic Party. They had to speed up the process. Her advisers drafted an endorsement for Biden's team to consider and reconnected with the Rehoboth Beach crew.

"We will do some kind of statement later today," Donilon said, with Biden listening in. Biden and his camp wanted to make sure that his own statement was given a chance to breathe. "It won't be too much time," he assured Harris.

We have to be able to go after these delegates immediately, she thought. *We'll only have the leverage to get them if he endorses now.*

"How about something like this?" Harris said, sharing the draft her aides had written.

"Okay," Donilon said. "Send us that and we'll make it a tweet."

Two p.m. would be good, she thought.

★

Driving to Jackson's, a Sumter, South Carolina, restaurant known for its beef pot with oxtails, to celebrate his eighty-fourth birthday, Representative Jim Clyburn's phone rang. He had been expecting to get this call—Biden telling him it was over—the previous day. Biden read his statement to Clyburn.

"What do you think?" the president asked.

"It's a good statement," Clyburn said, easing into his criticism. "I agree with it. But I'm disappointed. I think there's something missing."

"What's that?" Biden asked.

"I don't think you can leave the field without endorsing a successor," Clyburn replied. "If you don't endorse Kamala, you will be making an admission that you made a mistake when you picked her in the first place."

"I'm going to endorse her," Biden reassured Clyburn. "I'm going to leave this statement as it is."

Clyburn began thinking about the aftermath. He couldn't tell his own aides to start writing a Harris endorsement because Biden's decision was still a secret. But he knew that he couldn't wait long once the news was public.

Obama had scheduled a 5:30 p.m. call with him. *Obama's going to try to rope me into some kind of mini-primary*, Clyburn thought. *It will be easier to fend him off if I've already endorsed Harris.* When Obama called that evening, the conversation lasted less than a minute. Clyburn said the party should unify behind Harris and that "anything else will lead to a real tough convention, which will lead to defeat at the polls."

★

In Rehoboth Beach, the zero hour drew closer, but time seemed to speed up and slow down all at once. Biden's family and closest aides had ridden with him on a decades-long political trek full of highs—and a few lows. It was finally coming to an end. Yet they couldn't stop to process the meaning of that. Neither could Biden. At one point, the prime minister of Slovenia called. Biden secured his agreement to sign off on releasing prisoners as part of a complicated multicountry swap that would bring home jailed Americans, including *Wall Street Journal* reporter Evan Gershkovich, from Russia.

From the Washington suburbs, O'Malley Dillon dialed deputy campaign manager Rob Flaherty but got transferred to voicemail. It was 1:05 p.m., and he was hiking in Alapocas Run State Park in Wilmington with his wife, who had just started climbing up a rock wall. Flaherty noticed he had missed O'Malley Dillon and called her back.

"How fast can you get to a computer?" she asked.

"I'm probably thirty minutes away," Flaherty replied.

"He's going to drop out, and we're going to have to post his letter at one forty-five," O'Malley Dillon said, the urgency in her voice coming through the phone loud and clear. "You need to not tell anybody, and *you* need to post it."

"I don't actually have the keys to post anything," he said. "I have people for that."

Flaherty hung up and called Parker Butler, a young gunner on the digital team who handled the campaign's social media accounts. He told Butler to be ready for a statement updating the country on Biden's health. Next Flaherty told his wife, a fellow campaign aide, that they needed to hightail it home. But he didn't tell her why. She used GPS to locate the closest road, and they called an Uber. On the ride home, Flaherty received the text of the statement and read it. Arriving at his apartment at 1:33 p.m., he sent Biden's still-secret message to Butler. "You cannot say a goddamn word," Flaherty warned.

Biden signed in to the conference call with senior White House and campaign staff from his screened-in porch at 1:45 p.m. Tomasini, just out of sight inside, swiped down on her phone over and over to refresh her X feed. When Butler posted the tweet, as directed, she swung into Biden's view and gave him a thumbs-up sign. It was out in the world. There was no turning back.

"I just can't fight Democrats and Republicans at the same time," he said on the call.

★

Nancy Pelosi and Phil Murphy had eaten lunch while talking politics at a table in Jon Bon Jovi's Red Bank, New Jersey, restaurant, JBJ Soul Kitchen, which provides meals for the needy. Pelosi had won a charity auction bid to work with Bon Jovi at the restaurant, and he had invited Phil and Tammy Murphy to join them. Pelosi's grandkids bused tables and washed dishes while Pelosi, wearing a lavender pantsuit, and Murphy, in a blue shirt and white pants, gossiped about Biden's future.

"What do you think he'll do?" she asked in a low tone. Murphy thought he would eventually get out. Both of them believed that was the right move. But Pelosi insisted that she wasn't maneuvering behind the scenes to make it happen. "I'm not making any calls. People call me," she said. "Everyone thinks I'm behind this. I just want to win."

After lunch, Pelosi and the Murphys said their goodbyes at the governor's house, which was just a few minutes away from Bon Jovi's restaurant. Pelosi climbed into her black SUV for the three-and-a-half-hour ride to Washington. Phil Murphy went upstairs to use the bathroom. Tammy Murphy shouted up to him: "Biden dropped out!"

Inside the SUV, Pelosi's phone lit up with notifications of Biden's withdrawal. She asked aides to verify that it was not a fake. Then she dialed Murphy.

"Nancy?" he said, amused.

She replied wryly: "Do you think they had a microphone at our lunch?"

★

Harris did not have time for a pinch-me moment, at least not yet. Her aides set up a modern war room on her dining room table, with laptops and cell phones at the ready, and called for reinforcements to help wrangle delegates. Two precocious grandnieces buzzed around the adults—apparently oblivious to the stakes of a blitz to make the vice president the first woman of color to lead a major party's presidential ticket.

Harris already had the most important piece in place: Biden. Sure, she was his vice president. And yeah, it would have looked bad to pass over her—hypocritical even, since he'd been so sore for so long about Obama hanging him out to dry in 2016. Hell, Biden even factored in the party unity aspect: if Democrats picked someone else, they could lose Black voters by the millions. But the most satisfying aspect of his decision to endorse had little to do with Harris. "It was a fuck-you to Obama's plan," said one person close to both men. "At that moment, you have very few things you control, and that's the one thing he had control over, and he chose to stick it to Obama."

In truth, there was little love lost between the Biden and Harris camps. First Lady Jill Biden had never gotten over Harris hammering her husband over school busing on a debate stage in 2019—all but calling him racist—and neither had Biden's old guard. The first lady's staff "holds the grudges that she can't outwardly hold," said one White House official. Over the previous three weeks, Biden's team had inflicted serious reputational damage on Harris with Democratic insiders—to say nothing of the three-plus years before that.

She had hurt herself too. Harris was tough on staff, even by Washington standards, and they spun in and out of her orbit at an alarming rate. She tended to interrogate them about matters large and small, asking questions until she eventually found one they could not answer. It made her feel intellectually superior—a sign of an underlying lack of confidence in herself—said one longtime aide who had worked with other politicians. "She can be ice cold," this person said.

Her advisers held different views on the trait, with some explaining it as an attention to precision that she did not just demand from aides. "She's very hard on herself," said one senior Harris staffer. She found little support in Biden's West Wing, where unnamed officials piled on when she stumbled in public appearances. It was standard operating procedure for out-of-power Republicans to rip a vice president. But from the day she took office, Harris had to fend off friendly fire from a city full of Democrats interested in advancing the 2028 hopes of different candidates—and in making sure she never outshined Biden.

Biden's team had played on her reputation to help save him. In the middle of July, with more Democrats clamoring for his exit, the Biden-Harris campaign conducted "data trackers"—basically rapid-fire polls—of how Harris and other potential Biden alternatives stacked up. The point was to show that she wasn't ready for prime time. Not surprisingly, she fared worse than Biden, who had better name recognition and had been campaigning actively for the presidency. Biden's closest aides used these polls to scare party elites away from pushing for a change at the top of the ticket—and to reassure Biden that he was the best choice for the party. On Sunday, July 21, Harris became Biden's best hope for vindication. Before that, she was the threat his campaign brandished to keep Democrats lined up behind him.

"They wanted to sow doubt that she was ever going to be able to put it together," said one Harris adviser. Harris grinned and bore it. She would only hurt her reputation if she showed anything but loyalty to Biden when he was on the ropes. She often spoke publicly of her affection for him, and there were few signs that the principals did not get along well. But now that he had thrown in the towel, she knew locking down delegates would be harder because of the way his team disparaged her to fellow Democrats.

That had been a sore point for years, long before the debate. Like most vice presidents, she was given a shit-sandwich portfolio stocked with issues, like illegal border crossings, that the president couldn't solve. By July 2021, less than six months into her job, Harris slipped under the even mark in favorability surveys, eventually dropping well below 40 percent approval, and stayed underwater.

In 2022 and 2023, some elite Democrats chattered about the pros and cons of replacing Harris on the ballot. The talk was never serious, but it underscored the degree to which Democratic insiders worried that she would be a drag on Biden—with Republicans arguing that the next person in line to the presidency mattered more with an elderly commander in chief. Some Democrats thought she was incapable of winning if she had to take over for him.

"It doesn't take a genius to say, 'Look, with his age, we have to really think about this,'" John Morgan, the Florida donor, told the *New York Times* in February 2023.

Harris was well aware of how she was perceived by many Americans, including no small number of fellow Democrats. The caricature of a bumbling vice president is a familiar one in American politics. *Saturday Night Live* lampooned Gerald Ford, a former college football star, tripping over his own feet. Dan Quayle's spelling challenges, George H. W. Bush's "wimp factor," and Biden's penchant for gaffes all made fodder for late-night comics and columnists alike. But the artists filling in pictures of Harris used details such as her race and gender—"an affirmative action hire"—to dismiss her political skills and accomplishments.

The main plank of the case for her, even among many of those who made it, revolved around the idea that the party would implode if it bypassed a Black woman vice president. Pelosi, the Democrat who put the most public pressure on Biden, didn't want her. "Her assessment was there were other, better candidates who didn't have Harris's negatives, but that anyone would be better for House and Senate races than Biden," said one Pelosi confidant. In private conversations, Obama flat-out told allies she would lose to Trump.

"I think they felt Kamala was weaker than she is," said one Republican Trump ally who knows Biden, Obama, Harris, and Pelosi.

Had Biden been most concerned and clear-eyed about keeping Trump out of the White House, he might have chosen not to seek re-election at all. His approval ratings had dipped underwater for good following the fatal withdrawal from Afghanistan. He failed to sell his legislative wins as economic engines. About three-quarters of voters thought the country was on the wrong track. And most of them believed he was too old to serve another term.

If he had run calculations on the best way to position Democrats for November after the debate, he might have dropped out immediately and allowed more time for a competition. But in both cases, he misread the writing on the wall. By the time he got out, Democratic leaders and voters were sick of infighting, scared of losing, and eager to turn their focus back to beating Trump. That teed up Harris's team to activate a rapidly growing national network of allies.

★

Harris was under no illusion about her party: its leaders wanted a new candidate, but there was no clear consensus that it had to be her. She would have to win a behind-the-scenes fight to force that consensus, and there was no time to waste. But her first call from 1 Observatory Circle missed its target. Husband Doug Emhoff was three thousand miles away, sipping coffee with friends from his West Hollywood SoulCycle class, when one of them showed him Biden's statement on an iPhone. The second gentleman had left his own cell phone in his Secret Service SUV.

"Gotta go!" Emhoff said, tearing out to the car to find his phone. It had several messages, all of which said versions of "Call Kamala!"

When he did, she asked a question familiar to many husbands: "Where the fuck were you?"

"I need you right now," Harris said. "Get to work!"

That's exactly what she and her top advisers were doing in Washington. Harris sat in the middle of the dining room table, with West on one side and Voles on the other. They sent out a bat signal to a coterie of political associates around the country to jump on a Zoom call, while more aides and Harris family members began to congregate in the dining room. Kristin Bertolina Faust, a veteran California political consultant who was close to Harris, joined the videoconference from Cavallo Point lodge in San Francisco, looking out at the Golden Gate Bridge. Maya Harris, the vice president's sister, hopped a train from New York so that she could pitch in.

The only pause in the action came when Harris called her pastor, Amos Brown, and put him on speakerphone. Her aides stopped in their tracks. The vice president closed her eyes as Brown said a prayer over her, the gravity of the tasks ahead—locking down a nomination, fighting Trump for the presidency, and possibly running the country—fully sinking in for the first time.

Divvying up Jones's call sheet, Harris and her team started dialing for endorsements. Harris took the big names: former presidents, governors, House and Senate leaders, and the heads of the Black, Hispanic, Asian American and Pacific Islander (AAPI), and progressive caucuses. The others split up rank-and-file lawmakers, convention delegates, and donors. Harris made her own calls and took cell phone handoffs from West and various aides when they reached prominent Democrats. Among the first she connected with: Bill and Hillary Clinton.

Vacationing on Martha's Vineyard with friends, the Clintons had already made up their minds. The vice president's inner circle included a set of former Clinton aides who remained close to the former first couple. More than that, Bill and Hillary still wanted to see a woman elected for the first time—even if it wouldn't be Hillary. Harris spoke first to Bill and then to Hillary. They both committed to her on the spot. They even offered to come to Washington to help brainstorm. Biden's tweet backing Harris posted at 2:13 p.m. The Clintons followed suit with their own tweet less than an hour later. Half the living presidents in the Democratic Party were already in Harris's corner.

"There's something about a former president of the United States and former secretary of state saying, 'Listen, you're it,'" said one Harris adviser who described excitement coursing through the vice president's residence when the Clintons jumped on board. "There was something very powerful about it. It gave us more confidence that the plan we were putting in place was working. It was so reassuring."

But Obama still had deep misgivings about Harris—and a hankering for an intraparty fight. "He did not think she should be the candidate," said one confidant. He liked the idea of Michigan governor Gretchen Whitmer at the top of the ticket and Maryland governor Wes Moore at the bottom—a combination that would still allow Democrats to rally around a woman and a person of color—but he was mostly certain he didn't want a coronation of Harris.

When Harris connected with him early that afternoon, she stepped out of the dining room so that they could speak privately. She told him she was running and that she would work to win the nomination, whatever it took. She didn't expect him to endorse her, but she asked what he planned to do.

"I don't want to get in and put a finger on the scale," Obama said.

"I respect that," Harris said, disappointed but not surprised. "That's fine."

He told the world he wasn't ready to get behind Harris in a Medium post linked to a tweet at 3:44 p.m. "We will be navigating uncharted waters in the days ahead," Obama wrote. "But I have extraordinary confidence that the leaders of our party will be able to create a process from which an outstanding nominee emerges."

If Harris couldn't count on Obama, she was determined to stock her new version of the old campaign with his brain trust. Jim Messina, who ran Obama's 2012 reelection bid, was catching trout and a decent alcohol buzz on the Flathead River in northwest Montana when Harris's team called. He had to be fished out of the river to dial back on a satellite phone. Harris wanted either him or David Plouffe, the manager of Obama's 2008 campaign, to temporarily give up their lucrative day jobs and join up as paid help.

★

In state capitals across the country, governors assessed their chances of winning a round of speed-dating with Democratic voters. The list of potential hopefuls included California's Gavin Newsom, Whitmer, Pennsylvania's Josh Shapiro, New Jersey's Phil Murphy, and Illinois's J. B. Pritzker. Separate from the Harris operation, Democratic National Committee chairman Jaime Harrison called a roster of would-be candidates to inform them of the process—and get a bead on who might actually run.

"It would have been very cheap. It would have been quick. A rocket ship for your career and no loss," said one Democratic former governor.

"If this had been a year earlier, twenty people would have gotten in," said one governor who had kicked the tires on a 2024 bid.

Unknown to most, Whitmer already had told Harris she wouldn't run. But an endorsement was a different question. At an event in the "Downriver" region south of Detroit, Whitmer huddled in a hold room with Representative Debbie Dingell to process their options.

"You sure you're not running?" Dingell asked. Politicians, of course, had been known to change their minds. But Whitmer had a pragmatist's view of how hard it would be to win the nomination, bring the party together, and then beat Trump. Besides, she had familiarized herself with the party rules and thought Harris had the inside track.

"Yes," she told Dingell.

"Well," Dingell said, "I'm going to show loyalty to Joe Biden and I'm going to support the person he wants. But I'm not doing it if you're not."

Dingell and Whitmer's sister, Liz Whitmer Gereghty, signaled where the governor was headed by posting endorsements of Harris on X. By the time Harris called, Whitmer's support was a formality.

"You have my vote," Whitmer said, but she held back on promising an endorsement until later in the day.

Harris discovered a theme emerging from some of the most prominent governors. Instead of jumping to endorse her or laying out their own thoughts, several asked her to explain how she thought the nomination process should play out. Was she open to going through a mini-primary or a contested convention? Harris smiled to herself. *I'm lapping them,* she thought, *and they are asking when the race starts.*

"This is the process," she said. "Whoever can get a majority of the pledged delegates will be the nominee. I'm trying to shore up the support of the majority of the pledged delegates." Then she put everyone on the spot: "Will you endorse me?" Most of the governor-size dominoes fell over the next several hours. They simply didn't see a path for themselves, especially with Biden, the Clintons, and a growing number of party luminaries coalescing around Harris.

Harris held crucial advantages beyond their backing: a level of incumbency, a call sheet of delegates, and Democrats' fear of creating a backlash by skipping over a Black woman. Because her name was already on the Biden-Harris campaign, there would be no legal complication in transferring the war chest to her. That alone was enough to put a chill on potential rivals. Biden's endorsement also meant that his campaign team felt obliged to swing in behind Harris, even though she was not yet the party's nominee.

From Rehoboth Beach, Biden dialed high-leverage allies to thank them for their support and encourage them to unify behind Harris. "They were both hitting the ground running," said one Biden aide who counted fifty contacts he made Sunday. "She was calling folks. He was calling folks."

★

In Wilmington, Biden campaign aides braced for Pritzker to jump in. The press-friendly governor had been eerily quiet for too long.

"Pritzker would not take our call," said one Harris aide. The Biden and Harris camps concluded that he was a real threat. Why else would he dodge her? They drew up plans to welcome him to the race with an uppercut.

"I was ready to go fuck up J. B. Pritzker," said a Biden aide who was tasked with writing a draft statement attacking the Illinois governor.

When Harris finally reached Pritzker, he sidestepped her entreaty for an endorsement. Look, he said, I want to figure out if I need to remain neutral because Chicago is the host city for the convention. It was such an outlandishly contrived response that it would have made a red herring blush full crimson.

There was no room for anyone to run, and Harris was not going to let prospective rivals hide.

★

Nikki Fried, the chair of the Florida Democratic Party, found herself out of place again when Biden dropped out. She had been at a Janet Jackson concert when the big call from Donna Brazile had come three days earlier. This time she had picked the wrong time for an airboat ride with her family deep into the Everglades.

Returning to her car afterward, she grabbed her phone as she slid onto the driver's-side seat.

"Oh, shit," she said, looking down at the screen to see all the missed calls and news notifications.

Her fiancé's three sons, amped up from the adventure, screamed at one another in the back seat.

"Shut the fuck up!" she blurted out.

"What's up?" her fiancé asked.

"I need you to drive," she replied, switching seats with him.

Fried might not have been ready at that moment, but she had prepared for it. On Friday, the day after her talk with Brazile, Fried had dialed Ken Martin, who led the committee of state party chairs. Commiserating over the state of the race, and how it was tearing their state parties apart, they had discussed how to handle a possible Biden exit.

"If Joe decides to step aside, the party chairs must have an oversized influence on how this plays out," Fried had said at the time. She worried that a nomination completely driven by Washington insiders would hurt the party in the fall. "This has got to feel like it came from the base of the party, the grassroots side of things." Fried and Martin had agreed that the state party chairs should move as a unit at that time.

Late Sunday afternoon, Martin held a call with all the chairs, and they decided to issue a unanimous endorsement of the vice president that night. With that decision locked down, Fried checked in with the Florida delegation and found support for Harris at better than 90 percent. Similar results poured in to state party chairs across the country. Biden's delegates didn't want a fight. They wanted his vice president.

In a matter of hours, Harris's shock-and-awe whip operation effectively iced the nomination. For the many Democrats concerned about her political acumen, it was hard to deny she passed her first test with an A-plus. She had outgunned, outrun, and outdone Obama and Pelosi. They hacked up Biden. She proved too strong for them. Donald Trump presented a bigger challenge.

★

In 2023 and the first half of 2024, Trump had predicted to anyone who would listen—friends, aides, and interviewers—that Democrats would yank Biden from the race and replace him with a better candidate. As time wore on, with Biden cruising to renomination and the Democratic convention drawing nearer, some of his senior advisers cautioned that scenario was becoming less likely. After all, Biden had almost all the delegates in his column, and heading into the June debate, he had given every sign that he relished the coming rematch.

Shortly before Trump walked onto the debate stage that night, Jason Miller, one of his senior advisers, tried to pump him up. A hype man at heart, the goateed Miller, dressed always in suits as highly tailored as his hyperbole, told Trump to "go for the jugular."

Trump pushed back: "I don't want to hit him too hard and knock him out."

"If you go in there halfway or seventy-five percent, you'll win," Miller said. "But the editorials the next day will say 'if you'd only done this or that.' You have to go in, do the best you can, and let the chips fall."

Biden was the chip Miller didn't anticipate falling—at least not all the way to the floor. Trump had been right all along, even if Hollywood's greatest screenwriters couldn't have scripted the machinations that culminated in Biden's exit. In one sense, Republicans were ready for the candidate swap.

The fear of a switcheroo lurked close enough that Trump's campaign already had begun compiling political research on various Democratic candidates, including Harris. "We had started to test her, do opposition research on her at a deep level, test messages against her, test our performance against her," said one of Trump's top campaign advisers. The outlines of a campaign against her were clear from the jump: a continuation of the "failed" Biden presidency with a more extreme leftward tilt. The vault was already stocked with clips of her endorsing the administration's agenda, from "Bidenomics" to the withdrawal from Afghanistan. Her progressive-minded campaign for the 2020 Democratic presidential nomination—which ended before the first caucus—provided fodder for the extremism argument.

In short, Harris looked like a disaster to Trump's top aides. They thought Democrats would spin their wheel for a while and land on Shapiro. He presented a greater threat to Trump, they thought—better on Israel, better in Pennsylvania, and better to attract Republicans. "He makes up a lot of her gaps," one of them said.

When Biden sent out his statement, Wiles was at home in Ponte Vedra Beach, Florida, ironing her clothes for the next week. Most of Trump's top aides steered clear of the office on summer Sundays, and they had to jump on a conference call to plot their next moves. "We were shocked," one senior Trump adviser said. "Not caught off guard, just shocked in that it's such a momentous political thing."

James Blair, the campaign's political director, raised the possibility of tampering with the Democrats. He had obtained a list of Democratic delegates. If Trump allies made calls to some of them pretending to represent Harris rivals, it might sow chaos. "We weighed engaging in an antiwhipping operation and trying to fracture the Democratic Party further," said one Trump adviser. The idea was quickly scrapped.

Even with modest preparation, Trump and his advisers didn't know exactly what to expect from Harris. Her blitz of the delegates belied her reputation for ham-handedness. It would take time to assess her abilities, and voters' reactions to her. But Trump advisers felt confident that the overarching factors in the race—the shape of the electorate, dissatisfaction with the economy, and voters' desire for change—would not shift dramatically. Even if they did, Trump had been beating the same drums for nearly a decade. He wouldn't suddenly abandon his commitment to cracking down on illegal immigration, aversion to foreign wars, or advocacy for tariffs. He believed that he had presided over a robust economy—until Covid unraveled it—and that Biden's policies provoked inflation. The inflation message was key. He wouldn't back off that because Democrats swapped candidates.

What changed for both parties between 2020 and 2024 was the need to find new voters. Four years earlier, historically high turnout produced a total of almost 160 million votes. Only so many of those voters would be open to switching jerseys in 2024. The Trump camp pegged that share at 11 percent across the seven battleground states: Pennsylvania, Michigan, Wisconsin, Georgia, North Carolina, Arizona, and Nevada.

The Trump camp's persuadable-voter set was more likely to be young, male, nonwhite, and politically independent, compared to the rest of the electorate. Because they were younger, that meant they were more likely to watch streaming services or receive political messaging via text and direct mail than over cable television. The other group Trump's campaign homed in on comprised hard-to-reach nonvoters. Basically, they were hunting for people who liked Trump but were unlikely to receive traditional political communications.

A newcomer to the political arena—Barron Trump—played a major behind-the-scenes role in engaging both sets of voters. Over the summer, the Trump campaign hired Alex Bruesewitz, a political strategist and MAGA-flavored social media warrior who had been working at the main Trump PAC. He was still getting his feet wet during the Republican National Convention but quickly turned to pitching ideas for engaging Trump with new audiences. One day he parked himself on the couch in Alvarez's office and made the case for the president to appear with Theo Von, a popular comic whose podcast, *This Past Weekend*, is broadcast in video format on YouTube.

After pressing Bruesewitz for numbers—he said Trump would reach exponentially more potential voters with Von than on a cable news interview—Alvarez agreed. Bruesewitz dialed the former president, who was on the golf course.

"You know, I'm calling because I want to talk to you about doing a podcast with a superhot comedian," Bruesewitz said.

"Tell me about him," Trump directed. Bruesewitz gave him a thumbnail of Von's background and reach.

"Is it a big deal?" Trump asked.

"It's a big deal," Bruesewitz replied.

"Run it by Barron," Trump said. "If Barron likes it, we'll do it."

Bruesewitz hung up. He and Alvarez exchanged quizzical glances. It was close to a yes, but now they had to figure out how to get the former president's eighteen-year-old son on the phone. Barron Trump, whose mother had always tried to keep him out of the spotlight, had become a valued adviser to his father—often giving the elder Trump articles to read and acting as a tour guide to the younger generation. There was always plenty of chatter inside the Trump campaign about the latest do-ings of Don Jr., Eric, Lara, Ivanka, and Jared Kushner, all of whom toiled in the political arena. But Barron was a different beast.

"You don't talk about Barron," said one Trump campaign aide. "You don't talk to Barron. He's not like the other kids."

Bruesewitz and Alvarez didn't even know how to get his number. Alvarez suggested calling Don Jr.

"No," Bruesewitz countered. "You know who will be the most help-ful here is Jared," the former president's son-in-law. They reached out to Kushner, who told them to wait for him to confirm that Barron was okay with talking to them. Trump had just signed off on it, but Kushner still wanted to make sure. Once that was done, he shared Barron's number.

They connected with Barron and asked him whether he thought his father should go on with Von.

"Yeah," he said immediately. "You know who else you have to do? Adin Ross."

While Democrats fought one another in the early summer months, Trump's campaign launched an alternative media blitz—slowly at first—that would allow him to connect virtually with millions of people on a cultural level deeper than the politics of a presidential election. In a few days, Harris's campaign would tell America that she was all in on "brat summer." Trump was already locking in on his own bro summer. And while he hunted for new votes on modern platforms, Obama forced Har-ris to turn back to the technology of his era just to get his endorsement.

★

Harris had long pined for Obama's imprimatur. But for the most part, he couldn't be bothered with her.

In Chicago's Grant Park, on the night he claimed the presidency in

2008, Harris wandered outside a VIP tent set up for elected officials. She tried to force herself into one reserved for Obama's friends and family. "She was adamant about it," said one person who recalled her eagerness to get inside "the bubble." But Harris, then the San Francisco district attorney, was turned away because she was neither family nor friend.

Five years later, when she moved up to statewide office and he was in his second term as president, Obama called Harris "by far the best-looking attorney general in the country" at a fundraising event. The incident sparked a tempest-in-the-teapot hurricane of condemnation for the president, and Harris let him twist for a day, declining to comment. The most important woman in Obama's life, his wife, Michelle, found irritation in both his remark and Harris's silence. In order to win Harris's forgiveness, the president was forced to call her and apologize.

Even as vice president, Harris pursued Obama's stamp of approval, with little success, in ways direct and indirect. As she looked up and down a holiday party invitation list one year, she noticed that the hosts of *Pod Save America*—the podcast run by former Obama comms staffers—weren't on it. They had criticized her as a 2020 primary candidate and in her time as vice president. They were not her friends. Still, Harris wanted to make sure they weren't left out.

"Where's Jon Favreau and Dan Pfeiffer?" she asked an aide. "We're inviting them." They were added to the list—but they didn't show up.

"There's this need, and she's not unique in this, a need for people to be loved by the Obamas, to be blessed by them," said one Harris adviser.

But the vice president was not blessed by Obama. Along with Pelosi, major donors, and a tramload of governors, he had wanted to set up an open nomination process. So, while Harris liked to say the Obamas were her "friends," it was a loose description of the reality, even in an arena in which politicians often called their adversaries by the term. "She didn't keep up with them," one of her aides said, noting that Harris had tea with the Obamas a couple of times during her vice presidency. But Harris did not solicit their counsel in the way that other savvy politicians did. "She didn't ask them questions. She didn't build up a strong relationship there." That resulted from her own self-doubt, the aide said.

Harris "didn't want to be seen as not knowing something" or "to be exposed."

It came as no surprise to Harris that Obama wasn't the first to jump on her bandwagon. He found out there was little if any traction among the delegates for the mini-primary idea—but only after trying to round up support for it. As a candidate who ran an outsider 2008 primary campaign while benefiting from the backing of institutional heavyweights, the fight-it-out version of the nomination process was consistent with his brand and his broad worldview. But as a practical matter, the mini-primary was Obama's way of trying to kneecap Harris.

By 5:30 p.m. Sunday, it should have been clear to Obama that his swing had lost the power to smash bone. That's when he called Clyburn, hoping to lobby for the mini-primary, and instead heard a pitch for Harris.

As the hours rolled by, and it became clear that she was well on her way to seizing the nomination by storm, Obama's opposition to her grew more confounding. Harris was "very annoyed" with him, according to a confidant. They had plenty of donors and political allies in common. The rest of the party threw in with her. Where was Obama?

Doesn't he see what's happening? she thought. Harris felt hurt that he thought so little of her. That pain turned to anger. *What's holding him back?*

Over the next couple of days, Obama connected with Harris a few times. Suddenly, he was in a position where his actions against Biden and Harris could diminish him in the eyes of Democratic elites. Whether she won or lost—and he didn't think the former would happen—his reputation for loyalty to the party was on the line. He needed to make things right, or at least better, with Harris. "There was a little bit of mending that had to be done," said one person close to the former president. Obama told Harris he was impressed by how fast she got out of the gate and offered to help her on the campaign trail. That was as close as the former president would get to apologizing for his effort to end her career.

No matter how mad she was, Harris needed him—and Michelle. They were the most sought-after campaign-trail surrogates in the

Democratic Party. The only Democrat since Franklin Roosevelt to win back-to-back elections with a majority of both the popular vote and the Electoral College, Obama commanded the kind of coalition that Harris hoped to replicate. She was also inheriting a trailing campaign run by one of Obama's former aides—O'Malley Dillon—and had her eyes on Plouffe and Messina as possible adds that could make her new team stronger.

O'Malley Dillon, presiding over a campaign hemorrhaging cash, thought she could save a few bucks—and generate some grassroots giving—by turning the Obamas' endorsement of Harris into a shareable video clip rather than a simple tweet or major campaign event.

Harris aides were taken aback when they heard what they believed was a demand from the Obamas. The former first couple was purportedly insisting on a campy behind-the-scenes video of Harris taking their call. She would be on camera, but not the Obamas, and Harris would have to clear her calendar to align with theirs.

"It was like, 'Here's the window of time that Michelle and Barack have for you to take this call, and it can't be on video because Michelle's not going to be camera-ready,'" said one aide familiar with the discussions. "'They want you on video, recording the call, so you have to be on camera.'"

Harris's longtime advisers pushed back, asking why the Obamas wouldn't just put out a paper statement or a tweet. A bewildered Obama aide replied that the video was the Harris campaign's idea.

"Jen wanted a video because we were hard up for cash," said one person familiar with the snafu, noting that there were concerns in Wilmington that the campaign might not make payroll in August. "But she didn't tell anybody. She wasn't transparent about it. Logistically, it was a pain in the butt."

To seem real, Harris had to fake surprise and enthusiasm about what should have been an obvious endorsement from both Obamas. It took days of intense negotiations to strike a deal on the simplest act in politics. The whole frame, including the script, was designed to elevate the Obamas by making it look like she was begging for their blessing. This was typical bullshit.

But for Harris, the optics of unity had taken on the utmost importance. So the quality and authenticity of the endorsement moment took a back seat. With a camera filming, Harris held her phone to her ear.

Each of the Obamas said they were proud of her.

Harris responded with gratitude for their support and ended the call with a question: "We're going to have some fun with this too, aren't we?"

★

Eight days after he dropped out, Biden flew to Texas to attend an event at the LBJ Presidential Library in Austin and a memorial service for the late representative Sheila Jackson Lee (D-TX). Lyndon Baines Johnson was the last Democratic president to abandon a reelection bid, in 1968. The Vietnam War had taken a toll on him with northern Democrats, and civil rights had done the same in the South. But Johnson had seen the writing on the wall far earlier in the process and let others fight it out in the primary.

Aboard Air Force One with some of his closest political friends—Coons, Clyburn, and Al Sharpton among them—Biden expressed his gratitude for their firm support during his period of turmoil.

"Al, you stuck with me," Biden said. "You never tried to force me out."

"Mr. President, I was glad to," Sharpton replied.

Biden told Sharpton he would never forget the loyalty. Then he started naming the people he would never forgive for their betrayal. The first name out of his mouth: "Nancy Pelosi."

CHAPTER 11

FUCKERY

FEW PRESIDENTIAL HOPEFULS HAVE EVER EXPERIENCED THE EXUBERANT embrace Kamala Harris felt in her opening days as the de facto nominee. Charli XCX, the British pop star, labeled Harris "brat"—a good term, the olds would soon learn—the night of the switch. Money poured in from the sidelines, and suddenly no one worried about making August payroll. Endorsements piled up. The media gushed over the Democrats' new hope. Harris's first rallies, a week apart in Milwaukee and Atlanta, were packed with people and energy. A unified anti-Trump coalition, thirsty for an exciting new candidate, launched her campaign straight into the thermosphere.

"When we fight, we win!" she told each crowd, turning a phrase she had used before into a rallying cry for that coalition.

But inside the campaign, a very different reality took hold. The transition was anything but smooth, and the trouble started at the top. The choice of a campaign chief would be one of Harris's first and most consequential decisions. Jennifer O'Malley Dillon, a polarizing figure who had guided Biden to victory in 2020, sat atop a series of silos that made the Department of Homeland Security's organizational chart look rational. JOD, as she was known in political circles, had consolidated authority over the reelection campaign, the Democratic National Committee, and the White House political office during four years in Biden's orbit.

She had a well-earned reputation for kissing up, kicking down, and freezing out—how she treated superiors, dissenting subordinates, and people she perceived as rivals for power, respectively. She surrounded herself with a guard of loyalist lieutenants—"spies," said one Harris adviser—who helped her gather information, micromanage decisions, and avoid direct contact with anyone who might criticize her.

"People do not speak truth to Jen, because they have learned through the years that if you speak truth, you get kicked out of the room," said one person who worked with O'Malley Dillon on multiple campaigns.

Change would be at the heart of Harris's argument to the American people, but it was not immediately clear whether her campaign would reflect that. On the day of the switch, Harris spoke to O'Malley Dillon by phone. JOD had kept up a positive professional and personal relationship with the vice president in a White House where courtesies to Harris were in short supply. She was one of the few people in Biden's orbit who could claim to have solid bonds with both the first lady and the vice president. But the names of potential replacements were already circulating at the vice president's dining room table: former Obama campaign managers David Plouffe and Jim Messina, as well as former EMILYs List president Stephanie Schriock. It would not be hard for a new candidate to justify replacing the old guy's campaign chief, and JOD knew that when she picked up her phone.

"I want you to stay," Harris said.

That was hardly a full vote of confidence. If anyone knew the million ways to kneecap a high-level political aide, it was O'Malley Dillon. Staying could mean continuing to run the campaign without interference. But it could also mean being formally demoted or informally "layered" by someone who would come in with a new title and take over her job. She could be farmed out to a super PAC or the DNC—or, like Mike Donilon, returned to the Biden White House.

"I'm sure you're going to want your own person," O'Malley Dillon said deferentially, her voice audible to Harris advisers at the vice president's house. "I understand that."

Harris was not yet sure what she was going to do with O'Malley Dillon. Harris had been scarred by three-plus years of the president's aides dumping on her to one another—and at times to the media. She did not blame JOD for the West Wing's treatment of her. But when Biden was on the rocks, the O'Malley Dillon–run campaign had argued publicly and privately that the vice president was an inferior candidate. Rob Flaherty, a deputy campaign manager who was particularly close to O'Malley Dillon, had written a memo within hours of the Biden-Trump debate that undercut Harris.

Yet when O'Malley Dillon worked at the White House, she had shown more reverence for the vice president than some West Wing colleagues. "Kamala had a good relationship with JOD when JOD was at the White House," said one Harris adviser. "I'm not saying Kamala had that with all of Biden's senior advisers, but JOD would come in and brief her. They had a lot of respect for one another."

Harris wanted to hit pause and consider her options. In the interim, she needed to avoid a mutiny on the campaign. To do both, she had to convince O'Malley Dillon to stay in place for the moment. "This is all very sudden," Harris said. "I have to figure out exactly what the composition of the team is, but I need you to remain involved."

Harris had not fired JOD outright. Many Democratic insiders— including some donors, strategists, and Biden campaign aides—hoped that JOD would get the ax. Many of them felt that JOD had been dishonest about Biden's capabilities and about the state of the race. Money bundlers believed she had gaslit them in the days after the debate, pushing back on legitimate questions about Biden's path to victory. And there was no shortage of Democrats who thought she was simply running a bad campaign.

But there would be costs to replacing her. For starters, there was no one in Harris's inner circle both capable of running a billion-dollar-plus national presidential campaign and willing to do it. It was also going to be painful enough for Biden's Wilmington staff to convert to a new candidate; asking them to follow a new campaign manager might be too much.

That was certainly true for the top JOD lieutenants. They believed she had demonstrated loyalty to Biden, Harris, and the party for four years, particularly on the most tumultuous day in memory. She had ordered her team to transition the campaign's branding, social media presence, and fundraising apparatus from Biden to Harris—even though she was not the nominee. After a few hours of Harris advisers whipping delegates and building irreversible momentum, the old Biden campaign started promoting endorsements. From Wilmington, it felt like the two sides were moving in concert, "like trains on parallel tracks" with aides "throwing baggage to each other" on Sunday night, said one person involved in the effort. JOD's inner circle wanted to see her loyalty repaid. "If Jen were not kept," one of her confidants said, "a bunch of us would have probably gone." Explicit or implicit, the threat of a leadership exodus had to be weighed against the potential benefits of new blood.

On the other hand, O'Malley Dillon's abrasively dismissive treatment of people she regarded as inferior had been rubbing campaign professionals raw for years. The handful of Harris aides working on the vice president's end of the campaign had been crammed into one tiny sixth-floor office in a back corner of the sprawling headquarters complex, which spanned parts of two buildings in Wilmington. They were not even an afterthought, said one senior Biden aide. "We had an advance person for the vice president on the campaign," the aide said. "I didn't even fucking know that." What the Harris aides knew was that they were both out of sight and out of mind.

By the time Harris arrived at campaign headquarters on Monday afternoon, little more than twenty-four hours after Biden bowed out, she believed she didn't have much of a choice. "What was she going to do? You have this whole apparatus and a hundred and seven days," said one senior Harris adviser. Even though O'Malley Dillon had been presiding over a losing campaign, and even though Harris would market herself as a change agent, she felt that the risks of disruption outweighed the benefits. "We're heading into August," said one person familiar with Harris's thinking. "You couldn't really do a wholesale change." Still, the deal was not yet sealed.

Before taking a lectern to give a pep talk to rows of cheering aides standing at their desks, Harris huddled with O'Malley Dillon in a conference room at the back of the campaign's "Brandywine" office in Wilmington. The meeting was supposed to last five minutes. It ran close to half an hour.

O'Malley Dillon set her conditions for staying on the team. She was open to adding an adviser, like Plouffe, who had been her boss on the first Obama campaign. But she would not accept being demoted, formally or informally. She would not report up to a new supervisor. "I will stay if you think that's what best," O'Malley Dillon said. "If you want to have someone else come in, I'll be fine with that. I will help transition."

The threat hung in the air, unspoken: if Harris layered her, JOD might walk and take her deputies with her.

"The vice president didn't call her bluff," said one Harris adviser who believed that O'Malley Dillon was never going to take her ball and go home. Win or lose, that would have looked disloyal. While Harris had not yet worked out who would sit in what chair in her own mind, O'Malley Dillon had given the structure a lot of thought. She laid out her thoughts on how to blend Harris's lieutenants into the existing campaign team. The level of consideration and detail recommended her for the job. So did the resilience O'Malley Dillon had demonstrated during the previous month.

Harris did not want to waste time. Naming a top aide would show that she had fully taken the reins of the party and its presidential campaign.

"If you're comfortable with it," Harris said as they wrapped up, "I'm going to go out there and announce you to everyone." Her first big decision as a presidential candidate chased stability rather than change.

★

There would be more drama in both the Harris and Trump camps as the candidates and their teams adjusted to this second major shakeup of the race in less than a month. For the Harris campaign, friction hit fast. The vice president wanted to integrate some of her trusted advisers into the existing Biden operation. A doctor could more fluidly have sewn a second living head onto a human body.

On his first day in the office, Harris aide Sergio Gonzales showed up for the 9 a.m. senior staff meeting, run by Julie Chavez Rodriguez. "Thank you for all you have done to get us to this point," he said to his new colleagues. "The vice president thanks you. Her team thanks you. There will be changes to come, but we are so grateful." He seemed to thank everyone but Harvey Weinstein.

My God, he's giving his Oscar speech, thought one Biden holdover. *Does this guy think he's my boss now? Maybe he is my boss.*

Suddenly, Biden originals took a different view of the out-of-the-way workroom that had been a receptacle for the vice president's staff when she was number two on the campaign. Now it felt like a command center where Harris aides were plotting a soft coup of the operation. Past a phone booth and around the corner from the first lady's office, as many as six Harris aides holed up together. They did that because it was the only space allotted for them. In the opening days of the merger, the Harris staff office became a metaphor for the uncertainty, tension, and suspicion that gripped both sides.

Low-level conflict started immediately. Some Harris aides felt that the Biden campaign had been too slow to start working for her on the Sunday of the switch. Given that Biden's inner circle had threatened donors with the prospects of a Harris candidacy, and that O'Malley Dillon was closely tied to Obama, it was not totally unreasonable for them to worry that the president's campaign might not jump into line.

At the same time, Harris's landing team might not have fully appreciated the technical complexities of rebranding a presidential campaign on a midsummer Sunday with no advance notice. That required making lightning-fast decisions, like whether the candidate would be "Kamala" or "Harris" on social media accounts, creating a logo, and, with some bumps, making sure that a tsunami of donations could flow into the campaign's coffers. Every hiccup hit the Harris team like an affront to the candidate. "They thought we were trying to fuck them by putting the press release announcing the switch on Biden-Harris letterhead," one Biden original said of the Harris folks.

Each side looked at the other and thought: *Who the fuck do these guys think they are?* "We were like, we got you guys here," said one high-ranking Biden adviser. Along the way, Harris aides well remembered, they and their candidate had been treated like oddball in-laws. Flaherty, the deputy campaign manager, had sent a memo a couple of days after the debate effectively arguing that Harris couldn't beat Trump. "We all have our pants down," one Biden aide said.

"It looks good on the outside. People are totally excited. Folks are stoked," the aide said. "The energy of the country is so great, but inside the campaign, it felt horrible. Everything is a turf fight now, and it's lawless."

O'Malley Dillon cautioned her nervous lieutenants to let her take the lead in establishing control of the fief. "You have to put your mask on before you put your kid's mask on," she told them, perhaps inadvertently likening the tense situation to an airline disaster.

It was an airplane—Air Force Two—that O'Malley Dillon saw as her best vehicle for establishing authority. In the coming weeks, she would use her face time with Harris in flight and in Washington to develop a stronger bond and earn the vice president's trust. Then she could more easily assert herself and her team. But in the opening phase of the switch, Biden aides looked at the Harris transplants like a JV team that had been called up to the varsity squad to play in a national championship game. "There's a group of people who have been with her for a long time but have plateaued," said one Biden aide who kept his spot after the candidate swap.

"There was frustration on both sides," said a senior Harris adviser. "People in the campaign in Wilmington were like, *Who are these people who now think they are in charge?* And our folks were thinking, *Wait a minute, we should get a little more here, have a little more respect.* There was truth on both sides."

Kristin Bertolina Faust, one of California's top consultants and a personal friend to Harris, flew east for what she thought would be a role as co-chair of the Harris campaign's finance team. In her first week in Washington, she ran into interference from finance chair Rufus Gifford and fundraisers at the Democratic National Committee. Then she read a story in the *New York Times* suggesting that another California fundraiser would take on a role very similar to the one she had accepted.

This is going to be some fuckery, Bertolina Faust thought.

Even so, Faust headed home to California to pack clothes so she could move to the East Coast for the rest of the campaign. With her return to California, friends worried that she had thrown up her hands and decided not to join the team. Having picked up on her frustration, Tony West, the vice president's brother-in-law, called to check in that Friday.

"How's it going?" he asked.

"Rufus is really resistant," she said. "He does not want me to have a title. It's a whole thing." Bertolina Faust went on to explain that she had been cut out of the loop on a national fundraising call and found out about it from donors just in time to scramble to send a staffer to assist Harris.

West chuckled. "All right," he said. "Rufus is on the plane with her tomorrow. Let me talk to her."

The next morning, he called back with Harris on the line. The vice president, and newly minted presidential candidate, found herself dealing directly with what seemed like childish games. There was a nonzero chance that her own people would get boxed out—or simply give up—if she didn't.

"I'm going to see Rufus," Harris said. "I will make it very clear why you're here and why it matters to me."

On an hourlong Air Force Two flight from western Massachusetts to Andrews Air Force Base Saturday evening, Harris huddled with Gifford to discuss the campaign's finances and its personnel. They were returning from a $1.5 million fundraising event in Pittsfield, Massachusetts, cohosted by former governor Deval Patrick and attended by musician James Taylor. Most of the conversation revolved around ways to energize grassroots giving with merchandising and branding, and to push big-dollar donors to pump more money into the campaign. But before long, Harris segued into her own longtime donors and Bertolina Faust's role.

"Kristin's going to come in here," Harris said. "We want her to work hand in hand with you. Her skill set is going to be different than yours. I need her to look out for my people."

Gifford nodded his agreement, but drew a line. "I want to maintain my title, and I don't want anybody over me."

Gifford got the message and worked more cooperatively after that. But in nearly every department, Harris add-ons faced intransigence. Longtime Harris aides Stephanie Young and Kirsten Allen ran into dismissiveness from communications director Michael Tyler and other top brass on the campaign.

"Even the folks that had a harder time in the transition because it was perceived that they weren't fans of the VP, all of those people survived," said one holdover. "They all maintained their titles. There were very few people who were layered." The one major exception: T. J. Ducklo, who had worked for Biden in the West Wing and on both of his campaigns, was pushed completely out.

O'Malley Dillon's cliquish, top-down leadership style—*Mean Girls*, campaign edition—had long been held in check by the guardrails of Biden's pooh-bahs. But they were gone, and she ran roughshod over even the most established and well-connected Harris confidants. "She's tough, she loves tough women," one Harris adviser said of the vice president. "But I don't think she understood that JOD was a dictator." Beyond that, Harris worried that the infighting could sink her campaign and make her look bad in the process. The backbiting on her 2019 campaign scarred her so badly that she barely mentioned her sister Maya, who helped run that campaign and remained her closest adviser in 2024.

During the graceless denouement of her first presidential campaign, Harris's operation devolved into infighting that spilled into public. It was never clear to her aides whether her sister or the campaign manager, Juan Rodriguez, was in charge, and often they gave contradictory instructions. The debacle left a lasting impression in political circles that the candidate could not manage her own operation—one that was reinforced by staff turnover in her vice presidential office—and she was determined not to let internal drama dominate this fragile bid.

Sheila Nix and Lorraine Voles clamped down on the bullshit, warning Harris aides not to elevate small grievances—any grievances—with the Biden crowd. "This won't be 2019," one Harris adviser said of their message. "We're not going to cause drama. We're all going to go along to get along." The fear of fucking things up for Harris ran deep. "Everybody got in a space where they were afraid to rock the boat," said a second Harris adviser, "or didn't think rocking the boat would make any difference."

The result was a paradigm that cemented O'Malley Dillon's authority and relegated the Harris team to "Burn Book" status. "The people that were in power previously, they just continue doing what they're doing," one of the Harris advisers said.

JOD asserted her authority in other ways that were not related to the merger of the two camps. One campaign aide was surprised to hear highly respected pollster Jefrey Pollock back down on his numbers when

O'Malley Dillon challenged them in a meeting about Wisconsin. Her analytics team painted a rosier picture. Why was his poll more bleak? JOD wanted to know. "Jef starts making excuses for his own fucking poll," said one person who was on the virtual call.

There were fewer than 107 days before the November election. Harris fans feared it wasn't enough time for her to establish herself and win. Democratic skeptics thought it might be too long: her warts would reveal themselves in a matter of months, if not weeks, they argued. With the party convention less than a month away, both types of Democrats and Trump campaign officials expected she would benefit from the hype surrounding her entry into the race, her selection of a vice presidential nominee, and the convention itself. But then what?

★

"Given what has happened over the past couple of days and her impending VP choice, there is no question that Harris will get her bump earlier than the Democrats' Convention," Tony Fabrizio, the Trump campaign pollster wrote in a memo on July 23. "And that bump is likely to start showing itself over the next few days and will last a while until the race settles back down."

On the surface, Fabrizio's memo represented a reasonable stab at analyzing a scenario that he acknowledged "is totally uncharted territory and has no modern historical parallel." But it was also a message to his candidate: the next few weeks will look ugly, but hold tight. That wasn't Trump's forte. Even though he had long thought Biden would not finish the race, the aftermath was nerve-racking.

From the time of the debate to the candidate switch, Trump had expanded his lead in the RealClearPolitics average of national polls from 1.5 points to 3.1 points. In historical terms, it was a small shift—incremental enough that Biden had been able to hold on for nearly a month. But in modern terms, against a backdrop of two straight elections that were decided by fewer than 80,000 votes over three states, the Trump bump was significant—especially given his history of outperforming national poll averages.

It was even more pronounced in two of the three Blue Wall states—

Pennsylvania and Wisconsin—that were crucial to Democrats' chances of holding the White House. In Wisconsin, Trump went from a tie to a 2.9-point lead; in Pennsylvania, he rose from a 2.8-point lead to a 4.5-point lead. In Michigan, the change matched the national trend exactly, leaving Trump with a 2.1-point margin.

Both campaigns saw Pennsylvania as the most likely to decide the outcome if the race ended close to a dead heat. Aptly, it was the keystone in the Blue Wall. Democrats would win if Harris could hold the three Blue Wall states plus a single electoral vote from Nebraska's Second Congressional District. Nebraska was one of two states, along with Maine, that awarded two electoral votes to the statewide winner and one apiece for each of the state's congressional districts.

On the other hand, if all the other states held the same as the 2020 map, Trump would win the election by flipping Pennsylvania and Georgia into his column. When the Biden-Harris switch happened, Trump had a 3.8-point lead in Georgia, down from 4 points on debate day, but a relatively comfortable spread all the same.

Before she could get too invested in the details of the electoral map, Harris had to make what was traditionally considered to be the most important decision facing a nominee—and do it, like everything else, on a truncated timeline. Conventional wisdom holds that vice presidential candidates matter very little. There's no evidence to suggest that a modern number two can even deliver his or her own home state. With a race featuring Trump, the most consequential figure of the era, and Harris, vying to become the first woman to win the presidency, the bottom of the ticket mattered even less. With one caveat: voters could form opinions on the presidential nominee's judgment based on the choice of a running mate. As a result, most nominees followed the Hippocratic Oath: do no harm.

On the night of the switch, Pelosi had just gotten off the phone with Harris when a former House colleague called to pitch himself for the second slot on the ticket.

"I'm the one who can do this," Tim Walz, the Minnesota governor, exclaimed. The career teacher had gotten his political start by upsetting a veteran Republican House incumbent in the 2006 Democratic wave that handed Pelosi the Speaker's gavel the first time.

Only a week or so earlier, he had called her while he was stuck in the Salt Lake City airport for several hours. After Walz gave her a report on what voters were saying to him at the Utah airport, she pointed out that, as chair of the Democratic Governors Association and the chief executive of his state, he should have found a private plane to take him home. It was a waste of precious buckraking hours to sit at an airport waiting for a commercial flight, she thought. Walz had been well liked in the House, and obviously by the majority of voters in his district and the state. But he was hardly the world's most skilled politician.

That didn't deter Walz, whose nearly bald dome, framed by snow-white hair on the sides, made him look older than his sixty years. He'd won six elections to the House and two to the governorship without a blemish on his record. He'd spent almost a quarter of a century in the Army National Guard, and he believed he could be the attack dog Harris needed to savage Trump.

"I know how to go after this guy," he told Pelosi. "I'm not afraid of him. I'm the one. I'm the one who can do it!" She would hear from a lot of politicians who wanted either the first or second spot on the ticket. Walz might have been the most eager. Walz worked former House colleagues to back his bid and launched a media tour. By the end of the week, he had gone viral with an MSNBC interview in which he called Trump and Vance "weird," a term that quickly caught fire in Democratic circles.

Harris had just fifteen days to make a decision, and she tapped former U.S. attorney general Eric Holder to lead the vetting team. The process boiled down to three rounds: a background check by lawyers at Holder's firm, Covington & Burling; meetings between those who made the first cut and a small group of Harris advisers; and, for the select few, a final face-to-face sit-down with Harris.

She narrowed her choices down to about a half-dozen candidates by the end of July, all of them white men, and homed in on three real contenders: Walz, Pennsylvania governor Josh Shapiro, and Arizona senator Mark Kelly.

In 2020, when she beat out a crowded field to join Biden's ticket, Harris advisers ran a dark-arts operation to undermine the competition, circulating negative information on her rivals. "We stabbed Karen Bass a little bit. We stabbed Susan Rice a little bit. We stabbed Stacey Abrams a little bit," one adviser said of the effort four years earlier. "We stabbed Gretchen Whitmer."

The 2024 veepstakes would be no different. It too was full of fuckery—on fast forward.

Kelly had to fend off rumors that he was unfaithful to his wife, former representative Gabby Giffords, who barely survived a shooting massacre. No one ever presented evidence to the vetting team about a specific liaison, but the risk of a scandal loomed in the background of discussion about him.

One Walz ally promoted the Minnesota governor to the Harris vetting team and then stuck a knife in Shapiro. The Pennsylvania governor could not be trusted to be loyal to Harris, the Walz ally explained. He related a story to the vetting team about Shapiro driving his political patron, former representative Joe Hoeffel, out of politics. It is hard to stand out as overly ambitious among politicians, but the description stuck to Shapiro like a KICK ME sign.

Still, Shapiro offered an attractive set of attributes. He fit the prototype: a white, male governor under the age of sixty-five. Not only had he won election in a swing state, it was the key state. And he was relatively popular in Pennsylvania, with a poll from Emerson College and *The Hill* newspaper showing that 49 percent in his home state approved of him, while only 31 percent disapproved. More than 1 in 5 Republicans said they approved of him. He was a talented public speaker, even though his Obama-like affect felt like a cheap and forced imitation.

Trump advisers worried that Harris would pick him. They had thought Democrats would put him at the top of the ticket. While Trump's brain trust was not sure that Shapiro could deliver Pennsylvania, they weren't certain that he couldn't. Perhaps as important, Democrats were deeply divided over Israel's war in Gaza. Trump hoped to capitalize on that with Jewish voters, many of whom had drifted to the political right in the wake of the October 7, 2023, terrorist attack on Israel. Picking

Shapiro, who is Jewish and unapologetically pro-Israel, would compli-
cate Trump's argument that he would be better for Israel than Harris.

The war had given Biden fits. He simultaneously backed Israel's
right to defend itself and lobbied Prime Minister Benjamin Netanyahu
to limit the bombardment of Gaza. That angered a lot of Jewish voters, especially when Biden's private commentary about Netanyahu—he
called the Israeli leader an "asshole"—made the rounds. At the same
time, Biden took heat from pro-Palestinian activists—including a set of
White House interns—who fumed about U.S. military aid continuing
to flow to Israel as the civilian death toll in Gaza mounted. In the fall
and spring, pro-Palestinian protesters took over American college cam-
puses.

Democratic leaders were terrified that pro-Palestinian protesters
would disrupt their August convention and expose the deepest, most
painful rift in their party at a high-profile event designed to be a unifying force. Biden wasn't winning with either side, and, as vice president,
Harris had not distanced herself from his policy in any substantive way.
Her aides said that, behind the scenes, she had urged Biden to pay more
attention to civilians in Gaza, but it was not an issue that she raised
publicly.

Even as Biden swept to victory in the Democratic primaries in 2024,
the Gaza war proved embarrassing and divisive. He won just 81 percent of Michigan Democrats' votes, with 13 percent opting for "uncommitted" as part of a coordinated campaign to demonstrate the power
of pro-Palestinian activists. What Harris might gain in Pennsylvania
by picking Shapiro, she could lose in Michigan. In all likelihood, she
needed both states to win the presidency.

Publicly, Walz supporters found other ways to criticize Kelly and
Shapiro. Shawn Fain, the United Auto Workers president, argued it took
Kelly too long to back a pro-labor bill in the Senate and that Shapiro's
support for school vouchers was problematic. But the real issue for Shapiro was the perceived consequence of picking a pro-Israel Jewish running mate in the midst of a Middle East war. Many Democratic-leaning
Arab American voters would not only balk, but they might stay home
or vote for Trump. "I made sure they knew how the community would

react," said one Democratic elected official familiar with the state's Arab American voters, "and that it could cost them Michigan."

Voters' views were not the only considerations, and maybe, at least at some level, not the most important ones for Harris. Candidates who met virtually or in person with Harris's vetting squad—a group that included Tony West, Cedric Richmond, Nevada senator Catherine Cortez Masto, and former Biden labor secretary Marty Walsh—noticed the tenor of the questions leaned heavily toward whether the man in question could play second fiddle to Harris. Biden's team had harbored similar concerns about Harris four years earlier: Would she be loyal to him and would she make sure she didn't outshine him on the campaign trail or in the White House? Like Shapiro, she had once been seen as an overly ambitious rocket ship of a politician with potentially more star power than the presidential nominee. That helped explain West Wing aides' treatment of her early in the Biden administration. With an aging president who had promised to be a bridge, they could not afford to let her rise too much.

Harris had promised to be loyal, embedding the Biden code of the street so deeply in her core that she had trouble disagreeing with him in public or in private throughout his presidency. As the first woman of color to be nominated by a major party, it was arguably more important to her that a middle-aged white-guy running mate refrain from fighting her for power and acclaim. It would be easier for one of them to diminish her stature than for her to have done the same to Biden.

Walz was pretty thrilled just to be considered, and that came through in every interaction he had with the vetting team, with the media, and with other politicians. But Shapiro took a very different tack. Five minutes into his meeting with the small vet set, Shapiro launched into an explanation of which policies he thought he should have control over. *He thinks this is a negotiation*, one of the Harris advisers thought. Looking around, the adviser could see the shock was universal. What Shapiro was doing seemed intentional. "I'm not sure I could be a number two," he said.

He was in an awkward position. Two years into his first term as governor, and in good position for reelection in 2026, winning the veepstakes could be a death sentence for his own presidential aspirations. If she chose him and they won, his best-case scenario for his own bid would be trying to win a fourth straight Democratic term in 2032. Neither party had held the presidency that long since Franklin Roosevelt and Harry Truman captured five consecutive elections for the Democrats. If Harris picked Shapiro and they lost, he might be the baby thrown out with the bathwater—deemed a loser, just for the chance to campaign for VP for three months. More than anyone, he knew that Trump was on a trajectory to win Pennsylvania and the election. Biden had not led in a single reputable independent poll in the state in 2024, and Trump's margin had only grown over the previous weeks.

But Shapiro could hardly have turned down the opportunity to be vetted. Mentions are mentions, and the process elevated his stature within the party and around the country. Besides, it would look disloyal to the party if the governor of the most important swing state simply refused to be considered. One adviser who was present used a single word to describe Shapiro's attitude: "arrogance." The same adviser took the performance as "honesty, not self-sabotage." Perhaps Shapiro was just being himself. But whether he was motivated primarily by staying pristine for the 2028 Democratic presidential primary or simply expressing views of the vice presidency that did not align with Harris's, the effect was the same. Her advisers counseled her to stay away from Shapiro, and she did.

Harris met separately with her finalists at the vice president's residence on Sunday, August 4, a parade that kept the media focused—as it had been for two weeks—squarely on her. By that point, the decision was all but made—more than a formality but less than an open question. Harris clicked with Walz, as most of her advisers predicted she would. He put her at ease. "She wasn't going to have to wake up worried if he was knifing her," one campaign adviser said.

Harris aides quietly went to work updating materials on Walz and planning a rollout for Tuesday. There was so much to do. The two-week window was shorter than normal not just for making a selection but for logistics. Walz needed a private plane—he had never flown on one—a Secret Service detail, and a lot of instruction on the operations of a national political campaign. Veteran Harris adviser Liz Allen, who would serve as chief of staff to the running mate, booked a flight to Minnesota and a train ticket to Pennsylvania, Shapiro's home state, a move designed to keep the identity of the VP pick a secret for as long as possible. But news of Harris's decision leaked an hour earlier than planned, and Allen was still in transit to East Cliff, the Minnesota governor's temporary residence in St. Paul, when it did.

Walz had a lot of questions as he and his family scrambled to get to the airport for a flight to Philly and the new ticket's first rally that night. "How many suits do I need to pack?" he asked. "Can my wife come with me for the first night? Can my daughter come for the whole week?" From the outset, he worried about his ability to hit his marks on this new, bigger stage. *How do I make sure I don't fuck this up?* he thought. On the flight east, his new aides handed him his remarks for the rally. Looking them over as he sat next to his wife, Gwen, Walz made no significant changes. He just wanted to execute as well as possible on the campaign's plans for him. "You guys captured me pretty well," he said, unaware of the frantic work Harris advisers had put into writing a speech for a candidate they didn't know.

The Walzes met up with Harris and Emhoff in a hold room at Temple University's Liacouras Center, taking a moment to get to know one another before stepping out onstage in front of more than ten thousand Democrats who were thrilled to have a new lineup for taking on Trump. Green as he was in the national political arena, Walz gave Harris something she needed. "There was something that day that made her ascendancy much more whole and real," said one Harris campaign aide who was there. "It completed the picture." For the first time, with a VP candidate riding shotgun, it was more clear that she was number one.

★

Trump was not sure exactly how to attack his opposite number—or, more to the point, whether his team's strategy would work. The introduction of Vance as his VP pick had been a mini-nightmare, with Democrats and the news media digging up old Vance commentary, including disparagement of "childless cat ladies" and a portrayal of Trump as an American Hitler. Walz's "weird" formulation seemed to stick to Vance.

Like Fabrizio had predicted, Harris gave the Democrats a bounce. No one could have projected the record fundraising haul that accompanied her entry into the race. By the end of July, she could claim to have collected more than $300 million in less than two weeks for various accounts connected to the campaign. Nor was it easy to foresee the speed with which Democratic voters who had soured on Biden came back into the fold.

Trump freaked out, mostly about his inability—once again—to seize attention. For nearly a decade, he had dominated headlines with as little effort as it took to write a social media post. But for more than a month, and with the exception of his shooting and the Republican convention, he found himself relegated to the back burner. His team developed a concise attack against Harris: "weak, failed, dangerously liberal." It wasn't doing the trick—or at least Trump didn't think so.

On July 31, he took matters into his own hands during a panel interview at a National Association of Black Journalists convention. In an already combative session, he questioned Harris's racial identity. "She was always of Indian heritage, and she was only promoting Indian heritage," he said. "I did not know she was Black until a number of years ago when she happened to turn Black, and now she wants to be known as Black."

It didn't stop there. "I respect either one," he said, "but she obviously doesn't." He added his own question: "Is she Indian or is she Black?" Harris, the daughter of a Jamaican father and an Indian mother, had always been clear about her background. Injecting her race into the discussion, Trump implied that she was ashamed of her heritage unless it was politically advantageous to embrace it—a wink and nod that Black voters shouldn't trust her.

It was certainly part of the Trump campaign's strategy to boost his standing with voters of color, and depress hers, but not through such public and explicit messaging. He risked turning off more voters than he gained. People who knew Trump well said the episode was a sign that he had lost faith in his campaign. "When he goes off script, when he says things that you wince at because they are so base and so unnecessary," said one former senior Trump campaign adviser, "that's because he doesn't trust the plan that's in front of him or the messengers of that plan."

From a horse-race perspective, neither the campaign nor the candidate was doing anything effective enough to slow Harris's roll. On August 5, two weeks after she entered the race, Harris caught Trump in the RealClearPolitics average of national polls. She even grabbed the lead by two-tenths of a point. She closed his lead in Pennsylvania to less than 2 points and pushed past him in Michigan and Wisconsin. Harris had done more than make up the ground Biden lost while he weighed whether to stay in the fight. For the first time in months, Trump worried that he might be consigned to the dustbin of history as a one-term president and two-time loser.

All of this made Trump angry and itchy. That was usually lousy news for his top aides. He had switched campaign managers in the summers of 2016 and 2020, and his four former White House chiefs of staff had lasted an average of one year in their jobs. Wiles, LaCivita, and Miller, the three senior advisers who ran his 2024 campaign from the start, had wisely avoided giving anyone the title campaign manager. In a de facto sense, Wiles served in that role, but she never gave Trump the target title for a classic shakeup. In early August, the campaign rumor mill started spinning with reports that he was dissatisfied with his management team.

Vultures circled in the air, typically on Trump Force One, whispering the sweet nothings that usually swayed the former president: *You're right. The polling drop isn't your fault. Your team is failing you. Maybe they're lining their own pockets at the expense of your campaign. It's time to make a change.*

"Corey fed him a line of bullshit, and Trump was like 'yeah, go ahead, make sure that money is being spent properly,'" one senior campaign aide said. "Corey" was Corey Lewandowski, the first of several campaign chiefs for Trump's 2016 bid and a bit of a foxhole buddy for the former president. A surrogate for Trump on television, Lewandowski, fifty-one, had remained in Trump's orbit the old-fashioned way: sycophancy. But Wiles had been careful to keep the official campaign staff streamlined, in part for budgetary reasons and in part to avoid exactly the kind of drama that followed Lewandowski like a shadow. He wasn't on payroll in Mar-a-Lago, but he had been given a contract at the Republican National Committee.

Kellyanne Conway, the third campaign manager on Trump's 2016 team, met with Trump on August 2 and offered strategy advice—focus on policy, not personal invective against Harris. That both echoed the counsel of his advisers and rankled them because it felt like an implication that they weren't serving him well. At a time when Trump worried that things weren't going well, two of his former campaign managers came out of the woodwork to raise suspicions about his staff.

"He was just rattled throughout the course of the honeymoon period—not shaking in his boots—but he let a buddy come back in," a top Trump aide said of Lewandowski's return.

The resurfacing of Lewandowski and Conway coincided with a growing rift between Susie Wiles and deputy campaign manager Justin Caporale, the intense and hyperorganized aide who oversaw Trump's traveling road show—scheduling, planning, and executing the rallies, fundraisers, and major events for the ex-president. Wiles and Caporale had been close for years but clashed privately over operational control of Trump's campaigning.

Caporale thought Trump rallies were getting stale, and he agitated for more interactive events. Wiles thought he had a point but shut him down, knowing how much the rallies meant to the boss. Caporale did not handle that well. "If he disagrees with someone for a long period of time, he can't be respectful about it," one campaign adviser said of Caporale's interactions with Wiles. "And he pissed her off." Caporale, seeing a lifeline, aligned himself with Lewandowski.

Trump was getting pressure from donors and friends to right the ship. *I have to do something, and Corey might be the least bad option*, he thought. Lewandowski secured a "senior adviser" title and parked himself in Palm Beach, interviewing campaign officials about their jobs and the budget. He was conducting an audit at Trump's behest, he told anyone who would listen. Wiles, for the moment, played along.

"We were transparent with him," said one top Trump campaign aide. "He went to the president privately and tried the age-old 'They're stealing money and all their decisions are stupid.' And he also told the president that he should fire the entire top shelf of the campaign, like literally twelve to fifteen people."

Lewandowski's interrogations hurt morale, according to one manager who heard from junior aides. They felt "bummed out" and confused about who was in charge, the manager said, adding that he offered straightforward advice: "Stay loyal to Susie and don't worry about anything else. Because Susie will stay loyal to the president."

The audit was bogus, entirely fabricated to get Wiles and LaCivita fired, the campaign pros thought. "He was trying to motherfuck them," one senior official said.

On the Harris campaign, O'Malley Dillon was making an art of fuckery. But on the Trump side, Wiles would only tolerate so much of it.

CHAPTER 12

MAR-A-LAGO VS. KAMALOT

IN EARLY SUMMER 2022, DONALD TRUMP POLLED HIS ADVISERS AND friends about the timing and logistics of launching a third bid for the presidency, not whether it made sense to run. "I've laid out my case why I think he should do it," longtime Trump adviser Jason Miller told NBC News in June. "I think that there being clarity about what his intentions are [is important] so he can start building that operation while it's still fresh in people's minds and they're still active—a lot of that can be converted into 2024 action."

There was talk in his inner circle about a possible July 4 launch, four months ahead of the midterm elections. But some advisers cautioned that would be too early—that it would distract from Republican efforts to win Congress, dilute the spotlight on him, and potentially give Joe Biden traction at a time when he was struggling. "The clearest path is to have a cage-match rematch," another veteran adviser said. "If you have that rematch too early, it could actually help Biden a little bit. . . . Trump in modest doses has been good for Trump."

Despite the postpartum boredom of sitting on the sidelines, and his eagerness to jump back into the fight, Trump agreed to wait. But one week after Republicans underperformed expectations in the November midterms, Trump beckoned friends and family to the main ballroom at Mar-a-Lago. Between the gold-accented marble columns and below three massive chandeliers, guests listened to Trump lay out the foundation of his argument for a change—back to him—in the White House.

The expectation that Trump would run again did nothing to diminish from the audacity of the undertaking. He left office with a 29 percent approval rating after the January 6, 2021, storming of the Capitol, according to the Pew Research Center. Only one ousted president, Grover Cleveland, had ever reclaimed the White House, back in 1892. Establishment Republicans in Washington blamed him for the party's lackluster showing in the midterms. And Club for Growth Action, driven by heavyweight economic conservative donors, put out polling the day before Trump's announcement purporting to show that he trailed Florida governor Ron DeSantis in primary contests in four politically important states.

But Trump had a ride-or-die base and a story to tell. He had left Biden and Harris a country poised to roar back from Covid, he told the faithful at Mar-a-Lago. "All the incoming administration—all they had to do was just sit back and watch," he said. "Inflation was nonexistent. Our southern border was by far the strongest ever." He touched on other issues, including the Afghanistan withdrawal, oil drilling, and competition from China. But he set the main supports for his platform, which for many voters were interlocked, two years before the 2024 election. He would focus on stopping inflation and immigration.

These themes, consistent with Trump's 2016 message, reflected the needs that psychologist Abraham Maslow identified as the basic motivators of human behavior. Inflation made it harder for people to satisfy physiological needs, such as food, clothing, and shelter. Illegal immigration, at least as Trump presented it in broad terms and anecdotes, threatened their safety. As a bonus, Trump linked illegal immigration to fears that jobs—and economic security—were being taken away from citizens by outsiders.

Trump rode his message through the Republican primaries, in which a handful of challengers failed to articulate a compelling reason for the GOP to switch horses. Like Obi Wan Kenobi, attempts to strike him down only made him stronger. Both Biden and Trump had contributed to inflation, pushing trillions of dollars into the economy during a period of supply chain shocks. But inflation—a predictable outcome of rising demand and falling supply—had only hit hard during Biden's presidency.

He and his economic team hurt their own credibility with the public, telling Americans not to believe their lying wallets. First, they denied inflation was happening, then they called it "transitory." Whatever that meant, it didn't make groceries or household goods any cheaper. In the summer of 2022, Biden responded to public frustration by wrapping a law focused on climate change in a deceptive title: "The Inflation Reduction Act." The following year, he would concede that he wished he "hadn't called it that." Like any VP, Harris carried the administration's message, promoting "Bidenomics" as a cure for the nation's pocketbook ills.

By the time 2024 rolled around, Biden was still trying to sell his economy as a success to voters. The brutal truth about inflation, more than any other economic factor, is that sticker shock is obvious to everyone. Whether buying milk or a megayacht, voters could feel the pain of higher prices. Biden told them it was not as bad as it seemed, and he chose to fight for reelection on a different set of battlegrounds.

In 2020, Biden promised to "restore the soul of America," framing Trump as a threat to the nation's values and democracy itself. He convinced himself that his message delivered him to the White House, even though Trump's chaotic handling of Covid—and the economic calamity it wrought—played a clearer role in his election. Biden lucked into the presidency on the back of a pandemic that broke Trump. But he misread his win as an embrace of his defense of democracy and put that issue at the forefront of his reelection campaign. Along with much of the Democratic Party, he also misread the meaning of the midterm elections.

In the shadow of the *Dobbs* decision, which overturned federal protections for abortion rights, Democrats rallied abortion rights supporters to hold back a projected Republican wave. The GOP still took control of the House, but by a smaller-than-anticipated margin. Democrats gained a seat in the Senate, breaking a 50–50 tie. By historical standards, it was an excellent year for the president's party in his first midterm election.

But there were reasons to doubt that the issue would be as effective for Biden and his party in 2024. For starters, midterm elections are low-turnout affairs dominated by the type of high-information voters who increasingly leaned toward Democrats in the Trump era. Beyond that, the *Dobbs* decision wouldn't be as fresh two years later. And Biden, a Catholic whose views on abortion had changed over the years, was never particularly comfortable talking about it.

As the midterm results encouraged Democrats to vociferously oppose any restrictions on abortion, Trump moved to the center on the issue after wrapping up the Republican nomination. Over the years, he had held a variety of views, from full-on support for abortion rights to saying women should be punished for having the procedure. He was consistent, however, in pointing out that he appointed justices who voted to reverse the long-standing *Roe v. Wade* precedent on abortion.

With *Dobbs* in place, social conservatives—and Republican legislators—pushed for new state laws banning or tightly restricting abortion. At the federal level, some lawmakers and activist groups wanted to impose a national ban on abortions past a certain number of weeks of pregnancy. After the midterms, Trump had said Republicans lost because some of them did not endorse abortion-ban exemptions in cases of rape, incest, and when the life of the expectant mother was in danger. But for a long time, Trump tiptoed around the idea of a national ban.

In April, with his GOP rivals eating his dust and only the general election to worry about, Vince Haley convinced Trump to come out against a national ban. Haley, the top policy adviser on the campaign, prepared a slide deck for Trump that showed the existing laws in swing states. Not surprisingly, they had more liberal abortion policies than the heavily Republican areas that were pushing for state and national bans. The upshot: Trump would threaten to take rights away from swing-state voters if he backed a national ban and make it easier for abortion rights supporters to vote for him if he didn't.

On April 8, Trump released a video saying the issue should be left to the states—a light rebuke of the national-ban crowd in his own party. "The states will determine by vote or legislation, or perhaps both, and whatever they decide must be the law of the land." It wasn't so much that Trump thought he would convert progressive activists to his side. But he might be able to blunt the force of Democratic attacks by positioning himself more to the center of the political spectrum while he framed them as extremely liberal. Abortion was perhaps the clearest example of this dynamic. Biden and Harris backed no legal restrictions on abortion.

Before the June debate, Trump, his agenda, and his message were beating Biden. Persuadable voters had misgivings about Trump and his antics, but they worried more about Biden's capabilities and his record. When Democrats switched candidates, it gave Harris an opening to make major changes to the policy and messaging that had failed Biden.

She had the party's liberals from the get-go. "When Biden was the candidate, our door-knocking universe had a lot more progressives in it because we needed to persuade our own people," said one senior Harris campaign official. "After the candidate switch, the universe changed a lot because suddenly we were doing a lot better with the hard left."

For the same reason, Trump advisers rushed to staple Harris to Biden and then mix in positions from her past that placed her to the left of him. The idea was to make her own every bit of his record and the parts of her record that were outside the mainstream. They still believed a basic contrast on policy was the key to a Trump victory, and, if they were right, Harris gave them a better target.

But there was a risk that Harris's new-kid-on-the-block surge in the polls could turn into a tidal wave—especially if she continued to get sweetheart coverage from the media. Trump fumed about her treatment in the press, and his disappearance from it, as well as the ground she was making up with voters. "You know, some of his old-time friends call him up and say, 'Donald, what the fuck are you doing?'" said one high-ranking Trump aide. "And he was getting frustrated because the polling was tightening."

Just a few weeks earlier, Trump had come out of his convention as a world-beater. He had unified his party, defeated a would-be assassin, and punched Biden so hard in the teeth—not just during the debate, but over the course of the campaign—that the president could no longer seek reelection. Trump had won too soon, early enough that Democrats could swap out their candidate and put in a fresh fighter. Until the polls started turning, he was confident he could beat Harris too. But now she was closing in on him. "They rigged it," he complained to his aides. "The Democratic Party pulled a coup."

Disaffected Democrats rushed back to Harris. When Biden was struggling, Trump aides had cast hungry eyes at Virginia and Minnesota—states where they thought they could expand the electoral map. Harris put a fork in those states. Trump had seen a version of this movie before—in 2020, when he believed he was cruising to reelection before the pandemic hit. He had Lewandowski and others in his ear, telling him what he wanted to hear: his campaign was failing him.

Trump's advisers needed to calm him. Even if they were right that Harris's sugar high wouldn't last, they might not survive long enough in their jobs to see their prophecy fulfilled. Trump was on the warpath. "The more he sits around and stews, the worse it is for us," said one high-level aide. "He was pissed."

Trump was mad because he couldn't break through the media's new obsession with Harris and because his lead had disappeared, creating a virtuous cycle for her and a vicious one for him. For the sake of the campaign, and in the interest of keeping their own jobs, his advisers understood they had to show him that they were working to reverse both. Trump campaign operatives were busy building their operations in states and developing new messaging around Harris for television, the mail, and other outlets. But those activities weren't as visible to Trump as television news coverage and polls. At the same time, the portion of the press corps covering Trump had less access to him in early August because he was mostly off the campaign trail.

As the brutal summer heat descended on communities across the country, Wiles decided to kill several birds with one stone—or at least redirect them. On August 8, she and a handful of Trump's senior aides summoned reporters from leading print and television outlets to Florida for a state-of-the-race briefing. In a first-floor conference room of the West Palm Beach Hilton, with blue-swirl carpeting and a screen for slide-deck presentations, they spent three hours making the case that the fundamentals of the campaign had not really shifted—that the Harris rocket would fall back to earth.

"She owns every single decision" of the Biden-Harris administration, one of his senior advisers said from the end of a U-shaped arrangement of conference tables. Harris had said she was "the last person in the room" when Biden decided to pull troops out of Afghanistan, the adviser said. Next, he previewed attacks that would "utilize her own words" and be delivered to voters through a combination of television advertising, social media, peer-to-peer conversations, and direct mail.

The last mode—the U.S. mail—was the first vehicle for dumping on Harris. In an age of cutting-edge political communication, Wiles, senior adviser Chris LaCivita, pollster Tony Fabrizio, and political director James Blair turned to the oldest form of voter contact to get a leg up on the competition. Long before Harris's entry, Trump's team cast its eyes toward voters who were hard to reach by traditional means. In collecting data about the electorate, they determined that old-fashioned mailers—laying the groundwork for, and reinforcing, themes carried through broadcast and digital advertising—were likely to be received, read, and believed.

"Because everybody has a mailbox, you can send the exact same messages in a longer form," one of the advisers explained later. Even better, the mailers didn't draw the same attention from the rival campaign that TV ads did. It was a better way to quietly persuade voters.

The long presentation, covering polling, voter targeting, messaging, and other aspects of the campaign, came to an abrupt end as the buses pulled up to the Hilton. It was one thing to *hope* that the briefing would generate stories about Trump. But to seal the deal, Trump brought the media to Mar-a-Lago for a sprawling press conference.

Beneath the gold-paneled ceiling of his home's cavernous living room, amid arches, columns, urns, and vaguely religious murals, Trump stepped up to a lectern in a navy suit and extra-long red tie. He could hardly wait to unload.

"Kamala's record is horrible," he said little more than a minute into his opening remarks. "She's a radical-left person at a level that nobody's seen." Then he turned to her judgment in choosing Walz. "She picked a radical-left man," he said. "He's going for things that nobody's ever heard of, heavy into the transgender world, heavy into lots of different worlds having to do with safety."

It wasn't as smooth as a thirty-second TV ad, but Trump had made his point: he was going to push Harris and Walz to the left at every turn. He went back and forth with reporters for more than an hour, touching on the economy, immigration, crime, and the prospect of debates with Harris. He said he had agreed to three of them and looked forward to her joining him onstage. Also, he picked at the fresh Democratic scab—

Biden's exit. "Whether he could win or he couldn't win, he had the right to run," Trump said of the onetime rival he had cast as the worst president in American history. "They took it away."

Harris had yet to sit for a single interview since Biden dropped out—a fact increasingly highlighted by her critics and the media. So far, she had done a handful of swing-state rallies—including her first joint appearance with new vice presidential candidate Walz—with short, scripted stump speeches. But here was Trump, wheeling and dealing, with cameras pointed at him and reporters free to ask anything they wanted. It was his first media circus since the candidate switch, and the looming question was how he would approach Harris, compared to Biden.

"I haven't recalibrated strategy at all," he said. "It's the same policies. Open borders, weak on crime. I think she's worse than Biden because he got forced into the position. She was there long before. She destroyed San Francisco. She destroyed California as the AG."

But what would happen to his efforts to court Black voters now that he was facing a Black candidate?

"It changes around a little bit. I'm getting other voters. . . . I seem to be doing very well with Black males," he said. "It's possible that I won't do as well with Black women, but I do seem to be doing very well with other segments, extremely well with Hispanic. Jewish voters, way up. White males, way up. White males have gone through the roof." Black women, he added, would end up liking him better, "because I'm going to give them security, safety, and jobs" and "a good economy." For most of a decade, Trump had been campaigning on the same themes, which fit neatly under his twin slogans of "Make America Great Again" and "America First."

The last time Harris had run for president, in 2019, her bid had been hamstrung by the absence of a clear, overarching argument for what she could deliver to voters—as well as the internal drama that resulted from an aimless campaign. Most voters didn't get a chance to know her before she dropped out of that primary, and, as vice president, the public did not pay much attention to her. To the extent that it did, her approval ratings tracked a little lower than Biden's. On the day of the switch, her approval rating in a polling average compiled by *The Hill* and Decision Desk HQ stood at 42.4 percent, 10 points below her disapproval rating.

By August 4, her favorable score outpaced her unfavorable score, 47 percent to 46.7 percent.

It was obvious from the positive momentum that voters were giving Harris a chance to reintroduce herself to them. On the same day she moved into positive territory, Impact Research, one of her campaign's polling firms, sent a private memo to Wilmington inboxes that analyzed survey data to make four recommendations about her message:

- Introduce the vice president's middle-class background and prosecutorial experience to connect her with voters, help inoculate her against attacks that she is too liberal, and qualify her to stand on her own outside of President Biden;
- Define her priorities and vision for the future centered on improving people's lives through pocketbook issues, restoring abortion rights, and creating opportunities for all;
- Forcefully rebut attacks from the Trump campaign, specifically that she is dangerously liberal, bad for the economy, and will make us less safe (border + crime); and
- Drive a strong contrast against the danger posed by a Trump term, and the risks of him implementing Project 2025 and the threat of an abortion ban.

Each plank came with its own subset of supporting points. The memo had more bullets than an ammo emporium. What the pollsters did not provide—what Harris still didn't have—was a core cause for her candidacy. She was running for president because Biden stepped aside, she was next in line, and she had enough political clout to lock down the nomination. She had also inherited Biden's campaign operation and agenda. The items on the polling memo amounted to shiny ornaments, but there was not yet a Christmas tree to hang them on.

Trump advisers could see that forest clearly. "We had to marry her to Joe Biden," one of the former president's communications aides said of the Republican campaign's thinking at the time. "She was going to try to distance herself from him, and we had to make her own every single failure of the administration."

Trump expected Harris to break from Biden because the president's approval numbers had been in the toilet for years. Democratic leaders in Washington convinced themselves that his policies were popular and that voters were turned off only by his age. But polls showed that the vast majority of voters thought the country was headed off a cliff. A CNBC survey conducted the first week of August found that 22 percent of registered voters believed America was on the right track, while 66 percent said the wrong track.

Both candidates understood the importance of being seen as the bigger change agent. For Trump, that meant continuing to promise an antidote to the Biden-Harris years. For Harris, there was more flexibility to define her brand of change. She could risk looking hypocritical by making clean breaks with Biden on policies she had supported as vice president, rejecting parts of their record to forge her own agenda. She could identify new issues to run on that avoided the pitfalls of turning her back on the Biden era. Or she could rely on voters to see her gender, her genes, and her "lived experience"—a middle-class upbringing, schools outside the Ivy League, and a career as a prosecutor—as symbols of change.

Biden and his loyalists took the first option off the table. He would say publicly that Harris should do what she must to win. But privately, including in conversations with her, he repeated an admonition: let there be no daylight between us. "No daylight" was the phrase he had used as a vice presidential candidate in 2008 to bind Republican nominee John McCain to an unpopular president, George W. Bush.

Almost everywhere she went, Harris walked among former Biden aides who sought to defend his presidency. Her campaign was run by a former White House deputy chief of staff—whom she had just empowered to box out her own confidants—and a phalanx of department heads who had served Biden until the previous month.

By circumstance, there was one exception: her debate prep team. Before Trump named JD Vance as his running mate, and before the Trump-Biden debate, Harris put together a squad to help her get ready for a vice presidential debate. To lead the group, she tapped two women who had trained her for her matchup against Vice President Mike Pence in 2020: Washington lawyer Karen Dunn, who was not related to Anita Dunn, and longtime policy adviser Rohini Kosoglu.

Starting in mid-June, Harris sat in writers'-room-style sessions with a band of close confidants that one aide referred to as "Kamalot": Dunn, Kosoglu, former representative Cedric Richmond, Democratic National Convention chair Minyon Moore, California-based political consultant Sean Clegg, Tony West, Lorraine Voles, Sheila Nix, and communications aides Brian Fallon and Kirsten Allen.

In part because they didn't know who her opponent would be, and in part because the running mate's role is to attack the other party's presidential candidate, the Kamalot crew focused on crafting arguments against Trump. Dunn and Kosoglu mapped out twenty topics, and the group workshopped each issue into its own one-page study guide. Their early work was of little concern to the Biden campaign team, which was naturally more focused on getting him ready for his debate with Trump—and then trying to save his candidacy.

In later weeks, when it was time to start rehearsing, the Harris squad met at Howard University. Over the course of June, July, and August—as Harris rose from the bottom of the ticket to the top—they developed what one participant said became "the foundation for her presidential campaign." When Harris spoke at her first rally as the presidential candidate in Wisconsin in late July, twin pillars of her speech were lines that had come out of the writers' room: "We are not going back" and "I know Donald Trump's type."

But there were limits to what the Kamalot crew could do to position Harris substantively as a break from Biden. Shortly after she took the reins of the campaign, her advisers met with veteran Biden policy hands. Clegg, who had worked with Harris going back to her days in California, was shocked at the messaging materials he had seen coming from the campaign and was looking forward to engaging on the economic plans. *There's no fucking future in our message*, he thought. *Campaigns are about the future. And we have no fucking future economic message.*

Harris turned early to Brian Deese, who had spearheaded Biden's economic agenda as director of the White House's National Economic Council. She trusted him from his days in the administration and wanted him to have "a role whenever she was talking about the economy," said one senior Harris aide. Deese counseled that Harris should not roll out any plans that were not already in the president's budget. The stated purpose was to make sure that her promises did not "score"— Washingtonspeak for cost—too much.

Trump had a website full of videos promising popular policies that would run up annual deficits and the national debt by trillions of dollars. Seemingly every day, he added to that pile. Harris's new campaign team—the old Biden guard—put on their green eyeshades just when she needed to be motivating voters along the Blue Wall. Between the Kamalot team and the veteran Biden hands, a patchwork of small-bore ideas became her economic agenda.

Sure, Harris could play around the edges. She could speak loftily about an "opportunity economy," taking on corporate greed, and expanding the Child Tax Credit. But Biden's loyalists drew a hard line at anything that smacked of a rebuke of the president's record. Biden too had tried to sell his policies as a boon for the economy—from incentives for making computer chips and electric vehicles to major infrastructure projects—but had failed to convince voters.

"The people cooking the policy, these were all Biden people," said one Harris aide. Harris herself was no expert on the economy. Wall Street jargon hit her ears like a foreign language. And no matter how much coaching she got on the topic, it was never comfortable for her. But she could usually hit her marks in a speech.

On August 16, two days before the Democratic convention, and after weeks of unanswered questions about her plans for the issue most on voters' minds, she flew to Raleigh, North Carolina, to deliver an address on her economic agenda. She opened with an ode to Bidenomics. She concluded that "today, by virtually every measure, our economy is the strongest in the world." That, of course, had been true every day for generations. Harris touched on her promise of an "opportunity economy" and said Trump would take the country backward.

Harris told her audience at Wake Technical Community College that she would offer a $25,000 tax credit to first-time homebuyers. The Biden budget had proposed the same policy but at $15,000. She said she would restore the Child Tax Credit and expand it to $6,000 in the first year of a child's life—another tweak to a Biden policy.

But the key component of the address—a promise to implement a federal ban on price-gouging on groceries—turned into a public relations nightmare. "SOVIET Style Price Controls," Trump wrote on Truth Social. News outlets covered the pledge the same way. In her team's contortions to give her something new to talk about, it had landed on a narrow policy that painted her as a lefty on economics. She had been boxed in by the president, his former aides, and her own lack of a unique vision for the American economy.

She did not have the background to create a broad economic agenda. Neither Biden nor his former aides wanted her to formulate one. She would have to stick to personal characteristics to differentiate herself from a president who left many Americans worried about their ability to pay for necessities, much less luxuries.

"The consensus view that was provided to her was to focus on biographical and experiential differences," said one Harris adviser. "So that was the answer."

CHAPTER 13

"NO DAYLIGHT, KID"

W E GOTTA GET HIM ON!" STEVE RICCHETTI EXHORTED. "PEOPLE ARE leaving!"

It was getting late on Monday, August 19, the first night of the Democratic National Convention in Chicago, and President Joe Biden was in danger of finding out whether a speech delivered after prime time on the East Coast made a sound. Ricchetti, his trusted White House counselor, had already spent hours prodding convention officials—newly beholden to Vice President Kamala Harris—to skip over segments of the night's slow-developing program and put Biden onstage. If Harris's team couldn't do that, speaking to empty seats at the United Center and a diminished TV audience would be a brutal final humiliation for Biden.

This was supposed to have been his coronation. He had been looking forward to it for four years, ever since Covid robbed him of a crowd—the rowdy and adoring kind—at the 2020 Democratic National Convention. He was still a little bitter about that. But he had expected a remedy. Just twenty-nine days ago, this convention was going to be *his* convention. He was going to be at its center, perfectly placed to soak in the pomp and adulation he craved.

Now Biden just hoped to make it onstage before folks in the East Coast's so-called Acela Corridor went to bed. It had been a rocky opening day for convention officials. Protests against Israel's war in Gaza and long lines at the metal detectors delayed delegates' arrival to the arena. Convention leaders had to push back the opening gavel. Speakers ran past their allotted times, many of them refusing to interrupt applause. Shawn Fain, the president of the United Auto Workers, ran an end-around to expand his time in the spotlight. In addition to the remarks he gave the Harris campaign to load into a teleprompter, he pulled out extra pages and read from them. "It's getting hot in here," he said, quoting the hip-hop star Nelly and taking off his jacket to reveal a T-shirt that read TRUMP IS A SCAB. His performance excited the crowd, but it infuriated aides who were desperate to get back on schedule.

By the time Biden slid into his custom limousine to ride to the United Center at 8:30 p.m., it was already clear that his speaking slot would slip back. Because of the time difference, that meant at least part of his speech would be delivered deep into the night. Seething on the inside, Biden had to smile on the outside. He had high-profile visitors to greet.

Bill and Hillary Clinton found Biden backstage, where he was going over his speech in a holding area. Harris and Walz were already with him. The Clintons had not seen Biden since he dropped out, and they wanted to "give him a hug," said someone who witnessed the small gathering of Democratic royalty past and present. The group sang "Happy Birthday" to Bill Clinton, who turned seventy-eight that day, before breaking up.

But with each tick of the clock, Biden grew ever more irritated. These people were going to deny him his last big moment on the national political stage. He had slayed the MAGA dragon in 2020 and then, just a month ago, given everything up in a bid to save the party. There was no gratitude. They were all so eager to get rid of him. This final insult, his gold-watch retirement ceremony playing out to an emptying arena and a smaller TV audience, really burned. He wouldn't go down that quietly. He was going to fight for his due.

Ricchetti checked in regularly with campaign and convention officials to find out when the president might actually take the stage. "He's upset because the boss is upset," said one person who watched the dynamic play out. As the evening wore on, Biden and his team increasingly saw a darker side to the delays. "Steve was assuming somebody was out to fuck Biden," said one person who spoke with him.

That's how Ricchetti, one of the most powerful men in the country, found himself cajoling convention officials—half-ordering, half-pleading—to do what the president wanted. "He's going to be talking to no one!" Ricchetti exclaimed. "He's going to go on at midnight."

"He was calling, ringing everybody," one of the convention officials said. O'Malley Dillon, who spent time with the Biden team in the president's box at the convention hall and backstage, took the brunt of Ricchetti's fire. She and other campaign and convention staff were caught between Biden and Harris, forced to navigate a new reality that pitted the president's interests against the vice president's. Much as he might want it to be, the convention was not about Biden. O'Malley Dillon told Stephanie Cutter, the programming chief for the convention, that Biden's team was insisting that he be put in front of cameras more quickly. But Cutter, a close friend and longtime business partner of O'Malley Dillon, wasn't sure how to do that.

Cutter pointed to each of the speakers who had been picked by the president's team to lead up to him and asked the same question over and over: "Do you want me to cut this?" Cutter did what she could to speed things along. She slashed a planned performance by the singer James Taylor, a favorite of the Bidens, and a biographical video produced by filmmaker Dawn Porter about the president that had been touched up by Steven Spielberg. There were certain segments she could not jettison. Biden's personal friends, like Delaware senator Chris Coons, and family members would not be on the chopping block, for example. There was not much more she could do. First Lady Jill Biden and First Daughter Ashley Biden took speaking slots that ramped up to the president's address.

When Joe Biden finally took the stage at 11:25 p.m. on the East Coast, he recounted his reason for running in 2020—"to save democracy"—and boasted about his record. It sounded like the speech he had planned to give before he stepped aside, and some Democrats detected a note of fury in his voice.

"I'm glad he wasn't in prime time, because he was so fucking angry," said one Harris adviser who thought O'Malley Dillon could have done more to influence Biden. "There was hardly anything in there about Kamala Harris. We're going to have JOD in charge, and she can't even make her former boss's speech be about Kamala Harris?"

Biden did talk about Harris, but not in the most helpful way. "We've had one of the most extraordinary four years of progress ever," he said to cheers. "When I say 'we,' I mean Kamala and me." That was the foundation of a motif in the speech: over and over, he would name a policy and then say they had implemented it together. Trump hoped to tie Harris to Biden. Biden, still convinced of the persuasiveness of his own record, did that for Trump.

Most voters did not see Biden's first term as the most compelling recommendation to give him a second term. Harris would have to give them a different reason to elect her over Trump, and her Thursday-night acceptance speech—the first by a woman of color—would give her an opportunity to articulate it to an audience of tens of millions of Americans.

In the spring, she had tapped Adam Frankel, an author and veteran of the Obama White House speechwriting team, to draft her convention remarks. He was working on her vice presidential speech on the Sunday that Biden dropped out of the race, and both candidate and wordsmith had to pivot quickly from touting Biden to promoting her. "She knew going into it that the key moments on the campaign would be the convention speech and debates—however many debates there would be—and so she really prioritized it from the beginning," said one person close to Harris.

At the start, Frankel effectively interviewed Harris about her life, pulling out details to form a biographical section that would lay the groundwork for her to present herself as a change candidate. *This is my best chance to reintroduce myself,* she thought. Over the course of a month, they discussed the speech and sent drafts back and forth. *Trump talks about Making America Great Again, but I want voters to understand that I'm a patriot—that I believe this country is great and that I am a patriot,* she thought. Of course, her speech would touch on policy—but at a thirty-thousand-foot level, both because white papers don't inspire voters and because she had not yet fleshed out a detailed agenda. She would praise Biden, but not spend so much time on him as to make it even harder to differentiate herself.

All of that was important to Harris, but perhaps not as crucial as her tone on Trump. Democrats talked about him in apocalyptic and hyperbolic terms all too often and that was counterproductive, she thought. No matter the color of his hair, straw-man arguments did not work against Trump. She insisted that her remarks stick to the facts, building a case against him in prosecutorial fashion. *Add all the truths up,* she thought, *and it will be more effective. No need for hype. Clear and clinical. Keep your credibility by avoiding claims that can be disputed or refuted.*

"Show the math," she told Frankel.

After Harris arrived in the Windy City on Monday—three days before her address at the United Center—she hunkered down with a small group of aides in a basement ballroom at the Park Hyatt, on Michigan Avenue.

That day, Harris walked into the ballroom, a space made to look like the convention hall, complete with a podium and chairs set up where certain delegations would be sitting in the convention hall. Inside the ballroom, Harris did a conversational read-through of the speech instead of a performative practice. It was nothing like the one she would deliver on Thursday night, before the crowd and under the arena lights.

"Her attorney general staff nicknamed her Iverson," one senior adviser to Harris noted, referring to the basketball legend Allen Iverson. "She doesn't practice like she plays." Harris had been reviewing the speech multiple times a day throughout the week alongside top aides. Each time, she made tweaks, adding "very small bits and pieces to the speech," but not major rewrites.

On Thursday morning, hours before Harris would take the stage for one of the biggest political moments of her life, she and her convention speech crew had to practice in masks after Frankel tested positive for Covid-19. With Frankel holed up in his hotel room, he joined the group on Zoom for the final run-throughs of the speech. *The last thing the VP needs right now is to worry about Covid today,* Frankel thought, feeling horrible for creating the situation.

But it didn't seem to bother Harris, who immediately asked Frankel how he was feeling while suggesting remedies for him. At 8:37 p.m. the Harris motorcade sped through Chicago on an eleven-minute ride to the United Center, with the vice president sitting in the back of an SUV and making one last round of adjustments to her script. Wearing a navy pantsuit that flared at her ankles, Harris strode confidently into the backstage area, where Secret Service agents in full tactical gear, Democratic insiders, and the convention crew milled about. In her hands, Harris carried nothing more than the Democratic Party's hopes of defeating Trump.

By any measure, Harris was riding atop a political wave as she stepped to the wooden lectern on the United Center stage, with American flags behind her and to her sides. From her perspective, the screaming delegates in front of her served as the most obvious sign of the momentum at her back. They had been warmed up over previous nights by an all-star cast of Democratic luminaries, including the Obamas and the Clintons. Michelle Obama and Hillary Clinton, in particular, had primed the crowd—Hillary by pointing, as only she could, to the place Harris took in the pantheon of women in politics, and Michelle by ripping into Trump.

The electric atmosphere inside the convention hall reflected what Harris had seen on the campaign trail. It had been hard at times for her to fill rooms as a vice presidential candidate. As the leader of a party overjoyed by the candidate switch, she was getting used to seeing thousands of faces when she spoke.

But polling carried the most telling data points. On the night of her acceptance speech, she held a 1.5 percentage-point lead over Trump in the RealClearPolitics average of national polls. The race had moved 4.5 points in the Democrats' direction in the fifty-six days since Biden's debate flop. There was every reason for her to think that she would be in the fight of her life down the stretch. But there was also reason, in this moment of excitement and party unity, to believe she could win.

The history she made, just by accepting the nomination, was lost on no one in the building. Harris never wanted voters to see her through the lenses of race, ethnicity, and gender. She thought that undermined her achievements. "Kamala has always been a person who says, 'I'm not going to be reduced to that. I'm not going to be reduced to your demographic,'" said one longtime adviser. But she did ask her aides to find a way to pay homage to Shirley Chisholm, the New York congresswoman who, at the 1972 Democratic convention, became the first Black woman to win delegates. She landed on a reference so subtle that few, if any, voters made the connection.

"I see an America where we hold fast to the fearless belief that built our nation and inspired the world," Harris said in defining her brand of patriotism. "An America where we care for one another, look out for one another, and recognize that we have so much more in common than what separates us. That none of us—none of us has to fail for all of us to succeed. And that in unity, there is strength." Chisholm had delivered the last line during the roll call vote at the 1972 convention, seeking the right to speak so that she could throw her support to the party's nominee, South Dakota senator George McGovern.

No one argued for Harris leaning into her race and gender—especially with Republicans casting her as a "DEI" candidate—but when she broke from Biden on personal characteristics, rather than policy, it implicitly highlighted those aspects of her candidacy. In other words, if she simply was a different person than Biden, it was hard for voters not to notice her race and gender.

In his suite at the Trump International Hotel in Las Vegas, surrounded by advisers, Trump interrupted a debate-prep session to focus on Harris's speech and respond to her in real time on Truth Social. Natalie Harp, a gatekeeper and gofer in his traveling entourage, tapped out the messages he dictated on a laptop. Former Democratic presidential candidate Tulsi Gabbard; Florida representative Matt Gaetz; and advisers Susie Wiles, Jason Miller, and Stephen Miller sat arrayed around Trump at a dining table and in an adjacent living room.

Trump attacked Harris for the number of "thank-yous" she said at the start of her remarks. He torched her for going after Project 2025. The plan, a nine-hundred-page compilation of conservative policy ideas cooked up by former Trump aides and their allies, had caused heartburn for the Republican's campaign. Many of the proposals were part of Trump's stated agenda, but some of them—for example, outlawing pornography—risked alienating swing voters. It was relatively easy for Democrats to use the whole book to portray Trump as an extremist.

Trump and his campaign disavowed the project in late July, and Harris mentioning it in her convention speech set him off. So did accusing him of trying to cut Medicare and Social Security. He responded to hit after hit. At times he took suggestions from Gaetz and others to formulate his posts. When Harris finished, Trump called in to Fox News to preview a theme he would return to on the campaign trail: "Why didn't she do the things that she's complaining about?" he said. "She could have done it three and a half years ago."

Unlike his Democratic rivals, Trump rejected the very idea that he should formally prepare for debates. So his occasional sessions, like the one in Las Vegas, typically consisted of freewheeling conversations with a handful of official and unofficial advisers. Despite the change in polls, and his overall anxiety about the state of the race, he felt even more confident than usual heading into a September matchup with Harris. After all, he had knocked the last Democrat he faced clean out of the ring. He was also on the verge of picking up the support of an important booster.

On August 23, the day after the Democratic convention ended, Robert F. Kennedy Jr. suspended his independent bid for the presidency. Many of his Democratic-leaning supporters had already lined up behind Harris, meaning that his third-party candidacy could derail Trump. Though he registered in the low to mid single digits of most multi-candidate surveys, he was in a position to play spoiler. Kennedy, son of the slain former attorney general, senator, and presidential candidate, had built a following through an unorthodox coalition that included vaccine skeptics. Trump had long pursued Kennedy's endorsement, and its delivery promised to give him new voters.

It was a rare blip of good news for Trump in the summer of Harris's ascent. A private Hart Research Associates survey taken for the Harris campaign from August 26 through August 28 showed her leading Trump by 2 percentage points across battleground states. Even if polls were off, there was no doubt that the race had moved in the Democrats' direction.

But the survey contained red flags for Harris, perils that the Trump team could see more clearly. Voters were most likely to cite inflation and immigration as their top concerns. Those were also the issues on which Trump had the biggest edge. By a 54 percent to 37 percent spread, they preferred Trump on dealing with immigration and border security. Respondents also said he would be better at handling inflation, by a 48 percent to 39 percent margin. More broadly, they picked him as best positioned to deal with the economy (50 percent to 41 percent) and crime (47 percent to 42 percent), even though he had been convicted in New York and the first bullet point in Harris's biography was her work as a prosecutor.

Voters also thought he would be a stronger leader—48 percent to 43 percent. Harris led on most of the attributes tested, including handling abortion (56 percent to 32 percent) and having the mental stability to serve as president (50 percent to 38 percent), but not on the policies that mattered most to the highest share of the electorate.

Even a cursory read of the data suggested that she was ahead despite trailing Trump on the key issues, and that she would need to persuade more voters that she would be better for their pocketbooks than Trump. "The results from this exercise are an important reminder that this election is first and foremost about economics," the pollsters wrote in an underlined sentence—at the bottom of the third page of a memo accompanying the survey.

The underlying numbers were one reason for Harris campaign aides to worry about the sustainability of her sugar-rush surge. She also had been given little exposure to voters, rising with guardrails around her public appearances. More than a month into her candidacy, Harris still had not participated in an interview with a major media outlet or held a formal press conference. David Plouffe, who acted as a narrative-setter and in-house consultant to O'Malley Dillon, liked to talk about the art of running for president as a "decathlon," in which the political athlete had to compete in a series of contests—convention speeches, debates, press conferences, and the like—to win. Cutter, a former aide to presidents Clinton and Obama who had cofounded a political consulting firm with O'Malley Dillon, was tapped to coach the vice president for one set of events: a round of high-stakes postconvention interviews.

It was hard to remember exactly how many campaigns Cutter had played major roles in—going back at least to John Kerry in 2004—and she would not let Harris or anyone else forget that she had the most experience. *Why is Stephanie doing all the talking?* one adviser thought while watching her handle Harris by dictating answers to various questions. *Did she read the background material or is she workshopping this on the fly? The VP isn't getting any reps in.*

The day before Harris's first interview, a joint appearance with Tim Walz, she dived into the recurring question of whether and when she would let daylight shine between herself and Biden. Cutter launched into a proposed preamble—a list of all the items that made Harris proud of her work with Biden.

"Wait, wait, wait!" said Sean Clegg, a longtime Harris adviser whom the vice president had brought in to help Frankel with the convention speech, work on her debate prep team, and counsel her on interviews. "Let's not do this. Let's not go down memory lane." That was the last time he was invited to media prep. Cutter, another Harris confidant later joked, cut him out.

When Harris sat down with Walz and CNN's Dana Bash the last week of August, the segment produced a little bit of news: Harris said she would name a Republican to serve in her Cabinet. She also said that she no longer supported a ban on fracking. Her 2019 call to end the practice threatened to hurt her in Pennsylvania, even though she had adopted Biden's no-ban policy as his vice presidential candidate in 2020. But the first portion of the one-on-two interview—the part more viewers were likely to watch—featured Harris reciting a laundry list of Biden's policies.

Sitting next to Walz in a chair that seemed to place her below him and heaping praise on Biden's record, Harris did not look like a candidate seeking the highest office in the land. The whole scene reinforced the criticism that the vice president was either incapable, or afraid, of answering tough questions on her own. For the rest of the campaign, her team required that she be provided a chair that met certain specifications: "Leg height no less than 15 inches; floor to top of seat height no less than 18.9 inches; arms on chairs may not be very high, arms must fall at a natural height; chairs must be firm."

No matter how firm her chair, the question facing Harris was whether she could build a sturdy platform. Her rallies and convention speech had not answered the question of why she was running for president—or how her vision for the country would deliver for voters—other than having been next in line. She was running out of major moments to explain a vision to a broad audience. Her September 10 debate with Trump would offer another opportunity—perhaps a last chance before voters cast early ballots—to establish that key part of her narrative.

All the same, Harris was on a roll. She had locked in her delegates, closed down a rollicking convention, and pushed past Trump to take a lead in most polls. Aides to both Harris and Trump expected her to enjoy a honeymoon period. Few of them thought it would last this long. Trump believed it would come to an end on the debate stage at Philadelphia's National Constitution Center.

If there was one thing Trump didn't count on, it was how hard Harris would work to get ready for him. He mocked her for taking five days off the campaign trail to sequester in a hotel and rehearse. But she had been training for him for months. When her prep team started meeting at her house in June, she didn't have an opponent for the VP debate. For that reason, and because the VP's job is to tear into the other party's presidential candidate, much of her focus went into Trump. She had all that under her belt when she hunkered down for "debate camp" at the Omni William Penn, a regal early-twentieth-century hotel across the way from Pittsburgh's Mellon Square, on September 5.

On a commuter flight from Washington to Pittsburgh that morning, several members of her debate team spotted what appeared to be an auspicious omen. Former vice president Mike Pence, keeping a low profile under the brim of a baseball cap, sat one row behind Philippe Reines. When the plane landed, Rohini Kosoglu motioned to Reines, a longtime Hillary Clinton aide who had been brought into Harris's fold to play the role of Trump.

"That's Mike Pence," Kosoglu said in a low tone.

Reines's brow furrowed. "The former vice president?" he asked.

"No, the other one," Kosoglu teased. She had not seen Pence since that time a fly landed in his hair during a 2020 debate against Harris. Kosoglu had been backstage that night, certain for a moment that the fly was a spot on the television screen.

After exiting the plane, Reines waited for Pence on the walkway to their gate. "Mr. Vice President, I just want to introduce myself," Reines said, "because this is a pretty funny coincidence." Pence kept a poker face when Reines asked if he should send the former vice president's regards to Harris. "Great," Reines said. "I'll take that as an endorsement."

As the rest of the Harris team deplaned, Reines pointed them out to Pence and asked if he had any tips for the group. For the first time, Pence's demeanor changed. He had been stoic. Now he offered his take. "She's very good on the attack," Pence said. "Less so on her record."

On a Frankenstein's monster of a debate prep team, which included longtime Harris confidants, advisers from what had recently been Biden's campaign, and White House officials, Reines stuck out as a particularly unlikely appendage.

Square-faced, with dark hair graying at the temples, he was a Hillary Clinton man, through and through. In 2016 he had nailed a Trump portrayal for Clinton. Karen Dunn, who headed up Harris's debate prep with Kosoglu, wanted him to reprise the Trump role. When Biden dropped out in June, Reines was in the midst of drafting a memo to Harris's aides on JD Vance—in case Trump picked Vance for his ticket—and had been growing out his beard to more closely resemble the Ohio senator. At the time, Biden campaign officials were far less concerned about Harris's debate prep than the president's. Now all the focus was on Harris.

Reines approached the assignment with the commitment of Joaquin Phoenix. At a tanning salon, he told the attendant he wanted to look like Trump—"but not in a Halloween kind of way." They tried one coat of spray tan on his face and neck. It didn't do the trick. Next he went to a Sephora store. No dice. His stylist told him she couldn't dye his hair Trump's color without lasting effect. He searched Amazon wigs for something that would work. In the end, Reines just soaked his hair with gel, combed the sides back, and pulled the top forward at an extreme angle. For the mock sessions in Pittsburgh, he wore a dark suit and knotted an extra-long red tie at his collar.

Inside the William Penn's grand ballroom, with its soaring ceilings and a gilded indoor balcony, Harris and Reines stood behind lecterns on a full replica of the actual debate set. The lights were turned down low, giving the 6,000-square-foot cavern the feel of a theater. Video cameras fed tight shots of the debaters to monitors. By this point they had been through so many rounds of table-read-style sessions focused on particular topics that the content of the back-and-forth was well honed. Reines focused on behaving like Trump. Unlike most in his party, he believed the former president was extraordinarily predictable. He largely avoided making eye contact with Harris, knowing that Trump would refuse to look at her. He interrupted her at times, knowing Trump might do that.

Harris and her team batted around ideas for how to respond to the Biden question: What made her different from the unpopular president? She was deeply reluctant to diverge from him in any real way. Some in her orbit attributed that to unfailing loyalty to the man who picked her first as vice president and then endorsed her for his job. Others blamed Biden, his White House aides, and a campaign leadership that remained devoted to him. These advisers said Biden pressured her explicitly and implicitly to avoid embarrassing him. Harris received "mixed messages" from the White House—Biden on one side and his staff on the other—according to one senior Harris adviser.

There was some element of truth to all of it, but ultimately Harris believed it was her duty to stand by the president, and Biden would never let her forget it.

I am part of the administration, Harris thought. *I sat in the Oval Office for all of these big decisions. Even when I disagree, it is my job to rally behind the president, and I always have. How could I change that now? How dishonest would that look? How dishonest would it be? I can't say "I wish he would have done this" or "I wouldn't have done it that way."*

"That was just never going to happen," said one top Harris adviser who spoke to her about the roles of vice president and candidate. "It's just not her."

Even if Harris was willing to pay a political price, some of her advisers believed she could split the distance between a lifetime commitment to Biden and a full divorce. Maybe a trial separation would do the trick.

"The answer needed to be something like, 'Look, I think the president needed to be a lot more aggressive addressing the cost of living, and that's what I'm going to do, and that's what my plans do,'" said one adviser who participated in the sessions. "People are pissed at Biden about the failure and tone-deafness on the economy." What Harris landed on—another iteration of the idea that she differed from Biden only in personal characteristics—was "I am not Joe Biden, and I am certainly not Donald Trump."

The mock sessions were grueling, even for a lawyer who had spent years of her life engaged in legal battles. Four days in, Harris hit a wall. Worn down, she paused the practice for a Sunday walk through Pittsburgh with her husband, Doug Emhoff. "You have to know when to just stop," said one person who attended the sessions. "We felt like this is just too much for any human to bear." Cutting short the plan for Pittsburgh, she flew to Philadelphia on Monday, the day before the debate. After nearly two months of nonstop activity, Harris needed a breather.

Tuesday afternoon, hours before she would step on the stage with Trump, Harris and her advisers found a small room in her hotel for a final tune-up. Reines wanted to signal that this would be a lighter round of sparring. For the first time, he did not dress up as Trump. He wore a baseball cap. And he committed the cardinal sin in Harris's world: he showed up late. Standing at lecterns positioned close together, they recited well-worn lines to each other.

"We only have time for one closing statement," Dunn said, playing the role of moderator. Harris drew back to go into her practiced spiel, only to be surprised by Dunn's next line. "We'll now hear from the former president."

"Oh," Harris said, raising her eyebrows.

"The media says I lie twice a minute, but they don't give me any credit for sometimes telling the truth," Reines said. "So for a few minutes, I am going to tell the truth.

"What kind of crazy politician is always on time?" he said, referring to Harris. He launched into a rant on the price of bacon—a feature of previous sessions. Pulling his arms in tight and scrunching his shoulders together—a mouselike pose—Reines spoke in a squeaky voice. "Even though I'm big and loud, I'm really a very small, scared person," he said. "I'm a very sick man. I suffer from neurosyphilis."

Then, changing his voice back to his normal baritone, Reines riffed off the top of his head about Harris, looking directly at her for the first time. He closed with a twist on the "radical" term he had thrown at her in months of prep sessions. "You are *radically ready*," he said. "You got this!"

Harris walked over and hugged him.

That evening, before the debate, Biden called to give Harris a different kind of pep talk—and another reminder about the loyalty he demanded. No longer able to defend his own record, he expected Harris to protect his legacy. Whether she won or lost the election, he thought, she would only harm him by publicly distancing herself from him—especially during a debate that would be watched by millions of Americans. To the extent that she wanted to forge her own path, Biden had no interest in giving her room to do so. He needed just three words to convey how much all of that mattered to him.

"No daylight, kid," Biden said.

CHAPTER 14

MOTHAFUCKA

SO, BE COGNIZANT," DONALD TRUMP SAID, "BUT DON'T GO CRAZY?"

Two hours before his debate with Harris, Trump wanted to make sure he understood the rules of the road. Standing at his lectern during a walk-through of the small studio at Philadelphia's National Constitution Center, he confirmed with organizers that his microphone would not be cut off if one of his answers ran a little bit long. He should be aware of the clock and try to stick to it but not worry about going over.

Harris had spent the previous five days in Pennsylvania rehearsing every aspect of her first-ever meeting with Trump, down to how, if at all, she would greet him. Trump whisked in that evening on Trump Force One with all the concern of a college senior auditing an elective—or of a candidate who had bludgeoned his last debate rival to political death. His advisers worried that he was too cocky and not focused enough on Harris. Whatever her flaws, her fuse box wasn't going to blow like Biden's had. On the flight from Palm Beach, they went over a handful of key points they thought still needed emphasis after a short series of undisciplined prep sessions in previous days.

Harris still had not laid out a comprehensive agenda for the country. Trump and his advisers thought that was a major vulnerability that he needed to exploit. "All of a sudden, she was like Miss I-Have-A-Plan, but wouldn't really articulate her plan," one Trump adviser said. That made it harder for him to draw sharp contrasts with her on policy—where his advisers always thought he would succeed against his Democratic foe, whether it was Biden or Harris. If she couldn't say what she would do for the country in a coherent way, Trump could point that out. If she started listing her plans, he could ask why she and Biden had not implemented them in their time in office. *Win-win*, Trump thought.

Just before go-time, Harris gathered with a small clutch of family and advisers in a tented temporary greenroom. She told them she had called her pastor to pray and that she was ready for this, the biggest political test of her life. Then she took a moment to herself, engaging her mental mechanism, before ABC News moderator David Muir called the candidates to the stage. Trump made a beeline for his lectern. Harris walked past hers, to meet him behind his.

"Kamala Harris," she said, extending her hand. She had practiced various versions of the walk-out moment at debate camp. Would he ignore her? Should she ignore him? She landed on confronting him with courtesy, part of a broader strategy of trying to get in his head. "Have a good debate," she said.

"Nice to see you," Trump replied, taking her hand and shaking it. "Have fun."

The plan to knock her rival off-kilter developed over the course of several weeks, with a good portion of it coming from a former White House official whose eleven-day run as Trump's communications director made his last name a standard measurement of time in Washington: Anthony Scaramucci.

Over a weekend in mid-August, Karen Dunn and Rohini Kosoglu connected with Scaramucci, who had known Trump for years. Speaking to them from his home in the Hamptons for six hours over two days, Scaramucci mapped out the sensitive parts of Trump's psyche, from the size of the crowds at his rallies to his intellect and how he was viewed by foreign dignitaries. His thoughts, scrawled in blue pen beneath the heading "under his skin," became part of the debate-prep bible and Harris's fusillade onstage.

"People start leaving his rallies early out of exhaustion and boredom," "World leaders are laughing at Donald Trump," and "Not everybody got handed $400 million on a silver platter and then filed bankruptcy six times"—the latter, a line that Philippe Reines fashioned with Harris adding the silver platter—were among the bamboo shoots Harris jabbed under Trump's fingernails.

Agitated each time, he spent precious minutes defending himself against personal attacks that had nothing to do with the policy issues his advisers wanted him to stay focused on. She was on such a roll that she came close to improvising a compound rhetorical bomb. When Muir asked Harris about her level of culpability for the botched U.S. withdrawal from Afghanistan, she pivoted to a takedown of Trump's handling of the peace deal that brought it about. He had negotiated the pullout, she said. It was a terrible agreement, she added, needling the man who prided himself as the best dealmaker in the world. But there was more, she believed, to be outraged about.

The word flashed through Harris's head. She even started to say it, as she looked dead-eyed at Trump. "And this"—*mothafucka*, she thought, her face contorting as she caught herself—"former president, as president, invited them to Camp David." In her telling, he had desecrated hallowed ground by bringing in the leaders of a terrorist group for a photo op—a slap in the face to the Americans they had killed and to the military.

Scaramucci had given another bit of counsel to Harris's team in August. Dunn and Kosoglu asked him whether it made sense for the vice president to fact-check Trump in real time if he said things that were not true. "That's not her job," Scaramucci advised. "Her job is to get out her economic, immigration, social policy messages. If she starts to fact-check him, she's going to look like a substitute teacher. And that's going to diminish her."

Harris left that to Muir and his co-moderator, Linsey Davis. They corrected Trump repeatedly when he made false assertions, declining to give Harris the same treatment when she bent the truth. Infuriated, Trump aides Chris LaCivita, Jason Miller, and Justin Caporale demanded an audience with John Santucci, a top ABC producer, in the middle of the debate. The atmosphere around Trump's campaign was already tense, with outsiders like Corey Lewandowski telling the boss that his aides were failing him. The top campaign aides saw Trump's face tighten as they watched the fact-checking from a hold room. They knew they had to intervene—or at least try.

"What the fuck is this?" LaCivita, a retired marine, bellowed at Santucci when the campaign convoy caught up to him in a hallway outside the studio. "That is a fuck job!"

"We are in the control room. We are in the ears," Santucci said, suggesting that executives were pressing the moderators to dial it back. "We are trying."

By the traditional measures of debate optics, Harris ran circles around Trump. She deployed her attacks as planned, unnerved him, and kept her cool. Most of all, viewers could plainly see that she relished the fight. But this wasn't like the Trump-Biden debate, where one candidate responded like a punch-drunk boxer. Despite getting distracted at times by tangents, and sparring with the moderators, Trump landed serious blows that previewed his fall campaign.

"Now she wants to do transgender operations on illegal aliens that are in prison," Trump said. "This is a radical-left liberal that would do this. She wants to confiscate your guns and she will never allow fracking in Pennsylvania." Most important, he framed his economic record in terms that rang true with many persuadable voters. "Everybody knows what I'm going to do—cut taxes very substantially and create a great economy like I did before," he said. "We had the greatest economy. We got hit with a pandemic."

In one exchange that drew a rebuke from the moderators, Trump talked up a conspiracy theory about Haitian immigrants in Springfield, Ohio. "In Springfield, they're eating the dogs. The people that came in. They're eating the cats," Trump said. "They're eating the pets of the people that live there." The whole concept smacked of racism and xenophobia. No one in Springfield was making pet-touffée. Yet Trump's false example spoke more broadly to very real fears about immigration creating burdens for communities.

At the same time, the debate further revealed the holes in Harris's platform. She dodged the very first question—whether Americans were better off than they had been four years earlier. It was a softball, drawn directly from Ronald Reagan's 1980 campaign against Jimmy Carter. Harris answered in 330 words, none of which suggested that the economy had improved during the Biden-Harris term or offered a broad-based framework for how she would make it better.

Still, there was little question in either camp about who had "won" the debate—even if Trump would never acknowledge that he lost at anything. He told on himself by rushing in a motorcade from the Constitution Center to the nearby "spin room"—where he could address hundreds of reporters at once.

Before stepping into the spacious rectangular media hall, Trump stopped behind a curtain to talk to his running mate.

"The story they're going to try to spin—you've got all the momentum right now—is she stopped the momentum. That's bullshit," Vance told his new boss, ignoring weeks of polling showing that Harris had the momentum.

"I think I killed her," Trump replied.

"I think you killed her," Vance replied, like a storm trooper under the influence of a Jedi mind trick.

Trump then conferred with Senator Marco Rubio, who stuck to his conviction that he should not sugarcoat things for Trump. "I think the way people here analyze it and the way real voters analyze it are very, very different," Rubio said. It was an honest answer—both in articulating the truth that voters and the media can have different reactions to debates and in stopping short of suggesting Trump had won in a romp.

"I thought it was the best," Trump told Rubio. "Love you, man. Thanks, Marco."

When Trump stepped into the spin room, journalists formed a twenty-foot circle, several rows deep, around him. Kosoglu caught sight of the former president, surprised that he had chosen to speak for himself in a space usually filled with surrogates. *He got his ass kicked, and he knows it*, she thought. Harris aides high-fived, chattering about how she had "baited" Trump into talking about people feeding on pets.

"Guys, we didn't bait him into it," Clegg said. "He came to say that."

By that time, Harris aides were already telling the media that she wanted to debate Trump at least once more. On one level, that was a show of their view that she had won. But it was also a tell: she needed more major moments to seal the deal with voters. Trump, dominating the spin room like only he could, simultaneously complained about the moderators and suggested that he had won. "It basically was three-on-

one," he said. "She wants to do another one because she got beaten to-night." At the same time, he refused to commit to another meeting.

Harris could not tell how well she had done. She had been giving speeches at rallies and the convention, where an audience gave her immediate feedback. But this debate was held in a closed studio. As she entered the tented greenroom, she could see wide smiles on the faces of family and friends, who applauded her like a returning heroine.

"You hit it out of the park!" West exclaimed.

"Really?" she said. "I really did?"

On her way out of the Constitution Center, West elbowed Harris and said he knew she had almost called Trump a motherfucker. Harris broke into a smile, shot her brother-in-law a knowing glance, and laughed.

Trump was hitting full tailspin. He simply could not believe the turnaround—and began to fear that, for the second time in two elections, a magic carpet was being pulled out from underneath him. He was positioned to win in 2020 until a once-in-a-lifetime pandemic battered public faith in him. This time Democrats swapped candidates mid-campaign, and voters did not seem inclined to punish them for upending the game board or for hiding Biden's frailties in the first place. "He felt really confident coming out of the Republican convention, coming out of the debate with Biden, the Democrats are eating their party alive," said one senior Trump aide. "Then she overperformed."

It was infuriating, and he trained his anger on his staff. "When he screws up," said one longtime Trump confidant, "he blames somebody else." Already Lewandowski had infiltrated the Palm Beach headquarters, creating a sense of fear within the Trump campaign organization. Trump's traveling crew had added more faces since then, with 2020 Democratic presidential candidate Tulsi Gabbard and Representative Matt Gaetz, a Florida Republican, helping with debate prep. But it was his inclusion of Laura Loomer, a far-right social media influencer, that signaled his flailing and guaranteed another bad news cycle on the heels of the debate.

Loomer, one of Trump's most constant and controversial cheerleaders, had flown from Palm Beach to Philadelphia with Trump on the day of the debate, and on to New York for September 11 memorial events the following day. Outraged Democrats and Republicans bashed Trump for sullying the anniversary with a woman who openly questioned whether the 2001 terrorist assault on the United States was an "inside job."

The guardrails were off. Trump's top advisers no longer had the luxury of wasting political capital to keep Trump away from the most extreme influences on him. "The people that have the authority to stop it are hanging on to their jobs," a former Trump campaign official who maintained ties to the 2024 operation said at the time. "So are you going to pick that fight with him?"

On the other side of the political field, Harris felt like she had hit full stride. Democrats had come back home quickly when she took over for Biden. Cash continued to pour into the campaign and outside groups supporting it. She would cross the billion-dollar fundraising threshold by the end of September, saving the finances of an outfit that had once stared into the abyss of a red-ink October. She believed the early tension between Biden's old team and her longtime advisers had been mostly wiped away by the unifying force of success.

For nearly two months, she had enjoyed an uninterrupted wave of media attention—the vast majority of it positive—as she moved from locking in the nomination to naming a running mate to the convention and a bang-up debate performance.

"The convention and the debate were her epicenters," said one of Harris's closest advisers. "They set her up for the win."

CHAPTER 15

THE TURN

IT WAS TIME FOR DONALD TRUMP TO SACK SOMEONE.

He summoned Corey Lewandowski to the four-seater table on Trump Force One during a West Coast swing a few days after the debate. Susie Wiles and Chris LaCivita, the senior advisers whom Lewandowski hoped to replace, were already perched near the boss. Giving up at least thirty pounds to LaCivita and a world of gravitas to Wiles, Lewandowski looked small approaching the adult table.

Another aide walked up to listen in, and Wiles, in uncharacteristically dramatic fashion, pointed her finger to the back of the cabin—an admonition to stay away. Several other campaign staffers snuck into the plane's second bedroom to avoid the scene.

Lewandowski had accused Wiles and LaCivita of mismanaging the campaign budget, leaving Trump vulnerable at a time when Harris was outraising him by gobsmacking sums. He took particular issue with the budget for mailers, which the senior campaign staff saw as a key part of their strategy for reaching hard-to-contact voters. Justin Caporale, the deputy campaign manager, had joined in, trying to push Wiles out. This was the showdown that Trumpworld had awaited with apprehension. Unbeknownst to Lewandowski, Wiles and LaCivita had outflanked him, having already met with Trump that morning to go over the finances in detail. They would answer any questions, they said, but Lewandowski had become a distraction.

Considering his options on the plane, Trump paused for a moment. He had gained a new level of fame as the executive who told hopefuls "You're fired!" on the NBC television show *The Apprentice*. As a candidate and as president, he talked tough about who should lose their jobs, face prosecution, or be sent out of the country. But in real life, he hated confrontation. He had heard an earful already from Lewandowski and other informal advisers about the need for a campaign shakeup.

On one hand, he feared looking weak—or even losing—if he did not make a change. On the other, Wiles and LaCivita had guided him through the primaries, the political perils of his trials, and knocking Joe Biden out of the race. Their plans had been solid, and they had been loyal. *Corey's loyal*, Trump thought, *but he's a catastrophe. How do I make that clear without pissing him off?*

"They're in charge, Corey," Trump said flatly. "They stay in charge." Lewandowski, kneeling at the table, listened like a chastened schoolboy. He had trashed Wiles and LaCivita to Trump and to others in the ex-president's circle. Now he held his tongue. "You need to go on TV and go win New Hampshire," Trump continued. "Be a surrogate. That's what you're supposed to do." Lewandowski was not kicked off the plane mid-flight, but he was not given a ride home.

LaCivita blamed Lewandowski when he found himself, a month or so later, showing documents to Trump to prove that he had not—as had been reported in the Daily Beast—made nearly $20 million from the campaign. It was a hard-to-believe sum, but Trump wanted to make sure he was not being taken for a ride. On Trump Force One, LaCivita defended himself by producing receipts. Trump accepted LaCivita's evidence and advised him to sue the news outlet.

A rotating band of self-styled Trump whisperers would never completely leave his orbit, jockeying with one another and the campaign's leadership for bits of affirmation and power—"constant fuckery," as one top Trump aide put it. But in laying down the law with Lewandowski—effectively banishing him to a state that didn't really matter to the outcome of the race—Trump once again showed his commitment to running a more professional operation than he had in the past. In the midst of the shakiest period so far, he opted for stability and did that decisively.

★

Despite the extended honeymoon, Harris aides discovered a troubling trend in their data—or, more precisely, the absence of a trend.

The debate had given her a statistically insignificant bump in national polling—less than a point in the RealClearPolitics average. While many Democrats had come home to the party after the switcheroo, she was no longer building her coalition. She had effectively hit a ceiling. They either needed to find more of the kind of hard-to-reach voters that the Trump team pursued through the summer or else pull Republican-leaning likely voters into the Harris column. They probably had to do both if she could hope to beat Trump.

Plouffe, who integrated into the campaign smoothly as an adviser, spoke often of the importance of "moments." That meant opportunities for Harris to use big events like the VP pick, the convention, and the debate to change the dynamics of the campaign. When he had run Obama's operation back in 2008, there had been more of them: multiple debates with Republican nominee John McCain and a high-profile bank bailout fight among them. Looking at the calendar, there were no more natural moments left, unless Trump agreed to another debate. And he simply was not interested in subjecting himself to that again.

"There had been something every few weeks, and we were seeing growth from each of those moments," said one high-ranking Harris campaign aide who watched her numbers freeze in mid-September and looked at the relatively open October calendar with apprehension. "I don't think it was something that happened. I think it was something that didn't happen."

Both campaigns would have to make their own headlines—a game that Trump had dominated for the past decade—rely on advertising, and scrape for votes on the ground in swing states. The gravity of the situation struck home in Harris's state campaigns in September, when Wilmington abruptly ordered them to change the calculus of which voters they targeted for calls and door-knocking.

Typically, a presidential campaign spent the early months of the general election trying to persuade likely swing voters to side with their candidate. Later on, as early voting started, the campaigns would shift to mobilizing friendly voters to go to the polls. "You want to be having these persuasion conversations and laying the groundwork, and then do a final kind of push for persuasion up until maybe August," said one veteran hand who worked on the campaign. "But then you've got to start moving into mobilization."

The vast majority of Democrats would vote for a koala bear if it was wearing a *D* jersey. But the candidate switch altered the calculations for enough voters that Harris's team decided it had to do persuasion and mobilization at the same time. It was an unorthodox solution for a very unique problem, one rooted in the late selection of the nominee. Even knowing all that, state teams were shocked when they got new orders from the campaign leadership to expand the universe of prospective voters considered to be "persuadable."

Using laptop loads of personal data—from magazine subscriptions to voting histories—modern presidential campaigns assign a 0–100 score to each voter in two separate categories: likelihood of voting and likelihood of voting for the campaign's candidate. Late one week in September, the national office told state teams to start reaching out to a much wider swath of likely Republican voters.

"They lowered the support score for our persuasion universe to twenty and up," said a campaign official in one state. What that meant in theory was contacting voters who had a 2-in-10 likelihood of backing Harris. In practice, it meant that the Harris campaign in Virginia knocked on the door of the executive director of the state Republican Party, according to a person familiar with the incident. The idea of sending young volunteers to houses with MAGA signs in the yard—or homes where everyone had voted in Republican primaries in recent years—did not sit well with some of the state campaign officials. More than that, it told state officials that all the chatter about a Harris honeymoon masked deep concerns at headquarters.

"It seems like a little bit of a panic," one state-level campaign aide said of using door knocks to win converts. "It's more likely they pull a gun on you than say, 'Oh, let me hear what your policy platform is.' One in ten thousand doors you knock, somebody is a Trump voter, you talk to them for five minutes and they decide, 'You know what? I've seen the light. I'm going to be for Kamala.'"

In at least one state, the frame changed so that the target support score ranged from a floor of 20 percent to a ceiling of 80 percent, meaning that nearly all of the voter contact was aimed at persuading the middle 60 percent of the electorate and none of it at mobilizing the 20 percent who leaned most heavily toward Harris. The scores, of course, were imperfect predictors of actual human behavior at an individual level.

By using large data sets, the campaign could affect strategic decisions by gathering survey information—electronically, by phone, and at front doors—to match expectations with results and adjust accordingly. The basic concepts are common to presidential campaigns—Trump's team used data in similar ways—but the secret sauce for each algorithm is different. And how data is used—to inform strategy or dictate it—varies from camp to camp. No data set was going to tell Trump what to say about tariffs or immigration.

For Harris activists in the swing states, trying to convert Trump voters was disheartening. At best, it was a buzzkill. At worst, it felt like it might be dangerous. "Revolt is the wrong way to put it, but a lot of states lost a lot of volunteers over that period," said one of the state-level campaign officials. David Plouffe and Mitch Stewart, an O'Malley Dillon lieutenant brought in for the general election to help with battleground states, pushed the plan, according to the official. "This was a great idea that Mitch and David thought of, and they thought 'Oh, we can get these marginal people.' But in practice, it was such a disaster that they quickly—within three weeks—pulled back on it."

★

While the Harris team grasped at straws to find more voters, Biden grabbed a totem of Trump's movement and crowned himself with it. Visiting a volunteer fire department in Shanksville, Pennsylvania, on September 11, Biden bantered with Trump voters in the town where passengers had downed United Airlines Flight 93, hijacked by terrorists twenty-three years earlier. Finding one wearing a red "Trump 2024" hat, Biden offered up a cap with the presidential seal and signed it.

He asked for the Trump hat in return. "Put it on!" several people in the crowd shouted. "I ain't going that far," Biden replied. Then he did exactly that. Placing the cap atop one he was already wearing, Biden smiled broadly for cameras.

Without any context at all, it looked like Biden was endorsing Trump. With context, it was not much better—an outgoing president burnishing his own brand with a bipartisan gesture while his vice president argued that democracy would fall if voters did not choose her side. The possibility of sabotage was too painful, and too remote, for Harris aides to entertain. But some of her loyalists worried that Biden had just created a "permission structure" to swing voters to conclude that "Trump is not so unacceptable," said one campaign aide.

Where the Harris campaign saw an unfortunate series of events, Trump's aides—and an online army of his social media warriors—saw an opportunity too good to pass up. Various pictures and videos of Biden wearing the Trump hat garnered millions of views on social media platforms, including at least one that falsely asserted Biden had actually endorsed his old rival. That dovetailed with a broader theme pushed by conservative media and activists, in direct and indirect ways, to undermine Harris: that Biden did not want her to win.

Inside Trump's Palm Beach headquarters, the Harris hullabaloo moved on two tracks: perception and reality. The metanarrative of an iconic new candidate surging to a lead felt reminiscent of Barack Obama's arrival on the national political scene in 2008, even if Trump aides believed—or hoped—that Harris would fade as voters saw more of her. Trump's senior advisers adjusted to her bump in the polls by abandoning visions of competing in peripheral states such as Minnesota, Virginia, and New Jersey. Trump was in love with the idea of winning them, but it made little strategic or tactical sense to waste limited resources on states he did not need to take back the presidency.

Even with Harris dominating news coverage and picking up more support than Biden lost in public surveys, the Trump team's internal poll numbers simply did not change enough to cause panic. He had led Biden by a little, opened up a bigger margin after the first debate, and now found himself locked in a close race with Harris. To the extent that Trump had fallen behind in enough battleground states on a given day to lose the Electoral College, it was brief and by statistically insignificant margins.

"It wasn't that our internal polling bottomed out," a senior Trump aide familiar with the numbers said. "It was the public perception that the bottom was falling out that we had to deal with." In politics, there is always a danger that perception will become reality, and that is what Trump and his team had to guard against in the fall.

★

Consistency gave Trump's high command confidence, even when Harris took off. That same consistency worried top Harris aides when her numbers stopped going up. The basic shape of the Trump coalition carried through from the 2016 and 2020 elections: more white, more rural, more male, and less college-educated. But he had barely won the presidency in 2016 and had lost it in 2020. He needed to expand his base, and his pollster and data analysts determined early on that the electorate had shifted in ways that gave him new opportunities. That was particularly true with young Black men and young Hispanic men, many of whom were unhappy with Biden's economy and put off by his age.

"Latinos have just been coming of age at a faster rate than the rest of America, and what that means is they're not influenced, like their mothers, grandmothers, fathers, and grandfathers by just being able to watch three television channels, being more Spanish-dominant, and being closer to the immigrant experience," said one Democratic strategist who noticed the same trends as the Trump team. "They start falling in line with people in their socioeconomic status, which is non-college-educated working class, which got swooped up in the appeal of Donald Trump."

Ruben Gallego, the Democratic Senate candidate in Arizona, felt the cultural shift too and decided that he would make a point of leaning into it. Gallego, a forty-four-year-old Marine combat veteran, rented out a youth boxing gym in Glendale in May to screen a pay-per-view Las Vegas title fight between Canelo Alvarez, a legendary Mexican boxer, and Jaime Munguia. Gallego's campaign arranged for a food truck and picnic tables outside, and invited members of the community to watch the boxing match for free. The Senate candidate and his young son threw punches at a heavy bag, along with other fathers and sons. Throughout the campaign, he set up similar events catering to young, working-class men—many of them Hispanic—as he tried to gain an advantage over Republican Kari Lake.

Trump did not have to win the majority of Black or Hispanic voters, but cutting into Democrats' traditional edge would boost his chances. His data analysts believed there was a softening of support for Democrats among Black men under fifty years old that took root in 2020 but did not begin to blossom until 2024. Trump's aides had a variety of hypotheses for what they were seeing in surveys and shifting coalitions in the off-year and midterm elections in the previous three years. But they were certain that more young Black men—a lot more—were less attached to Democrats.

"There's a lot of different things that happen that cause an African American man under the age of fifty to become more open to supporting President Trump," said one Trump adviser. "But we saw it, and then we amplified it."

That took a variety of forms. In June, Representative Byron Donalds, a forty-five-year-old rising star in Florida and national politics, launched a series of barbershop conversations for Trump's campaign in swing-state metropolises, including Atlanta, Detroit, and Philadelphia. Trump called in to the first one. He held a tele-rally specifically for Black voters. Before a rally at Georgia State University in early August, Trump's campaign contacted Black voters identified as potential supporters to invite them to the event. A couple of days after that, Trump said in a streaming interview with Adin Ross that the rapper Young Thug, facing criminal charges in Georgia, was being "treated very unfairly"—playing on his own experiences and his allegations that the justice system is corrupt. Young Thug later struck a plea deal on charges involving gang activity, drugs, and guns that led to his release on probation after spending nearly three years in jail during an unusually long trial.

Critics did not have to search hard to find racial tropes in some of Trump's appeals, including when he questioned Harris's identity. But no matter the modes of amplification or the specific messages, the biggest underlying issue for persuadable young Black men who sided with Trump was the same as for the rest of the electorate: the economy, headlined by inflation. In that way, Trump's overarching message appealed to a growing set of voters across demographics, and his aides looked for creative ways to cement the new bonds. "It started kind of on its own, but we just drove it hard when we identified it," the adviser said.

Harris campaign officials in the states noticed the same dynamic taking shape, even as Wilmington was slow to respond to it. Unlike 2008, when Black voters rushed to the polls to vote for Obama, the first Black president, there was no guarantee of a repeat with Harris. One state-based campaign official was befuddled by handbills the national office sent late in the campaign that were targeted to Black men.

"I did have specific literature for Black men. And I was like, what is this for?" the state campaign official said. "Like, do we take it out canvassing? And if I happen to knock on the door of a Black man, I give him this lit?" There didn't seem to be a real plan for targeting Black men—or a broad message to appeal to them—just partially customized literature. Even the Harris policies aimed at Black men seemed to be scattershot in nature. She promised to give "fully forgivable" loans of up to $20,000 to start businesses, fight for job-training programs, protect crypto assets, launch a health-equity program focused on diseases that disproportionately affect Black men—including prostate cancer—and legalize pot.

For millions of Black men, that agenda missed the mark. "They weren't concerned about what Kamala Harris was doing to build businesses in the Black community," one state campaign aide said of Black men who leaned toward Trump. "Every single one of them said one word and fucking one word only: *stimmy*." The aide tried to argue that Biden had also sent stimulus checks. "They'd say, 'No, he didn't. I got one with Trump's name on it.'"

It was not just Black men. Trump's campaign aides tried to reinforce his economic message in every community and demographic where they thought it would stick. And they were careful not to do what they believed had happened in 2020—target the wrong voters and turn out people who would cast ballots for his rival. They were on the hunt for likely Trump voters regardless of race, ethnicity, or zip code. "We were working Black voters, veterans, gun owners, and higher-income and lower-income voters with more individualized programs that reach into a lot of those suburban and urban areas too," said a second Trump adviser.

Like the Harris campaign, the Trump team used big data to score voters. His aides were pleasantly surprised that across two dozen rounds of polling, which allowed them to apply actual voter data to their models, their projections matched up almost perfectly with the reality. Knowing where the race stood was not the same as winning, but accuracy was critical to making smart tactical decisions. On September 15, according to the RealClearPolitics average of surveys, Harris held infinitesimal leads in the Blue Wall states and Nevada, with Trump leading in Georgia, Arizona, and North Carolina. Under that scenario, Harris would win the election.

★

With the rougher-than-expected debate behind him, a final campaign sprint ahead, and the fear of another shocking defeat weighing heavily, Trump took a breather from the trail on September 15. He would never say he needed to recharge his battery, but he did. Shortly after the sun hit its peak on a 90-degree day, Trump approached the first tee at Trump International Golf Club in West Palm Beach with Steve Witkoff, a friend, donor, and fellow billionaire real estate developer who had sent his jet to pick up JD Vance for the Ohio senator's final meeting with Trump before the VP pick.

Earlier in the year, Witkoff had brokered a détente between Trump and Florida governor Ron DeSantis following their nasty primary fight, which had left Trump in retribution mode and DeSantis licking his wounds. Witkoff took it upon himself to reach out to DeSantis, without Trump's knowledge, to feel the governor out about meeting with the former president. Through intermediaries, DeSantis said no. Witkoff was relentless, eventually talking to the governor directly. He offered to host the two politicians, once close allies, at his own golf club, Shell Bay in Hallandale Beach.

Once DeSantis agreed, Witkoff had to sell Trump on the idea. Heading into the general election, it made sense for Trump to repair the party's rifts—a process he had already started with GOP donors who had opposed him in the primary. Mending fences with DeSantis would only help recoup his voters and widen the bridge to his contributors. But there was a lot of bad blood between the two men. DeSantis, in particular, fumed over Laura Loomer, the pro-Trump activist, accusing his wife, Casey DeSantis, of overhyping a bout with cancer to win sympathy.

Witkoff closed his golf club one morning in the spring to host Trump and DeSantis for breakfast. For an hour, Trump lit into DeSantis, who owed his governorship to the then-president's 2018 primary endorsement. Trump expected DeSantis to apologize for the betrayal of running against him and all that had happened during the primary. The proud governor of Florida, cut from similar cloth as Trump, refused to do it. But DeSantis turned the conversation in the second hour, pledging to encourage his donors to give to Trump, act as a surrogate in the fall campaign, and help secure Florida's electoral votes.

"They kind of hugged it out at the end," said a person familiar with the meeting.

Witkoff, a natural diplomat, had a way of putting Trump at ease, and the combination of his company and a mid-September round of golf promised to do that for the former president. The two men had just finished the fifth hole when Trump heard loud popping sounds in the distance. It had been little more than two months since a failed assassin fired a bullet across his ear. His protective detail dived on top of him and then rushed to pull him off the course and find cover. Secret Service snipers whisked past Witkoff and set up tripods.

The gunfire Trump heard came from Secret Service agents. They had spotted a man with a semiautomatic rifle, pointed at Trump from about four hundred yards away. The suspect did not get off a shot before fleeing in a car. Police arrested Ryan Routh, who would be charged by federal prosecutors with trying to assassinate Trump. For the second time in a single campaign season, the former president escaped an attempt on his life.

Trump called JD Vance shortly after the incident and before it was publicly reported to tell his number two what had happened. In Wilmington, Harris aides discussed the protocol for the campaign, given that it had paused attacks on Trump after the first assassination attempt.

"Our feeling was we shouldn't overreact to it," one of her advisers said, explaining why the campaign did not suspend its activities. "The nature of it wasn't as close a call. It didn't warrant that dramatic of a response by us."

Harris called Trump two days later to express concern for him. Democrats blamed Trump for violence during his term and after it—pointing to the January 6, 2021, U.S. Capitol riot as the first exhibit. He and his surrogates said Democrats' rhetoric about him—using words like *fascist*, which he also applied to Harris—made him a target. But during their brief conversation, Harris told Trump that there was "no place for political violence" against anyone. Trump thanked her for calling. She was struck by his gentle tone. He could be very charming when it suited him.

The Secret Service, under increasing scrutiny following the twin assassination attempts on a protectee, tried to put new restrictions on both candidates. While the agency did not have the authority to ban campaign activities, its guidelines and warnings were taken seriously in the Trump and Harris camps. Trump would have to stop playing golf. The candidates' ability to have unscripted interactions with voters—drop-ins at local restaurants that were a staple of barnstorming—would be sharply limited. No one wanted to take any chances in the middle of a fight for the presidency that had become as acrimonious as it was close.

Americans were so deeply and evenly polarized that few events had much discernible effect on swaying voters in one direction or the other. Biden had been able to hold on for so long because the numbers did not swing immediately and dramatically after his epic fail on the debate stage. Trump did not fully freak out about Harris's rise because he had not trailed her by a statistically significant margin. In an election full of startling moments, but remarkably static voter sentiments, the second try at killing one of the candidates was just another event that did not change the math on its own.

But it helped Trump and hurt Harris in another way. "It did kind of force the media to talk about something besides Kamala Harris's rise," said one Trump adviser.

★

That would happen again when the media and voters turned their focus to the vice presidential debate. Set for October 1, Tim Walz might as well have marked it on his calendar with a Mr. Yuk poison-control sticker. As soon as Harris picked him, aides advised Walz that he would have just a few big moments to worry about—the launch rally, his convention speech, and the debate. He was fine standing onstage and giving a stump speech, but that debate terrified him.

"He was very in his head about the debate from the very beginning," said one Walz adviser. "He just believed that it was not his forte."

It was easy to throw unanswered rhetorical bombs at his adversaries on television or at a rally. But it was harder to be an attack dog when he had to play defense at the same time. "You have to be prepared to defend your record, but, also in service of the campaign position, the vice president's position, and, arguably this was more difficult because you're dealing with the whole Biden record, plus the Harris views and whether they differ," the aide said. "All of those things were lurking."

Even prep sessions, with transportation secretary Pete Buttigieg playing Vance, overwhelmed Walz. He couldn't sleep at night. Aides had to remind him to eat. Vance, by comparison, relished the big stage. His tune-up for the debate included a round of interviews with mainstream media outlets that the Trump campaign viewed as enemy territory, giving the wonkish Vance a chance to road-test his responses to tough questions. He took a loose approach to his first two prep sessions, workshopping his answers with aides in hourlong Zoom calls. He subjected himself to a murder board—aides peppering him with sharp questions—and wrapped up with a mock debate against Representative Tom Emmer of Minnesota. He and his team tried to keep the project as casual as possible.

Vance had been through the wringer in his early days on the campaign trail, with old clips of him attacking whole classes of people and Trump circulating widely in the media. The U.S., he had said in a 2021 interview with Tucker Carlson, was being run in part by "a bunch of childless cat ladies who are miserable at their own lives and the choices that they've made and so they want to make the rest of the country miserable too." A false claim that he had written about having sex with a couch bounced around the internet and made it into Walz's remarks. The label "weird" stuck to him in most circles.

Vance's advisers thought the caricature—mean and odd—could be turned into an advantage in the debate. All Vance had to do was protect Trump's flank and do it in a way that seemed warm and normal. That could disarm Walz and color voters' view of Vance with a different light.

When they met in a CBS studio in Manhattan, Walz's nervousness showed. He struggled to answer an opening question on Middle East policy. Vance smoothly handled everything that was thrown at him in the opening stages of the debate, often turning to his own biography— the subject of his bestselling memoir—to remind voters that his mother had been addicted to opioids, that he served in the military, and that he had used the GI Bill to pay for school.

Each candidate took whacks at the other side's presidential nominee, but Vance extended olive branches to Walz personally. In one exchange on housing, Vance said he agreed with a lot of what Walz had to say— though not all of it—which appeared to soften Walz. Many of the arrows his team fashioned for use against Vance were left in his quiver. He didn't like hand-to-hand debate combat.

"His human nature really took over," one Walz aide lamented.

Vance had just one bad episode, and it happened after many viewers had tuned out. Toward the end of the debate, he was pressed on the January 6 attack on the Capitol and whether Trump had lost the last election. Vance said that Trump "peacefully gave over power" despite the riot and refused to concede that Biden had won fair and square. It reminded some voters of why they did not trust Trump with the presidency.

But to the extent that the VP pick matters in a presidential election— and there's little evidence that it does—the choice says something about the person vying for the Oval Office. Republicans were reassured by Vance's performance. Democrats were left to worry what voters would think about Walz. If he could not handle the pressure of a vice presidential debate, maybe he wasn't the best pick to sit one heartbeat away from the presidency.

★

Four days later, with Vance at his side, Trump returned to Butler Farm Show, site of the first attempt on his life, for a rally. For many of Trump's aides, it was a highly emotional moment—a mix of trauma, defiance, and pride in the resilience of their candidate and his movement.

But amid the activity in a crowded set of backstage tents, where a group of Trumpworld celebrities waited to be brought to the stage, there was little sign from the ex-president that this rally was different from any others. In the main operations tent, with a pair of screens showing a newscast and a bird's-eye view of the venue, Trump joked with his aides. He checked in with his speechwriting team to make final edits to his remarks.

We should be stopping to pray or at least mark what happened here in July, thought one Trump aide. "He seemed completely oblivious to it," the aide said. "It was so normal, it was eerie."

It was exactly one month from Election Day, and Trump and billionaire Elon Musk—who would spend a quarter of a billion dollars in support of the campaign—repeated the rallying cry the former president issued in the minutes after he was shot: "Fight! Fight! Fight!"

CHAPTER 16

TEXAS HOLD 'EM

KAMALA HARRIS TRIED TO KILL TWO BIRDS WITH ONE *JOE ROGAN EXPE-rience.*

She had spent much of September getting her feet wet by sitting for friendly interviews with mainstream media figures and podcasters whose audiences leaned heavily toward Democratic-dominated demographics. In short, she was playing a lot of home games—and not always winning.

It was hard for her to answer foundational questions about her platform, at least in part because she built her campaign ship midvoyage. At an even deeper level, Harris still refused to separate herself from Biden in any real way in public. Some of that stemmed from her own sense of duty and loyalty to the man who made her vice president and endorsed her when he stepped aside.

Biden's chief of staff, Jeff Zients, repeatedly told top Harris campaign advisers to do what was necessary to put Harris over the top—even if that meant disagreeing with Biden or not inviting him to her campaign events. "Zients was definitely 'Do what you need to do,'" said one top Harris aide. "Whether it was something small, like scheduling or not campaigning together, I would go to Jeff."

Biden chafed at his very limited role in the fall, but the White House staff tried to balance that against the Harris campaign's desire to keep him out of the spotlight. Harris was already tied too tightly to him, and his insistence on loyalty was already in her head.

No daylight, she thought.

Unlike Trump, Harris required intensive prep sessions before major interviews, sometimes taking time over multiple days to get ready. Before an October 8 appearance on ABC's *The View*—perhaps the most welcoming television venue in the country for her—Harris considered the question of how to show she was different from Biden without making either of them look bad.

Her plan was to note that a vice president typically stands with the president, and that she would honor that tradition, but talk about "what I would do differently going forward." She would transition from that into a contrast between their biographies and say that she planned to put a Republican in her Cabinet, which Biden had not done.

That was hardly a clean break from Biden, but Harris started in that direction when *The View* cohost Sunny Hostin asked about any issues where the president and vice president disagreed. Harris was not ready for the follow-up, though. Reading from notes, Hostin pressed Harris on whether there was anything specifically she would have done "differently than President Biden during the past four years."

Harris paused for a beat. Her jaw tightened, and her eyes looked upward as though she were trying to access information. Shaking her head lightly from side to side, she spoke nine words that would haunt her campaign. "There is not a thing that comes to mind," she said.

What the hell was that? Stephanie Cutter thought. *That's not what we practiced.*

"It provided the money shot" for Trump's ad makers, said one Harris confidant. "And it was her own bad moment."

Harris and Trump did not agree on much. But they both seemed bent on keeping her tethered to Biden and his record. The nature of Harris's late entry into the race explained, at least in part, her early difficulty in finding a platform and a narrative of her own. Most candidates did that in the planning stages of a run for the presidency. She was thrust into the race because she was next in line when Biden dropped out. And now, more than two months into her candidacy, she had done little to erase the impression that her reason for running was one of circumstance. There was no good explanation for why the backup to an octogenarian president had not mapped out her own narrative as part of a political go-bag.

Harris wanted voters to give her power, but she had not said what she would do with it. Softball interviews only served to underscore the idea that she was hiding from scrutiny and to funnel her message to voters she already had in the bank. This presented a conundrum for her aides. She wasn't performing well in easy interviews. And at the same time, if she wanted to expand her support—which she needed to do—she would have to expose herself to tough questioning. That was particularly important with men—specifically young men—who were not buying what she was selling.

The obvious answer: Joe Rogan. Representative Eric Swalwell, a fellow California Democrat who had attended Harris's wedding to Doug Emhoff, began back-channel discussions with friends of Rogan the first week of September. They thought the master podcaster would be open to Harris—and that it would be a good showcase for her. In late September or early October, Harris aides reached out to Rogan's team through Spotify.

Rogan, a late-1990s sitcom star turned bro-with-a-brain podcaster, boasted a subscriber base that amounted to a total eclipse of the genre's universe, with nearly 15 million signed up just on Spotify. His 2018 interview with Elon Musk, during which the Tesla and SpaceX founder smoked pot and sipped whiskey, garnered tens of millions of views on YouTube and crashed the next-generation car company's stock. The vast majority of Rogan's guests and listeners were white men, presenting Harris with a potentially golden opportunity to prove her mettle by walking into the lion's den.

On October 11, Harris's deputy campaign manager Rob Flaherty, the O'Malley Dillon lieutenant in charge of digital strategy, made the first Zoom call to start negotiating with Rogan's reps. He did not know what to expect. *These might be juiced-up, UFC-looking supplement people*, he thought. He was surprised—perhaps a tad disappointed—to find out that Rogan's associates were more like Hollywood agents. In that vein, they outlined his conditions for an interview: no staff in the studio, no topic restrictions, and she would have to sign a waiver.

There was one more item in the small print: Harris would have to come to Austin, Texas. Rogan's reps said that might be negotiable, but he had only once done an interview with an out-of-studio guest. That was leaker Edward Snowden, who was wanted in the United States.

Along with Stephanie Cutter and Brian Fallon, Flaherty offered up that Harris would be happy to talk about social media censorship, weed, and other issues they thought would be of most interest to his listeners. From their perspective, it was a suggestion of possible topics, not an exhaustive or exclusive list. That's not what Rogan wanted to talk about. "Joe just wants to talk about the economy, the border, and abortion," one of his reps said, according to a person familiar with the negotiations. After two Zoom sessions, Flaherty called the Rogan intermediaries with an offer.

Could Rogan join Harris in Michigan? he asked, proposing a date later in the week. No go, his reps said after reaching him on a weeklong hunting trip. Austin or nothing.

"That's going to be tough," Flaherty said. "We're only a few weeks out from the election." Harris had less than zero reason to be in Texas. It was not a battleground state. Her campaign was flush with cash—so it made no sense to take her off the trail to raise money. She was in battleground-or-bust mode. Plus, a detour to Texas might smell like desperation to the press and a waste of money to donors.

O'Malley Dillon thought she could break the internal impasse. Harris would be in Atlanta on October 24 with Barack Obama and Bruce Springsteen. O'Malley Dillon decided the campaign could fly the vice president to Houston for a rally—under the cover of visiting a state with one of the nation's most restrictive abortion laws—to put her in position to pop into Austin. JOD dispatched an advance team to the Texas capital to do a walk-through of Rogan's studio and get ready for a Harris arrival. She authorized her negotiating team to give Rogan what he demanded—an in-studio interview in Austin—on October 25.

For all of Trump's work to reach apolitical voters through podcasts, YouTube, and other outlets, Harris positioned herself to score a coup by grabbing the biggest megaphone of them all. If she did, she would be exploiting a rift between Rogan and Trump. Rogan had called Trump a "man baby" and a "threat to democracy" in 2022, vowing not to interview the former president. At the time, the beef was just one more sign of the social stigma attached to Trump after the January 6 assault on the Capitol, said one longtime Trump adviser. But when Rogan appeared to endorse Robert F. Kennedy Jr. in August, Trump fired back on Truth

Social: "It will be interesting to see how loudly Joe Rogan gets BOOED the next time he enters the UFC Ring??? MAGA2024."

Rogan was hardly Mr. Popular inside Harris's camp. Tony West, Minyon Moore, and others argued against putting her on the podcast, especially after her first venture into politically tough terrain—an interview with Fox's Bret Baier in the middle of the Rogan negotiations—bombed. There was no telling what Rogan might ask her or how he would treat her. Plus, his "antiwoke" crusade had made him a pariah on the hard left. They were overruled by the O'Malley Dillon crew, but not because the concerns were considered invalid. "Even for those of us who were in favor of it, it was a close call," said one of the Harris advisers involved in the back-and-forth.

The Harris high command was not built to lob Hail Mary passes. Its leaders, starting with O'Malley Dillon, cut their teeth on campaigns that ridiculed fellow Democrats for "bed-wetting" whether crises were imagined or real. Seeking an interview on a popular podcast hardly qualified as a desperation throw downfield. But it was outside the comfort zone for a campaign leadership that had kept its candidate hermetically sealed in the manufacturer's box, like she would retain more value without exposure to air and sunlight.

On October 10, two days after Harris flubbed on *The View* and the day before Flaherty's first Zoom with Rogan's team, the campaign's weekly internal analytics assessment of the race—a 129-page document—projected Harris winning exactly 270 electoral votes. She was on track to take the Blue Wall and Nebraska's Second District—but lose the rest of the swing states—at least according to her own analysts. Deputy campaign manager Becca Siegel and chief analytics officer Meg Schwenzfeier had been just a tad too rosy in their final projection for Biden in 2020—accurately predicting victories in the swing states he won but also forecasting a North Carolina triumph that did not materialize.

Beneath the top-line numbers, though, the analytics showed why it was so important for Harris to reach the type of voters who listened to Rogan. In battleground states, Trump led Harris by 10.6 percentage points among men and trailed her by 9.3 percentage points among women, according to her team's figures. In both gender splits, Trump did about 2 points better against Harris in the battlegrounds—the area of greatest concentration for the campaigns—than in national polling. He led her among young men, was tied with Hispanic men, and trailed her among Black men by a smaller margin than Biden beat him by in 2020.

Black men who liked Trump were 4 percent more likely to vote in 2024 than in 2020. That was not a particularly large difference, but it reflected a broader wave in the survey research. In nearly every imaginable subset of the electorate, Trump's fans were more likely to vote in 2024 than 2020. Overall, his vote likelihood score was 3 percentage points higher for 2024 than 2020. That wasn't true for Democrats, who found that voters who leaned in their direction were no more likely to cast ballots in 2024. Trump had the energy and the enthusiasm, and a promising foothold with young men. His favorability numbers were also ticking upward, according to the survey data, as Harris's started to slip. In other words, nostalgia for his presidency was growing.

★

In late September and throughout October, as voters started casting early ballots and the television ad war heated up, Trump's team rolled out several versions of an ad that turned a little-known Harris position into a graphic and visceral metaphor for the broader argument that she would push an extreme, liberal social agenda at voters' expense.

Back in August, with Harris flying high, Trump's senior advisers asked veteran Republican admaker Patrick McCarthy to slide from the Trump super PAC MAGA Inc. to the campaign. They had been impressed with the hard-hitting negative ads McCarthy made for MAGA Inc. and wanted to infuse the campaign with that kind of edge in the closing months. On a Friday afternoon in mid-September, McCarthy took a break from a lakefront reunion with college buddies to connect with his firm's team. They were about to do a round of testing on prospective ads, and he wanted to put something new in the mix.

"What's the craziest thing we've got on her?" McCarthy asked. The question was not totally out of left field—his firm actually kept a file called "crazy" with potential ad material that would portray Harris as a radical. The group tossed around issues before landing on a 2019 questionnaire Harris had filled out for the American Civil Liberties Union in her first bid for the presidency. She had pledged to make sure that transgender people who relied on the government for medical care—including those in prison and in immigration detention—would be able to have surgeries at taxpayer expense.

It seemed too good to be true, and perhaps too much for voters to believe. Many candidates would stay away from leveling a charge that could backfire by hurting their own credibility, but Trump had already raised this one at the debate. Besides, there was an available video clip of Harris explaining her position to a trans rights activist.

Sipping on his second glass of wine as afternoon faded into evening, McCarthy weighed whether to cut the ad, spend the money to test it, and potentially present it to Chris LaCivita, who managed the air war for the campaign. Over the course of the evening, McCarthy and his team discussed ways to punch up the ad—to make it even more memorable—with a tagline. "The pronouns," one of them suggested. Harris touted her *she/her* pronouns. Trump made fun of the explosion of pronouns, telling Fox News earlier in the year, "I don't want pronouns."

McCarthy and his team wanted the full contrast and landed on a catchy turn of phrase that both hit the trans issue and made a larger point about the two candidates: "President Trump is for you; Kamala Harris is for they/them." It was good, but would the campaign high command sign off on it?

Fuck it, McCarthy thought. *We're working for the Trump campaign. What would the boss do?* Obviously, Trump would try to savage his rival with the most powerful weapon at hand. "Let's try it," he told his team. "Let's see if they'll let us do it."

The ad tested well, and LaCivita showed it to Trump later that week on Trump Force One. The former president approved of the direction but balked at one element. To guard against voters dismissing the claim as too ridiculous to be true—could Harris really want strapped taxpayers to fund transgender surgeries for prisoners?—McCarthy had included a clip of CNN's Erin Burnett saying it was accurate.

"I don't want her in the ad," Trump said of the host, who had often been critical of him. McCarthy cut Burnett out, replacing her part in the ad with images of Harris and Sam Brinton, a nonbinary former Biden Energy Department official who was charged with stealing luggage, sharing the screen with a *New York Times* affirmation of the veracity of Trump's claim. LaCivita made one tweak, reversing the order of the tag line to read "Kamala Harris is for they/them; President Trump is for you."

Airing during NFL games and later the World Series, the ads used Harris's own words to show her as a potential danger to voters. Soft on gender. Soft on crime. Soft on immigration. Reckless with taxpayer dollars. In other words, she was an extremist. In one version, McCarthy used a clip of radio host Charlamagne Tha God talking derisively about her position. "We were upping our streaming to Black males," said one person familiar with Trump's ad strategy.

In the giant, sucking vacuum that served as Harris's agenda, Trump aides were thrilled to fill in the space with items from a record that placed her squarely to the left of Biden. They saw added value in protecting, and possibly expanding, their lead with men. "It has particular resonance with men," one of Trump's top advisers said. "While Kamala Harris is desperately trying to make up a massive gender gap with men, this may create issues for her in trying to bridge that gap."

What befuddled many Democrats was the Harris campaign's refusal to push back on the charges. Even if they were true—and the facts were airtight—football-watching Democrats shook their heads every time they saw one of the trans ads. Some of them called the campaign to complain and push for a strong response.

O'Malley Dillon and her lieutenants toyed with possible rebuttals, testing about a dozen ads with focus groups. But those ads did not test well—or at least not well enough to light a fire under Harris's aides. Focus groups didn't love the pushback ads, so Harris's team didn't put money behind them. "There was an overreliance on anecdotal qualitative comments from focus groups that people felt like the ads were not believable," said one Harris adviser who thought it was a mistake to base the strategy around focus-group tests.

One of Harris's most experienced allies tried and failed to make the case to Wilmington. Barnstorming battleground states for Harris, Bill

Clinton chatted with voters across the country—in big cities and small towns. Working rope line after rope line, he heard the same topic on a loop: the trans ad. *Does Harris really want that? Would she let boys play in girls' sports? What are her values?* Like everyone else who watched sports on TV, Bill had seen them—a lot—during his travels.

He felt the risk to Harris in his gut. Voters cared most about their financial situations—"It's the economy, stupid" had been his campaign mantra—and she couldn't break through on that if all the chatter around her focused on whether she was a radical social warrior. *Why the fuck isn't the campaign pushing back on this?* he thought.

Bill did not want to see something and not say something. He pushed a bunch of buttons, reaching out to O'Malley Dillon, Tony West, and Second Gentleman Doug Emhoff. When Bill called JOD from a hotel in California in October, she said the data suggested that the ad was not having much of an impact on the race. His eyes and ears, she implied, were deceiving him. In 2016, Hillary's campaign leaders dismissed Bill in the same way—using the black box of data analytics to tell him his brand of politics was dead. Back then too he had used his political tuner to find warning signals in swing states. He was living history again.

But this was not his wife's campaign. Most of the decision-makers were not Hillary's people. They were not Harris's people. Hell, they were not even really Biden's people. The campaign was being run by former lieutenants to the president who tried to stop Harris from winning the nomination: Barack Obama. They did not have much use for Bill Clinton. He was not alone. The campaign got pressure privately and publicly from allies to answer Trump's charge. But O'Malley Dillon had put her foot down.

"The strategic decision was not to directly rebut this thing," said a senior Harris campaign official who participated in the internal debate about how to respond. Instead of punching back directly, Harris's advisers decided to pivot by focusing on her own messaging on the economy and other issues. That infuriated allies who were watching Trump take a chunk out of Harris without paying any political price. "The polling showed warning signs the campaign ignored—namely her declining favorability, which owed to the completely unrebutted swiftboating of Kamala Harris in paid media," said one Harris confidant.

It was not just the Harris campaign that refused to fight back on her behalf. The main Democratic presidential super PAC, Future Forward, held back its spending until the latter stages of the campaign—after narratives about Harris began to set—and chose not to dump negative ads on Trump's head. In the summer, as Biden's inner circle worked to push Anita Dunn out of the White House, the president suggested that she move to the political action committee. Dunn had earlier blessed Future Forward as the vehicle of choice for pro-Biden donors who could cut massive checks.

"We built a coalition, a broad coalition, that was the Biden coalition," said one person involved with one of a constellation of outside groups that worked in concert in 2020 to elect Biden. "Anita Dunn said, 'No, we got one group. It's Future Forward,' and Future Forward got awarded all the money," this person said. When Dunn was still working for Biden, Future Forward's donors tried to choke him out of the race. To many Democrats, it was not clear what drove Future Forward's decision-making, besides extensive ad-testing that heavily prioritized data over common political sense. "There is a human dimension to these things that doesn't show up in an online test," said one senior Harris campaign adviser. "They never gave us air cover—ever."

Future Forward sat on the vast majority of its money until the last several weeks of the campaign, with very little of what it spent devoted to hitting Trump. Through the end of the election, according to Federal Election Commission records, Future Forward poured $443.5 million into ads backing Harris and $646,000 into spots that attacked Trump.

Harris campaign officials had to wait for the other advertising shoe to drop. When David Plouffe saw Harris on *The View*, his reaction was immediate and foreboding. "That's going to be in an ad out like tomorrow," he told colleagues. It would actually take a little more than a week. "We were all a little surprised that they didn't do it sooner."

But when the attack came, it was furious over land and air. Trump's team sent out mailers with a split screen of Biden and Harris punctuated by the quotation from *The View*. On October 16, Trump started running ads with the clip. "When she gave us the gift of the *View* interview, we were able to anchor her to the Biden administration in her own words, which is something we were trying to do anyway," said one of Trump's top advisers. "She just gave us that gift to sort of solidify the groundwork that we'd already been laying, and it also had the additional effect of highlighting her relatively substance-free campaign."

For the entirety of the campaign, dating back to before the Republican primaries, Trump's advisers had believed he could win if the nomination and general election fights were about policy. It was a strategy born of the simple truth that persuadable voters liked his policy ideas more than his persona.

But polling inside both campaigns, and in independent surveys, showed that his personal favorability ratings started to tick slightly upward in the fall. Strikingly, more voters remembered his presidency in positive terms than had approved of it when he was in office. The matchup with Harris—and four years of Biden—created a small but measurable Trump nostalgia bump.

★

The absence of traditional late-campaign moments—namely debates—meant that the two candidates had to compete against each other for voters' attention in unorthodox ways. That was home turf for Trump, who can drive news cycles like Max Verstappen drives Formula 1 race cars. Both candidates stepped up their rally schedules, though the big headline events were not terribly cost-efficient in terms of converting votes. Rallies were perilous for Trump because no matter how much time he spent talking about his policy ideas, he often went off-script in ways that hijacked the message his advisers hoped to pound into voters' minds.

That was part of the thinking behind a series of tax-cutting policy proposals he unveiled over the summer—no taxes on tips in June, no taxes on Social Security payments in July, and no taxes on overtime pay in September. Harris matched him on tips, but his Social Security promise—like many of his pledges—would have blown too big a hole in the budget for her to copy it.

Necessity proved to be the mother of invention for the Big Mac of Trump's fall events. During Harris's honeymoon phase, Trump's advisers spent hours tossing around ideas for how to get cameras pointed at him. "We've got to break through with big, splashy events, things that force coverage," one of his senior aides said.

One concept had the dual purpose of showcasing Trump's concern for working-class voters while also trolling Harris. She had said that she worked at McDonald's when she was a young woman, but her campaign had no receipts—no pay stubs, no photos, no corroborating witnesses—to prove it. Her aides ridiculed reporters who asked about it.

On October 20, little more than two weeks out from Election Day, Trump cleared out a McDonald's franchise about twenty miles north of Philadelphia. Wearing a red tie and white dress shirt, Trump put on an apron as employees watched the former president learn the finer points of their jobs. He pulled a basket out of a deep fryer, dumping the fries into a metal basin so they could be sorted into boxes. Then he took a turn at the drive-thru window, passing meals to prescreened customers.

The hours he spent at his favorite fast-food joint probably did not secure many votes at the drive-thru, but they earned him wall-to-wall television coverage and reinforced the message that he was focused on kitchen-table issues.

Harris went in a very different direction the following day, highlighting her focus on democracy—an issue more abstract than the self-actualization at the top of Maslow's Hierarchy of Needs. At three events in three cities on October 21, the vice president sat down for conversation-style rallies with Liz Cheney, a onetime House Republican leader who had turned on Trump and lost her job over it. Harris and Cheney made for strange political bedfellows, agreeing on virtually nothing but their disdain for Trump.

The Harris campaign was trying to find new GOP voters—particularly suburban women—and attract media attention. The Cheney experiment was always more likely to work for the latter than the former. Most Democrats hated Cheney's father, former vice president Dick Cheney, for leading the nation into a forever war in Iraq. So did many Republicans.

★

If the Harris-Cheney marriage felt like a head-scratcher for Democratic operatives outside the campaign, the October 22 announcement that Harris would hold a Houston rally felt like a palm-to-face moment. She was going to lose Texas, by a lot, and a visit would not force Trump to spend his limited campaign money there.

Her aides scheduled the rally for a Friday night in the fall—October 25—*in Texas!* It was as if no one on her team knew that the night reserved for high school football was more sacred than Easter in the state. Plouffe responded to the criticism publicly, explaining that Harris wanted to shine a spotlight on a place where she believed Trump's anti-abortion policies had done the most damage to women's health.

Only a few people knew the real reason: the whole Houston rally was built to put her in proximity to Rogan. The ongoing negotiations on that were touch-and-go. Flaherty had called his Rogan contacts on October 18.

"We could do Friday, the twenty-fifth," Flaherty said.

"Wish we had known about this sooner, because he has the twenty-fifth blocked out as a personal day," one of Rogan's reps said.

"What about Saturday morning?" Flaherty countered.

"Only if it's before eight thirty a.m.," came the tough reply.

The tone is different, Flaherty thought. *The vice president of the United States is offering to come to your fucking show, and you keep putting up more hoops.* Harris's team still wanted to make it work, but a new wariness set in.

On October 22, around the time the Harris camp announced the rally, the Associated Press reported that Trump would be Rogan's guest on Friday—the "personal day" Rogan had reserved. Mutual friends Elon Musk and Dana White had convinced Trump and Rogan to bury their dispute, according to a Trump aide. There would be no Harris interview. In this wild hand of Texas Hold 'Em, Harris aides thought they had one more ace to play. Beyoncé was in Houston and willing to perform at the rally. "The plan changed like twenty times that day, and they landed on her singing 'Freedom' a cappella before Harris walked onstage," said one person familiar with the back-and-forth between the campaign and Beyoncé's team.

As consolation prizes go, a Beyoncé performance ranked pretty high. She was a bigger star than Rogan—a bona fide global diva—and "Freedom" was the campaign's theme song. But Beyoncé would not give Harris the potential benefits of a Rogan interview: demonstration of her willingness to go outside her comfort zone and connection to a new and politically valuable audience. Worse for Harris, Beyoncé refused to perform. She would speak. But she would not sing.

No Rogan. No "Freedom." The campaign kept its poker face, but it had played out a losing hand. Trump spent three hours with Rogan in an interview that instantly went viral. The contrast amounted to a "traumatic event," said one Harris aide, "that I will never forget." But it wasn't quite over. Rogan would later blame the missed connection on Harris and accuse her of refusing to talk about marijuana, even though her platform included legalization.

Harris aides made a final stab, offering to let Rogan talk with Harris in Washington, D.C., the day after a closing-argument speech at the foot of the White House. Rogan's team balked, citing the Austin-only condition.

Flaherty had seen enough. "You get one trip to Texas within three weeks of the election," he told Rogan's associates. "You don't get two."

CHAPTER 17

GARBAGE TIME

Donald Trump never learned to love early voting.

In 2020, he told Republicans not to vote by mail or show up at the polls ahead of Election Day—a message he drove home so thoroughly that some of his own campaign aides blamed it for his 2020 defeat and two Senate losses in Georgia in January 2021. *There are too many steps in the process, too many opportunities for funny business,* he thought. *Voting should be done in person on Election Day. Period.*

He felt robbed in 2020. Despite collecting more votes than his advisers said he needed to win, he had lost. It was shocking, especially considering that he got 17.8 percent more votes than he had in 2016. But Joe Biden improved the Democratic vote total by 23.4 percent over Hillary Clinton's tally. Rather than look in the mirror, Trump looked for excuses. He blamed voter fraud, and he believed at least some of it had been done under the cover of an explosion of early balloting.

His base believed it too, and fixing a rigged game became a central theme of the political comeback narrative he began to weave in 2021. This, of course, presented a glaring and very sensitive problem for his 2024 campaign team. It was one thing for him to rail against the electoral system—and even to continue to falsely claim that the last election was stolen—but he would only harm himself if he kept telling Republicans not to use all available means to vote.

No one understood this tension better than Susie Wiles. For decades she had worked in the political trenches of Florida, where GOP mastery of early voting in recent years had helped turn the state from a battleground to more reliably Republican turf. It would not be easy to disabuse Trump of the idea that early voting invited fraud—much less that he should tell his base to do it.

Wiles did not have to change Trump's mind on a dime, but his electoral fate might rest on him eventually getting to yes. So, in conversations that began as early as the spring of 2024, she slowly socialized the concept with him. There were plenty of arguments to choose from, not least of which was the damage he'd done to himself in 2020, but Wiles opted for one that would appeal to his business sense.

Along with political aides James Blair and Alex Latcham, Wiles showed Trump data from primary states where early voting was allowed. Every time one of his voters cast a ballot before Election Day, she explained, the campaign could stop spending money to lobby that voter to go to the polls. It was presented as a cost-saving measure—operatives in both parties referred to the practice as "banking the vote"—which forced Trump to weigh that value against his reflexive distrust of early voting.

Trump could see the upside in Republican primaries, where GOP officials were in charge. But he was deeply wary of Democratic-run states in the general election. The early votes are secure, his aides tried to assure him. He did not really buy that—certainly not at first and not with regard to mail-in votes—but his mind opened to the possibility of encouraging his voters to cast ballots early.

"Susie started to plant that bug in his head," said one Trump adviser, "and it was just constant reinforcement."

The topic tore at Trump. Not only did he personally oppose early voting, but he worried that his voters would see him as a hypocrite if he suddenly embraced it.

In early June, he signed off on the Republican National Committee launching a "Swamp the Vote" program. "Whether you vote absentee, by mail, early in-person, or on Election Day, you must swamp the radical Democrats with massive turnout," Trump said in a direct-to-camera video promoting the program. But he often contradicted his own message. "They have early voting, late voting, everything is so ridiculous," Trump said in Palm Beach in July. "We should have one-day voting, paper ballots, voter ID, and certification of citizenship. And that's what we're striving for."

"You could see him wrestling with it," said one adviser who noted that Trump would tell audiences that he was being counseled by Wiles—against his instincts—to embrace early voting. He was right that his core voters had listened to him in 2020. A Pew Research Center survey in May showed that 37 percent of Republicans supported open rules for early voting, compared to 82 percent of Democrats. But in August, he cast an early ballot in Florida's downballot primary, sending a signal to skeptical base voters. And in September and October, as states collected early ballots, Trump leaned harder into endorsing early voting.

"Susie was the main driving force behind that," said one Trump camp insider.

While Trump led the GOP toward greater comfort with new modes of voting—demonstrating again that he could turn his base at will, if not always at full speed—Republicans faced a new fear that Trump voters would not be able to cast ballots in a key swing state.

In late September, Hurricane Helene ripped through western North Carolina, causing devastating and fatal floods that forced voters out of their homes. Aside from the blue dot of relatively liberal Asheville, the affected region was overwhelmingly Republican. Trump had won the swing state by fewer than 100,000 votes in 2020, and there was a chance that divine intervention—or at least a major weather event—could be responsible for flipping it into Harris's hands.

But North Carolina changed its election rules to grant new flexibility to voters affected by the hurricane, just like states had rewritten laws—to Trump's chagrin—during the Covid election of 2020. The new rules made for a fairer fight, decided by voters rather than Mother Nature.

Heading into mid-October, Trump campaign advisers were not sure how the candidate's evolution on early voting would affect the race. But as key states started to publish statistics, a wave of excitement pushed through the campaign's Palm Beach headquarters. Georgia and North Carolina both reported record first-day voting totals. Nevadans also rushed to cast their ballots.

Tim Saler, the chief data consultant to the campaign, rose early each morning to assess the new numbers coming in. His main vice, if it could be counted as that at an HQ operation littered with Zyn nicotine tins, was Diet Coke. On the surface, Saler liked what he was seeing.

Contrary to conventional wisdom, he had been tracking a significant uptick in early voting among Republicans in the off-year and midterm elections of 2021, 2022, and 2023. The pandemic had turned early voting into a virtue signal for Democrats in 2020. Now increases in preelection turnout were much more likely to signal growing Republican participation, he thought. Even though the states reported only total numbers of early votes, sometimes breaking them down by party registration, there was a way for the campaign to project how many were for Trump.

Through polling, the campaign identified specific voters who had already cast ballots for Trump. Armed with that data, Saler and his team fed the numbers into their model of the electorate to estimate how many of the early ballots had been cast for their candidate across a given state. Democrats did much the same thing. What neither side could know, for sure, was whether the early vote was simply a cannibalization of Election Day ballots. In other words, early voters could just be people who would have shown up to the polls on Election Day anyway.

When Harris aides floated that hypothesis to the media, Saler thought it was a sign that they were seeing the same pro-Trump results as he was. If they thought they were winning the early vote, Harris advisers would not play down its importance. Trump passed Harris in the RealClearPolitics average of polls by one-tenth of a point on October 26. In past elections, Trump's actual level of support had been understated in the averages. In 2020, for example, Biden led Trump by 7.2 points in the RCP average on Election Day. Biden ended up winning by 4.5 points across the country— and about 44,000 votes over three states in the Electoral College.

More important, Trump had opened up leads in each of the battle-ground states: 2.2 points in Georgia; 1.5 points in Arizona; nine-tenths of a point in North Carolina; six-tenths of a point in Pennsylvania; half a point in Nevada; three-tenths of a point in Wisconsin; and two-tenths of a point in Michigan. The margins were so small that either candidate could still win, but—especially given the traditional underestimation of Trump's strength—the breeze was at Trump's back ten days out from the election.

★

For years Trump had dreamed of commanding the stage at Manhattan's premier venue for sports, concerts, and political events: Madison Square Garden. He was a native New Yorker, and the arena held a unique importance in his imagination. Various iterations of the Garden had hosted P. T. Barnum's circus, one hundred and fifty sold-out Billy Joel shows, several national political conventions, pro- and anti-Nazi rallies, the Westminster dog show, and the home games of the NBA's Knicks and the NHL's Rangers. When Trump was ten, Rev. Billy Graham launched his famous "New York Crusade" there.

For Trump it represented acceptance, even veneration, in his hometown. He had been growing more nostalgic in the final stages of the race. For the first time in nearly a decade, win or lose, he would no longer be a candidate soon. The series of trademark rallies that fed his ego and fueled controversy—a cultural phenomenon in themselves—would come to an end. "It's the capstone rally," one Trump adviser said. And by stepping outside the battlegrounds to deliver his closing argument at an iconic venue, Trump could guarantee both media coverage and voter attention.

Feeling good about his chances, Trump also saw the rally and its reach as part of a strategy to do something he had failed to do in his previous two bids for the presidency: win the national popular vote. It stuck in his craw that he had lost the beauty contest to Hillary Clinton and Joe Biden. This time, if he took the Electoral College and the popular vote, no one could delegitimize his victory, he thought. And tallying more votes would make it easier to claim a mandate.

Harris surrogates preemptively tarred the rally as an homage to a World War II–era pro-Nazi gathering at MSG. Hillary Clinton told CNN that Trump would be "actually reenacting" the 1939 rally. Trump advisers pointed out that Bill Clinton had accepted the 1992 Democratic nomination there. But the left and the media leaned heavily into the idea that Trump picked the spot in order to send a signal to white supremacists. He promptly bolstered their argument—or at least one of his surrogates did.

It wasn't at all unusual for major Trump rallies to feature a rogue's gallery of MAGA celebrities. In addition to politicians and Trump family members, the MSG lineup included Elon Musk, Dana White, Tucker Carlson, and Rudy Giuliani. As a surprise, the live audience would be treated to a stump speech by Hulk Hogan, the wrestling icon who partnered up with Mr. T. to win a marquee tag team match at the very first Wrestlemania, at Madison Square Garden in 1985.

But the Trump campaign's fascination with reaching out to young men hit a snag early in the day. Like Trump himself, comedian Tony Hinchcliffe—host of the popular *Kill Tony* podcast and onetime member of Rogan's circle—was a veteran of the celebrity roast circuit. He had a history of injecting race into his stand-up act, including calling a fellow comic a "filthy little fucking chink."

The night before the rally, Hinchcliffe, a boyish-faced forty-year-old with thick brown hair and a wispy goatee, performed a surprise set at the Stand, a comedy club and restaurant near New York's Union Square. Testing out his material for the Sunday rally, Hinchcliffe called Puerto Rico a "floating island of garbage." The joke bombed, but Kill Tony promised the crowd that it would slay "at tomorrow's rally."

Reading from a teleprompter at Madison Square Garden, Hinchcliffe repeated his attack on the American territory. Nearly 6 million people living in the continental U.S., including several hundred thousand in swing-state Pennsylvania, could trace their roots to the island. Trump staffers pointed fingers at one another—many of them in the direction of Alex Bruesewitz, the social media guru who had helped convince Trump to court more podcasters.

It is inconceivable that only one person was responsible for putting Hinchcliffe onstage, with a script loaded into a teleprompter, for Trump's closing-argument rally. But the internal blame game pointed to a sense of panic in Trump's inner circle. Putting a comedian onstage was an unforced error, and the joke threatened to hijack Trump's efforts to court Latino voters, including Puerto Ricans, and drive home his closing messages in the final days of voting.

The boss has been looking forward to an MSG rally since before the Iowa caucuses, and this guy comes in and shatters it in five minutes, thought one frustrated Trump aide. *This could cost us votes.*

Wiles's ethos, laid out at every turn, was that Trump's campaign staff existed to help him win the presidency. This blunder cut against her admonitions to avoid getting in Trump's way. "Ultimately, this was a staff error," said a Trump adviser. "We should be able to control everybody but the principal. If Donald Trump wants to get up there and say what he says, that's his prerogative. But if a staffer invites some dipshit comedian, that's a staff problem. And that's where I get upset."

The Harris campaign pounced, promoting a video of the vice president pledging her support for Puerto Ricans and detailing policies she supported that she believed would help both the island and Puerto Ricans living stateside. Bad Bunny, the Puerto Rican rapper with a monster following, reposted her video and issued an endorsement that her campaign had long been pursuing. Jennifer Lopez and Ricky Martin were among those who followed suit.

Democrats had predicted the October 27 MSG event would look like a modern-day Klan rally, and Trump's campaign walked right into that trap. The rest of the lineup did not help either. Carlson aimed directly at Harris's racial and ethnic makeup, falsely saying she would be "the first Samoan-Malaysian, low-IQ former California prosecutor ever to be elected president." Harris was neither Samoan, Malaysian, nor low-IQ.

But calling Puerto Rico "garbage" evoked memories of Hillary Clinton's formulation that half of Trump's supporters could be categorized as a "basket of deplorables," a phrase that Trump's 2016 campaign hung around her neck to frame her as an elitist—and a nasty one at that. The Harris campaign needed a spark. Maybe this would be it. *Maybe.*

★

Two evenings after Trump's MSG affair, Harris took the stage on a patch of land at the foot of the White House known as the Ellipse. With the White House lit up behind her, Harris looked out at tens of thousands of supporters—many of them federal government workers who hoped she would become their new boss. To raucous cheers, she flashed them her signature megawatt smile and pressed her hands together in a gesture of gratitude.

Aside from the camera-friendly backdrop of the White House, this was symbolically significant turf. Nearly four years earlier, on January 6, Trump had held an unprecedented rally here. Usually, defeated presidents slinked out of Washington quietly, humbled—or at least quieted—by the loss. None of them gathered their voters for a rally. None of them would have entertained the idea of whipping the crowd into a frenzy by calling the election rigged and encouraging them to march to the Capitol.

But on that day, Trump was still trying to stop Vice President Mike Pence from certifying the election result. He promised to join the masses at the Capitol—he did not—and then watched them sack the Capitol from the comfort of the small dining room connected to the Oval Office. Biden and his top aides became convinced that voters cared most about defending democracy—after all, he had won while adopting that line of argument in his 2020 campaign, and at least for a short while, Republican elected officials and a share of the GOP electorate distanced themselves from Trump.

By choosing to speak from the Ellipse one week from Election Day, Harris signaled her commitment to the Democratic view that a Trump victory would topple democracy in the U.S. In polls, many Democrats identified that as their top issue. And why wouldn't they? For about eight years, their party's leaders had been telling them that the biggest threat faced by the country was Trump destroying the republic. But Harris's closing argument was not really about Trump and democracy—or at least it was not supposed to be.

This has to be forward-looking, Harris thought when she set out to plan the speech. *I need to get some of my bio in here—let people know why I fight for the things I fight for—and it needs a heavy dose of my economic messaging. And maybe some contrast with Trump, but not some big takedown.*

After three months on the campaign trail, she was still trying to define herself, and her priorities, to the electorate. She was still trying to put together a narrative, piece by piece. There was, according to one of her aides, "a lot of stuff mixed in." No one in the country wondered what Trump wanted to do, how he planned to do it, or what his conception of "America First" meant. And despite her difficulty in weaving a competing narrative, the two candidates were within whispering distance of each other in public polls. Trump was coming off the Madison Square Garden disaster, which some aides in both campaigns saw as a late-breaking threat to his chances.

Harris's choice of venue set an expectation that she would talk about Trump, democracy, and January 6—that she would close on a battle hymn for the republic. There were a lot of reasons to speak from the spot, not the least of which was the likelihood that she could draw a big crowd from the city and its near-in suburbs, which were both heavily Democratic. By the time she took the stage, her speechwriters had topped her remarks with a run of anti-Trump rhetoric that reflected the location.

"Look, we know who Donald Trump is," she started. "He is the person who stood at this very spot," she continued, pointing her forefingers toward the ground in front of her, "and sent an armed mob to the United States Capitol to overturn the will of the people in a free and fair election." Loud boos broke out in the crowd. But for anyone watching at home, hoping to learn what Harris might do to bring down prices or cut their taxes, the policy substance would have to wait until later in the speech.

Harris aides would only have to wait a little longer to see their carefully planned closing argument upended from just a few thousand feet away in the White House. On a teleconference call, held during Harris's speech, Joe Biden responded to Trump's MSG rally by saying, "The only garbage I see floating out there is his supporters."

Why are you doing anything public-facing during her speech?! Why are you competing with us, dude? one senior Harris campaign aide thought when he saw the video circulating online. *Fuck, here we go!*

"It was a gift," said a senior Trump aide. In just a few seconds of commentary, Biden stole the spotlight from Harris and bailed out Trump. The White House scrambled to doctor the transcript of his virtual call to reflect Biden's insistence that he meant to refer only to Hinchcliffe—as in "his supporter's" garbage.

Biden's intent did not matter nearly as much as his words—available for all to see in viral clips. It did not sound like he used the possessive form, certainly not to Trump fans who believed—or wanted to believe—they had been called "garbage" by the sitting president of the United States. At least Hillary Clinton had shown enough compassion to apply her "basket of deplorables" label to only half of Trump's base.

Trump aides sprung into action, seeing a golden opportunity to buttress several of the candidate's messages at once. They reached out to Dan Roddan, a waste management expert and former local official in Suamico, Wisconsin, to find out if it was possible to deliver a garbage truck to the Green Bay airport the day after Harris's speech. He contacted Andrew Brisson, president of Loadmaster, a waste-vehicle manufacturer in Michigan's Upper Peninsula. The two men met up and drove a couple of hours to Green Bay, where they rolled onto the tarmac and waited for Trump.

The former president almost botched the made-for-viral-distribution video clip, missing on his first two tries to grab the door handle. Finally getting it right, he climbed into the cab. Like the McDonald's moment earlier in the month, Trump and his advisers found an easy way to communicate that he stood with workers. At the same time, the juxtaposition of Harris's speech and Biden's remarks helped him keep them tied together. And again he showed a political dexterity that the heavily scripted Harris seemed to lack. Over the span of a few days, he turned the word *garbage* from a negative into a positive—and did so by tying it to his message for working-class voters in the Blue Wall states.

"He obviously had a national message, but when he would go to states, he was so good at talking about local wedge issues in a way that we never could," said a Harris campaign official who recalled a staffer in Michigan complaining that the vice president's team was "running a campaign for Axios and *Politico*"—Washington-insider publications—"and not for Michigan."

"Our leadership was always very adamant that everything was about national message," the aide said.

★

Heading into the final week of the campaign, senior Harris campaign officials noticed a shift among a key voting bloc. Among the shrinking set of late-deciding voters, more of them were breaking for Harris than before. The incremental changes were most pronounced in the Sunbelt states.

That was a double-edged sword. Harris's clearest path to the presidency ran through the Blue Wall states. But where she was seeing numbers move in her direction—in the Southeast and Southwest—she had more ground to make up. The margins were small enough in each of the swing states that it was possible she could win all of them, lose all of them, or end up with a mixed bag that might or might not amount to a victory. Harris campaign officials used the data to talk up "momentum" with fellow Democrats and the media.

That narrative got an unexpected boost on Saturday, November 2—three days before polls closed. J. Ann Selzer, the most prominent and respected pollster in Iowa, released a survey showing Harris with a three-point lead, 47 percent to 44 percent, in the Hawkeye State. Iowa wasn't previously considered competitive.

The Democratic twitterati celebrated the news as a sign that Harris was on the verge of swamping Trump. Some Republicans freaked out, similarly worried that it might be an eleventh-hour omen. Trump's team glanced at the survey and determined quickly that it was off base. Accustomed to independent pollsters missing on the Trump vote, they attributed the unusual result to a series of errors they had seen before. "All of the bad habits just compounded into this nuclear explosion of drama," said one senior Trump aide.

Senior Harris advisers split over the meaning. Some dismissed it. Others took the poll more seriously, coupling it with the movement among late-breaking voters to conclude the race was coming to them. *Oh shit*, one of them thought. *We can pull this fucking thing off.*

James Blair, the political director for the Trump team, had been through enough elections—win and lose—to have developed a three-prong way of looking at Election Day. There were elections where the campaign leadership knew the candidate was cooked and just hoped to limit the pain. There were elections that could go either way. And there were elections where all of the fundamentals pointed to a victory. Consulting with Tim Saler, the chief data consultant, in the hours before Election Day, Blair concluded this was the third type. Looking at all the numbers, he told his colleagues Trump was positioned to win. "We will likely sweep," he told them. It could be hard to tell in Trumpworld when bravado was warranted and when it was just consistent with the culture.

Saler, a master of microdata and macrodata, took a measure of pleasure in watching the returns come in from the first town to vote—Dixville Notch, New Hampshire. Situated about twenty-five miles from the Canadian border, with a population of fewer than ten people, Dixville Notch had found a way to make itself known in the political world by opening its polls at midnight. All six voters cast their ballots in the first minutes of Election Day. The vote split 3–3. Saler smiled to himself. In 2020, Trump had lost the niche notch 5–0. It was hardly definitive, but it felt good.

Several hours earlier, the top brass on the Harris campaign gathered on a Zoom call for a final projection of the race. O'Malley Dillon opened the meeting and quickly threw control over to Meg Schwenzfeier, the data analytics chief. Schwenzfeier walked the group through a slide deck.

In a cautious fashion that the rest of the Harris aides had become familiar with, Schwenzfeier presented the numbers. Harris was on track to lose Georgia, North Carolina, Arizona, and Nevada, and she was poised to win Michigan and Wisconsin. All of the states were close enough to go either way if Election Day produced small deviations from the projections.

In Pennsylvania, the state that had been blanketed with ads, candidate visits, and media attention—the state where Trump had been shot and Harris had introduced her vice presidential pick—the snapshot showed Harris trailing by less than one-tenth of a point. The final Electoral College projection, committed to the slide deck, had Trump winning 287–251. Yet the margin in the pivotal state was so narrow as to be statistically meaningless.

Inside the Harris campaign, the race looked like a toss-up, and she and her aides believed momentum was on her side. Harris discussed the final estimates with a few of her closest confidants and summed up all the information in one thought: *We're going to win this election.*

CHAPTER 18

"JUST TAKE THE 270"

HOLD ON!" TONY WEST WARNED.

West and his wife, Maya Harris, had lived through Election Night 2016. It was seared into their minds like it was burned into the collective consciousness of the Democratic Party. On that night, President Barack Obama and top campaign officials pressured Hillary Clinton to concede, even as some of her most trusted political hands begged her to wait until all the votes—or at least enough of them—had been counted. The margins were so close in the Blue Wall states. Hillary listened to Obama, and to her own heart, and called an end to the election in the wee hours of November 9, 2016.

Now Harris turned to her brother-in-law, sitting next to her on a sofa at One Observatory Circle, for a gut check. She had spent much of the night upstairs in her bedroom and personal office space as election returns rushed in. Shortly before midnight, Harris took a call from campaign chief Jennifer O'Malley Dillon and campaign chief of staff Sheila Nix with the latest update.

Harris had prepared to travel to Howard University to address supporters at her alma mater—and across the country—when it became clear that she was in a good position to win. It was likely, she had been told by campaign officials, that the race would still not be called at that point. Swing states might need hours, or even days, to render decisive results. She would go to Howard and help tide over the masses with upbeat remarks. Maybe, if everything broke right, she would be able to declare victory there before the night was out. Now, though, as she checked in with O'Malley Dillon and Nix, the message was different.

"It probably doesn't make sense for you to go to Howard," Nix said over her cell phone from a different part of the vice president's residence. This call was coming from inside the house.

"Pennsylvania looks like it is going to Trump," O'Malley Dillon said from a Washington hotel. "We're seeing some of the return here in the suburbs and the rural areas, and while we had anticipated this to be close, we've looked at it every way we could, and we just don't see a path anymore. The AP may call it soon."

Harris was not the type to study precinct-level data. But she knew, for certain, what O'Malley Dillon and Nix meant to communicate. Already her southern path to the presidency—the long shot—had been cut off by North Carolina and Georgia lining up behind Trump. A loss in Pennsylvania would tip the election to him.

We're going to lose, Harris thought for the first time. "Are you sure?" Harris asked. "Is it close?" JOD was sure.

Hanging up the phone, Harris tried to focus her mind on executing the next steps. She walked down the stairs at the center of her house, turning right to follow the dogleg steps to the landing. She could see family members lounging on couches and chairs that had been pulled into a reception area earlier in the day for a private watch party. CNN and MSNBC played on twin television sets. The room had grown quiet over the hours, a somber mood setting in more deeply with each new batch of votes showing Trump overperforming his targets. Harris walked in to find her family sitting shiva for her campaign.

Dressed in a pantsuit, she sat down on the sofa next to West. Her voice had lost its lilt, weighed down by the gravity of the moment and her sense of foreboding about the next item on her to-do list.

"I have to call Trump," she said, her eyes betraying a state of shock. It was half statement and half question.

This is not what she had expected, not at all. Her advisers had told her that she had all the momentum. Late deciders were breaking her way. She might even win all seven of the battlegrounds. Besides, at packed rallies over the final week, she had felt the energy of crowds in her bones and seen their excitement with her own eyes.

Everything added up to a win, she thought, *except the actual votes.* Trump had lived through a similar scenario in 2020, floored by an outcome that simply did not comport with what he expected heading into Election Day. A sense of foreboding spread through Harris as she contemplated an act that had been unthinkable to her only hours earlier: conceding to Trump.

West pushed back. This was about more than one swing state, and it was about more than one election. Harris represented the Democratic Party and all the people who had voted for her—Democrats, Republicans, and independents—and against Trump. They would not want her to give up if there was any chance left of winning. But he also had to consider the optics of a slow-rolled concession, especially if his sister-in-law hoped to continue her political career at the national level or in California.

There was no reason, West said, for her to jump the gun. He had discussed this very scenario with veterans of Hillary's campaign, including his wife and Minyon Moore, in the days leading up to the election. Moore had been adamant about keeping Obama out of Harris's ear on Election Night to prevent a repeat of 2016. "Call Obama and tell him 'do not call the candidate and tell her to concede,'" Moore had said. "You gotta shut him down quick."

A lawyer who had once served as the third-highest-ranking official at the Justice Department, West counseled Harris that it made sense to assess whether there had been any voting irregularities or mistakes in the reporting before ending the election with a concession. "It's fine if you call him after the call has been made," West said of the Associated Press's official declaration of a winner. "But there's no rush." After all, it had been 1,459 days since AP had declared the 2020 race for Biden, and Trump still had not called the president to concede.

"Until he gets 270," West said, "you don't have to concede."

★

Donald Trump's third and final Election Day marked the end of a campaign era defined entirely by him, from the MAGA movement he harnessed to the backlash that he inspired.

He had known next to nothing about electoral politics when he descended a golden escalator at Trump Tower in Manhattan in June 2015, hurling himself into the arena by accusing Mexico of sending its worst to America. "They're bringing drugs. They're bringing crime. They're rapists," he said, adding as an afterthought, "And some, I assume, are good people."

His abrasive talk attracted attention. His ideas, which defied partisan orthodoxies, shocked the establishment of both parties. So did his ability to build and maintain a loyal voting bloc. That base stuck with him through four years in the presidency, the Covid-19 pandemic, his 2020 loss, the January 6 impeachment, four indictments, a conviction, a contested 2024 Republican primary, two assassination attempts, and a general election fight against the Democratic tag team of Joe Biden and Kamala Harris.

Everything started with the MAGA movement voters who flocked to his rallies, wore his hats, and spread his message to their friends and families. But Trump learned the hard way in 2020 that he needed more than his base to win a second term. It was one of many lessons—and perhaps the most consequential—that he took with him when he left the White House in January 2021. But he had learned a lot about running the White House too. He had lost key votes in Congress, watched his Cabinet secretaries and White House officials quietly undercut his agenda, shaken public confidence with his response to the pandemic, and left himself open to countless investigations.

"He's now more knowledgeable about what it takes to be president after his first term," Susie Wiles told NBC News in a February interview. "He's more knowledgeable about how to interact with the media. His personnel instincts are, I think, better honed. The new skills are inside the package of the same Donald Trump."

As he left Mar-a-Lago to cast a vote for himself on the morning of November 5, he believed—or at least hoped—this Election Day would give him a second chance to implement his America First agenda. Flanked by his wife, former first lady Melania Trump, at his polling place, the once and possibly future president reflected momentarily on his feelings about the close of his career as a candidate. "Sad," he said. "And very fulfilled."

From there he headed to his West Palm Beach, Florida, headquarters so that he could thank the younger folks who had poured months—and in some cases years—into helping him reclaim the Oval Office. In a hallway, he checked in with senior aides, including pollster Tony Fabrizio, political director James Blair, and chief data consultant Tim Saler, so that he could get a read on their assessment of his chances.

There was still work left to do, but the vibe was strong. Earlier that morning, Blair had ordered up a batch of millions of text messages to send to voters touting a fresh endorsement from Joe Rogan. Unlike voters swayed by TV ads, mailers, or watching the former president debate, Rogan cited Elon Musk as the most effective persuasion agent for Trump. He posted his endorsement to X, and Blair saw it as a tool to boost last-minute turnout.

Trump, who had senior advisers Chris LaCivita and Wiles with him, asked his political mechanics how things looked under the hood. Saler knew enough to avoid making specific predictions; Trump had been told a "win number" for his total turnout in 2020 that had proved wrong. Anything Saler said could be used against him at a later date if things went sideways.

"Cautiously optimistic," Saler replied.

Trump nodded his head. No matter how many times he predicted victory publicly, he was actually a little superstitious. Wiles had already given him her readout: "It might not be as quick as we thought. It might take a little longer into the night, but never fear." Trump had neither agreed, nor argued. When Trump left the hallway, Fabrizio interpreted the boss's expressions and body language for Saler. "He feels good," Fabrizio said. "He thinks he's going to win."

Trump had thought that in 2020 too.

★

In her final days on the campaign trail, Kamala Harris had felt a surge of enthusiasm in her crowds. The Democratic campaign pros told her the numbers were moving in her direction. The outcome rested on a knife's edge, they said, but the race was coming her way. Tony West took in all the information from the campaign and shorthanded it for her: "The trend is our friend."

Harris was poised to become the first woman elected president, and to put a permanent end to the Trump era. This embodiment of the American melting pot, a daughter of Jamaican and Indian parents, raised in a middle-class neighborhood and bused to an integrated school, stood near the mountaintop of history. Armed with the energy of the trail and the data of her campaign's number-crunchers, she believed with every fiber of her being that she would ascend the summit.

The main questions in her mind, as she left her house to phone-bank at the Democratic National Committee that afternoon, were how long it would take for her to be declared the winner, and whether Trump would falsely claim that he had been defrauded again.

Already O'Malley Dillon and her deputies had set up a "boiler room" in a subbasement of the Marriot Marquis hotel, just across the way from the Washington Convention Center. From there the campaign's top brass would monitor election results and direct traffic across the country on Election Night.

These operatives could have done the same work from Wilmington, where pipes and drapes were set up on the sixth floor to create a warren of miniature boiler rooms for lower-ranking aides. But if Harris won—and her top aides had convinced themselves, their candidate, and the rest of the Democratic Party that she could—they wanted to be close enough to bask in the credit.

A couple of blocks away, at the chic Conrad Hotel, Nancy Pelosi set up shop in a suite with her husband, daughters Christine and Alexandra, several aides, and a couple of close friends. She too looked forward to a celebration of Harris—and of a new Democratic majority in the House. Her summer maneuvers to push Biden out of the race, she thought, were about to pay off.

Downstairs at the Conrad, Harris's finance team made preparations for a VIP watch party, with election-themed lights and balloons. Harris donors and aides expected to mingle, throw back drinks, and keep an eye on the results before heading to Howard University to watch Harris claim the presidency. Black cars and buses lined up outside the hotel in the early evening.

Howard, a little more than a mile north of the Conrad in the LeDroit Park neighborhood, set up an outdoor rally space for Harris supporters to watch vote tallies come in. Over the weekend, Harris had learned that longtime adviser Sean Clegg planned to stay in California for Election Day. He had been cut out of the campaign, even more abruptly and fully than most of the retinue of Harris insiders who had been sidelined by the O'Malley Dillon crew. Harris called Clegg from Air Force Two on her way to New York for a quick hit on *Saturday Night Live*—a mirror act with Maya Rudolph—and urged him to come to the nation's capital.

In a makeshift hold room at Howard, Clegg joined the Kamalot crowd—Rohini Kosoglu, Brian Nelson, Karen Dunn, and Philippe Reines—to sip wine and wait for results. Washington, D.C., was ready for Kamala.

In the early evening, Harris summoned family and a couple of close friends to the vice president's residence—about twenty people in all—for a takeout meal in the dining room. A small clutch of her aides gathered in the back of the house to give the vice president and her family space to kibbitz before swing states started to report vote counts.

★

Mar-a-Lago was already a madhouse when a handful of Trump aides arrived from headquarters early in the evening to set up their "war room."

Club members and Trumpworld figures spilled into the room, making it impossible for his aides to run a focused political operation. They retreated to Trump's personal office, high above the grand ballroom, and settled in. They were already feeling good about the early signs from Election Day.

When news outlets had started reporting the first exit polls about an hour earlier, senior adviser Jason Miller had called Trump. Eager to be the bearer of positive news, Miller reached Trump in the former president's suite at Mar-a-Lago. The data team had looked at the exits and extrapolated that, if the numbers were accurate, Trump was on track to win.

"Michigan is the only state where we think we're behind," Miller told him.

"What's wrong with Michigan?" Trump asked. Miller had brought a plateful of chocolate-dipped strawberries, and Trump homed in on the one sour grape.

"Sir, don't dwell on that," Miller said. "Right now, you're going back to the White House."

"Okay," Trump said, skipping over Miller's point that the current projection had him exceeding the electoral-vote threshold he needed. "Maybe the Michigan numbers will tick up a little bit."

"Sir," Miller pleaded, "just take the two seventy."

Still, none of the actual votes had been counted. Sometimes exit polls were off by a little bit. Sometimes they were off by a lot. These numbers held positive portents, but they were hardly conclusive.

Miller packed into Trump's office with Wiles, LaCivita, Fabrizio, Blair, pollster Travis Tunis, policy adviser Stephen Miller, veteran Trump adviser Taylor Budowich, former Georgia senator David Perdue, and Natalie Harp, who made a name for herself on the campaign plane—"the human printer"—by lugging around a printer and a generator to make sure Trump had whatever he needed on paper.

It was a tight fit in Trump's office, and there was little in the way of food. Rigatoni disappeared quickly from a small plate into LaCivita's mouth. Bottles of water quickly emptied from Trump's refrigerator. Over the course of the night, RNC co-chairs Lara Trump and Michael Whatley drifted in and out, as did Lara's husband, Eric. Senator JD Vance, the vice presidential candidate, who had been given a bungalow on the property to watch results with family and friends, popped in at one point.

The scene was a far cry from Election Night 2020 at the White House, when boozy Trump friends decamped to the White House Map Room while his aides tried to ignore them and keep tabs on the battleground states. That night, Rudy Giuliani had to be led into the China Room, away from the action, where he ranted about supposed fraud and insisted that Trump's aides encourage the president to declare victory.

Trump's 2024 operation had been run in a much more professional manner. As he reached the doorstep of the greatest comeback in American political history, the war room in his personal office reflected the silencing of the chaos.

★

As usual, the party scene at Mar-a-Lago, where Trump was always the center of attention, put him at ease. From television the guests could tell that there were no big surprises as Georgia and North Carolina reported vote tallies.

Trump wanted a little more inside intel, so he ducked into his office to check in with his campaign team. They had left the chair behind his desk open—or, more precisely, no one dared to sit in it.

"Um?" Trump grunted his question. The wait was killing him. The night felt almost as long as the four years he had spent anticipating it. There were hundreds of people in the ballroom. Why wasn't this coming faster? Wiles detected the nervousness in her boss.

"This is gonna just take a little longer," she said. "Don't worry."

"Nothing concerning you?" he said, kicking the tires. Of course there were concerns. They all felt good about his chances, but none of the Blue Wall states had come in yet. Still, no one wanted to give him any detail that might become an Election Night obsession for him. The best way to manage a hands-on boss was to avoid handing him something to squeeze.

"Nothing concerning us, sir," she said.

"No complaints right now?" he poked. They could use some more of those eight-ounce glass Diet Coke bottles that seemed ubiquitous at Mar-a-Lago but were nowhere to be found. But those could be secured without the former president's help.

"No complaints," she reported.

★

Georgia and North Carolina, the first two swing states to close their polls and begin reporting reams of votes, showed marginal movement toward Trump across geographical lines.

In Georgia, for example, Trump's performance improved in nearly 85 percent of the state's counties, compared to 2020, when he lost the state by fewer than 12,000 votes. The shift was clear in the rural counties that reported all of their votes early, with Trump adding to his raw vote total in many of them. But even as he got trounced in urban areas, Trump improved his share of the vote in Atlanta's Fulton County and some of the close-in suburban counties, such as DeKalb and Gwinnett.

A similar dynamic took hold in North Carolina, with Trump adding voters and margin across wide swaths of the state in suburban and rural communities while taking a higher share of the electorate in major Democratic counties, such as Wake and Mecklenburg. In Mecklenburg County, home to Charlotte, Harris won 65.2 percent of the vote, down from Biden's 66.7 percent in 2020. Trump jumped from 31.6 percent to 32.5 percent.

The trend lines were good for Trump and bad for Harris. She wasn't turning out enough voters in metropolitan areas to offset his bumps outside them. At the Marriott Marquis, her aides first noticed troubling data points in the returns from Florida, which was not in play. But the shifts were not pronounced enough in the two early swing states for Trump aides to pop champagne bottles or Harris aides to start drowning their sorrows with harder drinks.

Between Harris's family and a growing number of aides arriving through the night, the vice president's residence started to fill up. The staff worked out of an office in the back of the house and in the library. But it was hard for senior leaders to have private conversations with O'Malley Dillon and others in the Marquis boiler room from the house. Lorraine Voles, Sheila Nix, climate adviser Ike Irby, and comms staffer Kirsten Allen exited the back door and clambered into Voles's sleek black hybrid Audi A3.

The Georgia results were giving Voles heartburn. *This really is not good*, she had thought as she watched counties outside of Atlanta come in. The four aides in the Audi each dialed their own sources within the campaign to try to get a better picture of where the race stood. Nothing they heard made them feel any better. The possibility of defeat hung like a cloud of cigar smoke in the sports car.

Long before the Associated Press called North Carolina for Trump shortly after 11 p.m. on the East Coast, the campaigns and political insiders around the country could tell that Trump had taken two of the seven battlegrounds off the table. He had won North Carolina in 2020, but Georgia, where he had begged election officials to find more votes for him after that year's election, was a flip in his direction. Now he just needed to win Pennsylvania or a combination of the remaining swing states to take back the Oval Office.

★

Jennifer O'Malley Dillon had kept her cool as Georgia and North Carolina showed the data team's projections had been a little too rosy. Going in, they had believed both states were more likely to fall to Trump than Harris, and the small delta between the campaign's estimates and the actual vote shares in those states was well within a reasonable expectation of accuracy. On a videoconference call in the 9 p.m. hour, Harris aides discussed the incoming figures and determined that there was no cause for panic.

But O'Malley Dillon's blood slowly heated to a boil as Pennsylvania periodically released new batches of votes. Anecdotal reports out of Philadelphia convinced some campaign officials that turnout in the state's biggest city might be strong enough to deliver a Harris victory. But as the night progressed, that conclusion looked less and less solid.

By the eleven o'clock hour, Harris was missing her vote targets across the state by enough to raise the question of whether Trump had already won. But that's not exactly what upset O'Malley Dillon. Instead, she was vexed by her prized data analytics operation—the outfit that informed nearly every campaign decision, from where to send the candidate to how much to spend on television in midsize markets. Her team was not giving her the information, or the analysis, that she wanted.

The campaign, together with the DNC, had raised and spent roughly $2 billion—not counting the money big-swinging Democratic donors routed through outside groups—in building a juggernaut that made the Death Star look like a speck of dust. Trump's operation spent about half that, a model of precise efficiency by comparison. Now the number-crunchers couldn't—or wouldn't—tell O'Malley Dillon what the incoming vote data meant.

Sitting around a conference table in a subbasement of the Marriott

Marquis, the campaign's top brass watched O'Malley Dillon go to work on her top analytics lieutenants, Becca Siegel and Meg Schwenzfeier. The crowd of onlookers included David Plouffe, Quentin Fulks, Stephanie Cutter, Rob Flaherty, Mitch Stewart, Brian Fallon, and Liz Allen.

O'Malley Dillon pressed the data team to interpret the latest vote dump from Pennsylvania. Did the numbers mean Trump had won? If not, how long would it take to make a call? She had to decide whether to push Harris to Howard to preempt a possible early Trump declaration of victory or hold her candidate back. It would be devastating—an indelible personal stain—if Harris told supporters there was a pathway to win only to be quickly contradicted by the race being called for Trump.

O'Malley Dillon had a lot of decisions to make, and she needed the right information. So far, the data wasn't clear. Or at least the analytics team wasn't. Not long ago, Siegel and Schwenzfeier had sounded bullish about turnout in Pennsylvania, which lined up with eyeball reports of high mobilization in other parts of the state. Now they were uncertain.

"It had just been a couple of hours earlier when I was looking at like a six-hour line of college students in fucking Altoona, Pennsylvania," one senior campaign official said with a bit of hyperbole about the wait time. "But once it switched, man, it went down quick and hard."

As O'Malley Dillon began to grill her, the color drained from Schwenzfeier's face, turning it a paler white against her blondish locks.

Schwenzfeier spit out bits of data from around the state.

"But where is the race?" O'Malley Dillon asked, her tone insistent but the volume of her voice even. "What does your gut tell you?"

Schwenzfeier tried again. Turnout in Philadelphia was only a little bit lower than 2020, she said, but Trump was winning more of it. It would be slightly up in Bucks County—but Trump was doing better there too.

"We never saw that in the models," O'Malley Dillon said of the softness. "What can we expect in the rest of the state?"

"The rural vote is coming in a little slower," Schwenzfeier offered.

They were speaking different languages. O'Malley Dillon just wanted to know whether Harris was going to lose Pennsylvania and the election, how long it would take to know, and why the campaign had not anticipated Trump hitting higher percentages in precinct after precinct.

Siegel and Schwenzfeier responded in lawyerly fashion, refusing to commit to a position on the global questions O'Malley Dillon wanted to resolve.

"What does that mean?" she asked each time one of her analytics aides answered her with a number or an equivocation. Go back, she finally said, and figure it out. Siegel and Schwenzfeier retreated to a small room reserved for them nearby and collected their thoughts.

They returned a little while later with the interpretations O'Malley Dillon had been seeking: We're not going to win Pennsylvania. We're probably not going to win Michigan. It's too close to call in Wisconsin. The air went out of the room. O'Malley Dillon felt her gut drop.

"We went from having reports from the boiler room of 'votes are just slow to come in, we're going to be fine' to 'oh, fuck, we just got a bad batch of data and we don't think there's a path,'" said one senior Harris campaign official who was getting updates from the Marquis.

O'Malley Dillon, now pacing like a general planning a surrender, filled the void with a series of logistical orders. The campaign sent Cedric Richmond, the former Louisiana congressman, to Howard to address the crowd there. Her own mission was the most unpleasant: she had to tell the candidate that the campaign had failed her—given her false hope about the outcome—and had handed the reins of the nation back to Donald J. Trump.

At the vice president's residence, Second Gentleman Doug Emhoff came down the stairs from the family's personal quarters and spoke briefly to Voles and Nix. Like his wife, he was stunned. He had few words to describe their disappointment. "It's bad," he said.

The house was still packed with staff, including a photographer and a videographer who had been there to record behind-the-scenes images of the historic election of the first woman to lead the free world. Now, in her moment of defeat, Harris did not need a carnival of onlookers milling about her house. "We've got to get these people out," Voles said to Nix. "They've got to go home."

Reconnecting with the vice president by phone, O'Malley Dillon, Voles, and Nix learned that Harris was not ready to concede. She had agreed with West's take. She did not want to miss any opening.

"Could we be in a recount?" Harris asked.

O'Malley Dillon had conferred with campaign lawyers at the Marquis. They were not in recount territory.

"We've looked at it again," she told the crestfallen candidate.

"Trump's not coming out right now, and they haven't called it," Nix said. "So you should just go to bed."

Trump trounced Harris up and down the battlegrounds, sweeping seven of them. In 2020, Biden had won all of those states but North Carolina. In absolute terms, the margin was small by historical standards—less than two points in each of the Blue Wall states. But in the Trump era, when the prior two elections had been decided by less than 80,000 votes spread across three states, the 2024 result was convincing. In such deeply and evenly divided partisan times, there is only so much that the electorate can shift. The vast majority of voters would stick with their party regardless of the candidate. Trump moved the needle as far as he could.

Not only did he win all of the competitive states, but he increased his share of the electorate across the vast majority of demographic and geographic sets. Exit polls showed that he tore into the traditional Democratic advantages with Latino and Asian American voters, increasing his share of Latinos from 32 percent to 46 percent and his share of Asian Americans from 34 percent to 40 percent. With a Black woman as his rival, he incrementally boosted his performance with African American voters, from 12 percent to 13 percent nationally, with men moving from 19 percent to 21 percent.

Perhaps more surprising, given all the attention to Trump's edge with men and Harris's with women, he did more to close the gender gap with women than to expand it with men. After losing women to Biden by 15 percentage points—57 percent to 42 percent—he only lost to Harris by a 53 percent to 45 percent margin, according to exit polls. Among men, Trump jumped to a 55 percent to 43 percent spread, from 53 percent to 45 percent in 2020.

Urban areas held steady over four years, but Trump flipped Biden's narrow edge in the suburbs into a 4-point win in 2024. In rural areas, Trump voters came rushing out of the fields to go to the polls. He won them by 30 points—64 percent to 34 percent—which was double his margin in 2020.

All of this happened while Trump articulated a very consistent message about his plans at rallies, over broadcast television, in ads on streaming channels, in texts to voters, and in mailers. By the end of the election, no one wondered what Trump was promising to do. The choice he offered was a clean break from the unpopular Biden administration—from its policies on the economy to immigration and the wars in Ukraine and the Middle East.

Harris, looking over her shoulder at Biden, categorically refused to separate herself from him. To the extent that there was daylight, it was provided by the Trump campaign using her own words to portray her as more liberal than Biden. Harris promised to find "a new way forward" and "turn the page." But many voters could only see her flipping backward through the history books—to the beginning of the Biden administration.

Trump focused on tactile issues for voters: economic and physical security. First with Biden, and then with Harris, Democrats asked voters to concentrate on preserving democracy. Then Democrats tore down a president of their own party—and replaced him with a new candidate—because they thought he was going to lose. Not only did that move vitiate the ballots of primary voters, but it felt to many Americans like an undemocratic rigging of the electoral game.

For four years, Democrats had told voters not to believe their lying eyes.

"You can't gaslight the American people about Afghanistan, gaslight them about inflation, gaslight them about the president's decline and think none of that's going to add up to a political problem," said one veteran Democratic strategist who worked on past presidential campaigns.

The Democrats even lied to themselves, according to one Harris campaign aide who struggled to explain why the high command told everyone Harris was positioned to win. "The gaslighting on this campaign was unreal," the aide said.

★

Sitting on a couch in his suite at Washington's Mayflower Hotel, Tim Walz fell silent.

Moments earlier, Sam Cornale, Walz's traveling chief of staff, had been on the phone with Liz Allen, the longtime Beltway operative who was a senior adviser to the governor. The two discussed the latest bad batch of data that had come through to the boiler room at the Marriott Marquis.

"They don't think there's a path," Allen told her counterpart. "The AP is close to calling Pennsylvania."

Cornale knew what he had to do. He walked up to Walz's suite and then entered the living room section, bearing the news the Minnesota governor hadn't seen coming. The moment was something Cornale's political science classes failed to cover: how to break the news to a vice presidential candidate that he had lost. And lost to Donald Trump. *This doesn't feel great*, Cornale thought.

It's not looking good, Cornale said, cutting to the chase without hesitation, holding his cell phone with Allen piped in on speaker.

Walz, surrounded by his wife, Gwen, and a couple of senior aides from the governor's office, barely said a word. He stared into space, processing the weight of Cornale's words.

"He was really stoic. He thought they were gonna win," said one source familiar with the governor's thinking. "And he, you know, has never lost a race. And he said 'you get a feel for these things.'"

Gwen Walz was the only one doing the talking for Minnesota's first couple. "We will do whatever is needed," she said. "We will get through this."

The conversation was perfunctory, turning quickly to the logistics of the coming hours.

Allen then spoke, offering some operational details. "Here's what we think is going to happen. We think it's going to be called in the early-morning hours. So you are no longer going to speak tonight, we can release your motorcade driver. The vice president will speak tomorrow. We'll send Cedric out tonight."

"You can tell your family to go to bed," Allen said.

Sorry, Governor, Cornale said. We'll be back in touch on next steps for tomorrow and we'll do our best to get you out of here.

★

The crew in Trump's office at Mar-a-Lago could see the same numbers as the Harris team. But news agencies were not calling the race. It was frustrating, for them and for Trump. At one point Wiles went down to the ballroom to find Trump.

"Nothing's different, but it's going to take a little while," she said, again. "Don't be discouraged. Just do what you do."

Then, all at once, enough votes were in to be certain that it really would only be a matter of time before Trump was declared the president-elect. "Okay, everybody," he said, "let's load up." The Mar-a-Lago ball-room crowd herded onto buses for the short trip to the Palm Beach County Convention Center. It was too slow for Trump. *This is taking forever*, he thought.

Finally, in the wee hours, Trump's motorcade set out for the victory rally. Backstage, amid a maze of temporary rooms, it seemed like every-one who had ever shaken his hand was present. JD Vance sat in his own hold room.

The face of the next generation of the MAGA movement, bearded and boyish all at once, had developed a close enough relationship with Donald Trump Jr. that the former president's son and his kids were spending time with the VP pick. So was Tucker Carlson, the right-wing media impresario who had remade himself from a nerdy establishment conservative into an icon of radical antiestablishment Republican pop-ulism.

After Trump's false claim of victory on Election Night in 2020, sev-eral days before that race was called for Biden, no one wanted to get ahead of an official declaration by the Associated Press. When AP made that call, just before 2:30 a.m., Vance's hold room exploded in celebra-tion. Don Jr. sported what one onlooker described as a shit-eating grin while Vance and his friends hugged and high-fived.

Wiles squeezed herself into Trump's hold room to tell him that it was time to go onstage. "Congratulations!" she said. Four years of built-up tension evaporated in an instant. The normally stone-faced Trump beamed, smiling ear to ear.

Amid the jubilation backstage, only one Trumpworld figure seemed unhappy. Eight years after he had been sacked as campaign manager, Corey Lewandowski wangled his way into the campaign headquarters over the summer and tried to take over. Wiles had shut him down, and most of the campaign team had moved past that tenuous moment when Harris was surging, Trump was anxious, and the whole leadership sat on the hot seat. Chris LaCivita had neither forgotten nor forgiven. He blamed Lewandowski for trash-talking him to the boss and for media reporting that wildly overstated how much LaCivita was being paid for his campaign work.

As denizens of Trumpworld congratulated one another on the victory, LaCivita told Justin Caporale, the deputy campaign manager, that Lewandowski should not be given a place of prominence on the stage.

"I can't do that," Caporale said.

"You can't?" LaCivita asked. "Or you won't?"

"I won't," Caporale clarified.

Though he had aligned with Lewandowski against the top campaign leaders over the summer, Wiles and LaCivita both maintained deep respect for Caporale's ability to manage major operations. His actions would be dealt with subtly—he would be denied a senior post in the White House and instead given a job supporting Trump from the outside—but Lewandowski, in LaCivita's estimation, deserved public humiliation.

When Lewandowski approached, he tried to shake LaCivita's hand.

"Congratulations!" Lewandowski said. LaCivita refused to shake.

"I've never said an ill word about you," Lewandowski protested.

LaCivita wasn't having it. Lewandowski had tried to ratfuck him repeatedly. Towering over Lewandowski, LaCivita jabbed his index finger into Lewandowski's chest.

"Fuck you, fuck you, and fuck you," LaCivita elegized. "I'm going to gut you like a motherfucking fish. You're nothing. You're a piece of shit. You messed with the wrong fucking guy."

If LaCivita focused on retribution, Trump turned away from it—at least for the time being—when he finally declared victory at 2:33 a.m. He commended his movement, praised allies including Vance and Elon Musk, and vowed to heal the country. "Every single day," he said, "I will be fighting for you."

Trump's win was an epic comeback with just one parallel in American history. But the story behind it was more than improbable. Trump had been a pariah to all but the most loyal members of his MAGA movement less than four years earlier. He had endured more hardship than any presidential candidate—much of it self-inflicted—and stood higher than he ever had before. Not only did he take the Electoral College, but for the first time in three elections, he had also won the national popular vote.

Still, he did not see the arc as a comeback at all. He believed he was tasting his just dessert, the fruit not just of his labor but of the voters righting the wrong of 2020. Yet it took a moment for reality to sink in as he looked out at the jubilant crowd in front of him.

It happened, he thought. *It really did.*

Harris had not been able to shut down and go to sleep right away. Her thoughts raced, searching for a logical consistency they could not find. Closing her eyes, she ran through the past few days.

The crowds were big and enthusiastic, she thought. *The late polling was good. Everyone told me I was in position to win. Were they lying to me or just wrong?*

None of it added up. *This just doesn't compute*, she thought. *Can this be real? What the fuck happened?*

Kamala Harris had been gaslit too.

THE AFTERMATH

KAMALA HARRIS HAD PUT OFF THE INEVITABLE FOR LONG ENOUGH. WITH the Associated Press calling the race the night before, there had been no real pressure from Trump's camp or the media for her to formally concede. That had bought her some time. But she thought it was respectful to make the call before she spoke to the country from Howard University on Wednesday afternoon.

Harris had not given much consideration to her concession speech. She had not expected to give one. A draft written by Adam Frankel had gathered dust as Harris barnstormed the country and envisioned herself standing at the Capitol taking the oath of office. He sent it over late Tuesday night so that she could look at it in the morning. It was missing something essential, she told her aides, as they gathered at her home the morning after the election.

"I said, 'When we fight, we win,'" she reminded them. "And there are all these kids and families who come to the rallies who believe that. How do we reconcile the outcome for them?" She was talking through her own shock, developing an argument that could help her process the idea that she had fought and lost. "Sometimes the fight takes a while," she said. "That doesn't mean we won't win."

To highly tuned political ears, she might sound like a politician leaving the door open for a future run—for president in 2028 or California governor in 2026. But there also remained a real disconnect for Harris between the boom of excitement she had seen on the trail and the bust of Election Night. She was still reeling from the cognitive dissonance—

the brain-breaking conflict in data points—when Sheila Nix connected to Trump for the concession call late that morning. The denouement would have to wait a little bit longer, delayed by a technical glitch.

From her spot at one of the five desks in the staff's back office in the vice president's residence, Nix could not merge Trump's call with Harris, who was upstairs in her personal quarters. Even this final dispiriting task wasn't going according to plan. As Nix tried to figure out a workaround, Trump waxed nostalgic. "The phone companies," Trump said, "they're not like they used to be."

Lorraine Voles called Harris and held her phone next to Nix's, with the speaker functions activated on both, so the former and future president could speak with the vice president. "You gave me a run for my money," Trump said. "You're tough. You ran a great campaign." *I can see why some people think he's charming*, Nix thought.

"I want to make sure that you know we will help with the transition," Harris said. "It's important that you work to be a president for all Americans, and I appreciate what you said about unity and healing. We really need that as a country."

★

Democrats tried to break Donald Trump. Instead, they shattered again. They said they were saving the country, the presidency, and the Congress from Trump and his MAGA movement. They saved nothing, not even themselves. Democrats lost everything, including their friendships.

On December 9, a little more than a month after Election Day, Nancy Pelosi and her family attended a black-tie White House holiday party. It was only the second time she had seen Joe Biden since he exited the race—the first was a brief, cold greeting at Ethel Kennedy's October memorial service—and her presence was an indication of her status in Washington, not a thaw in Biden's feelings toward her.

The president and the former Speaker awkwardly held hands for an unusually unwarm photo-line snapshot, with nearly a foot separating her calf-length pink lace dress from the body of his tuxedo jacket. Harris and Emhoff, at the edge of a wide frame that also included Pelosi's husband and eldest daughter, made no effort to embrace any of the Pelosis.

First Lady Jill Biden didn't even pose for the shot. When Democratic insiders put out a contract on Biden's political life, Pelosi executed the hit. No one in the photo was confused about that, or her reluctance to back Harris for the nomination. Pelosi had appraised her betrayal as a selfless act of service to the higher goal of winning the House. It didn't work.

Senate Democratic leader Chuck Schumer did not want Pelosi to get all the credit for pushing Biden to the side, as soon as it looked like Harris had a chance to win. He started telling reporters in August that he had played a crucial role behind the scenes in urging Biden to get out. But that's not how other senior Democrats saw it. "He was silent until he went to see the president," one of them said, noting that Schumer was mocked in party circles for taking victory laps as Harris's poll numbers soared in the late summer. Schumer wanted Democrats to win the presidency, to save the Senate Democratic majority, and to keep himself viable as the leader of a caucus that was nearly unanimously opposed to Biden staying in. Schumer kept his spot atop the party leadership, but Democrats lost the presidency and the Senate.

Even Barack Obama, who had twice won the presidency, misfired badly. He subscribed to a magical hypothesis that Democrats could oust Biden, hold a speed-dating primary, and nominate someone other than Harris. He tried to make that happen even as she was locking down the delegates she needed. Obama usually wanted to float above the fray, taking credit and avoiding blame whenever possible. That didn't work either.

The Obama–Biden relationship was "irreparable" at the end of 2024, according to one Democratic insider who had worked for both men. Obama wanted to mend the damage, but Biden did not, the former aide said. A donor who is close to both presidents agreed with that assessment. "Their relationship will never be the same," the donor said. "It's never coming back." At one point in the summer, the Biden and Obama camps put them together on a phone call to frustrate a forthcoming news story that would have noted they had not spoken since Biden's withdrawal, according to two people familiar with the effort. "It was done to make it so aides could say 'Yes, they have spoken,'" one of the people said. One week before he left the White House, Biden named future aircraft carriers for presidents Bill Clinton and George W. Bush. Obama received neither that honor nor the Presidential Medal of Freedom, which Obama had once bestowed on Biden. Hillary Clinton, who had stood by Biden and then backed Harris, got a Medal of Freedom.

There was plenty of blame to go around in Democratic circles, but Biden found himself at the center of the Venn diagram. In late July—long before ballots were cast—a former high-ranking government official who is close to both Biden and Obama said the president damned his party by committing "the original sin" of running for a second term.

In 2020, Biden asked Americans to look at him as a caretaker, a competent political veteran who would temper the chaos of Trump's first term and serve as a bridge to the next generation. They elected him, barely, and then he reversed course by seeking reelection. In between, the American public lost faith in his competence, honesty, and cogency—judgments informed by his handling of domestic and foreign affairs, his refusal to level with consumers about inflation, and voters' own concerns about the effects of aging on his ability to do his job.

Before he met Trump on a debate stage in Atlanta in June 2024, Biden was on track to lose. But he continued to run anyway, even as the dominos continued to fall, and one by one, his fellow party leaders and donors turned against him. After the election, even as his closest aides said he had realized the die was cast and there was no way he could have defeated Donald Trump, he said the opposite. First, in private conversations with friends and close allies, he maintained he could have won. Then, he said it out loud, in an interview and to a gaggle of reporters at what would be his final face-to-face with the White House press corps.

"It's presumptuous to say that, but I think yes," Biden said when he was asked by USA Today reporter Susan Page if he could have prevailed, even as just about the entire electorate concluded the opposite. The comments angered Democrats up and down the party, but it was most triggering to Harris and her closest allies. "So basically, he was saying she sucked," one former Harris aide said in January. "You've done enough damage," the aide continued. "Just stop talking."

Biden's comments confounded even his top aides. "When, I think, he says stuff like that, it isn't based on . . . like, what happened," said one Biden aide who continued on with Harris after the candidate switch.

The first lady's venom was even more potent. Jill Biden, the keeper of the vindictive flame for the family, told the *Washington Post* in mid-January that she found Pelosi's actions "disappointing" because of the relationship between the two families. "We were friends for fifty years," Jill Biden said. A month earlier, and less than a week after the black-tie White Houe party, Pelosi had fallen in Europe and broken her hip. The first lady had nothing to do with the slip, but she wasn't interested in picking Pelosi up. For all of the comforting messages that poured in from national and world leaders, including Luxembourg's grand duke Henri and a string of Republicans, Pelosi did not receive a call from the Bidens. The slights were noticed.

"If I was Lady McBiden, I'd put on my big-girl pants, play the long game, and think about my husband's legacy," Alexandra Pelosi, one of the former speaker's daughters, told *Politico*. "There aren't that many people left in America who have something nice to say about Joe Biden. And Nancy Pelosi is one of them."

It was all a sad and stunning turn for Biden, who had so endeared himself to his party by defeating Trump in 2020. Back then, he had finally won the prize he had pursued for his entire adult life. He believed he had delivered policies that put him in a league with the nation's greatest presidents, even as voters told him the opposite. Now, as he prepared to leave the White House, he had lost almost everything: his presidency, his political career, his physical prowess, his acuity, and even some of his friends. What endured was the naked egotism that compelled him to seek a second term, continue to run when it was clear he could not win, and make wild claims that he would have beaten Trump again if only he had not dropped his bid.

He thought he had been done dirty. By Pelosi. By Obama. By donors. And even by Kamala Harris, the vice president who showed him nothing but loyalty and deference at her own expense. "She was a better friend to him than he was to her," one Harris adviser observed. One Biden friend said the anger toward Harris came more from the first lady than the president, who was not deployed as a campaign surrogate in the way his family would have liked. "She's really bitter at Harris," the friend said.

Biden insisted to friends that he would have prevailed where she failed. "There's a lot of modern revisionist history going on here," said one Biden confidant who spoke to the outgoing president in the days right after the election. "He firmly believes that he could have won, which is the most absurd fucking thing I've ever heard in modern politics."

In the end, Biden was, in fact, a bridge—from one Trump term to the next.

★

No one wanted to take responsibility for the party's second loss to Trump in three elections—least of all the campaign professionals who had told donors, voters, and even the candidate that they were poised to win.

Three weeks after Election Day, Jennifer O'Malley Dillon and her top deputies sought out a friendly audience for their first joint interview on what went wrong. Appearing on *Pod Save America* with former Obama aide Dan Pfeiffer, they painted the picture of a race that they were always destined to lose. "We were behind," David Plouffe, the senior Harris campaign adviser, said. "I think it surprised people because there were these public polls that came out in late September, early October, showing us with leads that we never saw." That didn't sound to many Democratic listeners quite the same as the proclamation that Plouffe made the day before the election, that Harris was poised to win *all* of the swing states.

While the campaign raised and shelled out more than $1.5 billion in 107 days under Harris, it ultimately wasn't enough, other advisers said on the podcast.

"It is easy to say with the kind of resources that we raised, we should have been able to do everything, but that's not the case," deputy campaign manager Quentin Fulks said. "You have to make decisions in the time frame that we were in in this race."

It was hard for Democratic voters to tell what was real. They had been led to believe Joe Biden was in fighting shape. But he wasn't. They had been led to believe he was locked in a dead-heat race with Trump. But he wasn't. They had been led to believe that Harris was in position to win. But she wasn't. And now they were being led to believe she never really had a chance. That wasn't really true either.

Harris started at a disadvantage, and she never overtook Trump. But there was a period in late August and early September where she had effectively evened the race—enough to make Trump nervous and Democratic insiders cautiously confident. Then Harris hit a ceiling. One of her senior aides described the loss as "death by a million cuts." Yet some were deeper than the rest.

★

Harris took longer to start processing the mechanics of her defeat. In the first days after the election, she cloistered with her family at the vice president's residence, eating comfort food and watching movies—*Land of Bad* and *Wise Guys* among them. There was nowhere else in the nation's capital to escape what one close associate described as the "public death" of continuing to perform the duties of an elected official after losing reelection.

Later in the month, Harris took a six-day vacation in Hawaii, before returning to Washington for a series of holiday parties. She kept O'Malley Dillon close at hand as she sifted through the various explanations for the loss and slowly began to think about her future. Harris was listening to friends who wanted her to run for governor of California in 2026 and those who thought she should enter the 2028 Democratic presidential primary field. O'Malley Dillon told her she could wait a year to decide on the governor's race. Longtime advisers raised their eyebrows at JOD's ability to stay in Harris's ear.

By December, Harris came to a counterintuitive conclusion. She could have won, she told friends, if only the election was later in the calendar—or she got in earlier. In other words, Joe Biden was to blame. If only he had not run. If only he had gotten out earlier. If only he hadn't been so unpopular. "It is very difficult if you're the incumbent vice president in a change election if your president can't break thirty-eight percent," said one ally who spoke to Harris regularly in the aftermath of the election and shared her view. "She thinks she needed a little more time," said a second ally.

There can be little doubt that Harris was handed a brutal assignment: campaign for 107 days on the back of a president with terrible approval numbers—and make sure there's no daylight. But she peaked well before Election Day. The more straightforward analysis is that extra time did not help her. "That is fucking bonkers," one Harris friend said of the vice president's take. "If Election Day was October first, we might have actually somehow pulled it off. Shorter was actually better, not longer."

Harris proved so ready for the hand-to-hand combat required to lock down the nomination that no one stepped up to fight her for it. But she was not at all prepared to present her case to the country. Disaffected Democrats rushed back into the fold in the summer months, after Biden's departure. The surge was real, and it brought Harris even with Trump. She had a chance to win, but she did not have the most fundamental premise of a presidential candidacy worked out: her reason for running. She did not articulate a vision for the country, or the concomitant policy matrix, that might have convinced enough voters to elect her. She did not have a counter to Trump's use of her own words and record to portray her as a liberal extremist.

"We were holding sand in the palm of our hand, and it was slipping out of the fingers slowly," said one Harris adviser. "I don't think we needed more time. We needed more sand. We needed more substance. And she did not have more substance."

★

Donald Trump, the second man to lose the presidency and then win it back, had taken nearly 50 percent of the vote. He wasted little time in making clear that he intended to wield 100 percent of the power—or as close to that as possible.

During the final weeks of the campaign, pundits had marveled at Trump's decision to hold rallies in states outside the main battlegrounds—California, Colorado, New Mexico, Virginia, and New York—as well as his spending on expensive national television ads. From the perspective of getting the most bang for his buck in the all-important Electoral College, those moves were wasteful. But Trump was obsessed with winning the most votes for the first time—and the mandate he believed that would give him. "No, no, no, no," he said when senior adviser Chris LaCivita noted that the national TV buys weren't the most efficient way to secure the presidency. "We can win *and* take the popular vote," Trump said. LaCivita pushed more cash into national ads.

When all the votes were counted, Trump beat Harris by 2.3 million ballots and about 1.5 percentage points. With also-ran candidates included, he ended with 49.7 percent of the vote—the highest share of his three campaigns. "Trump tapped into the anxiety of white people—and now a new generation of men," said one Democratic Party elder. "Trump saw them, and we did not. If we ignore them, continue to ignore them, or not understand what a real coalition is, then it's to our own peril."

Trump spent the transition period figuring out exactly how he would flex the muscles of the presidency, both in terms of policy and personnel. He pledged to use the powers of his office to execute a mass deportation program, give himself emergency authorities to address the economy, and issue pardons—including to people convicted of crimes related to the January 6, 2021, Capitol riot. He threatened to slap across-the-board tariffs on allies and talked openly of taking control of Greenland and the Panama Canal. His early Cabinet picks included a coterie of fringe political players with little experience in managing bureaucracies. And that was the point. "There's an emphasis on disruption," said one adviser close to Trump. "I wouldn't have predicted that he would have focused on that as he has, but he has. And he believes it will pay big dividends."

The day before he took the oath of office inside the Capitol, with his inauguration moved indoors because of cold and snowy weather in the nation's capital, Trump reflected on the battle scars he incurred in returning to the peak of power. Just four years earlier, his supporters had ransacked the Capitol in violent defiance of his defeat. Now, he had clawed his way back to that same building—the symbol of democracy across the globe—by winning an election in close but convincing fashion. To do that, he had to fight to restore his reputation, fight to dispatch Republican foes, fight for his freedom in the face of four separate criminal indictments, fight to beat both a president and a vice president of the other party, and survive a bullet.

Spotting some of his most committed fans at a pre-inauguration rally at Washington's Capital One Arena on January 19, Trump pointed them out to the crowd. This was the moment of reward for him, and for his MAGA base.

"We've been through so much together, and for the next four years, I will fight for you," he said.

★ ACKNOWLEDGMENTS ★

WE WERE NOT GOING TO WRITE A BOOK ABOUT THE 2024 ELECTION. AND then Joe Biden stepped onto a debate stage with Donald Trump and turned the political world upside down. Our editor, Mauro DiPreta, asked if we would be willing to put everything else on hold and jump headlong into reporting out what turned into a more intense *FIGHT*—inside the Democratic Party and for the future of America—than we ever could have imagined.

We are grateful to Mauro for his sharp questions, even temperament, and consistent encouragement—as well as his confidence in our ability to turn around an action-packed book on a condensed timeline. We remain indebted to our agent, Bridget Wagner Matzie, who took a chance on us more than a decade ago. After four books, she is much more than a literary agent to us. She is a close friend—close enough to tell us honestly what works and what doesn't in our drafts.

We can't thank Elleiana Green and Shravya Pant enough. Our bang-up researchers on this project, they proved eager, tireless, and insightful. We threw a variety of tasks at them, and they handled each with poise and professionalism.

We'd also like to thank our team at William Morrow: president and publisher Liate Stehlik, deputy publisher Ben Steinberg, vice president of publicity and integrated marketing strategy Kelly Rudolph, senior director of marketing Melissa Esner, director of marketing Liz Psaltis, director of publicity Megan Wilson, production editor Jeanie Lee, and assistant editor Allie Johnston.

But mostly, we are grateful to so many sources who agreed to talk to us, knowing that we would, once again, chronicle perhaps the most important election in our lifetime.

—JA & AP

I have been Stephanie Allen's husband for almost twenty years, and she amazes me more each day with her love, compassion, sense of humor, and endless desire to take and send pictures of our dog, Fluffy Tiger.

Our son, Asher, has developed into a sweet, funny, and delightfully contrarian young man, who performs far better in school than his father ever could. Asher, I'm proud of your curiosity, your entrepreneurialism, and your ability to juggle the demands of school, sports, and other extracurricular activities.

Our daughter, Emma, is a bundle of energy, whose creative talents—from acting in school plays to drawing—are flourishing. Emma, I am proud of you for your determination, your irrepressible spirit, and your desire to help family and friends.

Stephanie and I are both very proud of a trait our children share: good-heartedness. I love all three of you with every fiber of my being.

Amie, we did it again! You are more than a writing partner or a friend, you are family. We must be crazy to have accepted this assignment, and yet you kept us sane throughout the process. I wouldn't have done this with anyone else. I couldn't have done this with anyone else. Thank you for everything, always.

My parents, Ira and Marin Allen, continue to be invaluable sources of wisdom, strength, and childcare. They gave me everything, and I have only a free book to offer in return. My sister, Amanda Allen, "the good one," deserves a medal for giving this book a thorough scrub and offering brilliant insights into how to improve it. Thank you, Mom, Dad, and Amanda. I've loved you all much longer than anyone else. My father-in-law and mother-in-law, Bill and Ronnie Weintraub, provide love and support to all of us, and for that I am forever grateful.

I want to thank Rebecca Blumentstein, Catherine Kim, Carrie Budoff Brown, Tom Namako, Amanda Terkel, Natasha Korecki, Ali Vitali, Olympia Sonnier, Matt Dixon, Henry Gomez, Allan Smith, Jane Timm, Stephanie Ruhle, and all my colleagues at NBC News for giving me the support and space I needed to finish this book.

And, of course, a big shout-out to the family and friends who have given advice, listened to rants, and made it easier to finish this book: Chris Pearson, Adam and Tory Weintraub, Kristen Hawn, Ted Derheimer, David Mortlock, Justin Russell, Matthew Bartlett, Juliegrace Brufke, Del Wilber, Will Hessler, Dan McBride, Mark Bednar, Jesse Staal, Madison Andrus, Molly Jong-Fast, Kyle Hauptman, the Pearsons, the Bergmans, the Cohens, and Janet Crowder.

I am also thankful to Shelly's Backroom and TG Cigars and their staffs for tolerating my work in their gloriously smoke-filled rooms.

—JA

When we were asked if we were interested in doing another book on the election this summer, I immediately knew my coauthor's answer without even speaking to him. Nearly thirteen years after we came together to do our first book, I couldn't ask for a better partner in crime. Jon, I told you this repeatedly these past few months, but I am in awe of the way you produce journalism. Your writing, your reporting, your analysis, and the speed with which you do it all is most impressive. Thank you for your persistence, for your levity in the toughest moments, and most of all, your dear friendship.

I couldn't have done this again without Bob Cusack and Ian Swanson at *The Hill*. From the moment I told Bob and Ian I was working on another book—in the middle of the craziest election cycle to date!—they gave me their blessing, as they have done in the past. Most reporters have editors. Bob and Ian have long surpassed editor standing. They have become not only my close friends, they are family. I continue to be indebted to both of them for believing in me.

Speaking of family, my mom, Esther Parnes, as she has always done, stepped up to assist with childcare, making sure the laundry didn't pile up for weeks on end and my house didn't generally fall apart while I was completely checked out. And she did it all while keeping the tea, cookies, and love flowing. My sister, Sherry Parnes, was there as a sounding board throughout this process, offering thoughts, advice, and her unique perspective. She has a way of making me laugh like no one else can and, let me put it this way, her humor was much needed the past several months. My dad, Henry Parnes, offered his support, particularly late at night when I was running on empty. He also offered much needed "tutoring services" when I was too exhausted to help with math homework. I love you all!

Remy Maddox is my everything, as everyone knows. Whenever I am down, or too tired, or completely overworked, all I have to do is look at him and, like magic, I am a different person. He deserves all my love and appreciation for his patience and understanding these past few months. Remy, you will always be the best thing that ever happened to me. Don't ever forget that.

Sending more love to John and Cal, who started as bunk-bed and reading companions and have now become the best tour guides, co-chefs, and all around inspiration to their biggest and loudest fan.

And sending love and appreciation to Garri and Debbie Hendell (especially for taking good care of us during the DNC in Chicago), Abraham Zadi, Therese Yacobelli, Magny and Phillip Zadi, and the rest of the Zadi Zoo.

I have depended so much on my lovely friends, some of whom have been by my side for decades. Jarah Greenfield has remained the keeper of my innermost thoughts since we were twelve. On the roughest days, I know she's a phone call away, and that brings me immense comfort. Lesley Clark and Bridget Petruczok are my constant gut checks in politics and life. Craig Bode, who has been on the scene for nearly thirty years celebrating my best days and listening on my worst, pitched in as babysitter, chauffeur, and, much to my dismay, DJ.

Thank you also to my wonderful friends Dolly Hernandez, Michael Collins, Niall Stanage, Judy Kurtz, Kristin Owen, Amy Abernathy, Erika Bolstad, Libby Casey, M. E. Sprengelmeyer, Carrie Holland, Hanna Trudo, Chris Donovan, Chris Frates, Rebecca Morin, Nicole Gaudiano, Dan Merica, Marc Caputo, Mary Ann Akers, Stephen Neukam, Lauren Morello, Morgan Chalfant, Karin Tanabe, Julian Zelizer, Michelle Majure, Rachel Meltzer, and Daria Muresan for all your support and love.

And a special thank-you to the people who helped make my life a little easier this year. Looking at you, David and Carolyn Sitler (the very best neighbors), Debra Goldenring, Kristy Lynch, Danielle Manno, Meredith Dew, and Karim Saavedra.

Finally, I lost two dear people in my life since our last book project, and I can't express how many times I've thought of Jeremy Levine and Kirk Swanson—both of whom I had known since I was twelve—during the highs and lows of this process. Jeremy, who geeked out on politics, would often read my stories and was one of the first to send a note and text me about the latest news of the day. Jeremy would have loved this crazy election cycle, and he would have asked me a million questions about this book as it was being written. He will forever be one of my great loves, and I feel his absence and that profound void almost every day. Kirk, who battled cancer for years, often shone the brightest light, even as his own life was in turmoil and when he faced an immense amount of pain. Kirk taught me about the power of optimism and to "relish the opportunities horizon-bound" whenever change was afoot. He will always be one of the best people I know.

In many ways, this book is for both Jeremy and Kirk, the ultimate fighters.

—*AP*

★ NOTES ★

In reporting this book, we spoke to more than one hundred and fifty sources with insights into the Trump, Harris, and Biden campaigns, as well as the Biden White House. We spoke to these sources exclusively "on background" so that they could avoid the fear of retribution and speak frankly about sensitive topics. Often, we describe what someone thought. We cannot read minds, but many of our sources told us what they were thinking or shared what someone else said about his or her own thinking. In some cases, we received documents that shed light on what someone was thinking. Unless otherwise noted, voting data came from uselection atlas.org and state, county, and municipal websites; exit poll information came from the National Election Pool, a consortium of news agencies that conducts the polls; and polling averages came from RealClearPolitics. We drew heavily from the timeline and facts established by the U.S. Senate Committee on Homeland Security and Government Affairs' report "Investigation of U.S. Secret Service Planning and Security Failures Related to the July 13, 2024, Assassination Attempt" in the Chapter 7 depiction of Donald Trump's first rally in Butler, Pennsylvania. We also made extensive use of White House pool reports, which are available to the press and the public, for details on the activities of the president and vice president. We are endlessly grateful to the White House press corps for that vital reporting and to the University of California, Santa Barbara's American Presidency Project, which preserves it online.

CHAPTER 1: "THE QUIET PART OUT LOUD"

3   *Georgetown condo:* "Homes of the Bailout Stars," *Washingtonian,* December 1, 2008, https://www.washingtonian.com/2008/12/01/homes-of-the-bailout-stars/.

4   *House impeached him:* Lauren Egan and Rebecca Shabad, "House Impeaches Trump for Second Time; Senate Must Now Weigh Conviction," NBC News, January 13, 2021, https://www.nbcnews.com/politics/congress/house-poised -impeach-trump-second-time-incitement-insurrection-n1254051.

4   *mocked her husband:* Andrew Zhang, "Trump Mocks Pelosi Family as He Rallies Conservative Support in California," *Politico*, September 29, 2023, https:// www.politico.com/news/2023/09/29/trump-mocks-pelosi-family-as-he-ralli es-conservative-support-in-california-00119243.

5   *luxury condo:* Melissa Klein, "Rev. Al Sharpton Seen Maskless Around His New Luxury Upper East Side Building," *New York Post*, December 12, 2020, https://nypost.com/2020/12/12/rev-al-sharpton-seen-maskless-around-new -luxury-nyc-building/.

6   *presidential ambitions:* Michael Slackman, "Sharpton Runs for Presidency, and Influence," *New York Times*, December 5, 2003, https://www.nytimes .com/2003/12/05/us/sharpton-runs-for-presidency-and-influence.html.

6   *suffered through:* Darlene Superville, "Biden Honors the Memory of His First Wife and Baby Daughter Who Died in a 1972 Car Crash," Associated Press, December 18, 2024, https://apnews.com/article/biden-memorial-wife-daugh ter-killed-accident-delaware-a00f53d572a90386a55f206f59c7ff3e.

6   *win the White House:* "Presidential Election Results 2020: Biden Wins," *New York Times*, November 7, 2020, https://www.nytimes.com/interactive /2020/11/03/us/elections/results-president.html.

7   *no American troops:* Rebecca Shabad, "Families of Service Members Killed in 2021 Kabul Airport Attack Demand Accountability from Biden," NBC News, August 29, 2023, https://www.nbcnews.com/politics/joe-biden/fam ilies-service-members-killed-2021-kabul-airport-attack-demand-accou -rcna102436.

7   *during an attack:* "DOD Identifies Marine Corps, Navy and Army Casualties," Department of Defense press release, August 28, 2021, https://www.defense .gov/News/Releases/Release/Article/2756011/dod-identifies-marine-corps -navy-and-army-casualties/.

7   *plunging his approval ratings:* Gary Langer, "Biden's Job Approval Drops to 44% amid Broad Criticism on Afghanistan: Poll," ABC News, September 3, 2021, https://abcnews.go.com/Politics/bidens-job-approval-drops-44-amid -broad-criticism/story?id=79791303.

7   *"solitary person eligible":* "Read: Biden-Trump Debate Transcript," CNN, June 28, 2024, https://edition.cnn.com/2024/06/27/politics/read-biden -trump-debate-rush-transcript/index.html.

7   *"beat Medicare!":* Ibid.

7   *"He did beat Medicaid":* Ibid.

7   *"He beat it to death"*: Ibid.

8   *"don't know what he said"*: Ibid.

9   *onetime Biden intern*: Amna Nawaz et al., "Sen. Coons Reflects on Biden's Presidency and 'Selfless' Decision to Step Aside," PBS News, August 19, 2024, https://www.pbs.org/newshour/show/sen-coons-reflects-on-bidens-presidency-and-selfless-decision-to-step-aside.

12   *host Nicolle Wallace:* "Exclusive: Watch President Biden's Full Interview with MSNBC's Nicolle Wallace," MSNBC, June 29, 2023, https://www.youtube.com/watch?v=CmekpMxhFmg.

15   *over a sandbag*: Kevin Liptak, "White House Says Biden Is Fine After Tripping on Sandbag and Falling on Stage at Air Force Academy Commencement," CNN, June 1, 2023, https://edition.cnn.com/2023/06/01/politics/biden-us-air-force-academy-trip/index.html.

15   *HOKA shoes*: Diana Glebova, "Joe Biden's New 'Boat Anchor' Shoes Meant for Maximum 'Stability' as President's Falls Spark Concern," *New York Post*, March 18, 2024, https://nypost.com/2024/03/18/us-news/joe-bidens-new-boat-anchor-shoes-meant-for-maximum-stability/.

15   *wheel-up steps*: Tamara Keith, "Why Biden Is Now Routinely Taking the Short Stairs Up to Air Force One," NPR, August 31, 2023, https://www.npr.org/2023/08/31/1196803354/biden-air-force-one-short-stairs.

15   *grossly irresponsible*: M. J. Lee et al., "Angry and Stunned Democrats Blame Biden's Closest Advisers for Shielding Public from Full Extent of President's Decline," CNN, July 11, 2024, https://edition.cnn.com/2024/07/11/politics/joe-biden-age-decline-democrats-angry/index.html.

15   *wasn't going anywhere*: Ibid.

16   *special counsel Robert Hur*: Ryan J. Reilly et al., "Biden Won't Be Charged in Classified Docs Case; Special Counsel Cites Instances of 'Poor Memory,'" NBC News, February 8, 2024, https://www.nbcnews.com/politics/joe-biden/special-counsel-says-evidence-biden-willfully-retained-disclosed-class-rcna96666.

16   *struggled to recall*: Ibid.

16   *timing of his son's death*: Ibid.

17   *he froze*: "President Biden Appears to Freeze at White House Juneteenth Concert," Fox News, June 11, 2024, https://www.foxnews.com/video/6354800466112.

18   *normal pauses:* Jeff Murdock, "White House Says Videos Showing Biden Freezing, Appearing to Wander Are 'Cheap Fakes,'" *Washington Times*, June 17, 2024, https://www.washingtontimes.com/news/2024/jun/17/white-house-says-videos-showing-biden-freezing-app/.

18   *Silver screen idol:* George Clooney, "I Love Joe Biden. But We Need a New Nom-

inee," *New York Times*, July 10, 2024, https://www.nytimes.com/2024/07/10/opinion/joe-biden-democratic-nominee.html.

25 *used its power to insist:* Robert Tait, "No Props, No Notes, No Audience—but Trump-Biden Debate Will Have Ad Breaks," *The Guardian*, June 22, 2024, https://www.theguardian.com/us-news/article/2024/jun/22/biden-trump-presidential-debate.

27 *"feeling great":* Joseph A. Wulfsohn, "Jill Biden Privately Assured Donors 'Joe's Ready to Go' Ahead of Disastrous Debate: Report," Fox News, June 28, 2024, https://www.foxnews.com/media/jill-biden-privately-assured-donors-joes-ready-go-ahead-disastrous-debate-report.

CHAPTER 2: CONTINGENCY PLANS

30 *"whether he should continue":* Betsy Klein et al., "Biden's Debate Performance Sets Off Alarm Bells for Democrats," CNN, June 28, 2024, https://edition.cnn.com/2024/06/28/politics/joe-biden-debate-performance-panic/index.html.

34 *"collective lifetime":* Priscilla Alvarez, "Harris Rushes to Biden's Defense After Disappointing Debate," CNN, June 28, 2024, https://edition.cnn.com/2024/06/28/politics/harris-rushes-to-bidens-defense/index.html.

36 *"tell the truth":* Gabe Gutierrez et al., "'I Don't Debate as Well as I Used To': Biden Tries to Move On from His Tough Debate at an Energized Rally," NBC News, June 28, 2024, https://www.nbcnews.com/politics/2024-election/-get-back-biden-parlays-disappointing-debate-rallying-cry-supporters-rcna159480.

CHAPTER 3: "KEEP FIGHTING"

39 *"best debate ever":* Ibid.

39 *weigh his options:* Carol E. Lee et al., "'It's a Mess': Biden Turns to Family on His Path Forward After His Disastrous Debate," NBC News, June 29, 2024, https://www.nbcnews.com/politics/2024-election/biden-family-path-forward-disastrous-debate-mess-rcna159591.

40 *second ousted president:* "Grover Cleveland," White House Historical Association, https://www.whitehouse.gov/about-the-white-house/presidents/grover-cleveland/.

40 *four separate criminal cases:* Scott Wong, "Trump Allies Say Biden Is 'Weaponizing' DOJ Against His Chief 2024 Rival Following Indictment," NBC News, June 8, 2023, https://www.nbcnews.com/politics/donald-trump/trump-indictment-republicans-say-biden-weaponizing-doj-rcna87962.

42 *"It's not just political":* Jordain Carney, "Johnson Says Biden's Cabinet Should Discuss Invoking 25th Amendment," *Politico*, June 28, 2024, https://www.politico.com/live-updates/2024/06/28/congress/johnson-on-the-debate-house-gop-biden-trump-00165777.

43   *"no business running"*: Thomas Friedman, "Joe Biden Is a Good Man and a Good President. He Must Bow Out of the Race," *New York Times*, June 28, 2024, https://www.nytimes.com/2024/06/28/opinion/joe-biden-tom-fried man.html.

45   *Clyburn's endorsement*: Daniel Strauss, "'A Chain Reaction': How One Endorsement Set Joe Biden's Surge in Motion," *The Guardian*, March 4, 2020, https://www.theguardian.com/us-news/2020/mar/04/joe-biden-jim-clyburn -endorsement-super-tuesday.

45   *wasn't as popular*: "Do Americans Approve or Disapprove of Kamala Harris?" FiveThirtyEight, https://projects.fivethirtyeight.com/polls/approval/kamala -harris/.

46   *fit to be tied*: "Democratic Rep. Doggett Says Biden Needs to Drop Out of the Race or Trump Will Win," NPR, July 3, 2024, https://www.npr.org/2024/07/03 /nx-s1-5026987/rep-doggett-congress-democrat-call-biden-to-withdraw.

47   New York Times *editorial board*: "To Serve His Country, President Biden Should Leave the Race," editorial, *New York Times*, June 28, 2024, https:// www.nytimes.com/2024/06/28/opinion/biden-election-debate-trump.html.

50   *fiftieth birthday party*: Carlos Greer, "Bill Clinton, Nancy Pelosi Attend Hollywood Scion Casey Wasserman's 'Garish' 50th Birthday, Played by Imagine Dragons," *New York Post*, July 2, 2024, https://pagesix.com/2024/07/02/gos sip/nancy-pelosi-and-bill-clinton-celebrate-casey-wasserman-at-his-garish -50th-birthday-bash/.

50   *1994 crime bill*: "Examining Joe Biden's Record on Race: 1994 Crime Bill Sponsorship," NPR, October 13, 2020, https://www.npr.org/2020/10/13/923170325 /examining-joe-bidens-record-on-race-1994-crime-bill-sponsorship.

51   *wrote on X*: Hillary Clinton, X, June 28, 2024, https://x.com/HillaryClinton /status/1806686107632877647.

51   *delegate tracker*: Abby Livingston, "Allies Remember a Driven Hillary Rodham During 1972 Texas Campaign," *Texas Tribune*, May 16, 2015, https://www.tex astribune.org/2015/05/16/clintons-take-texas-1972/.

52   *"only about himself"*: Barack Obama, X, June 28, 2024, https://x.com/Barack Obama/status/1806758633230709017?lang=en.

56   *privately told friends*: Carol E. Lee et al., "'It's a Mess: Biden Turns to Family on His Path Forward After His Disastrous Debate," NBC News, June 29, 2024, https://www.nbcnews.com/politics/2024-election/biden-family-path -forward-disastrous-debate-mess-rcna159591.

58   *"abandoning Joe Biden right now"*: Katie Rogers and Peter Baker, "Biden's Family Tells Him to Keep Fighting as They Huddle at Camp David," *New York Times*, June 30, 2024, https://www.nytimes.com/2024/06/30/us/politics /biden-debate-anxious-democrats.html.

58 *"very honest and serious"*: Michelle Stoddart and Julia Reinstein, "Rep. Jamie Raskin: Democrats Having 'a Serious Conversation' Following Biden's Debate Performance," ABC News, June 30, 2024, https://abcnews.go.com/Politics/rep-jamie-raskin-democrats-conversation-bidens-debate-performance/story?id=111563163.

60 *draft her into*: Jonathan Martin, "Whitmer Disavows 'Draft Gretch' Movement—And Delivers a Warning to Biden," *Politico*, July 1, 2024, https://www.politico.com/news/magazine/2024/07/01/whitmer-biden-democrats-2028-00165995.

CHAPTER 4: "AN EPISODE OR A CONDITION"

61 *shadow primary*: Doug Stanglin, "Fact Check: Barack Obama Favored Hillary Clinton over Joe Biden in 2016," *USA Today*, November 27, 2020, https://www.usatoday.com/story/news/factcheck/2020/11/27/fact-check-barack-obama-favored-hillary-clinton-over-joe-biden-2016/6437725002/.

61 *wrote in a memoir*: Joe Biden, *Promise Me, Dad: A Year of Hope, Hardship and Purpose* (New York: Flatiron Books, 2017).

61 *insult to injury*: Jeff Zeleny, "Obama Congratulates Biden but Is Not Yet Endorsing Anyone," CNN, March 2, 2020, https://www.cnn.com/2020/03/01/politics/obama-biden-unify-democratic-party/index.html.

63 *overpreparation*: Trever Hunnicutt et al., "Joe Biden's Disastrous Debate Blamed on Bad Preparation, Exhaustion," Reuters, July 1, 2024, https://www.reuters.com/world/us/joe-bidens-disastrous-debate-blamed-bad-preparation-exhaustion-2024-06-30/.

64 *immunity from prosecution*: Trump v. United States, Supreme Court, July 1, 2024, https://www.supremecourt.gov/opinions/23pdf/23-939_e2pg.pdf.

64 *"WIN FOR OUR CONSTITUTION"*: Donald Trump, Truth Social, July 1, 2024, https://truthsocial.com/@realDonaldTrump/posts/112711754312482501.

64 *"I dissent"*: Trump v. United States, Supreme Court, July 1, 2024, https://www.supremecourt.gov/opinions/23pdf/23-939_e2pg.pdf.

65 *"limits of the presidential power"*: Joe Biden, "Remarks by President Biden on the Supreme Court's Immunity Ruling," White House, July 1, 2024, https://www.whitehouse.gov/briefing-room/speeches-remarks/2024/07/01/remarks-by-president-biden-on-the-supreme-courts-immunity-ruling/.

66 *without the president*: Tim Ryan, "Kamala Harris Should Be the Democratic Nominee for President in 2024, Opinion," *Newsweek*, July 1, 2024, https://www.newsweek.com/kamala-harris-should-democratic-nominee-president-2024-opinion-1919894.

67 *"episode or a condition"*: Rebecca Shabad, "Nancy Pelosi: It's a 'Legitimate Question' Whether Biden's Debate Performance Was a 'Condition' or Just

an 'Episode,'" NBC News, July 2, 2024, https://www.nbcnews.com/poli
tics/2024-election/nancy-pelosi-says-biden-trump-take-mental-fitness-tests
-rcna159993.

67   *urging the president to withdraw:* Leila Fadel and Majd Al-Waheidi, "Democratic Rep. Doggett Says Biden Needs to Drop Out of the Race or Trump Will
Win," NPR, July 3, 2024, https://www.npr.org/2024/07/03/nx-s1-5026987
/rep-doggett-congress-democrat-call-biden-to-withdraw.

68   *"his opinion":* "Press Briefing by Press Secretary Karine Jean-Pierre," White
House, July 2, 2024, https://www.whitehouse.gov/briefing-room/press
-briefings/2024/07/02/press-briefing-by-press-secretary-karine-jean-pierre
-july-2-2024/.

70   *Pence had fled:* Michael Blood and Jill Colvin, "Pence 'Proud' of His Role
Certifying 2020 Election Results," Associated Press, June 25, 2021, https://ap
news.com/article/joe-biden-michael-pence-constitutions-government-and
-politics-a8e29ab2c6bc5a5fecd9e4236eb8f3c3.

71   *Ohio law:* Trevor Hunnicutt and Jarrett Renshaw, "Democrats to Nominate
Biden Virtually to Bypass Quirk of Ohio Law," Reuters, May 28, 2024, https://
www.reuters.com/world/us/democrats-nominate-biden-virtually-bypass
-quirk-ohio-law-2024-05-28/.

72   *former Clinton White House:* Candice Norwood, "She Helped Create a More
Inclusive Democratic Party. Now She's Leading the Convention," The 19th,
August 13, 2024, https://19thnews.org/2024/08/minyon-moore-democratic
-national-convention-chair/.

72   *convention's rules panel:* Tamara Keith, "29 Days: How Democrats Had to
Overhaul Their Convention in a Hurry for Harris," NPR, August 16, 2024,
https://www.npr.org/2024/08/16/nx-s1-5052067/democratic-national
-convention-overhaul.

72   *"open competition":* Thomas Friedman, "The Question President Biden Needs
to Ask Himself. Now," *New York Times,* July 2, 2024, https://www.nytimes
.com/2024/07/02/opinion/biden-trump-step-aside.html.

74   *long conference table:* Nancy Cordes and Ed O'Keefe, "Biden Meets with Democratic Governors as White House Works to Shore Up Support," CBS News,
July 4, 2024, https://www.cbsnews.com/news/biden-democratic-governors
-meeting-after-debate/.

75   *events after 8 p.m.:* Ibid.

75   *interview with ABC News' George Stephanopoulos:* "ABC's George Stephanopoulos' Exclusive Interview with President Biden: Full Transcript," ABC
News, July 5, 2024, https://abcnews.go.com/Politics/abc-news-anchor-george
-stephanopoulos-exclusive-interview-biden/story?id=111695695.

75   *heavily Democratic Madison:* Rebecca Shabad et al., "Biden Doubles Down at

Wisconsin Rally: 'I'm Staying in the Race,'" NBC News, July 5, 2024, https:// www.nbcnews.com/politics/2024-election/biden-wisconsin-rally-staying-in -2024-election-race-debate-rcna160417.

75   *all-staff call:* "Press Briefing by Press Secretary Karine Jean-Pierre," White House, July 3, 2024, https://www.whitehouse.gov/briefing-room/press -briefings/2024/07/03/press-briefing-by-press-secretary-karine-jean-pierre -july-3-2024/.

76   *"just my brain":* Reid J. Epstein and Maggie Haberman, "Biden Tells Governors He Needs More Sleep and Less Work at Night," *New York Times,* July 4, 2024, https://www.nytimes.com/2024/07/04/us/politics/biden-governors-health .html.

76   *Independence Day celebration:* "President Biden and the First Lady Host a Fourth of July Celebration," White House, July 4, 2024, https://www.youtube .com/watch?v=Mgjk8B_32S4.

76   *Hamas-held hostages:* "Background Press Call on President Biden's Call with Prime Minister Netanyahu," White House, July 4, 2024, https://www.white house.gov/briefing-room/press-briefings/2024/07/04/background-press-call -on-president-bidens-call-with-prime-minister-netanyahu/.

76   *taped the ABC News interview:* "ABC's George Stephanopoulos' Exclusive Interview with President Biden: Full Transcript," ABC News, July 5, 2024, https://abcnews.go.com/Politics/abc-news-anchor-george-stephanopoulos -exclusive-interview-biden/story?id=111695695.

77   *"I don't think I did":* Ibid.

CHAPTER 5: THE ACE IN THE HOLE

78   *survived the Stephanopoulos interview:* Ibid.

78   *daily nighttime meeting:* Amie Parnes, "White House Chief of Staff Zients Reassures Staff amid Biden Turmoil," *The Hill,* July 3, 2024, https://thehill .com/homenews/administration/4754063-biden-debate-performance-white -house-chief/.

79   *appearance on* Morning Joe: "'I Am Not Going Anywhere': Biden Confirms He's Staying in the 2024 Race," MSNBC, July 8, 2024, https://www.msnbc .com/morning-joe/watch/-i-am-not-going-anywhere-biden-confirms-he-s -staying-in-2024-race-214393925734.

79   *NATO conference:* "Remarks by President Biden on the 75th Anniversary of the North Atlantic Treaty Organization Alliance," White House, July 9, 2024, https://www.whitehouse.gov/briefing-room/speeches-remarks/2024/07/09 /remarks-by-president-biden-on-the-75th-anniversary-of-the-north-atlantic -treaty-organization-alliance/.

80   *veteran of the convention floor fight:* Dave Davies, "How Ted Kennedy's '80

Challenge to President Carter 'Broke the Democratic Party,'" NPR, January 17, 2019, https://www.npr.org/2019/01/17/686186156/how-ted-kennedys-80-challenge-to-president-carter-broke-the-democratic-party.

80 *powder dry:* Julia Johnson, "Schumer Silent as Worries over Biden's Fitness Swell in Senate," Fox News, July 9, 2024, https://www.foxnews.com/politics/schumer-silent-worries-over-bidens-fitness-swell-senate.

81 *Jeffries convened:* Andrew Solender, "Top House Democrats Say Biden Should Drop Out in Call with Jeffries," Axios, July 7, 2024, https://www.axios.com/2024/07/07/top-house-democrats-say-biden-should-drop-out.

81 *sent his letter to Capitol Hill:* Joe Biden post on X, July 8, 2024, https://x.com/JoeBiden/status/1810301614965604827?lang=en.

81 *he would be on* Morning Joe: Isabella Ramírez and Myah Ward, "Biden Slams Dem Critics as 'Elites' During Surprise 'Morning Joe' Interview," *Politico,* July 8, 2024, https://www.politico.com/news/2024/07/08/joe-biden-morning-joe-interview-2024-00166784.

82 *"I'm getting so frustrated":* Ibid.

82 *preferred "someone else":* Kate Sullivan, "CNN Poll: 75% of Democratic Voters Want Someone Other than Biden in 2024," CNN, July 27, 2022, https://www.cnn.com/2022/07/26/politics/cnn-poll-biden-2024/index.html.

82 *new primary calendar:* Gibbs Knotts and Jordan Ragusa, "Why Democrats Moved South Carolina to the Start of the 2024 Presidential Campaign," New Hampshire Bulletin, February 7, 2023, https://newhampshirebulletin.com/2023/02/07/why-democrats-moved-south-carolina-to-the-start-of-the-2024-presidential-campaign/.

82 *Iowa caucuses:* Emma Barnett, "Iowa Democrats Move Caucus Results to Super Tuesday," NBC News, October 6, 2023, https://www.nbcnews.com/politics/2024-election/iowa-democrats-move-caucus-results-super-tuesday-rcna119222.

82 *Georgia and Michigan:* Will Weissert, "Democrats Vote to Change Order of 2024 Presidential Primary," Associated Press, February 4, 2023, https://www.pbs.org/newshour/politics/democrats-vote-to-change-order-of-2024-presidential-primary.

83 *"We have one job":* Joe Biden post on X, July 8, 2024, https://x.com/JoeBiden/status/1810301614965604827?lang=en.

83 *found the letter infuriating:* Steve Hunter, "U.S. Sen. Patty Murray Questions Whether Biden Should Stay in Race," Federal Way Mirror, July 8, 2024, https://www.federalwaymirror.com/northwest/u-s-sen-patty-murray-questions-whether-biden-should-stay-in-race/.

84 *"do more to demonstrate":* Joey Garrison, "Sen. Patty Murray Says Biden 'Must Do More' to Prove He's Strong Enough to Beat Trump," *USA Today,* July 8,

2024, https://www.usatoday.com/story/news/politics/elections/2024/07/08/sen-patty-murray-says-biden-must-do-more-to-prove-he-can-beat-trump/74333757007/.

84   *DNC headquarters:* Kevin Breuniger, "Another Democrat Urges Biden to Withdraw as Trump Debate Fallout Roils Campaign," CNBC, July 9, 2024, https://www.cnbc.com/2024/07/09/biden-campaign-democrats-updates.html.

85   *weekly luncheon:* Ursula Perano et al., "Senate Democrats Emerge from Party Meeting Stuck in Limbo on Biden," *Politico*, July 9, 2024, https://www.politico.com/live-updates/2024/07/09/congress/senate-democrats-meeting-biden-schumer-nominee-00167134.

85   *first-term antiestablishment Democrat:* Jon Levine, "John Fetterman Scolds Democrats for Fleeing Biden: 'Need to Get a Spine' or 'Grow a Set,'" *New York Post*, July 6, 2024, https://nypost.com/2024/07/06/us-news/john-fetterman-stands-by-biden-after-abc-interview-grow-a-spine/.

85   *suffered a stroke:* Annie Karni, "Fetterman, Recovering After Stroke, Labors to Adjust to Life in the Senate," *New York Times*, February 10, 2023, https://www.nytimes.com/2023/02/10/us/politics/john-fetterman-senate-stroke.html.

85   *changed its dress code:* Robert Jimison, "In a Sartorial About-Face, Senate Reverts to Tradition on Its Dress Code," *New York Times*, September 27, 2023, https://www.nytimes.com/2023/09/27/us/politics/fetterman-senate-dress-code.html.

86   *Schumer was taken aback:* Carl Hulse, "How Biden's Senate Allies Helped Push Him from the Race," *New York Times*, August 29, 2024, https://www.nytimes.com/2024/08/29/us/politics/senate-democrats-biden-drop-out.html.

86   *"it remains to be seen":* Ursula Perano et al., "Senate Democrats Emerge from Party Meeting Stuck in Limbo on Biden," *Politico*, July 9, 2024, https://www.politico.com/live-updates/2024/07/09/congress/senate-democrats-meeting-biden-schumer-nominee-00167134.

86   *Medal of Freedom:* Donald Judd and Michael Williams, "Biden Surprises NATO Secretary General Jens Stoltenberg with the Presidential Medal of Freedom," CNN, July 9, 2024, https://www.cnn.com/2024/07/09/politics/jens-stoltenberg-presidential-medal-of-freedom/index.html.

86   *prospective donors pulled out:* Gregory Krieg et al., "Donors Stress over Path Forward After Biden's Debate Performance," CNN, June 30, 2024, https://www.cnn.com/2024/06/29/politics/democratic-donors-biden-debate-election/index.html.

87   *"already disastrous":* Natasha Korecki, Jonathan Allen, and Monica Alba, "'It's Already Disastrous': Biden Campaign Fundraising Takes a Major Hit," NBC News, July 10, 2024, https://www.nbcnews.com/politics/2024-election/disastrous-biden-campaign-fundraising-takes-major-hit-rcna161214.

CHAPTER 6: ET TU, NANCY?

88   *for an interview on* Morning Joe: Rebecca Picciotto, "Pelosi Refuses to Say She Supports Biden as the Democratic Nominee," CNBC, July 10, 2024, https://www.cnbc.com/2024/07/10/pelosi-punts-biden-drop-out-rejects-critics-morning-joe.html.

89   *Kennedy's 1961 inauguration:* Ross Cristantiello, "Nancy Pelosi Attended JFK's Inauguration in 1961. This Is How She Remembers It," Boston.com, November 17, 2012, https://www.boston.com/news/politics/2022/11/17/nancy-pelosi-jfk-inauguration-1961/.

89   *"rhymed with the lessons":* "Statement from President Joe Biden on the 60th Anniversary of the Assassination of President John F. Kennedy," White House, November 22, 2023, https://www.whitehouse.gov/briefing-room/statements-releases/2023/11/22/statement-from-president-joe-biden-on-the-60th-anniversary-of-the-assassination-of-president-john-f-kennedy/.

89   *toiled to enact:* "Nancy Pelosi on Rekindling Her Friendship with President Biden," ABC News, August 23, 2024, https://abcnews.go.com/Politics/nancy-pelosi-rekindling-friendship-president-biden/story?id=113018994.

89   *victory in the House:* Rebecca Shabad and Alex Moe, "Pelosi Nominated as Speaker by House Democrats," NBC News, November 28, 2018, https://www.nbcnews.com/politics/congress/pelosi-nominated-speaker-house-democrats-n940786.

89   *hiding from the pro-Trump mob:* Eric Tucker, "New Jan. 6 Footage Shows Pelosi, Leaders as Crisis Unfolded," Associated Press, October 13, 2022, https://apnews.com/article/capitol-siege-united-states-presidential-elections-nancy-pelosi-election-2020-3ca391a6ca811b40e490909cbf45c5c9.

91   *"It's up to the president":* Rebecca Picciotto, "Pelosi Refuses to Say She Supports Biden as the Democratic Nominee," CNBC, July 10, 2024, https://www.cnbc.com/2024/07/10/pelosi-punts-biden-drop-out-rejects-critics-morning-joe.html.

92   *AFL-CIO headquarters:* "President Biden Attends Meeting with Union Leaders at AFL-CIO," C-SPAN, July 9, 2024, https://www.c-span.org/program/public-affairs-event/president-biden-attends-meeting-with-union-leaders-at-afl-cio/644544.

92   *posted an online story:* Jonathan Weisman and Michael D. Shear, "After Meeting with Biden, some A.F.L.-C.I.O. Leaders Remain Concerned About His Candidacy," *New York Times*, July 10, 2024, https://www.nytimes.com/live/2024/07/10/us/biden-trump-election.

93   *"an open process":* Sarah Ferris, "Pelosi Voiced Support for an Open Nomination Process If Biden Drops Out," *Politico*, July 19, 2024, https://www.politico.com/news/2024/07/19/pelosi-support-open-nomination-biden-drop-out-00169893.

93   *national polling*: Domenico Montanaro, "After Biden's Debate Performance, the Presidential Race Is Unchanged," NPR, July 12, 2024, https://www.npr.org/2024/07/12/nx-s1-5036518/biden-trump-poll.

95   *"We are not going to win"*: George Clooney, "I Love Joe Biden. But We Need a New Nominee," *New York Times*, July 10, 2024, https://www.nytimes.com/2024/07/10/opinion/joe-biden-democratic-nominee.html.

96   *Among Black, Hispanic, and progressive*: Kiara Alfonseca, "How Biden, Trump Are Fighting for Black and Hispanic Voters," ABC News, July 19, 2024, https://abcnews.go.com/Politics/biden-trump-fighting-black-hispanic-voters/story?id=112025242.

96   *$90 billion bailout*: Douglas Mackinnon, "When Did $90 Billion Become Nothing to Trump, DeSantis, Haley and the GOP?" *The Hill*, July 23, 2022, https://thehill.com/opinion/white-house/3570508-when-did-90-billion-become-nothing-to-trump-desantis-haley-and-the-gop/.

97   *alienated Arab American voters*: Nandita Bose and Trevor Hunnicutt, "Michigan's 100,000 'Uncommitted' Votes Challenge Biden's Israel Stance," Reuters, February 28, 2024, https://www.reuters.com/world/us/michigans-strong-uncommitted-vote-shows-israel-impact-biden-support-2024-02-28/.

97   *rally in Detroit*: "Remarks by President Biden at a Campaign Event," White House, July 12, 2024, https://www.whitehouse.gov/briefing-room/speeches-remarks/2024/07/12/remarks-by-president-biden-at-a-campaign-event-detroit-mi-3/.

98   *Biden should step aside*: June Kim et al., "How the Pressure Grew for Biden to Drop Out," *New York Times*, July 21, 2024, https://www.nytimes.com/interactive/2024/us/elections/biden-drop-out-democrats.html.

98   *against her late husband*: Tory Newmyer, "Waxman Defeats Dingell for Gavel," *Roll Call*, November 20, 2008, https://rollcall.com/2008/11/20/waxman-defeats-dingell-for-gavel/.

CHAPTER 7: "FIGHT! FIGHT! FIGHT!"

99   *right hand*: Gary Fineout, "Florida Republicans Are Thrilled About Susie Wiles—with One Big Exception," *Politico*, November 9, 2024, https://www.politico.com/news/2024/11/09/ron-desantis-susie-wiles-reaction-00188586.

99   *fired her*: Erin Doherty and Sophia Cai, "Susie Wiles' Journey to Be Trump's Gatekeeper," Axios, November 8, 2024, https://www.axios.com/2024/11/08/susie-wiles-trump-2024-white-house.

100   *the year he was charged*: "Keeping Track of the Trump Criminal Cases," *New York Times*, November 6, 2024, https://www.nytimes.com/interactive/2024/us/trump-investigations-charges-indictments.html.

100   *found liable*: Larry Neumeister, "Judge Upholds the $5 Million Jury Ver-

dict Against Trump in a Writer's Sex Abuse and Defamation Case," Associated Press, July 19, 2023, https://apnews.com/article/trump-rape-trial-columnist-carroll-4974ef026f3da61bc6f1b7ddda3ad10e.

100 *Her job, she thought:* Matt Dixon and Jonathan Allen, "Delays and Counterattacks: How the Trump Campaign Plans to Use His Court Dates for Political Gain," NBC News, March 14, 2024, https://www.nbcnews.com/politics/donald-trump/trump-campaign-court-dates-political-gain-rcna142804.

101 *His approval rating:* Gregory Korte, "Trump Ends Historically Unpopular Presidency with 34% Approval," Bloomberg, January 18, 2021, https://www.bloomberg.com/news/articles/2021-01-18/trump-ends-historically-unpopular-presidency-with-34-approval.

101 *voted to convict him:* Kathryn Watson, "Here Are the 7 Republicans Who Voted to Convict Trump," CBS News, February 14, 2021, https://www.cbsnews.com/news/trump-impeachment-republicans-voted-convict/.

101 *had been jailed:* Sara Murray, Katelyn Polantz, and Devan Cole, "Steve Bannon Begins Serving 4-Month Sentence in Federal Prison for Defying Congressional Subpoena," CNN, July 1, 2024, https://www.cnn.com/2024/07/01/politics/steve-bannon-report-to-prison/index.html.

102 *won pardons:* Amita Kelly, Ryan Lucas, and Vanessa Romo, "Trump Pardons Roger Stone, Paul Manafort and Charles Kushner," NPR, December 23, 2020, https://www.npr.org/2020/12/23/949820820/trump-pardons-roger-stone-paul-manafort-and-charles-kushner.

102 *served jail time:* Katelyn Polantz, "Rick Gates, Former Trump Campaign Aide Who Testified to Mueller, Sentenced to 45 Days in Jail," CNN, December 17, 2019, https://www.cnn.com/2019/12/17/politics/rick-gates-sentencing/index.html.

102 *outdoor rally:* Lizz Jassin, "Trump Shooter Classmate: Thomas Crooks Not 'Safe Fit' on Rifle Team," *The Hill*, August 3, 2024, https://thehill.com/homenews/state-watch/4809071-donald-trump-failed-assassination-attempt-shooter-classmate-rifle-team/.

102 *clear favorite:* "2024 Presidential Election Polls," *New York Times*, https://www.nytimes.com/interactive/2024/us/elections/polls-president.html.

102 *the Supreme Court handed him:* Amy Howe, "Justices Rule Trump Has Some Immunity from Prosecution," *SCOTUSblog*, July 1, 2024, https://www.scotusblog.com/2024/07/justices-rule-trump-has-some-immunity-from-prosecution/.

103 *he was rejected:* Lizz Jassin, "Trump Shooter Classmate: Thomas Crooks Not 'Safe Fit' on Rifle Team," *The Hill*, August 3, 2024, https://thehill.com/homenews/state-watch/4809071-donald-trump-failed-assassination-attempt-shooter-classmate-rifle-team/.

105   *"favorite chart"*: Philip Bump, "Updating (and Fixing) Trump's Favorite Chart," *Washington Post*, October 24, 2024, https://www.washingtonpost.com/poli tics/2024/10/24/trump-biden-immigration/.

107   *Butler staff had cleared*: Chris Hoffman, "Butler Memorial Hospital Applauds Quick Work of Staff to Treat Trump After Rally Shooting," CBS Pittsburgh, July 15, 2024, https://www.cbsnews.com/pittsburgh/news/butler-memorial -hospital-donald-trump-treatment-rally-shooting/#.

107   *Biden was at mass*: Emma Colton, "Biden Seen Leaving Church Minutes After Trump Shooting," Fox News, July 13, 2024, https://www.foxnews.com/poli tics/biden-seen-leaving-church-minutes-after-trump-shooting.

108   *In a one-on-one conversation*: Ryan Nobles, Monica Alba, Frank Thorp V, and Jonathan Allen, "Schumer had a 'Blunt' Private Conversation with Biden About the State of the 2024 Race," NBC News, July 17, 2024, https://www .nbcnews.com/politics/2024-election/schumer-blunt-private-conversation -biden-2024-race-rcna162446.

108   *"hear that crap"*: Sarah Ferris, "Biden Raised His Voice over House Dem Commander-in-Chief Concerns: 'I Don't Want to Hear That Crap,'" *Politico*, July 13, 2024, https://www.politico.com/news/2024/07/13/biden-raised-his -voice-over-house-dem-commander-in-chief-concerns-i-dont-want-to-hear -that-crap-00167975.

109   *he delivered*: Michael Williams, Priscilla Alvarez, and M. J. Lee, "Biden Says He's Grateful Trump Is Safe After Rally Shooting, Denounces Political Violence," CNN, July 13, 2024, https://www.cnn.com/2024/07/13/politics/joe -biden-reaction-trump-shooting/index.html.

CHAPTER 8: A VERY IMPORTANT PHONE CALL

110   *down to three*: Kevin Breuninger, "JD Vance Is Trump's VP Pick After Rubio and Burgum Were Passed Over for Running Mate," CNBC, July 15, 2024, https://www.cnbc.com/2024/07/15/donald-trump-vp-announcement.html.

111   Hillbilly Elegy: Tim Lammers, "How Did Critics React to Netflix's J.D. Vance Biopic 'Hillbilly Elegy?'" *Forbes*, July 15, 2024, https://www.forbes.com/sites /timlammers/2024/07/15/how-did-critics-react-to-netflixs-jd-vance-biopic -hillbilly-elegy/.

111   *Vance visited*: Jonathan Swan and Maggie Haberman, "How JD Vance Won Over Donald Trump," *New York Times*, July 16, 2024, https://www.nytimes .com/2024/07/16/us/politics/trump-vance-vp-decision.html.

112   *"busting JD's chops"*: Henry J. Gomez and Matt Dixon, "The Inside Story of How Trump Chose JD Vance as His Running Mate," NBC News, July 15, 2024, https://www.nbcnews.com/politics/donald-trump/trump-chose-jd-vance-ru nning-mate-vp-pick-rcna161982.

112 *bent his knee:* Jonathan Swan and Maggie Haberman, "How JD Vance Won Over Donald Trump," *New York Times*, July 16, 2024, https://www.nytimes.com/2024/07/16/us/politics/trump-vance-vp-decision.html.

112 *voted in lockstep:* Kaia Hubbard, "What to Know About JD Vance's Views and Policy Record," CBS News, October 2, 2024, https://www.cbsnews.com/news/jd-vance-views-policy-record-2024/.

112 *Vance also formed:* Sharon LaFraniere, "A Match Made in MAGA: How a Friendship Helped J. D. Vance Land on Trump's V.P. List," *New York Times*, April 27, 2024, https://www.nytimes.com/2024/04/27/us/politics/jd-vance-trump-vp.html.

112 *had been short-listed:* Juan Carlos Lopez, "VP Marco Rubio? The Man in Demand," CNN, January 27, 2012, https://www.cnn.com/2012/01/27/politics/vp-rubio/index.html.

112 *Trump supporters calling:* "Rioters Chant 'Hang Mike Pence' on Jan. 6, 2021," *Washington Post*, June 16, 2022, https://www.washingtonpost.com/video/politics/rioters-chant-hang-mike-pence-on-jan-6-2021/2022/06/16/3cc093f1-0eb7-427d-8073-b5874ca27e80_video.html.

112 *"small hands":* Jill Colvin, "Here's Why Each Contender on Trump's VP Shortlist May or May Not Be Picked," *PBS NewsHour*, June 23, 2024, https://www.pbs.org/newshour/politics/heres-why-each-contender-on-trumps-vp-shortlist-may-or-may-not-get-picked.

112 *Rubio worked:* Nancy Cook, "Ivanka Trump Scores Win with Senate Plan to Double Child Tax Credit," *Politico*, November 15, 2017, https://www.politico.com/story/2017/11/15/senate-tax-plan-child-tax-credit-ivanka-trump-244924.

112 *Cuban American Rubio:* Brendan Farrington, "Things to Know About Sen. Marco Rubio, Trump's Pick for Secretary of State," Associated Press, November 13, 2024, https://apnews.com/article/trump-marco-rubio-secretary-of-state-25664371f80dcf3332838352165e4d48.

112 *Rubio had tried and failed:* Reena Flores, "Marco Rubio Answers for His Failed 2013 Immigration Plans—Again," CBS News, February 27, 2015, https://www.cbsnews.com/news/marco-rubio-answers-for-his-failed-2013-immigration-plans-again/.

113 *often sided:* Nils Adler, "How Marco Rubio Has Shapeshifted to Embrace Trump's Foreign Policy," Al Jazeera, November 12, 2024, https://www.aljazeera.com/news/2024/11/12/how-marco-rubio-has-shapeshifted-to-embrace-trumps-foreign-policy.

113 *Rubio could resign:* Hannah Demissie, "Would Marco Rubio Need to Move Out of Florida if Trump Picks Him for Vice President?" ABC News, July 5, 2024, https://abcnews.go.com/Politics/marco-rubio-move-florida-trump-picks-vice-president/story?id=111583499.

114 *over the phone:* Henry J. Gomez and Matt Dixon, "The Inside Story of How Trump Chose JD Vance as His Running Mate," NBC News, July 15, 2024, https://www.nbcnews.com/politics/donald-trump/trump-chose-jd-vance-ru nning-mate-vp-pick-rcna161982.

115 *Trump didn't think:* Eric Deggans, "5 Takeaways by a Longtime NABJ Member from Trump's Appearance Before Black Journalists," NPR, August 1, 2024, https://www.npr.org/2024/08/01/nx-s1-5060269/trump-nabj-appearance -controversy.

115 *Pence had helped:* Aaron Blake, "In 2016, Mike Pence Was an Asset for Trump. In 2020, It's Not So Clear," *Washington Post*, October 7, 2020, https://www .washingtonpost.com/politics/2020/10/07/2016-mike-pence-was-an-asset -trump-2020-its-not-so-clear/.

115 *Pence and his lawyers had determined:* "Read Pence's Full Letter Saying He Can't Claim Unilateral Authority to Reject Electoral Votes," *PBS NewsHour*, January 6, 2021, https://www.pbs.org/newshour/politics/read-pences-full-lett er-saying-he-cant-claim-unilateral-authority-to-reject-electoral-votes.

115 *Trump felt betrayed:* Catherine Herridge, "Special Counsel's Interest in Sessions' Recusal Has Grown," CBS News, May 30, 2018, https://www.cbsnews .com/news/special-counsel-teams-interest-in-sessions-recusal-has-grown/.

115 *infuriated Trump:* Dareh Gregorian, "Former AG Barr Says Trump Was Enraged When Told Election Fraud Claims Were Baseless," NBC News, March 3, 2022, https://www.nbcnews.com/politics/donald-trump/former-ag-barr-said -trump-became-enraged-told-election-fraud-claims-no-rcna17750.

116 *kept her distance:* Jesse McKinley, "Ivanka Trump: A Rising Star in the 2024 Election," *New York Times*, October 29, 2024, https://www.nytimes .com/2024/10/29/style/ivanka-trump.html.

116 *Don Jr. had become:* Jonathan Allen, "The MAGA Wing of the Trump Family Takes Center Stage," NBC News, July 17, 2024, https://www.nbcnews .com/politics/donald-trump/maga-wing-trump-family-takes-center-stage -rcna161293.

118 *Trump broke the news:* Margie Cullen, "Trump Selects JD Vance as Running Mate: Read His Announcement," *USA Today*, July 15, 2024, https://www.usa today.com/story/news/politics/elections/2024/07/15/trump-vp-announceme nt-jd-vance/74414192007/.

120 *Trump stood:* "Full Transcript of Trump's RNC Speech," *New York Times*, July 19, 2024, https://www.nytimes.com/2024/07/19/us/politics/trump-rnc -speech-transcript.html.

122 *since George H. W. Bush:* "New Jersey Election Results," 270toWin, https:// www.270towin.com/states/New_Jersey.

122 *Trump had lost the state:* "New Jersey Election Results (2020)," CNN, https://www.cnn.com/election/2020/results/state/new-jersey.

122 *Hillary Clinton had beaten him:* "New Jersey Election Results (2016)," CNN, https://www.cnn.com/election/2016/results/states/new-jersey.

CHAPTER 9: "KARAOKE AT THE END OF THE WORLD"

124 *recorded Schiff's remarks:* Michael S. Schmidt and Mark Mazzetti, "Schiff Warned of Wipeout for Democrats If Biden Remains in Race," *New York Times*, July 16, 2024, https://www.nytimes.com/2024/07/16/us/politics/schiff -biden-democrats.html.

125 *interviews:* Michael D. Shear, "Biden Tests Positive for Covid," *New York Times*, July 17, 2024, https://www.nytimes.com/2024/07/17/us/politics/biden-covid -positive.html.

125 *while they waited:* Justin Walker, "Biden Visits Local Favorite Restaurant on Day 3 of Las Vegas Visit," 8NewsNow, July 17, 2024, https://www.8newsnow .com/news/local-news/biden-visits-local-favorite-restaurant-on-day-3-of -las-vegas-visit/.

125 *Harry Reid International Airport:* Meredith Deliso, "President Joe Biden Tests Positive for COVID-19, White House Says," ABC7, July 1, 2024, https://abc7 .com/post/joe-biden-tests-positive-covid-will-return-delaware/15065780/.

125 *appeared to lose his balance:* Zolan Kanno-Youngs, "From Buoyant to Frail: Two Days in Las Vegas as Biden Tests Positive," *New York Times*, July 18, 2024, https://www.nytimes.com/2024/07/18/us/politics/biden-covid-democrats .html.

130 *Organizing for Action:* Alex Seitz-Wald, "Obama-Aligned Organizing for Action Relaunches for Trump Era," NBC News, February 10, 2017, https://www .nbcnews.com/storyline/democrats-vs-trump/obama-aligned-organizing-act ion-relaunches-trump-era-n719311.

132 *subtweeted:* Andrew Bates post on X, July 18, 2024, https://x.com/AndrewJ Bates46/status/1814106474861252778.

132 *O'Malley Dillon went:* "'He's Not Going Anywhere': Biden-Harris Campaign Chair Insists Biden Is Staying in 2024 Race," NBC News, July 19, 2024, https:// www.msnbc.com/morning-joe/watch/biden-harris-campaign-chief-says-bid en-is-absolutely-in-this-race-215247429608.

133 *more than a dozen:* Scott Wong, Ali Vitali, and Rebecca Kaplan, "13 More Democrats, Including Pelosi Allies, Call for Biden to Exit 2024 Election," NBC News, July 19, 2024, https://www.nbcnews.com/politics/joe-biden/eight-dem ocrats-pelosi-allies-call-biden-exit-2024-election-rcna162726/.

133 *Clyburn's endorsement vaulted:* Peter Nicholas and Aaron Gilchrist, "Rep. Jim

Clyburn Helped Biden Win Young Black Voters in 2020. This Time, They're Not Listening," NBC News, January 30, 2024, https://www.nbcnews.com /politics/joe-biden/rep-jim-clyburn-biden-win-young-black-voters-2024 -election-rcna134512.

133 *The two men:* Ibid.

134 *hustled to the hospital:* Kevin Liptak et al., "President Donald Trump and First Lady Melania Trump Test Positive for Covid-19," CNN, October 2, 2020, https://www.cnn.com/2020/10/01/politics/hope-hicks-positive-coronavirus /index.html.

134 *maintain a light schedule:* Molly Ball, "How COVID-19 Changed Everything About the 2020 Election," *Time*, August 6, 2020, https://time.com /5876599/election-2020-coronavirus/.

134 *daily Trump press conferences:* David A. Graham, "The End of Trump's Coronavirus Briefings," *Atlantic*, April 27, 2020, https://www.theatlantic.com /ideas/archive/2020/04/end-trumps-coronavirus-briefing/610771/.

135 *Biden was slipping:* "July 2024 Swing State Polls," Emerson College Polling, July 18, 2024, https://emersoncollegepolling.com/july-2024-swing-state-polls/.

135 *Age had:* Mark Murray, "Biden's Age and Fitness Top the List of Voters' Concerns, Poll Finds," NBC News, February 6, 2024, https://www.nbcnews.com /politics/2024-election/bidens-age-fitness-top-list-voters-concerns-poll -finds-rcna137212.

135 *were panicking:* Andrew Solender, "Top House Democrats Privately Say Biden Should Drop Out," Axios, July 7, 2024, https://www.axios.com/2024/07/07 /top-house-democrats-say-biden-should-drop-out.

136 *Jon Tester of Montana:* Megan Lebowitz, Julie Tsirkin, Frank Thorp V, and Rebecca Kaplan, "Top House Democrats Privately Say Biden Should Drop Out," NBC News, July 18, 2024, https://www.nbcnews.com/politics/joe -biden/democratic-sen-jon-tester-calls-joe-biden-drop-out-2024-election -rcna162644.

136 *Sherrod Brown of Ohio:* Henry J. Gomez, "Ohio Sen. Sherrod Brown Calls for Biden to Drop Out of the 2024 Race," NBC News, July 19, 2024, https://www .nbcnews.com/politics/2024-election/ohio-sen-sherrod-brown-calls-biden -drop-2024-race-rcna162804.

CHAPTER 10: "YOU NEED TO ENDORSE ME"

143 *He had never lost:* Steven Levingston, "Joe Biden: Life Before the Presidency," Miller Center, University of Virginia, https://millercenter.org/president /biden/life-before-the-presidency.

149 *he'd been so sore:* Jonathan Lemire, Ursula Perano, Daniella Diaz, and Ryan

Lizza, "Biden Harbors Lingering Frustration at Pelosi, Obama, Schumer," *Politico*, August 14, 2024, https://www.politico.com/news/2024/08/14/biden-fru stration-obama-pelosi-00173883.

149 *had never gotten over:* Eric Bradner, "Exclusive: Jill Biden on Kamala Harris' Attack: The American People 'Didn't Buy It,'" CNN, July 18, 2019, https:// www.cnn.com/2019/07/08/politics/jill-biden-surprised-kamala-harris -debate/index.html.

150 *often spoke publicly:* Rebecca Shabad, "Kamala Harris Praises Biden at First Public Event Since He Endorsed Her for President," NBC News, July 22, 2024, https://www.nbcnews.com/politics/2024-election/kamala-harris-praises-bid en-first-public-event-endorsed-president-rcna163050.

151 *illegal border crossings:* Haley Ott, "A Look at Kamala Harris' Work on For- eign Policy as Vice President," CBS News, July 22, 2024, https://www.cbsnews .com/news/kamala-harris-foreign-policy-record-vice-president/.

151 *well below 40 percent:* Kamala Harris approval ratings, FiveThirtyEight, https://projects.fivethirtyeight.com/polls/approval/kamala-harris/.

151 *some elite Democrats chattered:* Zolan Kanno-Youngs, Katie Rogers, and Peter Baker, "Kamala Harris Is Trying to Define Her Vice Presidency. Even Her Allies Are Tired of Waiting," *New York Times*, February 6, 2023, https://www.nytimes .com/2023/02/06/us/politics/kamala-harris-vice-presidenct-legacy.html.

151 *Told the* New York Times: Ibid.

151 Saturday Night Live *lampooned:* Dave Itzkoff, "'Saturday Night Live': 11 De- fining Political Sketches," *New York Times*, October 3, 2024, https://www.ny times.com/2024/10/03/arts/television/saturday-night-live-politics.html.

151 *Dan Quayle's spelling challenges:* "How to Lose the Presidency: Dan Quayle Misspells Potato," History, April 29, 2016, https://www.youtube.com/wat ch?v=6tmoSGmvR1o.

151 *George H. W. Bush's "wimp factor":* Matt Taibbi, "A Brief History of Everything That Happened Because of George H.W. Bush's Insecurity," *Rolling Stone*, December 7, 2018, https://www.rollingstone.com/politics/politics-features /george-h-w-bush-wimp-766076/.

151 *"an affirmative action hire":* Terry Nicquel Ellis, "What Is DEI? Republicans Are Using the Term to Attack Kamala Harris, but Experts Say It's Widely Mis- understood," CNN, July 24, 2024, https://www.cnn.com/2024/07/24/politics /dei-kamala-harris/index.html.

152 *following the fatal withdrawal:* Margaret Talev and Dave Lawler, "Afghanistan Withdrawal Began Biden's Political Slide," Axios, August 15, 2022, https:// www.axios.com/2022/08/15/afghanistan-withdrawal-anniversary-biden -approval.

152   *He failed to sell:* Astead W. Herndon, "Why Joe Biden Isn't Getting Credit for the Economy," *New York Times*, May 23, 2024, https://www.nytimes.com/2024/05/23/podcasts/why-joe-biden-isnt-getting-credit-for-the-economy.html.

152   *About three-quarters:* Megan Brenan, "Biden's Approval Rating Hit New Low Before Exit from Race," Gallup, July 23, 2024, https://news.gallup.com/poll/647633/biden-approval-rating-hit-new-low-exit-race.aspx.

152   *And most of them believed:* Ibid.

152   *By the time he got out:* Edward-Isaac Dovere, "Democrats Fear Replacement Scenarios as Much as Keeping Biden," CNN, June 30, 2024, https://www.cnn.com/2024/06/30/politics/democratic-party-replacement-worries-joe-biden/index.html.

153   *Biden's tweet backing Harris:* Joe Biden post on X, July 21, 2024, https://x.com/JoeBiden/status/1815087772216303933.

153   *The Clintons followed suit:* Bill Clinton post on X, July 21, 2024, https://x.com/BillClinton/status/1815102085198958657.

154   *a Medium post:* Barack Obama post on Medium, July 21, 2024, https://barackobama.medium.com/my-statement-on-president-bidens-announcement-1eb78b3ba3fc.

156   *Most of the governor-size dominoes:* Reid J. Epstein, "Six Key Democratic Governors Endorse Kamala Harris," *New York Times*, July 22, 2024, https://www.nytimes.com/2024/07/22/us/politics/governors-endorse-harris.html.

156   *no legal complication:* Jessica Piper and Hailey Fuchs, "Kamala Harris Takes Over War Chest as Biden Campaign Becomes Harris for President," *Politico*, July 21, 2024, https://www.politico.com/news/2024/07/21/kamala-harris-biden-campaign-funds-00170136.

157   *better than 90 percent:* Max Greenwood, "Here's How Many Florida Democratic Delegates Have Already Pledged for Kamala Harris," *Tampa Bay Times*, July 22, 2024, https://www.tampabay.com/news/florida-politics/elections/2024/07/22/heres-how-many-florida-democratic-delegates-have-already-pledged-kamala-harris/.

157   *Similar results poured in:* Robert Yoon, "Who Will Win Delegates' Support to Be the Democratic Nominee? AP's Survey Tracks Who They're Backing," Associated Press, July 23, 2024, https://apnews.com/article/biden-harris-democratic-delegate-survey-10624977f1832da747c74d6408cc33c6.

158   *Biden had almost all:* Kenneth P. Vogel, "Amid Uncertainty, Biden Campaign Tries to Keep Control of Delegates," *New York Times*, July 18, 2024, https://www.nytimes.com/2024/07/18/us/politics/biden-delegates-democrats.html.

159   *"Bidenomics":* David Wright, "The One Harris Comment Trump and His Allies Have Spent $38 Million for Voters to See," CNN, September 15, 2024,

https://www.cnn.com/2024/09/15/politics/kamala-harris-bidenomics
-trump-advertisements/index.html.

159 *withdrawal from Afghanistan:* ET Online, "Old Video of Kamala Harris on
Afghanistan Goes Viral," *Economic Times*, August 27, 2024, https://economic
times.indiatimes.com/news/international/world-news/old-video-of-kamala
-harris-on-afghanistan-goes-viral/articleshow/112830913.cms.

159 *provided fodder:* Michael Gold and Simon J. Levien, "Fine-Tuning His Attacks
on Harris, Trump Tries Using Her Words Against Her," *New York Times*, August 10, 2024, https://www.nytimes.com/2024/08/10/us/politics/trump-rally
-montana.html.

159 *But Trump advisers felt confident:* David Jackson and Darren Samuelsohn,
"Donald Trump Has a New Strategy: Attack Kamala Harris (and Joe Biden),"
USA Today, July 21, 2024, https://www.usatoday.com/story/news/politics
/elections/2024/07/21/donald-trump-kamala-harris-attack/74491889007/.

159 *his commitment to cracking down:* Prizcilla Alvarez and Phil Mattingly,
"Mass Detention and Returning Migrants to Mexico: Donald Trump's Plans
on Immigration Are Coming into Focus," CNN, November 16, 2024, https://
www.cnn.com/2024/11/16/politics/donald-trump-immigration-plans/in
dex.html.

159 *aversion to foreign wars:* Benjamin C. Waterhouse, "Donald Trump: Foreign
Affairs," Miller Center, University of Virginia, accessed Janauary 3, 2025,
https://millercenter.org/president/trump/foreign-affairs.

159 *advocacy for tariffs:* Katie Lobosco and Annette Choi, "3 Charts That Help
Explain How Trump's Tariffs Would Work," CNN, December 9, 2024, https://
www.cnn.com/2024/10/13/politics/donald-trump-tariffs/index.html.

159 *He believed:* Laura Doan, "Trump Says Inflation Has Cost Households $28,000
Under Biden and Harris. Is That True?" CBS News, September 19, 2024,
https://www.cbsnews.com/news/trump-inflation-cost-households-28000
-biden-harris-fact-check.

160 *was the need to find new voters:* Josh Clinton and John Lapinski, "What
the Early Voting Data Shows About New Voters—a Group That Could
Swing the Election," NBC News, October 31, 2024, https://www.nbcnews
.com/politics/2024-election/early-voting-data-shows-new-voters-group
-swing-election-rcna178187.

160 *historically high turnout:* Olivia Munson, "How Many People Voted in the
2020 Presidential Election? The Numbers from Biden vs. Trump," *USA Today*, October 25, 2024, https://www.usatoday.com/story/news/politics/elec
tions/2024/10/25/how-many-people-voted-2020-election/75838131007/.

161 *she was all in on "brat summer":* Steven J. Horowitz, "Kamala Harris' Campaign Embraces 'Brat Summer' Following Charli XCX Endorsement," *Variety*,

July 22, 2024, https://variety.com/2024/music/news/kamala-harris-charli-xcx
-presidential-campaign-brat-summer-1236080386/.

162 *Obama called Harris:* "Obama Sorry Over Kamala Harris 'Good-Looking'
Comment," BBC, April 6, 2013, https://www.bbc.com/news/world-us-can
ada-22049070.

162 Pod Save America: Will Neal, "Pod Save America Accuses Joe Biden of 'Quiet
Quitting,'" Daily Beast, December 18, 2024, https://www.thedailybeast.com
/pod-save-america-accuses-joe-biden-of-quiet-quitting/.

162 *Along with Pelosi:* Sarah Ferris and Christopher Cadelago, "Pelosi Voiced Support for an Open Nomination Process If Biden Drops Out," *Politico*, July 19,
2024, https://www.politico.com/news/2024/07/19/pelosi-support-open-nom
ination-biden-drop-out-00169893.

162 *major donors:* Amanda L. Gordon and Heather Perlberg, "Harris Wins Soros
Backing While Other Billionaire Donors Want an Open Contest," Bloomberg
News, July 21, 2024, https://www.bloomberg.com/news/articles/2024-07-22
/rich-democrat-donors-question-rush-to-back-harris-after-biden-drops-out.

163 *outsider 2008 primary campaign:* Juliet Eilperin, "Obama, Who Once Stood
as Party Outsider, Now Works to Strengthen Democrats," *Washington Post*,
April 25, 2016, https://www.washingtonpost.com/politics/obama-who-once
-stood-as-party-outsider-now-works-to-strengthen-democrats/2016/04/25/34
0b3b0a-0589-11e6-bdcb-0133da18418d_story.html.

163 *political allies in common:* Brett Samuels, "Harris Beefs Up Campaign Staff
with Obama Veterans," *The Hill*, August 2, 2024, https://thehill.com/home
news/campaign/4807964-harris-campaign-staff-obama-veterans/.

164 *Harris hoped to replicate:* Sahil Kapur and Yamiche Alcindor, "Harris Seeks to
Recapture Obama-Era Energy as He Rallies for Her in Pennsylvania," NBC
News, October 10, 2024, accessed Janary 3, 2025, https://www.nbcnews.com
/politics/2024-election/harris-seeks-recapture-obama-era-energy-rallies
-pennsylvania-rcna174339.

CHAPTER 11: FUCKERY

166 *labeled Harris "brat":* Charli XCX, X, July 21, 2024, https://x.com/charli_xcx
/status/1815182384066707861?lang=en.

166 *Money poured in:* Eric Badner, "How Kamala Harris' Warp-Speed Campaign
Launch Has Changed the 2024 Race," CNN, July 26, 2024, https://www.cnn
.com/2024/07/26/politics/kamala-harris-election-campaign/index.html.

166 *Harris's first rallies:* Nnamdi Egwuonwu and Summer Concepcion, "Harris
Rips Trump Before Fired-Up Crowd at First Rally Since Launching Her Presidential Campaign," NBC News, July 23, 2024, https://www.nbcnews.com

/politics/2024-election/harris-heads-milwaukee-first-rally-launching-presid
ential-campaign-rcna162919.

166 *Milwaukee and Atlanta*: Matt Viser and Cleve R. Wootson Jr., "Harris Holds
Raucous Rally in Atlanta as She and Trump Battle for Georgia," *Washington
Post*, July 30, 2024, https://www.washingtonpost.com/politics/2024/07/30
/harris-raucous-rally-atlanta/.

166 *a polarizing figure*: Mike Wister, "Jen O'Malley Dillon," PBS, May 29, 2024,
https://www.pbs.org/wgbh/frontline/interview/jen-omalley-dillon/.

167 *Change would be at the heart*: Zeke Miller and Chris Megerian, "How Harris Balances Competing Messages as VP and Candidate," Associated Press,
August 26, 2024, https://apnews.com/article/kamala-harris-change-new-way
-forward-4e64f2b46287cb80c61f17a8d2efdf0f.

167 *like Mike Donilon*: "Longtime Biden Aide Mike Donilon Returning to
White House," Reuters, August 2, 2024, https://www.reuters.com/world/us
/longtime-biden-aide-mike-donilon-returning-white-house-2024-08-02/.

172 *one of California's top consultants*: Natasha Korecki, "First to NBC News: Harris
Brings On a New Campaign Fundraising Co-Chair," NBC News, August 8, 2024,
https://www.nbcnews.com/politics/2024-election/live-blog/harris-trump-presi
dential-election-live-updates-rcna164955/rcrd51552?canonicalCard=true.

174 *The backbiting on her 2019 campaign*: Christopher Cadelago, "'No Discipline. No Plan. No Strategy.' Kamala Harris Campaign in Meltdown," *Politico*, November 15, 2019, accesed January 3, 2025, https://www.politico.com
/news/2019/11/15/kamala-harris-campaign-2020-071105.

174 *who helped run that campaign*: Peter Nicholas and Katherine Doyle, "Kamala
Harris' 2020 Campaign Was a Mess. If She Replaces Biden, This Time Could
Be a Lot Different," NBC News, July 21, 2024, https://www.nbcnews.com/pol
itics/2024-election/harris-2020-campaign-was-mess-ended-ticket-time-lot
-different-rcna162737.

175 *Harris fans feared*: Peter Nicholas, Natasha Korecki, Monica Alba, and Matt
Dixon, "Harris Is Playing It Safe. Some Democrats Worry That Could Doom
Her Campaign," NBC News, October 4, 2024, https://www.nbcnews.com/pol
itics/2024-election/harris-playing-safe-democrats-worry-doom-campaign
-rcna173504.

175 *less than a month away*: Alix Martichoux, Sara Filips, and Addy Bink, "Biden
Drops Out of the 2024 Race: Now What Happens?" *The Hill*, July 21, 2024,
https://thehill.com/homenews/nexstar_media_wire/4784457-biden-drops
-out-of-the-2024-race-now-what-happens/.

176 *crucial to Democrats' chances*: Ronald Brownstein, "Why These Three States
Are the Most Consistent Tipping Point in American Politics," CNN, Septem-

ber 17, 2024, accessed Janaury 3, 2025, https://www.cnn.com/2024/09/17/politics/blue-wall-states-harris-trump-analysis/index.html.

176 *from Nebraska's Second Congressional District:* Nicholas Kerr and Brittany Shepherd, "How Nebraska's 'Blue Dot' Could Prove Pivotal in the Electoral College," ABC News, November 3, 2024, https://abcnews.go.com/Politics/nebraskas-blue-dot-prove-pivotal-electoral-college/story?id=115274378.

176 *one of two states:* George Fabe Russell, "Why Do Maine and Nebraska Split Their Electoral Votes?" *USA Today,* October 29, 2024, https://www.usatoday.com/story/news/politics/elections/2024/10/29/maine-nebraska-electoral-votes-split/75902884007/.

177 *The career teacher:* Sarah Ferris, Nicholas Wu, Meredith Lee Hill, and Daniella Diaz, "Why Pelosi and Other House Dems Were Privately Pushing Walz," *Politico,* August 6, 2024, https://www.politico.com/news/2024/08/06/pelosi-house-dems-pushing-walz-00172939.

177 *well liked in the House:* Sam Woodward and Riley Beggin, "Tough, Savvy, and All-Around 'Nice Guy': How Gov. Walz Gets Stuff Done," *USA Today,* August 21, 2024, https://www.usatoday.com/story/news/politics/elections/2024/08/21/tim-walz-political-policy-strategy/74767435007/.

177 *majority of voters:* Ariana Baio, "What Polling Shows About Tim Walz Approval from Voters Compared to JD Vance," *The Independent,* August 6, 2024, https://www.independent.co.uk/news/world/americas/us-politics/tim-walz-jd-vance-vp-polling-b2592117.html

177 *he called Trump and Vance "weird":* Sahil Kapur, Scott Wong, and Adam Edelman, "Tim Walz Has Friends in Congress. They Say His Political Chops Could Help Harris as VP," NBC News, July 30, 2024, https://www.nbcnews.com/politics/2024-election/tim-walz-kamala-harris-vice-president-pick-congress-rcna164349.

177 *she tapped former:* Christopher Cadelago, "Eric Holder Is Running Harris' Veep Vetting Process," *Politico,* July 22, 2024, https://www.politico.com/live-updates/2024/07/22/kamala-harris-campaign-biden-drop-out/a-familiar-name-vetting-vps-00170416.

177 *process boiled down:* Allison Detzel, "Eric Holder Takes MSNBC Inside Kamala Harris' VP Vetting Process," NBC News, August 21, 2024, https://www.msnbc.com/top-stories/latest/eric-holder-vice-president-barack-obama-tim-walz-rcna167641.

177 *sit-down with Harris:* Seung Min Kim, Bill Barrow, and Zeke Miller, "Picking a Running Mate: Inside the 16 Days Between Kamala Harris' Launch and Her Choice of Tim Walz," Associated Press, August 7, 2024, https://apnews.com/article/kamala-harris-picks-tim-walz-running-mate-a64a91ae84953e880c8d086316d07c54.

177 *She narrowed*: Ibid.

178 *who barely survived*: Alana Wise, "Gabby Giffords Recounts Her Own Shooting in DNC Remarks," NPR, August 22, 2024, https://www.npr.org/2024/08/22/g-s1-19204/gabby-giffords-dnc-speech-mark-kelly.

178 *a poll from Emerson College*: "July 2024 Swing State Polls: Harris Trails Trump in Arizona, Georgia, Michigan, Pennsylvania, Tied in Wisconsin," Emerson College Polling, July 25, 2024, https://emersoncollegepolling.com/july-2024-swing-state-polls-harris-trails-trump-in-arizona-georgia-michigan-pennsylvania-tied-in-wisconsin/.

178 *More than 1 in 5*: Ibid.

178 *cheap and forced imitation*: Dan Snyder, "Josh Shapiro Responds to JD Vance's Barack Obama Comparison, Deflects VP Speculation," CBS News, August 2, 2024, https://www.cbsnews.com/philadelphia/news/josh-shapiro-jd-vance-barack-obama-comparison/.

178 *Democrats were deeply divided*: Jason Lange and James Oliphant, "Democratic Divide on Gaza War, Campus Protests Hurting Biden, Reuters/Ipsos Poll Finds," Reuters, May 17, 2024, https://www.reuters.com/world/us/democratic-divide-gaza-war-campus-protests-hurting-biden-reutersipsos-poll-finds-2024-05-16/.

178 *drifted to the political right*: Marc Levy, "Some Jewish Voters in Presidential Swing States Reconsider Their Longtime Devotion to Democrats," Associated Press, October 21, 2024, https://apnews.com/article/jewish-voters-pennsylvania-2024-elections-trump-harris-09297d8c0843ae2b1698c9d2dfb80fd9.

179 *Picking Shapiro, who is Jewish*: Katie Glueck, "'I Am Proud of My Faith': Shapiro's Fiery Speech Ends on a Personal Note," *New York Times*, August 6, 2024, https://www.nytimes.com/2024/08/06/us/politics/josh-shapiro-harris-walz-rally.html.

179 *unapologetically pro-Israel*: Aliya Schneider and Max Marin, "Would Josh Shapiro's Stances on Israel Help or Hurt Kamala Harris' Ticket?" *Philadelphia Inquirer*, July 25, 2024, https://www.inquirer.com/politics/election/josh-shapiro-israel-kamala-harris-20240725.html.

179 *That angered a lot of Jewish voters*: Khaled Elgindy, "Biden's 'Bear Hug' of Israel Is a Failure," *Foreign Policy*, October 10, 2024, accessed Janaury 3, 2025, https://jewishinsider.com/2024/05/bidens-israel-threat-slammed-by-pro-israel-lawmakers-mainstream-jewish-groups/.

179 *called the Israeli leader an "asshole"*: Carol E. Lee, Jonathan Allen, Peter Nicholas, and Courtney Kube, "Biden Disparages Netanyahu in Private but Hasn't Significantly Changed U.S. Policy Toward Israel and Gaza," NBC News, February 12, 2024, https://www.nbcnews.com/news/investigations/biden-disparages-netanyahu-private-hasnt-changed-us-policy-israel-rcna138282.

179   *Biden took heat:* Elena Schneider and Jeff Coltin, "Pro-Palestinian Protesters Interrupted Biden's Glitzy New York Fundraiser," *Politico*, March 29, 2024, https://www.politico.com/news/2024/03/29/pro-palestinian-protesters-inter rupted-bidens-glitzy-new-york-fundraiser-00149706.

179   *White House interns:* Jonathan Allen, "White House Interns Demand a Middle East Cease-Fire in Letter to Biden," NBC News, December 5, 2023, https://www.nbcnews.com/politics/white-house/white-house-interns-demand-mid dle-east-cease-fire-letter-biden-rcna128264.

179   *pro-Palestinian protesters:* Kenichi Serino, "Pro-Palestinian Campus Protests Are Evolving. Here's What to Watch," PBS, May 20, 2024, https://www.pbs .org/newshour/politics/pro-palestinian-campus-protests-are-evolving-heres -what-to-watch.

179   *Harris had not distanced herself:* Clarissa-Jan Lim, "Let's Dispel the Myth That Harris Will Be Any Different from Biden on Gaza and Israel," NBC News, August 30, 2024, https://www.msnbc.com/top-stories/latest/kamala-harris-is rael-gaza-cnn-biden-rcna168949.

179   *13 percent opting for "uncommitted":* Reid J. Epstein and Shane Goldmacher, "Michigan Primary Takeaways: 'Uncommitted' Makes Itself Heard," *New York Times*, February 28, 2024, https://www.nytimes.com/2024/02/28/us/politics /michigan-primary-biden-trump.html.

179   *Shawn Fain:* Craig Mauger, "UAW President Voices Concerns about Kelly, Shapiro amid Harris' Running Mate Search," *Detroit News*, August 1, 2024, https://www.detroitnews.com/story/news/politics/2024/08/01/uaw-pres ident-shawn-fain-voices-concerns-about-mark-kelly-josh-shapiro-kamala -harris-vp-andy-beshear/74635714007/.

179   *the real issue for Shapiro:* Will Weissert, "Some Activists Step Up Criticism of Shapiro and Kelly as Harris Closes In on Naming a Running Mate," WHYY, August 3, 2024, https://whyy.org/articles/some-activists-step-up -criticism-of-shapiro-and-kelly-as-harris-closes-in-on-naming-a-running -mate/.

179   *Arab American voters would:* Joey Cappelletti, "Arab American Voters Struggle to Back Harris over U.S. Support for Israel's War in Gaza," PBS, October 29, 2024, https://www.pbs.org/newshour/politics/arab-american-voters -struggle-to-back-harris-over-u-s-support-for-israels-war-in-gaza.

180   *harbored similar concerns:* Shannon Pettypiece, "Kamala Harris Faces Challenging Dynamics in White House Full of Longtime Biden Allies," NBC News, December 20, 2020, https://nbcnews.com/politics/white-house/kamala-harris -faces-challenging-dynamics-white-house-full-longtime-biden-n1251611.

180   *she had once been seen:* Ibid.

180   *promised to be loyal:* Shelby Talcott, "Kamala Harris Struggles to Balance

'Change' and Loyalty to Joe Biden," Semafor, October 8, 2024, https://www
.yahoo.com/news/kamala-harris-struggles-balance-change-002833266
.html.

180 *the first woman of color:* "Kamala Harris Becomes First Woman of Color to
Accept a Major Party's Nomination for President," CBS Chicago, August 23,
2024, https://www.youtube.com/watch?v=XZxEXKH5Pos.

180 *in good position:* Julia Manchester, "Shapiro's 2028 Prospects Rise Sharply
After Harris Defeat," *The Hill*, November 23, 2024, https://thehill.com/home
news/state-watch/4986246-pennsylvania-gov-shapiro-2028-future/.

181 *Harris met separately:* Neil Vigdor, Jonathan Weisman, and Reid J. Epstein,
"Harris Meets with V.P. Finalists in Pivotal Test of Chemistry," *New York
Times*, August 4, 2024, https://www.nytimes.com/live/2024/08/04/us/harris
-trump-election.

182 *more than ten thousand Democrats:* Rebecca Morin, "Coach Walz's Prime-
time Debut: Four Takeaways from the First Harris-Walz Rally," *USA Today*, August 7, 2024, https://www.usatoday.com/story/news/politics/elec
tions/2024/08/07/kamala-harris-tim-walz-pennsylvania-rally-takeaways
/74698089007/.

182 *including disparagement:* Kit Maher and Eric Bradner, "Vance Says 'Childless
Cat Ladies' Comment Was 'Dumb' but His Point Stands," CNN, October 12,
2024, https://www.cnn.com/2024/10/12/politics/jd-vance-childless-cat-ladies
/index.html.

182 *portrayal of Trump as an American Hitler:* Gram Slattery and Helen Coster,
"JD Vance Once Compared Trump to Hitler. Now, He Is Trump's Vice
President–Elect," Reuters, November 6, 2024, https://www.reuters.com
/world/us/jd-vance-once-compared-trump-hitler-now-they-are-running
-mates-2024-07-15/.

183 *"weak, failed, dangerously liberal":* "Trump Needs to Paint Harris as 'Weak,
Failed, Dangerously Liberal': GOP Consultant," Fox News, September 10,
2024, https://www.foxnews.com/video/6361799979112.

183 *during a panel interview:* Eric Deggans, "5 Takeaways by a Longtime NABJ
Member from Trump's Appearance Before Black Journalists," NPR, August 1, 2024, https://www.npr.org/2024/08/01/nx-s1-5060269/trump-nabj
-appearance-controversy.

183 *"She was always of Indian heritage":* "Interview: Donald Trump Sits for Questions at the NABJ Convention in Chicago—July 31, 2024," *Roll Call*, July 31,
2024, https://rollcall.com/factbase/trump/transcript/donald-trump-interview
-national-association-black-journalists-nabj-chicago-july-31-2024/.

183 *strategy to boost:* Christian Paz, "The Republican Party Is Less White than Ever.
Thank Donald Trump," Vox, September 25, 2024, https://www.vox.com/2024

-elections/373535/3-theories-gop-donald-trump-nonwhite-voters-hispanic-black-latino-asian.

184 *Trump angry and itchy:* Michael C. Bender and Michael Gold, "Trump's Carefully Scripted Week Kept Veering Off Script," *New York Times*, August 24, 2024, https://www.nytimes.com/2024/08/24/us/politics/trump-campaign-2024.html.

184 *switched campaign managers:* Maggie Haberman, Alexander Burns, and Ashley Parker, "Donald Trump Fires Corey Lewandowski, His Campaign Manager," *New York Times*, June 20, 2016, https://www.nytimes.com/2016/06/21/us/politics/corey-lewandowski-donald-trump.html.

184 *2016 and 2020:* "Brad Parscale Replaced as Trump's Campaign Manager," BBC, July 16, 2020, https://www.bbc.com/news/world-us-canada-53426285.

184 *reports that he was dissatisfied:* Maggie Haberman and Jonathan Swan, "Inside the Worst Three Weeks of Donald Trump's 2024 Campaign," *New York Times*, August 10, 2024, https://www.nytimes.com/2024/08/10/us/politics/trump-campaign-election.html.

185 *offered strategy advice:* Hugo Lowell, "Top Trump Advisers in Turmoil After Campaign's Worst Month of 2024," *The Guardian*, August 15, 2024, https://www.theguardian.com/us-news/article/2024/aug/15/trump-campaign-leadership.

185 *Lewandowski secured a "senior adviser" title:* Sara Dorn, "Corey Lewandowski, Controversial Trump Ally, Returns to Campaign," *Forbes*, August 15, 2024, https://www.forbes.com/sites/saradorn/2024/08/15/corey-lewandowski-controversial-trump-ally-returns-to-campaign/.

CHAPTER 12: MAR-A-LAGO VS. KAMALOT

187 *Trump polled:* Jonathan Allen, "Trump on the Brink?" NBC News, June 5, 2022, https://www.nbcnews.com/politics/donald-trump/trump-brink-rcna31774.

187 *Trump beckoned:* Marc Caputo and Jonathan Allen, "Trump, Whose Lies About the 2020 Election Inspired an Insurrection, Announces Third White House Bid," NBC News, November 15, 2022, https://www.nbcnews.com/politics/donald-trump/trump-announce-president-2024-rcna36987.

187 *gold-accented marble columns:* Hannah Getahun and Kimberly Leonard, "See Inside the Ornate Mar-a-Lago Ballroom Where Guests Wearing 'Ultra MAGA' Hats Crowded In as Trump Announced His 2024 Presidential Bid," Yahoo! News, November 16, 2024, https://www.yahoo.com/news/look-mar-lagos-grand-ballroom-020540208.html.

188 *"sit back and watch":* "Former President Trump Announces 2024 Presidential Bid[;] Transcript," Rev, https://www.rev.com/transcripts/former-president-trump-announces-2024-presidential-bid-transcript.

188   *as Trump presented it:* Brian Bennett and Nik Popli, "What Donald Trump's Win Means for Immigration," *Time*, November 6, 2024, https://time.com/7171654/donald-trump-immigration-plan-2024/.

188   *Trump linked:* Josh Boak, "AP Fact Check: Trump Plays on Immigration Myths," Associated Press, February 8, 2019, https://www.pbs.org/newshour/politics/ap-fact-check-trump-plays-on-immigration-myths.

188   *challengers failed:* Michelle L. Price, "Trump Has Become the Last Republican Standing in the 2024 Primary. Here's How He Bulldozed the Field," Associated Press, March 6, 2024, https://apnews.com/article/trump-haley-election-2024-republicans-9736f3b504eef4da5a8ef7f8bbae9dfc.

188   *Both Biden and Trump:* Louis Jacobson, "Fact-Checking Donald Trump on the Scale and Causes of Inflation Under Biden, Harris," Poynter, September 13, 2024, https://www.poynter.org/fact-checking/2024/joe-biden-kamala-harris-worst-inflation-history-cost-families-28000-fact-check/.

188   *had contributed:* Paul Wiseman and Christopher Rugaber, "Trump's Economic Plans Would Worsen Inflation, Experts Say," Associated Press, October 15, 2024, https://apnews.com/article/trump-inflation-tariffs-taxes-immigration-federal-reserve-a18de763fcc01557258c7f33cab375ed.

188   *pushing trillions:* Jonathan Bydalk, "Who's Really to Blame for Inflation?" R Street, April 20, 2022, https://www.rstreet.org/commentary/whos-really-to-blame-for-inflation/.

188   *had only hit hard:* Max Zahn, "Republicans at RNC Blame Biden for Inflation. Economists Say It's Misleading," ABC News, July 18, 2024, https://abcnews.go.com/Business/republicans-rnc-blame-biden-inflation-economists-misleading/story?id=112022864.

188   *they called it "transitory":* Taylor Giorno, "Yellen Says She Regrets Saying Inflation Was 'Transitory,'" *The Hill*, March 13, 2024, https://thehill.com/business/4529787-yellen-regrets-saying-inflation-transitory/.

189   *promoting "Bidenomics":* Ibid.

189   *voters could feel:* Stephanie Perry and Patrick J. Egan, "NBC News Exit Poll: Voters Express Deep Concern About America's Democracy and Economy," NBC News, November 5, 2024, https://www.nbcnews.com/politics/2024-election/nbc-news-exit-poll-voters-express-concern-democracy-economy-rcna178602.

189   *Biden told them:* Daniel Dale, "Fact Check: Biden Again Falsely Claims Inflation Was 9% When He Became President," CNN, May 14, 2024, https://www.cnn.com/2024/05/14/politics/fact-check-biden-inflation-when-he-became-president/index.html.

189   *promised to "restore the soul of America":* Demetri Sevastopulo and Lauren Fedor, "Biden Pledges to 'Restore Soul of America' in Bipartisan Victory Speech,"

Financial Times, November 7, 2020, https://www.ft.com/content/95268089 -1178-4bbe-b41f-ce3e3d5dac8a.

189 *Democrats rallied:* Ashley Kirzinger et al., "How the Supreme Court's Dobbs Decision Played in 2022 Midterm Election: KFF/AP VoteCast Analysis," KFF, November 11, 2022, https://www.kff.org/report-section/how-the-supreme-co urts-dobbs-decision-played-in-2022-midterm-election-kff-ap-votecast-analy sis-findings/.

189 *projected Republican wave:* Zack Beauchamp, "The Supreme Court Lost Republicans the Midterms," Vox, November 10, 2022, https://www.vox .com/policy-and-politics/23451103/2022-midterms-results-data-analysis -abortion-dobbs-shor.

189 *The GOP still took:* Harry Enten, "How Joe Biden and the Democratic Party Defied Midterm History," CNN, November 13, 2022, https://www .cnn.com/2022/11/13/politics/democrats-biden-midterm-elections-senate -house/index.html.

189 *low-turnout affairs:* Drew Desilver, "Voter Turnout Always Drops Off for Mid-term Elections, but Why?" Pew Research Center, July 24, 2014, https://www .pewresearch.org/short-reads/2014/07/24/voter-turnout-always-drops-off -for-midterm-elections-but-why/.

189 *high-information voters:* "Voter Turnout Always Drops Off for Midterm Elec-tions, but Why?" Pew Research Center, August 23, 2022, https://www.pewre search.org/politics/2022/08/23/midterm-election-preferences-voter-engage ment-views-of-campaign-issues/.

189 *increasingly leaned:* Carroll Doherty and Jocelyn Kiley, "In Changing U.S. Electorate, Race and Education Remain Stark Dividing Lines," Pew Research Center, June 2, 2020, https://www.pewresearch.org/politics/2020/06/02/in-ch anging-u-s-electorate-race-and-education-remain-stark-dividing-lines/.

189 *views on abortion had changed:* Heidi Przybyla, "Joe Biden's Long Evolution on Abortion Rights Still Holds Surprises," NBC News, June 5, 2019, https:// www.nbcnews.com/politics/2020-election/biden-s-long-evolution-abortion -rights-still-holds-surprises-n1013846.

189 *never particularly comfortable:* Christine Fernando, "Biden's Big Speech Showed His Uneasy Approach to Abortion, an Issue Bound to Be Key in the Campaign," Associated Press, March 10, 2024, https://apnews.com/article /abortion-biden-2024-reproductive-rights-harris-494af752992ba88fa6e3d53 fbd54f716.

190 *Trump moved to the center:* Steve Contorno and Kate Sullivan, "15 Times Trump's Abortion Position Shifted over the Past 25 Years," CNN, April 10, 2024, https://www.cnn.com/2024/04/09/politics/trump-abortion-stances-ti meline/index.html.

190   *he had held:* Ibid.

190   *pushed for new state laws:* Allison McCann and Amy Schoenfeld Walker, "Tracking Abortion Bans Across the Country," *New York Times*, December 3, 2024, https://www.nytimes.com/interactive/2024/us/abortion-laws-roe-v-wade.html.

190   *wanted to impose:* Andrew Perez, "House Republicans Endorse National Abortion Ban," *Rolling Stone*, March 21, 2024, https://www.rollingstone.com/politics/politics-news/house-republicans-national-abortion-ban-endorse-1234991746/.

190   *Trump had said:* Eric Badner, "Trump, Who Paved Way for Roe v. Wade Reversal, Says Republicans 'Speak Very Inarticulately' About Abortion," CNN, September 17, 2023, https://edition.cnn.com/2023/09/17/politics/donald-trump-abortion-2024/index.html.

190   *Trump tiptoed:* Christine Fernando, "Anti-Abortion Leaders Undeterred as Trump for the First Time Says He'd Veto a Federal Abortion Ban," Associated Press, October 2, 2024, https://apnews.com/article/trump-harris-vance-walz-debate-2024-election-abortion-64c739e99ffa1ad51b973e420e1fe92d.

190   *Trump released:* Natasha Korecki, "A Timeline of Trump's Many, Many Positions on Abortion," NBC News, April 8, 2024, https://www.nbcnews.com/politics/donald-trump/trumps-many-abortion-positions-timeline-rcna146601.

190   *Biden and Harris backed:* "Fact Sheet: Biden-Harris Administration Continues the Fight for Reproductive Freedom," White House, March 7, 2024, https://www.whitehouse.gov/briefing-room/statements-releases/2024/03/07/fact-sheet-biden-harris-administration-continues-the-fight-for-reproductive-freedom/.

191   *Trump advisers rushed:* Erica L. Green, "As Trump Links Her to Biden, Harris Says, 'You're Running Against Me,'" *New York Times*, September 11, 2024, https://www.nytimes.com/2024/09/11/us/politics/harris-biden-trump-debate.html.

191   *Trump fumed:* Jill Colvin and Jonathan J. Cooper, "Trump Says He's 'Entitled to Personal Attacks' as He Hammers Harris on Inflation with Grocery Props," Associated Press, August 15, 2024, https://apnews.com/article/donald-trump-press-conference-9af8036585d6727b6bb07008c0690cdf.

191   *Trump aides had cast:* Olivia Rinaldi, "Trump Campaign Bets Big on Minnesota, Virginia with New Field Offices," CBS News, June 21, 2024, https://www.cbsnews.com/news/trump-campaign-to-open-new-field-offices-minnesota-virginia/.

191   *Harris put a fork in those states:* Sophia Cai and Torey Van Oot, "Trump Campaign Shifts as Its Path to Victory Narrows," Axios, September 5, 2024, https://www.axios.com/2024/09/05/trump-campaign-shifts-path-narrows.

192   *he was mostly off:* Sara Dorn, "Trump Significantly Ramping Up Campaign

Schedule Amdist Harris' Polling Surge," *Forbes*, August 26, 2024, https://www
.forbes.com/sites/saradorn/2024/08/26/trump-significantly-ramping-up-ca
mpaign-schedule-amid-harris-polling-surge/.

193   *his opening remarks:* "Press Conference: Donald Trump Speaks to Reporters at
Mar-a-Lago—August 8, 2024," *Roll Call*, August 8, 2024, https://rollcall.com
/factbase/trump/transcript/donald-trump-press-conference-palm-beach
-florida-august-8-2024/.

193   *touching on:* "Fact Focus: A Look at Claims Made by Trump at News Conference," Associated Press, August 8, 2024, https://apnews.com/article/trump
-news-conference-fact-check-misinformation-eb899c1fc734f5ecb42b8d0902
c5c004.

193   *He said he had agreed:* Ibid.

194   *Harris had yet to sit:* Rebecca Davis O'Brien, "Harris Has a Lot of Strengths.
Giving Interviews Isn't One of Them," *New York Times*, September 26, 2024,
https://www.nytimes.com/2024/09/26/us/politics/kamala-harris-interviews
-campaign.html.

194   *she had done:* Darlene Supervile, "Early Harris-Walz Rallies Feature Big
Crowds, Talk of 'Joy' and Unsolicited GOP Counterprogramming," Associated Press, August 11, 2024, https://apnews.com/article/harris-walz-rallies-ba
ttleground-states-vance-trump-7da99aace01fec1c784fba27fdbce558.

194   *short, scripted stump speeches:* Linda Qiu and Dylan Freedman, "How Stump
Speeches by Harris and Trump Differ (and Don't)," *New York Times*, September 13, 2024, https://www.nytimes.com/2024/09/13/us/elections/trump
-harris-speeches-accuracy.html.

194   *It was his first:* Ibid.

194   *"I haven't recalibrated":* Ibid

194   *"It changes around a little bit":* Ibid.

194   *had been hamstrung:* Melanie Mason and Michael Finnegan, "News Analysis:
Kamala Harris Drops Out. What Went Wrong?" *Los Angeles Times*, December 4, 2019, https://www.latimes.com/politics/story/2019-12-04/kamala-harr
is-what-went-wrong-analysis.

194   *the internal drama:* Christopher Cadelago, "'No Discipline. No Plan. No Strategy': Kamala Harris Campaign in Meltdown," *Politico*, November 15, 2019,
https://www.politico.com/news/2019/11/15/kamala-harris-campaign-2020
-071105.

194   *her approval ratings:* "Election Center," *The Hill*, https://elections2024.thehill
.com/.

196   *in the toilet for years:* "In Tight Presidential Race, Voters Are Broadly Critical
of Both Biden and Trump," Pew Research Center, April 24, 2022, https://www
.pewresearch.org/politics/2024/04/24/joe-bidens-approval-ratings/.

196   *CNBC survey:* Steve Liesman, "Trump Holds 2-Point Lead over Harris with a Big Advantage on Economy, CNBC Survey Shows," CNBC, August 8, 2024, https://www.cnbc.com/2024/08/08/trump-holds-2-point-lead-over-harris -with-a-big-advantage-on-economy-cnbc-survey-shows.html.

196   *middle-class upbringing:* Ibid.

196   *But privately:* Carol E. Lee, Natasha Korecki, Courtney Kube, and Monica Alba, "'It's Very Complex': Biden Struggles with Being Out of the National Conversation," NBC News, September 30, 2024, https://www.nbcnews.com /politics/2024-election/biden-struggles-national-conversation-rcna173036.

196   *who sought to defend his presidency:* Alex Thompson, "Tensions Rise Between Harris and Biden Teams as Election Nears," Axios, October 13, 2024, https:// www.axios.com/2024/10/13/kamala-harris-biden-campaign-tension.

196   *who had trained her:* J. Epstein Reid, "Harris's Debate Tutor: A Lawyer Unafraid of Telling Politicians Hard Truths," *New York Times*, September 11, 2024, https:// www.nytimes.com/2024/09/06/us/politics/karen-dunn-harris-debate-prep.html.

198   *Biden too had tried:* Josh Boak and Zeke Miller, "Biden Funded New Factories and Infrastructure Projects, but Trump Might Get to Cut the Ribbons," Associated Press, November 12, 2024, https://apnews.com/article/biden-trump-infr astructure-chips-inflation-economy-evs-c8bcb1eb5cdff1ce97f40416e6d88af3.

198   *had failed to convince voters:* Sylvan Lane, "Why 'Bidenomics' Is Falling Flat with Voters," *The Hill*, December 28, 2023, https://thehill.com /business/4376617-why-bidenomics-is-falling-flat-with-voters/.

198   *she flew:* "Vice President Kamala Harris Campaigns in Raleigh, North Carolina," C-SPAN, August 16, 2024, https://www.c-span.org/program/cam paign-2024/vice-president-kamala-harris-campaigns-in-raleigh-north -carolina/647596.

198   *Wake Technical Community College:* Chloe Courtney Bohl, "In Raleigh, Kamala Harris Unveils Economic Plan to Help Working- and Middle-Class Americans," Indyweek, August 16, 2024, https://indyweek.com/news/wake /in-raleigh-kamala-harris-unveils-economic-plan-to-help-working-and -middle-class-americans/.

198   *$25,000 tax credit:* Matt Brown and Makiya Seminera, "Watch: Harris Debuts Economic Proposals to Lower Costs for Americans," *PBS NewsHour*, August 16, 2024, https://www.pbs.org/newshour/politics/watch-live-harris-debu ts-economic-proposals-to-lower-costs-for-americans.

198   *The Biden budget:* Kathleen Howley, "Biden's $15,000 First-Time Homebuyer Tax Credit Explained," Housingwire, August 26, 2020, https://www.housing wire.com/articles/bidens-15000-first-time-homebuyer-tax-credit-explained/.

199   *She said she would restore:* Ibid.

199   *"SOVIET Style Price Controls":* Timothy H.J. Nerozzi, "Trump Accuses Har-

ris of 'Soviet Style' Policies Following Price Control Proposal," Fox News, August 17, 2024, https://www.foxnews.com/politics/trump-accuses-harris -soviet-style-policies-following-price-control-proposal.

199 *painted her as a lefty:* Josh Boak, Zeke Miller, and Steve Peoples, "Harris Is Making a 'Capitalist' Pitch to Boost the Economy as Trump Pushes Deeper into Populism," Associated Press, September 25, 2024, https://apnews.com /article/harris-trump-economy-taxes-middle-class-tariffs-bda4bfe7cb02c1c5 c2f6232bf05ad670.

CHAPTER 13: "NO DAYLIGHT, KID"

206 *Chisholm had delivered:* Sheila Hixson and Ruth Rose, eds., "The Official Proceedings of the Democratic National Convention, 1972," 395, https://name .umdl.umich.edu/AEW7024.0001.001.

206 *In his suite:* Justin Wells and Neal Edelstein, producers, *The Art of the Surge*, Episode 4, "There's Something Wrong There," Ashokan Studios in association with the Tucker Carlson Network.

206 *tapped out the messages:* Ibid.

206 *took suggestions from Gaetz:* Ibid.

207 *preview a theme:* Ibid.

207 *pursued Kennedy's endorsement:* Rachael Bade and Ryan Lizza, "Trump Met with Robert F. Kennedy Jr. to Seek Endorsement," *Politico*, July 15, 2024, https://www.politico.com/live-updates/2024/07/15/rnc-live-updates -coverage/trump-met-with-rfk-jr-00168412.

208 *John Kerry in 2004:* Molly Ball, "The Resurrection of Stephanie Cutter," *Atlantic*, May 30, 2012, https://www.theatlantic.com/politics/archive/2012/05 /the-resurrection-of-stephanie-cutter/257732/.

209 *name a Republican:* Kevin Liptak, "Harris Explains in Exclusive CNN Interview Why She's Shifted Her Position on Key Issues Since Her First Run for President," CNN, https://www.cnn.com/2024/08/29/politics/kamala-harris -tim-walz-cnntv/index.html.

210 *early-twentieth-century hotel:* Omni William Penn, Historic Hotels of America, National Trust for Historic Preservation, https://www.historichotels.org /us/hotels-resorts/omni-william-penn-hotel-pittsburgh/history.php.

211 *6,000-square-foot:* Omni Hotels, https://www.omnihotels.com/hotels/pitts burgh-william-penn/meetings.

CHAPTER 14: MOTHAFUCKA

215 *"So, be cognizant":* Justin Wells and Neal Edelstein, producers, *The Art of the Surge*, Episode 5, "Debategate 2024," Ashokan Studios in association with the Tucker Carlson Network.

217 *demanded an audience:* Ibid.

218 *bellowed at Santucci:* Ibid.

218 *Santucci said:* Ibid.

218 *330 words:* Transcript, ABC News presidential debate, September 10, 2024, https://abcnews.go.com/Politics/harris-trump-presidential-debate-trans cript/story?id=113560542.

219 *"The story":* Justin Wells and Neal Edelstein, producers, *The Art of The Surge*, Episode 5, "Debategate 2024," Ashokan Studios in association with the Tucker Carlson Network.

219 *"I killed her":* Ibid.

219 *"people here analyze":* Ibid.

220 *flown from Palm Beach:* "Laura Loomer, Who Promoted a 9/11 Conspiracy Theory, Joins Trump for Ceremonies Marking the Attacks," Associated Press, September 11, 2024, https://apnews.com/article/laura-loomer-trump-911 -conspiracy-theories-18198b8ea2ce567467acfd6bf7f19f1e.

221 *billion-dollar fundraising threshold:* Natasha Korecki, Jonathan Allen, and Carol E. Lee, "Harris' Political Operation Crosses $1 Billion Raised for the 2024 Election," NBC News, October 9, 2024.

CHAPTER 15: THE TURN

223 *had been reported:* Michael Isikoff, "Trump Campaign in Cash Crisis—as Campaign Chief's $19.2M Pay Revealed," Daily Beast, October 15, 2024, up-dated November 8, 2024, https://www.thedailybeast.com/donald-trumps-ca mpaign-manager-chris-lacivitas-llc-multi-million-payday-revealed/.

226 *Placing the cap:* "Biden's Moment Wearing a Trump Hat," *New York Times*, September 13, 2024, https://www.nytimes.com/video/us/politics /100000009691518/biden-trump-hat.html.

227 *too good: Reuters,* "Fact Check: Photo of Biden in Trump Cap Falsely Shared as Evidence of Endorsement," Reuters, September 19, 2024, https://www .reuters.com/fact-check/photo-biden-trump-cap-falsely-shared-evidence -endorsement-2024-09-20/.

228 *youth boxing gym:* Adrian Carasquillo, "Boxing, Tacos and TV: Democratic Senate Contender Aims to Win Back Latino Voters," *The Guardian*, May 3, 2024, https://www.theguardian.com/us-news/article/2024/may/03/ruben -gallego-arizona-senate-race.

229 *launched a series:* Faith Jessie, "Black Americans for Trump Meet at Rocky's Barbershop in Atlanta Ahead of Presidential Debate," WXIA-TV, June 27, 2024, https://www.11alive.com/article/news/politics/black-americans-trump -meet-rockys-barbershop-day-before-debate-ben-carson-businessmen/85-6 d35641c-1235-4ae1-b6eb-922eddeef6be.

229   *Trump called in:* Ibid.

229   *"treated very unfairly":* Ashley Quincin, "Young Thug Being Treated 'Very Unfairly' in Atlanta Gang Case, Trump Says," *Atlanta Journal-Constitution*, August 5, 2024, https://www.ajc.com/news/donald-trump-says-young-thug -being-treated-very-unfairly-in-atlanta-gang-racketeering-case/PT3DVI H5WVDGJLML2MMQJXUMOU/.

229   *struck a plea deal:* Erik Ortiz, "Young Thug Released After Changing Plea to Guilty in Georgia's Longest-Running Criminal Trial," NBC News, October 31, 2024, https://www.nbcnews.com/news/us-news/young-thug-changes-plea -guilty-georgias-longest-running-criminal-trial-rcna177873.

232   *overhyping a bout with cancer:* Laura Loomer, X, January 8, 2024, https://x .com/LauraLoomer/status/1744399259913290058.

232   *heard loud popping:* Garrett Haake and Patrick Smith, "Trump's Golf Partner Recalls Moment Secret Service Dived on Him During Apparent Assassina-tion Attempt," NBC News, September 17, 2024, https://www.nbcnews.com /news/us-news/trumps-golf-partner-recalls-moment-secret-service-dived -assassination-rcna171414.

232   *dived on top:* Ibid.

232   *four hundred yards away:* Ibid.

233   *new restrictions:* Natasha Korecki and Jake Traylor, "Fewer Diners and Ice Cream Shops: Trump and Harris Shift Strategies on the Trail amid Se-curity Threats," NBC News, October 21, 2024, https://www.nbcnews.com /politics/2024-election/trump-harris-shift-strategies-trail-security-threats -rcna176234.

CHAPTER 16: TEXAS HOLD 'EM

237   *Biden chafed:* Carol E. Lee, Natasha Korecki, Courtney Kube, and Monica Alba, "'It's Very Complex': Biden Struggles with Being Out of the National Conversation," NBC News, September 30, 2024, https://www.nbcnews.com /politics/2024-election/biden-struggles-national-conversation-rcna173036.

238   *"not a thing":* Megan Messerly, "'Not a Thing That Comes to Mind' for Harris on What She Would Have Done Differently from Biden," *Politico*, October 8, 2024, https://www.politico.com/news/2024/10/08/harris-biden-the-view-00 182883.

239   *15 million:* Ashley Carman, "Spotify Reveals Joe Rogan's Podcast Numbers," Bloomberg News, March 21, 2024, https://www.bloomberg.com/news/news letters/2024-03-21/spotify-reveals-podcast-numbers-for-joe-rogan-alex -cooper-travis-kelce.

240   *"man baby":* Grace Panetta, "Joe Rogan Calls Trump an 'Existential Threat to Democracy' and a 'Man Baby' on Drugs," Business Insider, July 19, 2022,

https://www.businessinsider.com/joe-rogan-trump-a-man-baby-on-drugs
-2022-7.

241 *"Rogan gets BOOED"*: Donald Trump, Truth Social, August 9, 2024, https://
truthsocial.com/@realDonaldTrump/posts/112933460513899494.

244 *charged with stealing luggage*: "Ryan Wesley Routh Indicted for Attempted
Assassination of Former President Trump," press release, U.S. Department of
Justice, September 24, 2024, https://www.justice.gov/opa/pr/ryan-wesley-rou
th-indicted-attempted-assassination-former-president-trump.

246 *started running ads*: Victor Nava, "Trump Campaign Releases New Ad Centered on Kamala Harris Telling 'The View' She'd Do 'Not a Thing' Different than
Biden," *New York Post*, October 16, 2024, https://nypost.com/2024/10/16/us
-news/trump-campaign-releases-new-ad-centered-on-kamala-harris-telling
-the-view-shed-do-not-a-thing-different-than-biden/.

247 *tick slightly upward*: Donald Trump Favorability, FiveThirtyEight, https://
projects.fivethirtyeight.com/polls/favorability/donald-trump/.

247 *remembered his presidency*: Mark Murray, "'Dead Heat': Trump Pulls Even
with Harris in NBC News Poll," NBC News, October 13, 2024, https://www
.nbcnews.com/politics/2024-election/dead-heat-trump-pulls-even-harris
-nbc-news-poll-rcna174201.

248 *McDonald's franchise*: Dee-Ann Durbin, "McDonald's Agreed to Trump Event
but Says It Isn't Endorsing a Presidential Candidate," Associated Press, October 21, 2024, https://apnew.com/article/mcdonalds-trump-campaign-harris
-fries-56a5773528e212df058f85ec0f264578.

249 *Plouffe responded*: Nicholas Nehamas, "Harris Will Campaign in Texas to Call
Attention to Abortion Rights," *New York Times*, October 22, 2024, https://www
.nytimes.com/2024/10/22/us/politics/harris-texas-abortion-trump.html.

250 *accuse her*: Ryan King, "Joe Rogan Claims Harris Wanted to Avoid Marijuana
Legalization Talk as Aides Feared Progressive Backlash: 'Thought It Was Hi-
larious,'" *New York Post*, November 13, 2024, https://nypost.com/2024/11/13
/us-news/joe-rogan-claims-harris-wanted-to-avoid-marijuana-legalization/.

CHAPTER 17: GARBAGE TIME

252 *In early June*: Kate Sullivan, "Trump Pushes Early and Mail-In Voting Ini-
tiative Ahead of November Despite Casting Doubt on Voting Methods for
Years," CNN, June 4, 2024, https://www.cnn.com/2024/06/04/politics/trump
-mail-in-early-voting/index.html.

253 *Pew Research*: Andrew Daniller, "Republicans, Democrats Continue to Differ
Sharply on Voting Access," Pew Research Center, July 9, 2024, https://www
.pewresearch.org/short-reads/2024/07/09/republicans-democrats-continue
-to-differ-sharply-on-voting-access/.

253   *cast an early ballot:* Brett Samuels, "Trump Casts Ballot During Early Voting for Florida Primary," *The Hill,* August 14, 2024, https://thehill.com/home news/campaign/4827686-trump-early-voting-florida-primary/.

253   *changed its election rules:* Jane C. Timm, "North Carolina Gives Counties Affected by Hurricane Helene Voting Flexibility," NBC News, October 7, 2024, https://www.nbcnews.com/politics/2024-election/north-carolina-voting-flex ibility-hurricane-helene-rcna174352.

253   *Georgia and North Carolina:* "Georgia Voters Smash Records on First Day of Early Voting," press release, Georgia Secretary of State, October 15, 2024, https://sos.ga.gov/news/georgia-voters-smash-records-first-day-early-voting; "North Carolina Sets Turnout Record for First Day of Early Voting," press release, North Carolina State Board of Elections, October 18, 2024, https:// www.ncsbe.gov/news/press-releases/2024/10/18/north-carolina-sets-turnout -record-first-day-early-voting.

254   *floated that hypothesis:* Reid J. Epstein, Lisa Lerer, and Maggie Haberman, "Harris Aides Quietly Grow More Bullish on Defeating Trump," *New York Times,* October 28, 2024, https://www.nytimes.com/2024/10/28/us/politics /kamala-harris-donald-trump-2024-election.html.

255   *P. T. Barnum's:* "History of Madison Square Garden," Madison Square Park Conservancy, August 1, 2014, https://madisonsquarepark.org/community /news/2021/04/history-of-madison-square-garden/.

255   *Billy Joel shows:* Rebecca Cohen, "Billy Joel Closed Out His Long Run at Madison Square Garden Thursday Night," NBC News, July 25, 2024, https:// www.nbcnews.com/pop-culture/celebrity/billy-joel-madison-square-garden -rcna163720.

255   *pro- and anti-Nazi:* Sarah Kate Kramer, "When Nazis Took Manhattan," NPR, February 20, 2019, https://www.npr.org/sections/codeswitch /2019/02/20/695941323/when-nazis-took-manhattan; "Anti-Nazi Protest in New York's Madison Square Garden," United States Holocaust Memorial Museum, https://encyclopedia.ushmm.org/content/en/photo/anti-nazi-protest -in-new-yorks-madison-square-garden.

255   *"New York Crusade":* "1957 New York Crusade," Billy Graham Library, June 1, 2012, https://billygrahamlibrary.org/1957-new-york-crusade/.

255   *"actually reenacting":* Joseph A. Wulfsohn, "Hillary Clinton Accuses Trump of 'Reenacting' Infamous Nazi Rally at Madison Square Garden: We Can't Ignore It," Fox News, October 24, 2024, https://www.foxnews.com/media/hil lary-clinton-accuses-trump-reenacting-infamous-nazi-rally-madison-square -garden.

256   *marquee tag team:* "Full Wrestlemania I Results," World Wrestling Entertainment, https://www.wwe.com/shows/wrestlemania/1/results.

256 *had a history:* Hershal Pandya, "Donald Trump Got the Tony Hinchcliffe He Hired," Vulture, October 29, 2024, https://www.vulture.com/article/tony-hinchcliffe-trump-rally-roast-jokes.html.

256 *surprise set:* Nicole Acevedo and Ignacio Torres, "Trump Rally Comedian Workshopped Racist Puerto Rico Line at NYC Comedy Club the Night Before," NBC News, October 28, 2024, https://www.nbcnews.com/news/latino/tony-hinchcliffe-trump-rally-racist-puerto-rico-remarks-rcna177587.

257 *Bad Bunny:* Tara Sutter, "Bad Bunny Shares Kamala Harris's Video on Puerto Rico on Instagram," *The Hill*, October 27, 2024, https://thehill.com/blogs/in-the-know/4956229-bad-bunny-kamala-harris-video-puerto-rico-instagram/.

257 *Jennifer Lopez and Ricky Martin:* Emily Zemler, "Jennifer Lopez, Ricky Martin Voice Support for Harris After Trump Rally Comments on Puerto Rico," *Rolling Stone*, October 28, 2024, https://www.rollingstone.com/music/music-news/jennifer-lopez-ricky-martin-kamala-harris-endorsement-puerto-rico-1235144561/.

257 *Carlson aimed directly:* Shane Goldmacher, Maggie Haberman, and Michael Gold, "Trump at the Garden: A Closing Carnival of Grievances, Misogyny and Racism," *New York Times*, October 27, 2024, https://www.nytimes.com/2024/10/27/us/trump-msg-rally.html.

259 *doctor the transcript:* Eli Stokols, "White House Altered Biden Transcript," *Politico*, November 1, 2024, https://www.politico.com/news/2024/11/01/white-house-altered-biden-transcript-00186762.

260 *They reached out:* Paul Steeno, "How Trump's Viral Garbage Truck Came to Be," WFRV via FOX59, November 3, 2024, https://fox59.com/news/national-world/how-trumps-viral-garbage-truck-came-to-be/.

261 *released a survey:* Brianne Pfannenstiel, "Iowa Poll: Kamala Harris Leapfrogs Donald Trump to Take Lead Near Election Day. Here's How," *Des Moines Register*, November 2, 2024, https://www.desmoinesregister.com/story/news/politics/iowa-poll/2024/11/02/iowa-poll-kamala-harris-leads-donald-trump-2024-presidential-race/75354033007/.

CHAPTER 18: "JUST TAKE THE 270"

265 *1,459 days since:* Nicole Meier, "Calling the 2020 Presidential Race State by State," Associated Press, November 8, 2020, https://www.ap.org/the-definitive-source/behind-the-news/calling-the-2020-presidential-race-state-by-state/.

266 *hurling himself:* Suzanne Gamboa, "Donald Trump Announces Presidential Bid by Trashing Mexico, Mexicans," NBC News, June 16, 2015, https://www.nbcnews.com/news/latino/donald-trump-announces-presidential-bid-trashing-mexico-mexicans-n376521.

266 *"They're rapists":* Ibid.

266 *"now more knowledgeable"*: Jonathan Allen and Matt Dixon, "'She Sits in a Tough Chair': Meet Susie Wiles, the Operative Trying to Guide Trump Through Four Indictments to the White House," NBC News, March 1, 2024, https://www.nbcnews.com/politics/2024-election/meet-susie-wiles-trump -four-indictments-white-house-campaign-manager-rcna140514.

266 *cast a vote*: Michael Gold, "Trump Votes and Says This Will Be His Last Campaign," *New York Times*, November 5, 2024, https://www.nytimes .com/2024/11/05/us/politics/trump-votes-florida.html.

266 *"Sad"*: Matt Papaycik, "'I Ran a Great Campaign,' Former President Donald Trump Says After Voting on Palm Beach," Associated Press, November 5, 2024, https://www.wptv.com/news/national-politics/america-votes/i-ran-a-great-ca mpaign-former-president-donald-trump-says-after-voting-on-palm-beach.

267 *Rogan cited Elon*: Joe Rogan, X, November 4, 2024, https://x.com/joerogan /status/1853614670764015762?lang=en.

269 *mirror act*: Megan Lebowitz, Monica Alba, Yamiche Alcindor, and Zoë Rich-ards, "Harris Makes a Surprise Appearance on 'Saturday Night Live,'" NBC News, November 3, 2024, https://www.nbcnews.com/politics/2024-election /kamala-harris-make-appearance-saturday-night-live-rcna178494.

270 *"human printer"*: Marc A. Caputo, "Meet Trump's 'Human Printer,'" The Bul-wark, May 22, 2024, https://www.thebulwark.com/p/meet-trumps-human -printer-natalie-harp.

271 *Trump's performance*: Maya Homan, "Election Day 2024 Map: How All 159 Georgia Counties Voted Compared to 2020," *Savannah Morning News*, No-vember 12, 2024, https://www.savannahnow.com/story/news/politics/elec tions/2024/11/12/explore-which-counties-determined-the-winner-of-the -2024-election/76205958007/.

272 *called North Carolina*: Brian Slodysko, "Why AP Called North Carolina for Trump," Associated Press, November 6, 2024, https://apnews.com/article /trump-harris-north-carolina-president-winner-explain-736bddfa4c0f1d479 700bf1615e79128.

273 *roughly $2 billion*: Theodore Schleifer and Albert Sun, "How Much Did Trump, Biden and Harris Raise? A Stunning $4.7 Billion," *New York Times*, December 6, 2024, https://www.nytimes.com/2024/12/06/us/politics/trump -harris-campaign-fundraising.html.

276 *Exit polls*: "Exit Polls," NBC News, December 17, 2024, https://www.nbcnews .com/politics/2024-elections/exit-polls.

276 *share of Latinos*: "Exit Polls 2020," NBC News, https://www.nbcnews.com /politics/2020-elections/exit-polls/; "Exit Polls," NBC News, December 17, 2024, https://www.nbcnews.com/politics/2024-elections/exit-polls.

276 *Asian Americans*: Ibid.

276   *African American voters:* Ibid.

276   *After losing women:* Ibid.

276   *Among men:* Ibid.

277   *In rural areas:* Ibid.

280   *"Fuck you":* Rachael Bade and Eugene Daniels, "Playbook: Trump Returns, and So Does the Drama," *Politico*, November 7, 2024, https://www.politico .com/newsletters/playbook/2024/11/07/trump-returns-and-so-does-the -drama-00188123.

EPILOGUE: THE AFTERMATH

285   *"It's presumptuous":* Susan Page, "In Exclusive Sit-Down Interview, Biden Reveals His Biggest Regret and the Compliment Trump Gave Him," *USA Today*, January 8, 2025, https://www.usatoday.com/story/news/po litics/elections/2025/01/08/exclusive-joe-biden-interview-donald-trump -election/77378693007/.

286   *told* Politico: Jonathan Martin, "'Lady McBiden': Alexandra Pelosi Blasts the First Lady," *Politico*, January 19, 2025, https://www.politico.com/news/maga zine/2025/01/19/lady-mcbiden-alexandra-pelosi-first-lady-00199164.